D1481015

*f*P

ALSO BY DAVID DREMAN

Psychology and the Stock Market:
Investment Strategy Beyond Random Walk

Contrarian Investment Strategy:
The Psychology of Stock-Market Success

The New Contrarian Investment Strategy

Contrarian Investment Strategies:
The Next Generation

CONTRARIAN INVESTMENT STRATEGIES

The Psychological Edge

DAVID DREMAN

FREE PRESS

New York London Toronto Sydney New Delhi

This publication contains the opinions and ideas of its author and is intended to provide useful advice in regard to the subject matter covered. It is sold with the understanding that in this publication the author and publisher are not engaged in rendering legal, financial, or other professional services. If the reader requires expert assistance or legal advice, a professional advisor should be consulted directly.

The strategies outlined in this book may not be suitable for every individual, and are not guaranteed or warranted to produce any particular results. The author and publisher specifically disclaim any responsibility for any liability, loss, or risk, personal or otherwise, which is incurred as a consequence, directly or indirectly, of the use and application of any of the contents of this book.

Free Press
A Division of Simon & Schuster, Inc.
1230 Avenue of the Americas
New York, NY 10020

Copyright © 1998, 2011 by David Dreman

All rights reserved, including the right to reproduce this book or portions thereof in any form whatsover. For information address Simon & Schuster Subsidiary Rights Department, 1230 Avenue of the Americas, New York, NY 10020.

First Free Press hardcover edition January 2012

FREE PRESS and colophon are trademarks of Simon & Schuster, Inc.

For information about special discounts for bulk purchases, please contact Simon & Schuster Special Sales at 1-866-506-1949 or business@simonandschuster.com.

The Simon & Schuster Speakers Bureau can bring authors to your live event. For more information or to book an event contact the Simon & Schuster Speakers Bureau at 1-866-248-3049 or visit our Web site at www.simonspeakers.com.

Designed by Katy Riegel

Manufactured in the United States of America

1   3   5   7   9   10   8   6   4   2

Library of Congress Cataloging-in-Publication Data
Dreman, David N.
Contrarian investment strategies : the psychological edge / David Dreman.
p.   cm.
1. Investment analysis.   2. Investments—Psychological aspects.   I. Title.
HG4521.D727 2012
332.601'9—dc23   2011023716

ISBN 978-0-7432-9796-7
ISBN 978-1-4516-2895-1 (ebook)

Revised and updated edition of *Contrarian Investment Strategies: The Next Generation.*

For Meredith and Ditto

Contents

PART IV: Market Overreaction: The New Investment Paradigm

PART V: The Challenges and Opportunities Ahead

CONTRARIAN
INVESTMENT STRATEGIES

Introduction

SOME THINGS SEEMED clear as I wrote this introduction in late August 2011. Although we have recently survived the worst economic and market period since the Great Depression, we are on anything but a solid footing today. Many market experts call the 2000–2009 period the "lost decade." People lost heavily in the dot-com crash of 2000–2002 and even more in the subprime crash of 2007–2008, which not only dented their remaining savings but also substantially knocked down the prices of their homes. So much for the idea that modern investment methods and critical information delivered in nanoseconds would make this nearly impossible.

By June 2011, stock prices doubled from their lows of March 2009. But it wasn't to last. After moving to its high of up 111 percent from the March 2009 low, the market took one of its sharpest dives in decades. From the July high through late September, the S&P 500 index free-fell almost 20 percent, a drop that cost investors more than three trillion dollars. The plunge was considered by many senior money managers to be the beginning of a new bear market as business activity concomitantly slowed dramatically. From almost universal investor agreement that the world economies and markets were improving, fears built up rapidly that we were entering a new recession. Most investors were bewildered and a good number were terrified. Who could blame them? Along with a frightening drop in prices reminiscent of September to December of

2008, volatility, exceptionally low for eighteen months, skyrocketed in four days in August 2011; the Dow Jones Industrial Average dropped 635 points, then rose 430 points, then dropped 520 points, and finally rose 423 points.

The result was confusion and panic rarely seen. Fearing a sharp recession, both Americans and foreigners poured into U.S. Treasuries even though they had been downgraded by Standard and Poor's, one of the nation's foremost credit-rating agencies, for the first time in U.S. history. Nevertheless investors rushed into them and into gold, which they regarded as the only secure investments available. Treasuries shot up a remarkable 15 percent from the beginning of the July 2011 stock market decline.

Hundreds of thousands of other investors bought gold, and in six months it rocketed from $1,400 to $1,900. Buying Treasuries because it was believed we were on the cusp of a major recession and buying gold because runaway inflation was expected in a highly overheated economy were diametrically opposite investor reactions to the same market events. It was like betting heavily on a horse to both win and come in trailing the pack in a major race. The investor, like the bettor in the analogy of the race, is almost destined to lose either way, because the house keeps a healthy percentage of both bets.

To further complicate recent developments, the over-two-month battle in July–August of 2011 to raise the U.S. debt limit, thereby preventing a U.S. default, which went down to the wire, shook the confidence of many large foreign investors in Treasuries from Russia to China to Japan, and again injected major fear into U.S. markets. The debt freeze has been estimated to eventually cost over one million domestic jobs, because state and municipal governments cannot get the money from the federal government to finance road and highway construction, maintenance, and other badly needed infrastructure projects. Our politicians certainly are far from winning public accolades for their performance. Recent public opinion polls have shown approval for congressional actions in the 20 percent range. Unfortunately the negativity does not stop there.

Many people of all political persuasions have serious questions about the quality of our economic leadership, at both the Treasury and the "independent" Federal Reserve—a concern that now stretches from the Clinton years through the Bush presidencies and the first two and a half years of the Obama administration—as well as a deep distrust of the investment bankers and banks who together came close to wiping out both our own and the global financial system in 2007 and 2008.* The Federal Reserve, for example, quietly loaned the biggest problematical banks 1.2 trillion dollars in 2008. Almost half of the largest borrowers were foreign banks. These loans were about the same amount as U.S. mortgage borrowers currently owe on 6.5 million delinquent and foreclosed mortgages.[1] The delinquent mortgage holders naturally received nothing, while many officers of the biggest troubled banks received mind-boggling bonuses and severance payments.

So where do markets and the economy stand today? The truth is that nobody knows. Horrible exogenous events can tempt you to give up your faith in the bullish case for stocks. Who could foresee the earthquake in Japan in March 2011 measuring 9.0 on the Richter scale or the giant tsunami that followed only minutes later, which created enormous devastation as well as taking thousands of lives? Those were followed within days by four adjacent nuclear plants of the Tokyo Electric Power Company being on the verge of a meltdown that threatened to take many thousands of additional lives and send markets worldwide plummeting because of the fear that this disaster would thwart global economic growth for years.

Small wonder that many people worry that even fiercer winds are not far off, while others, like myself, think the great storm is almost over and markets will continue to move higher over time, albeit with a full complement of bone-jarring such as we have just seen. One thing, though, is certain: the times are very different today from a little over a decade ago. All the investment standards we were comfortable with for many years appear to have fallen by the wayside. Many of today's financial teachings are actually toxic to your portfolio. For many generations, investors kept their money in bonds and believed they were investing prudently. Doing so today would bring about disaster. Treasury bills, supposedly the safest investment there is, have cost investors 77 percent of their purchasing power since 1946.

Can we depend on savvy and knowledgeable money managers to get us out of this quandary? No, that won't work either. They consistently underperform the market over time. John Bogle, the ex-chairman of the

---

* Throughout the text I use the term "Wall Street" to refer only to the banks and investment banks and some of the hedge funds that were instrumental in causing the financial crisis, and not the majority of money managers, analysts, mutual funds, and scores of other parts of the financial industry that had nothing to do with the debacle and were, along with their clients, hurt by it.

Vanguard Group of Mutual Funds, is an expert on mutual fund performance. Bogle heads Financial Markets Research Center, which showed
that between 1970 and 2005, a period of thirty-six years, only 2.5 percent
of the 355 equity mutual funds in existence in 1970 outperformed the
S&P 500 by at least 2 percent. A whopping 87 percent of the funds either
didn't survive or underperformed the market.[2]

Then what are we left with? Once again, as Plato noted more than
2,400 years ago, necessity will prove to be the mother of invention. The
sky is not falling; there will be some excellent opportunities ahead for
those who are not fixated on the past. I'm convinced that the country is
strong enough to put the last decade's devastating crashes behind it. It is
obvious that the mistakes and incompetence of the policy makers and the
level of greed that caused the subprime collapse cannot be brushed aside
and soon forgotten, but in this book we are concerned primarily with
how to rebuild your savings, how to structure your portfolio to withstand
likely conditions ahead, and how to take the proper actions that will let
your portfolio prosper again over time.

That is a tall order, requiring us to reexamine and fundamentally
challenge the investment theory most of us have used for generations. We
must keep what is useful but discard what doesn't work, basing this decision not on anecdotal reports but on solid empirical performance data. It
is, however, admittedly not a walk in the park.

In the opening chapters of this book, I will make the case that not
only the recent crashes but a host of powerful research findings to be
introduced have definitively proven that the efficient-market hypothesis
(EMH), the reigning investment paradigm, which states that sophisticated investors always keep prices where they should be, is incapable of
providing accurate explanations of why current investment theory has
failed, often miserably. Its basic assumptions are going to be thoroughly
analyzed, and as we analyze them, we'll see how they have been clearly refuted. The error at the heart of EMH, we will see, is that it simply does not
recognize that psychology plays a part in your investment decisions. The
efficient-market theorists—and most economists—do not believe that
psychology, with its "softening" of human rationality, should be allowed
a role in investment or economic decision making. Instead, it seems, they
have plastered the lipstick of complex mathematics onto an academically
abstract piggy to sell a lot of theoretical bacon. The deceit is certainly not
intentional; the theory's supporters believe it, despite numerous refuta-

tions of many of its premises. Science has always had a fair share of such sincere but mistaken researchers who simply won't give up on a cherished theory. In an important sense the book is a new investment paradigm or method of investing. A new paradigm is normally accepted only when an old one can no longer explain events heretofore believed to be fully explicated by it. We are at just such a crossroads today.

Appreciating the fundamental flaws in the investment strategies based on EMH will demand that we take a close look at one of the major sources of investment errors—the person you see in the mirror every morning. What psychology has to tell us about our investing behavior as individuals and within groups is, I think you will come to agree, both eye-opening and surprisingly useful in crafting an optimal investing strategy. Introducing a set of powerful psychological insights that help explain why investors so often make incorrect decisions and why the market is subject to so many booms and busts, it will provide ways to help us reject the siren call of many failed methods that are still the mainstay of contemporary investment practices; it will enable you to become a psychological investor. You will start looking at the "wacky" world of investing through a new sort of glasses: contrarian psychological shades (patent pending).

Program for This Book

I think readers would like to know at this point, in case you're faintly worried, that a dry academic debate or dull scholarly treatise is not on tap. You can relax. I will present the research findings in an easily understandable manner, not with complicated mathematical equations.

As you may already have noted, there are five parts in this book, each covering a major thematic area. Part I, "What State-of-the-Art Psychology Shows Us" looks at some of the most bizarre investment manias in history, crises that have helped us develop the new psychological insights into investors' behavior. From sophisticated French nobles in the early eighteenth century to contemporary investment bankers (circa 2006) wearing sleek Zegna suits, nothing has held back people who believe that enormous wealth is within their grasp. Yet fascinating as these stories are, our purpose here is very different. We want to see how a historical perspective can be transformed into a psychological one that might be predictive of the characteristics of future bubbles and allow us to avoid jumping on the next bandwagon.

Readers already conversant with psychology and stock market interactions will find some familiar themes and alarm bells in this work. But what is decidedly new for everyone is some recent psychological research that has pushed our understanding of investment strategies light-years ahead. Two new topics, Affect theory and neuroeconomics, are especially exciting to researchers, and neither has yet to be absorbed into Wall Street's conceptual tool kit.

The finding of how what is known as Affect works provides us with a powerful understanding of how people can so often be caught up in bubbles and come out almost penniless when they are over. Affect also works against investors in far more normal market conditions. We'll examine its influence, how it was discovered through psychological research, and the role that its various corollaries have played in distorting "rational" market behavior.

Then we'll take up a number of other psychological pitfalls that are waiting to snare the unwary investor. It turns out, for example, that people simply aren't very good statistical information processors, and that this deficiency leads them to make consistent and predictable investment errors. We'll also discover that the more we like an investment, the less risk we think it entails even if it is riddled with risk, and that in some well-known scenarios we consistently misplay odds when they are heavily against us. We'll also see how some aspects of psychology can continually trick us into buying securities that are red-hot just before they collapse and why so many of us continually play against bad odds.

We'll conclude by introducing two more heuristics (mental shortcuts), representativeness and availability, that cause systematic errors in our judgment. Both consistently take a good slice out of most investors' portfolios. Throughout, we will see how psychologically compelling these mental shortcuts are and how hardwired into our minds they happen to be. But by learning to recognize them in action, we can fend off their all-too-tight mental embrace.

In Part II, "The New Dark Ages," a critical review of the efficient-market hypothesis will help you develop a precise understanding of why the most recent market crashes have proved so destructive and why the latest one has lasted so long.

We will also deal with the efficient market's sidekick, risk analysis. It states that if you want higher return, you must take higher risk, defined as volatility. Less volatility will give you lower returns. Yet this essential portfolio protection, which you've been told for years would keep your savings secure, doesn't work and never did. We will also see that the risk evaluation methods employed today have failed miserably. The theory of risk that investors have depended on for decades to protect their portfolios is constructed on specious reasoning. Today we do not have a workable theory of risk to defend ourselves, nor have we had one in close to forty years. Small wonder that performance results have been so disappointing when bear markets come along. As will be detailed, this risk theory has been the chief culprit in the three shattering crashes since 1987 alone. We'll see why and look at something better, a new, workable theory of risk, which is well documented and will take in many of the important risk factors we are faced with today, as well as some new and potentially devastating ones that are not yet incorporated into investment teachings.

Along the way there are some hard lessons to be learned. For example, liquidity was completely sucked out of the system in 2008 and has only partially returned. We know that 60 percent of new jobs in the United States are created by companies with one hundred or fewer employees. Yet the banks, in spite of trillions of taxpayer dollars directly (and indirectly) funneled their way, have refused to lend to these job-creating firms. They couldn't, as far too much of their excess capital was invested in illiquid subprime mortgages. And guess what academic thinking encouraged them to have such small liquidity reserves? Yes, the efficient-market theorists strike again.

We'll wrap up this section with a humorous but far too precise comparison of EMH to the ancient Ptolemaic theory of planetary motions, with efficient-market advocates playing the role of ancient astronomers loudly insisting, with lots of equations and highly advanced mathematics, that the sun absolutely has to orbit around the earth. There could be no other way.

Part III, "Flawed Forecasting and Poor Investment Returns," shows that despite the great confidence in forecasting, analysts' forecasts through the years have been remarkably off the mark. Today's analysts are expected to fine-tune earnings estimates within 3 percent of actual reported earnings to prevent damaging earnings torpedoes after an earnings surprise. The evidence in these chapters of large groups of analysts' estimates over forty years demonstrates that earnings surprises are many times higher than the 3 percent analysts believe will not disrupt markets and are remarkably frequent.

Further evidence indicates that even the smallest earnings surprise can have a major effect on stock prices. Most important, the research strongly demonstrates that surprises benefit contrarian stocks and damage favorite stocks over time, providing strong new evidence supporting the use of contrarian strategies. Despite the robustness of these findings, analysts and money managers ignore them. We must not make the same mistake.

In Part IV, "Market Overreaction; The New Investment Paradigm," I introduce the contrarian strategies that will allow you to account for these psychological foibles and forecasting errors, showing that these strategies have stood the test of time and also did well through the "lost decade" and the first ten years of the twenty-first century, outperforming the market and "favorite" stocks. (The returns, though positive, were naturally lower, given the two severe crashes during this time; but there was no total devastation or major loss of capital, as so many experienced.) When the bear roared loudly, the contrarian investors could stay the course with considerable confidence. We will take a close look, in particular, at how they fared through the dot-com bubble of 1996–2000 and the financial crisis of 2007–2008. The book will also fine-tune the strategies in light of the 2007–2008 crash by adding some further investment guidelines and safety features.

A powerful hypothesis of investor behavior will also be presented, which explains why and how investors so often misvalue investments. It is called the investor overreaction hypothesis (IOH), and its thesis is that investors almost constantly overpay for stocks they like and just as consistently underpay for stocks they don't. The IOH so far has twelve testable points, with more likely to be added as research continues.

Part V, "The Challenges and Opportunities Ahead," looks at what we should expect from markets in the next few years. We'll also discuss the tools investors will need to handle the high-probability scenarios that will be described.

Our *tour d'horizon* of this brave new financial world will touch on what is likely to come. We may be saying farewell to the "Great Recession," but investors are a long way from exiting the perilous woods of inflation. As a forward-looking investor, you'll want to be fully equipped and knowledgeable about the critical financial issues that could engulf us at practically any point in the future.

The most important scenario is the major likelihood of serious inflation within two to five years, not only in the United States but also globally. We'll consider the best investments that are likely to preserve your capital and even flourish in an inflationary environment. Also, we'll review methods that investors in many other countries that have faced similar inflationary challenges have successfully followed to survive and prosper.

A Personal Note

You're going to run across an occasional brief note on my private or professional experiences. Some of these notes I hope are amusing, and some are moments I'd definitely prefer not to repeat. I thought that in a work that's so heavily indebted to the discipline of psychology, these personal reminiscences would lightly remind us that in the end we're all only human.

Sure, I've made more than a few investing choices I'd do over, and certainly not every single stock I've picked has come up a winner. I've had a few squirmy reminders that psychology affects me as much as the next guy. But as Warren Buffett once said, if a manager can bat .600 over time—get a hit six times out of ten—he or she will prove to be a big winner. In the end, fortunately, I was one of the few who outperformed the market over an extensive period of time.

Ultimately, the most essential thing you can take away from the entire book is this: the psychology-aware investor holds a superior advantage, not just more theoretical knowledge but a genuine practical investing edge. I hope that's an appealing reason to read on.

Inevitably, not all market analysts will agree with my analysis. New ideas, even when they are strongly backed by empirical investment and psychological research, will not be accepted by most, because they contradict and threaten to dethrone the theory of the day. It doesn't matter how good the new work proves to be or how badly the reigning ideas have failed; that's irrelevant to the true believers, who will try to hold their turf to the last dollar that you have. That's the way of paradigm change and probably has been since time immemorial. But fortunately the attacks are never on the reader; it's the writer who is always called out.

I have fielded criticism from academic and professional experts for more than thirty years, some of it containing sharp personal attacks. Nevertheless, though the fusillades may have sent a few of my feathers flying—not to mention on occasion raising my blood pressure to a frothy level—they have never been able to undermine the work.

I believe that it is vital that we never underestimate the role psychology plays in the market. It can be our best friend if we follow the proven contrarian strategies that protect us so well against psychological traps. It can also be our worst enemy if we try to outguess the traps, for example, saying something like, "Okay, this market will blow, but I'll just stay in a teeny bit longer" or "Heck, I've got my ten-bagger, I'll sell at eleven." Chances are those portfolios will end up at or near another financial Boot Hill. Psychology, no matter how much you've studied it or think you know it, can reduce both your ego and your net worth very quickly.

David Dreman
Aspen, Colorado
September 30, 2011

Part I

What State-of-the-Art Psychology Shows Us

Chapter 1

Planet of the Bubbles

Do you remember the days when investing was fun? I do. For me the late 1960s were a great time to be in New York City and in my midtwenties, just the right age. I started working as an analyst barely a year before the Go-Go Bubble developed. Anything we bought went up, not just 20 or 30 percent; hell, those didn't even count, they were a waste of our capital. Computer service companies, health care, semiconductor stocks, and scads more shot up ten-, twenty-, even a hundredfold. We were all becoming wildly rich—or so my young colleagues and I cockily thought for the next eighteen months.

We were a new generation, and this was a new market unlike any that had existed before. We laughed at the old fogies who bought blue-chip stocks and who shook a warning finger at us to sell before the bottom dropped out. Didn't they realize this was only the beginning? More and more analysts were recommending these sizzlers, and all the hot mutual funds were piling into them as their funds soared. Once again, as in the distant 1920s, everyone was buying stocks. As they continued to move higher, our euphoria was endless.

One of my friends (let's call him Tim) was at that time in group therapy—he said to straighten himself out, but from our talks it seemed more likely that he wanted to meet new interesting women. Whatever the case, the red-hot market permeated the group. Tim, intelligent, articulate, and not in the least reluctant to express his views, quickly became the center of attention. The sessions, led by a psychoanalyst who was an avid investor himself, turned more and more into stock-picking seminars. One group participant, a diffident middle-aged businessman still under Daddy's thumb, believed himself a financial failure. He bought one of Tim's suggestions—Recognition Equipment—as the price doubled, doubled again, and doubled yet again. He was suddenly the ultimate business success, a multimillionaire. The transformation in his self-confidence was amazing, so much so that Tim now had trouble maintaining his position as the group guru.

But the businessman's newfound financial empire was not destined to last. Suddenly the market turned down sharply, and he was heavily margined. When Recognition Equipment began collapsing, the stock quickly led him to bankruptcy, whereupon Tim was made to return the Piaget watch he had been given in appreciation. At that point my friend turned to the First Avenue bar scene, which he hoped would provide better self-realization. Still, we all remained confident. The market drop was only a sharp correction, we were certain. The stocks we held, unlike those of other investors, were sound. And had to go higher . . .

None of us escaped.

Most of my friends lost all of their gains and much of their capital. As the markets screamed downward, I slowly remembered that I was a value analyst and got out with a modicum of my gains still intact, as well as what I thought was a newly acquired ulcer; it turned out to be just badly shaken nerves. But I had been taught a lesson. The ride up was magnificent, but the ending was horrific. Despite my training and knowledge of bubbles, I too was zapped.

Though bubbles provide almost endless jubilation on the way up, the way down is like entering Dante's eighth circle of Hell. And bubbles are not simply market aberrations, occurring only occasionally. No, they are far more integral to market behavior than that, as we shall see. They sharply magnify overreactions that occur in markets and work persistently against investors' best interests. The dynamics of bubbles, and of the market reactions when they burst, have also stayed remarkably consistent over time. Unfortunately, we have not been good at learning from our mistakes.

Consider this scenario.

For almost two months the market continued to slide on increasing volume. The near-universal confidence that investors were simply beating through another correction in a market destined to move much higher was gradually changing into doubt. When rally after rally failed, that doubt turned to a deepening anxiety. Could something be very different this time?

Next came the margin calls! Financial instruments at the heart of the nation's growth and expansion plummeted for no apparent reason. Not just 2 or 3 percent but often 10 percent or more in a day. What was going on?

Rumors were rampant that now one major institution and now another was on the brink of collapse. Something had to be done to stop the stampede that threatened to turn into a panic on a scale no one had ever seen before. The president, reluctant to interfere, was called on by his top advisers to make a statement that the economic outlook was sound and to assure the nation that major prosperity lay ahead after this brief hiccup.

Assisting him in his efforts to calm the markets was his highly respected secretary of the Treasury, previously the head of one of the most formidable investment firms on Wall Street and a legend in his own time. Many other powerful market figures also threw their financial heft and hard-won reputations behind the secretary and the president.

The Treasury secretary worked with the leaders of some of the largest banks and with leading investment bankers in the country in an attempt to head off what was beginning to look like a financial disaster. A gigantic bailout plan was put together by the banks for immediate execution. The news sent stock prices soaring. Battered investors hoped this action would save the market and the financial industry, but the rally fizzled within a week and prices began to nose-dive. If the banks and the big-money pools couldn't find a fix, who could? Many professionals now saw the possibility, even the likelihood, of complete financial disintegration.

Surely this happened just prior to the infamous 2008 crash, right? But wait, this description also fits the tumultuous events before the October 1929 crash. Amazingly, the president could be either President George W. Bush or Herbert Hoover, and the Treasury secretary could be Henry "Hank" Paulson or Hoover's secretary, Andrew Mellon. (Mellon, who served through three administrations, was formerly the head of the Mellon Bank and the leading financier and industrialist of his day, with an income behind only those of John D. Rockefeller and Henry Ford.)

How badly did these crashes affect us? The 1929 crash and the ensuing Great Depression sent shock waves through the U.S. economy and
global economies that radically changed Americans' tolerance of the Wall
Street they knew. Within several years after 1929, major legislation was
passed to stop many of the egregious abuses that had been identified. Still,
none of the reforms restored confidence in the financial system for decades. As the nation approached World War II and Selective Service was
reintroduced in 1940, stockbrokers were designated the ninety-ninth out
of one hundred least important categories to be exempt from the draft.
Unemployment was near or over 20 percent for most of the 1930s, while
the value of the companies making up the Dow Jones Industrial Average
dropped from $150 billion in market value in 1929 to $17 billion in 1932,
down 89 percent.

The crash of 2007–2008 was as devastating in many ways, taking financial stocks down 83 percent in a little more than twenty-one months—
slightly more than half the time it took stocks to reach their lows of 1932.
The free fall in the value of assets so frightened lenders that they refused
to lend to banks that needed to borrow, and credit, the indispensable financial lubricant that had driven the wheels of commerce for centuries,
froze. Jean-Claude Trichet, the president of the European Central Bank,
remarked that it was the worst drop in credit since the Industrial Revolution. The industrial world was on the brink of a credit seizure it had not
experienced since the Dark Ages.

"Why Bother with Bubbles and Panics?"

That's what Fred Hills, an outstanding former editor at Simon & Schuster,
asked me in 1997, when I submitted my last manuscript to him. "Even my
twelve-year-old daughter knows about bubbles and panics," he continued.
Fred was dead-on. I'm sure that virtually every reader knows about manias and crashes. You've probably read about investors in Holland in the
1630s scrambling frantically to buy tulips and paying the equivalent of
$75,000 for a Semper Augustus, a rare bulb, during Tulip Mania. Maybe
you know the story of the printer in the 1720 English South Sea Bubble.
Envious of the promoters all around him who were coining money by
starting companies "to bring up hellfire for heating" or "to squeeze oil out

of radishes," he hatched his own scheme: "A company for carrying out an undertaking of great advantage, but nobody to know what it is."[1] When he opened his door for business at 9 A.M. the next day, long lines of people were waiting patiently to subscribe. The printer took every pound offered and wisely took a boat to the Continent that evening, never to be heard from again.*

Perhaps you've even heard of the Mississippi Bubble in France in 1720. The Mississippi Company promoter John Law was an expert at painting the canvas of concept. As one of his numerous spectacles to hype the stock, he marched many dozens of Indians through the streets of Paris bedecked in gold, diamonds, rubies, and sapphires, all supposedly coming from the almost unlimited mines of gold and precious stones in the mountains of Louisiana. The stock appreciated four thousand times before it collapsed in 1720.

When our forebears left for the New World with the hopes of escaping tyranny and persecution and finding a better life, Mr. Bubble took the perilous voyage with them and flourished as much as anyone on the journey. Bubbles and market meltdowns have occurred regularly since the nation's founding; the panics of 1785, 1792, 1819, 1837, 1857, 1873, 1893, and 1907 and the crashes of 1929, 1967, 1987, 2000, and, of course, 2008. Depending on the technical definition, more could be added.

These stories are all too familiar, it's true, but we will not be looking at bubbles through the eyes of an economic historian or simply retelling tales of the almost unbelievable levels of folly and self-delusion investors can reach. The purpose here is very different; a discussion of bubbles is essential to the investment methods we will examine in the book.

Contagion and crashes are, in fact, the starting point for our understanding of psychological behavior in the markets. After all, if everyone knows about financial bubbles, how can they keep on happening? Shouldn't economists have figured out by now how to watch for the equivalent of the engine warning light coming on?

We all know that it's very hard to pinpoint exactly when dangerous financial overheating will blow up the financial structure. We realize that stocks can become enormously overvalued, but still, most people don't

---

* Amazingly, an almost identical scheme was pulled off on a much larger scale in the 1996–2000 Internet bubble.

fold their cards and walk away with their mounting piles of chips. We just can't seem to get the timing right. This situation has not been helped by the prevailing wisdom touted by economists.

Economists following the efficient-market hypothesis (EMH) state that bubbles are impossible to predict. Market bubbles are something like stealth bombers, they say; you can't pick them up on radar, and you won't know what's hitting you until your investments are getting shellacked. No less an authority than Alan Greenspan, the former chairman of the Federal Reserve and the "prophet" of prosperity, concurs with this economic thinking: "It was very difficult to definitively identify a bubble until after the fact—that is, when its bursting confirmed its existence."[2] There is widespread agreement by economic scholars with his statement. But even worse, the popular theory states that bubbles are rational. In short, absurd pricing is always justified by the actions of totally rational, nonemotional investors, who keep prices exactly where they should be. As we'll see, this is an easy out. But it certainly protects the Fed's and academics' reputations. To accept it means that we are not capable of ever valuing anything accurately. So bye-bye to all theories of valuation, whether you are buying a home, purchasing stocks, or building a new plant. Any price is good—until it isn't. We will go into this rather tortuous logic in some detail later on, but it's obvious that investors often do not, in fact, keep prices where they should be.

Our purpose in this book is to change this thinking or at least to help change your thinking, and your investing decisions, by revealing its folly. In this chapter we'll take a quick ramble through history to show you a dozen of the main causes of bubbles and convince you that it is vital to come to a better understanding of how to spot them and avoid their carnage. Most of us looking back at earlier manias think that we could never make the same silly mistakes. I know I did when I first came to Wall Street in the late 1960s. In researching my earliest work, I logged a lot of hours at the New York Public Library and pulled out virtually every book I could find on bubbles and panics; I then read the daily financial section of both *The New York Times* and *The Wall Street Journal* for several years preceding the 1929 crash to get a real feel of these events. At first it looked so easy to make a killing by going against the obvious madness of these silly investors in the era of speakeasies, flagpole sitters, and "jazz babies" with short skirts and boyish figures. Didn't they know markets couldn't go up endlessly? Taking advantage of such folly would be a cinch.

It wasn't. It bears repeating that within a year of starting my career on the Street, I got caught up in the exact same foolishness, in the 1966–1969 Go-Go Bubble. That is a personal reason why I know that it is only through thoroughly understanding what causes manias, along with the continual overvaluations of popular stocks, that you can protect and possibly enhance your capital.

Some Common Characteristics of Manias

As we noted earlier, one of the most remarkable characteristics of speculative manias is their similarity from period to period, even if hundreds of years apart. Take the excessive use of credit as the first of many destructive characteristics most bubbles have in common.

Let's flash back again briefly to the 1929 and 2007–2008 crashes. Enormous leverage was employed in both periods, as it was in many bubbles in the past. In 1929, investors could buy stocks on 10 percent margin. Many investors back then bought investment trusts, which themselves employed large amounts of borrowing, in effect substantially increasing the 10 percent margin the buyer normally put down. By early 1929, the Federal Reserve was very concerned with speculation and raised the interest rates on margin loans to an astounding 20 percent. That put a damper on buying on margin for only an instant. After all, 20 percent a year is only 1.67 percent a month, and stocks' performance in the recent past had conditioned most investors to expect gains of 10 percent, 20 percent, or even more in months. Markets could only go higher, and quickly.

During the housing bubble that led to the 2007–2008 crash bankers margined themselves up to twenty-five to thirty times their capital, while investment bankers such as Bear Stearns, Lehman Brothers, Goldman Sachs, and Morgan Stanley were leveraged even more, up to thirty to forty times their capital, much of it in highly illiquid mortgage instruments. They believed that real estate markets could only move higher. With so much leverage, it took only a very small drop in the value of subprime mortgages for the bubble to burst.

Another similarity of manias is that virtually all of them have been bred in solid economic conditions, when investors' confidence was high. Each mania had sound beginnings and was built on a simple but intriguing concept but was then characterized by the almost complete abandonment of prudent principles that had been followed for decades, if not generations.

People believed each bubble offered opportunities far more enticing than they had ever seen before. In the classic South Sea and Mississippi bubbles, the lure was the endless flows of gold and jewels from the New World that would enrich speculators beyond their wildest dreams. In the technology bubbles of the 1960s, '70s, and '80s, it was the inexhaustible profits to be derived from the sales of innumerable numbers of semiconductors, computers, and other state-of-the-art technological products. Speculators mesmerized by the prospect of huge gains have quickly abandoned all valuation standards in bubble after bubble.

The seemingly inexorable rise in stock prices prior to the 1929 crash was called the "New Era." Earnings growth, it was said, would be so great that investors could toss all old-fashioned value standards aside, because things were really very different this time. In the Roaring Twenties, many major breakthroughs had occurred, from the invention of radio to the exciting promise of commercial aviation, and new and very profitable auto and industrial manufacturing techniques that could turn out almost unlimited amounts of goods and services. Those would continue to be scooped up by national and international markets, creating a remarkable new level of profitability on company stocks. During the 1996–2000 dot-com bubble, investors justified the enormously high stock prices by asserting that the dot coms had ushered in a "New Economy." Stock prices no longer had to be justified by the valuation standards that had been followed for generations. A new wave of much higher technological profitability now called for much higher valuations.

In every bubble, the experts have also been caught up in the speculation, not only condoning the rising prices but predicting much higher ones in the future. After all, in each case people thought they had good reason to believe that the opportunity this time was really far better than any other they had ever seen.

Another kind of flawed thinking common to all manias is the "Greater Fool Theory." In each mania some independent and skeptical thinkers were not overwhelmed by the euphoria of the time. They believed prices should never have reached the preposterous levels they had, that the crowd was really mad. But they thought things would get madder still; if prices had gone up tenfold and enthusiasm was soaring, why couldn't they go up fifteen- or twentyfold? Thus wrote a British member of Parliament in 1720 after being bankrupted by the South Sea Bubble: "I said, indeed, that ruin must soon come upon us, but I own it came two months sooner than I expected."[3]

In each mania excessively risky actions were justified as prudent. Those who did not go along were considered old fogies or even labeled "dinosaurs." I received this distinguished title myself from Jim Cramer, the market guru who has a daily show on CNBC. A month before they crashed, he said I did not understand the enormous potential of dot-com stocks. Fortunately for me, Jim's thinking about the bubble, not mine, turned out to be Stone Age that time round.

In every bubble, once the crowd begins to realize how wildly overpriced the stocks it rushed into are, there is a scramble to escape. A horrific panic ensues as the image changes from euphoria to doom. Rumors always play a major role, at first of fortunes being made and of good things to come and then later of prophecies of doom. Finally, prices fall back to where they started off or lower. The curtain has dropped, and the riveting drama is over.

Perhaps the most curious similarity of all is the sharp percentage drop from each high-water mark—on the order of 80 to 90 percent or more. Tables 1-1 and 1-2 illustrate this.

Have Bubbles Changed over Time?

I'm going to try to make a strong case that they haven't. If anything, bubbles have become much more frequent since the 1960s, the price swings more violent, and the damage to the financial system and economies, both in the United States and globally, significantly greater.

Table 1-1 shows the price drops from their peaks of four of the classic bubbles in market history: Tulip Mania (1637), the Mississippi Bubble (1720), the South Sea Bubble (1720), and the crash of 1929. The price of the Semper Augustus tulip plummeted 99 percent from its high. The price of Mississippi Company stock also fell 99 percent, while that of the South Sea Company plummeted 88 percent. Finally, in 1929–1932, the Dow Jones Industrial Average made the league of major financial disasters,

Table 1-1 Market Bubbles Through the Ages	High Price	Low Price	Price Decline from High (in Percent)
Holland, 1637 Semper Augustus (tulip bulb)	5,500[a]	50[a]	99%
England, 1720 South Sea Company	1,050[b]	129[b]	88%
France, 1720 Mississippi Company	18,000[c]	200[c]	99%
The Great Crash, 1929–1932 Dow Jones Industrial Average	381.2	41.2	89%

Source: © David Dreman, 2011. Currency used was that of each nation at that time: [a]florins; [b]pounds sterling; [c]livres.

dropping 89 percent between its high of 381 in September 1929 and its low of 41 in 1932.

Table 1-2 shows the six major market bubbles in the United States between 1960 and 2009. There were no manias between 1932 and 1960, perhaps because investors still carried the searing memories of 1929 and the Great Depression with them.

There were also at least three major real estate manias in this period, including a major S&L crisis in the mid-1980s, a commercial real estate collapse in the late 1980s, and early '90s (not shown), and of course the mother of crises, the subprime panic only a few years back. Nor does the table include a passel of major real estate bubbles such as the sale of large amounts of swampland in southern Florida in the land bubble of the mid-1920s. So high was the interest of buyers that the *Miami News* printed one edition of 504 pages that was almost all devoted to real estate ads. After that there was a collapse in real estate prices in the 1930s.

Also not included are numerous minor bubbles, among them several art frenzies (for some months in the late 1980s, Picasso paintings appreciated by about 1 percent a day). There were also stampedes into stamps, collectibles, precious metals, gold, diamonds, and coins, as well as a bevy of bubbles in the early 1990s in the Eastern European countries, after they overthrew their Communist governments. Those bring the total number of manias into the dozens since 1960, compared with only the three in Table 1-1 in the almost three hundred years prior to the 1929 crash.

Table 1-2
Contemporary Tulip Bubbles

	High Price (dollars)	Low Price (dollars)	Decline from High (in Percent)
IPO BUBBLE, 1961–1962			
AMF	63.31	15.63	75%
Automatic Canteen	44.52	9.75	78%
Brunswick	9.36	0.63	93%
Lionel	30.81	3.86	87%
Texas Instruments	0.85	0.20	76%
Transitron	42.38	6.25	85%
Adler Electronics	24.00	8.50	65%
Universal Electric Labs	18.00	1.38	92%
"GO-GO" MARKET, 1966–1969			
Control Data	29.12	4.81	83%
Electronic Data Systems	162.00	24.00	85%
Leasco Data Processing	53.96	6.60	88%
Ling-Temco-Vought	164.36	6.91	96%
Mohawk Data	111.00	18.13	84%
National Student Marketing	143.00	3.50	98%
Polaroid	72.88	25.19	65%
Recognition Equipment	102.00	12.00	88%
University Computing	442.92	52.63	88%
Itek	160.47	20.12	87%
Kalvar	73.00	11.00	85%
TWO-TIER MARKET, 1971–1974			
Kidder Peabody Nifty Fifty	—	—	81%
Avon	17.50	2.33	87%
Clorox	6.63	0.69	90%
Curtiss-Wright	7.41	0.63	92%
Data General	24.75	5.25	79%
Polaroid	74.75	7.06	91%
Rite Aid	3.55	0.16	96%
Simplicity	4.88	0.88	82%
Tropicana	60.38	6.50	89%
Wal-mart	0.07	0.01	79%
IBM	22.83	9.41	59%
Eastman Kodak	54.13	20.56	62%
TECHNOLOGY, 1979–1990			
Ask Corp	32.67	0.06	100%
Cullinet Software	33.38	4.13	88%
Floating Point Systems	46.00	0.44	99%
DOT-COM BUBBLE, 1996–2002			
NASDAQ 100 Index	4,704.73	804.64	83%
REAL ESTATE BUBBLE, 2007–2009			
S&P 500 Financial Select Sector SPDR	38.02	6.18	83%

Source: © David Dreman, 2011. Data Source: Center for Research in Security Prices (CRSP).

Many of the bubbles of recent years that are not shown in the tables were in dollar terms as large as or larger than some of the stock market bubbles shown.

As Table 1-2 also indicates, the dominant trend displayed in the six stock market bubbles since the 1960s is the increasingly prominent role of technology-related stocks, culminating in the infamous dot-com bubble of 1996–2000, by far the biggest technology bubble to this time. Technology stocks have had a special allure. Everyone had a general idea of what a big win IBM had been. It made over 11,000 percent on a buyer's original investment from 1945 to 1968 and was still growing. Why not buy the next IBM now? The promoters—oops, investment bankers—spun out thousands of new technology issues for buyers to snap up. Computer-leasing companies, for example, could quadruple or quintuple the money they made, buyers were told, by simply purchasing computers from IBM and leasing them at a lower rate. Leasco Data Processing Equipment Corporation and Levin-Townsend Computer Corporation made billions of dollars for their owners and the investment bankers before they went bust. Ten years later, most of those would-be IBMs had collapsed.

In a bubble any torrid concept will work. Investors in each mania have believed and followed pied pipers. One led them dancing to National Student Marketing Corporation (NSM), the hottest stock of the go-go market of the late 1960s. At one time it traded at nearly 100 times earnings because NSM promised to unleash the collective marketing power of hundreds of thousands of college students. What it could actually market—and how well—wasn't known. The "power" of NSM's "massive" marketing force consisted of maybe seven hundred part-time college students at its peak, but the story sounded believable, so the stock rose as high as $143 a share before reality kicked in. Then the share price dropped, like a bear on a 150-foot bungee cord, to three and change. But it didn't spring back.

Contemporary Crashes More Severe

So there are remarkable similarities in market bubbles, but there is also one important difference in the most recent booms and busts. Holland, France, and England were still prosperous after their bubbles imploded. Many speculators lost their homes, their businesses, precious metals, and other valuable assets, but the countries' economies remained strong and continued to grow stronger as the years passed. The bubbles from the 1960s to the early 1990s, although high for any period, also did little longer-term damage to the economy; the nation continued to prosper and grow. However, the last two bubbles in Table 1-2 are a very different species. Not only have more recent bubbles occurred much more frequently; they have also caused more damage. The dot-com bubble and crash of 1996–2002 is estimated to have cost investors $7 trillion and forced millions of people of retirement age to continue working because of major losses in their pension plans.

The enormous loss of wealth was also due to keeping interest rates far too low for much too long under first Chairman Greenspan and then Ben Bernanke, his successor at the Fed. This disastrous policy was instrumental in setting up the recent financial crisis, which is estimated to have caused losses of $25 trillion to $30 trillion in security values alone. Added to the cost were lost GDP, lost employment, and other major charges that brought the total loss much higher. We can also see that losses in contemporary manias are as high as and sometimes considerably higher than in those in centuries past. The price of South Sea Company stock appreciated 720 percent to its peak, while the price of tulips ran up 1,500 percent. The price of Qualcomm stock, by comparison, skyrocketed over 22,000 percent to its high, Yahoo! 18,000 percent, and Amazon.com 7,500 percent. Dozens of other dot-com stocks appreciated several thousand percent.

And all of this happened despite the fact that investors were the best educated in history. They commanded powerful state-of-the-art computers and instant communication and had up-to-the-nanosecond data at their fingertips, as well as the finest research money could buy. All the tools of logical decision making were better than ever; only the outcomes were among the worst on record. All of this is why gaining a better understanding of the psychology of both investors and the market is so crucial. The psychology of investors' overreaction is only now being researched in detail by scientists in the fields of cognitive psychology and neuroeconomics, and the work is providing new answers about why and how bubbles take place and, importantly, how the same forces that generate bubbles influence our investment decisions in any kind of market. This research has added greatly to the basic appreciation of the irrationality of investors' behavior popularized by some very astute pioneers.

▨ Understanding Bubbles: The Early Years

Far from faddish, modern psychological insights applicable to market behavior have grown over 170 years. One of the first steps of scientific method is accurate observation. This is as true in psychology as it is in chemistry, medicine, or other scientific fields. As far back as the 1840s, the Scottish journalist Charles Mackay used his astute powers of observation to develop the antecedents of behavioral finance. He wrote a remarkable book, *Extraordinary Popular Delusions and the Madness of Crowds,* first published in 1841 and still in print.

Mackay examined the three historic bubbles we have discussed—the Dutch Tulip Mania (1630s), the English South Sea Bubble (1720), and the French Mississippi Bubble (1720)—as well as other instances of crowd madness from alchemy to the burning of suspected witches and sorcerers at the stake. He declared, "We find that whole communities suddenly fix their minds upon one object, and go mad in its pursuit; that millions of people become simultaneously impressed with one delusion, and run after it. . . . Sober nations have all at once become desperate gamblers, and risked almost their existence upon the turn of a piece of paper. . . . Men, it has been well said, think in herds . . . go mad in herds, while they only recover their senses slowly, and one by one."[4] The characteristic he observed repeatedly was that when the enormous surge of speculative enthusiasm ends and the bubble begins to implode, the crowd becomes as extreme in its panic as it was euphoric. Caution and rationality are lost in the stampede to sell. In a market collapse, terrified investors are oblivious to fundamental value, just as they were when no price was too high to pay.[5] Mackay captured the flavor of mania and panic as well as any writer to this day.

Picking up from Mackay, Gustave Le Bon wrote *The Crowd: A Study of the Popular Mind,* published in English in 1896. Le Bon was a French social psychologist, sociologist, and amateur physicist. His book brilliantly caught the actions and moods of the crowd that Mackay had described. Le Bon wrote, "The sentiments and ideas of all the persons in the gathering take one and the same direction. . . . A collective mind is formed . . . presenting very clearly defined characteristics. The gathering has thus become . . . a psychological crowd."[6]

A most striking feature that Le Bon noted was a crowd's inability to separate the imaginary from the real: "A crowd thinks in images, and the image itself immediately calls up a series of other images, having no logical connection with the first. . . . It accepts as real the images evoked in its mind, though they most often have only a very distant relation with the observed fact. . . . Crowds being only capable of thinking in images are only able to be impressed by images."[7]

To a crowd, few images are more seductive than the promise of instant wealth. The picture of vast riches that would normally take a lifetime of hard work to accumulate, if you were lucky, being won effortlessly in just a few days or months is almost irresistible. Think of all of the house buyers in the early 2000s who took on huge mortgages they knew they really couldn't afford. There's no question that Mackay and Le Bon were outstanding observers far ahead of their time, but what wasn't available to them is the recent research that explains in more detail why crowds can be swept away to such levels of irrationality.

A Glimpse at the New Psychology

The psychological studies that explain a good part of these consistent and predictable behavioral errors began in the 1970s. That work eventually earned two of the leaders in the field, Daniel Kahneman and Vernon Smith, the Nobel Prize in Economics in 2002. Even more cutting-edge research began coming out after I published *Contrarian Investment Strategies: The Next Generation* in 1998. The new research provides major findings in both cognitive psychology and neuroeconomics that explain why bubbles are so powerful and repeat themselves so frequently, as well as why contrarian strategies have worked so well over time and should continue to outperform other approaches in the years ahead.

Just as psychiatrists have learned much about the functioning of the human mind through the study of disturbed patients, researchers in this field have investigated manias and crashes to gain valuable insights into financial decision making. Investment bubbles are the clearest examples of investors' overreaction because the disparity between value and price is at its most extreme.

I think this work is only the beginning in this exciting field.

This research helps greatly to explain why people become caught up in manias and bubbles and why it is so hard to recognize what's happening. So let us bid adieu to the wry and humorous images of eighteenth-century English duchesses and red-faced twenty-first-century investment bankers, all desperately scurrying after beckoning fortunes, and move on to the emotions that bring them to this state.

Chapter 2

The Perils of Affect

YES, IT'S AMUSING that investors poured money into all the historical bubbles described in the previous chapter. Even Bernie Madoff might envy the promoters back then. Their schemes were far less sophisticated than his, and if you got caught you didn't go to jail and have your underwear auctioned off to boot. But it's anything but funny to think of the millions of people who have taken brutal hits on their retirement funds and financial nest eggs.

Although the findings we'll consider about the psychology of investor and market behavior are increasingly followed by interested investors, the majority of economists, financial academics, and Wall Street professionals still dismiss the idea that psychology plays any role in investment decisions. I've written about and participated in parts of this work in cognitive psychology, sociology, and experimental psychology since the late 1970s, and there is no doubt that these findings are important to our understanding of market phenomena that entrap us repeatedly; this is why we'll look at them in some detail over the next two chapters.

Until a few years back, I continued to be perplexed by some key market events. Although a lot of the blanks had been filled in, an important piece still seemed missing from the puzzle. It's the piece we looked at in the previous chapter: why do crowds go as berserk as they do in manias and panics? How could they pay $75,000 (in today's purchasing power) for a rare tulip and then some months later refuse to pay $750 for it? How could investors shell out $150 a share for Red Hat, a sizzling computer software company, in early 2000, and only $3 a share not even two years later?

What is it that drives the supposedly totally rational investors of the late twentieth and early twenty-first centuries into speculative frenzies even more damaging than those of centuries ago?

Yes, cognitive psychology, social psychology, and a score of related disciplines have been extremely helpful in pointing out numerous psychological errors that investors make and how understanding these mistakes can both protect you and help to make you some very good money. Still, none of the psychological research could answer the question of how price movements can be so extreme or how euphoria can turn to panic in almost the blink of an eye.

▪ Affect: A Powerful New Psychological Influence

Fortunately, there are now answers. Beginning with work in the early 1980s and drawing increasing interest from researchers in the last two decades, new and dramatic findings have begun to emerge to answer this question. Not only do the answers form the core of our understanding of why bubbles occur so frequently and result in such enormous price movements in manias and panics; they also address many other market questions, some of which are critical to our investment decisions, as well as others that cut through the heart of contemporary risk analysis.

The most important discovery is that of Affect, or the Affect heuristic, as it is sometimes called, which has only recently been recognized as an important component of our judgment and decision making.* What the Affect findings have shown is that our strong likes, dislikes, and opinions, experienced as feelings such as happiness, sadness, excitement, and fear, can, either consciously or unconsciously, heavily influence our decision-making processes.

Affect can work either on its own or in tandem with our rational

---

* We will discuss cognitive heuristics in chapter 3.

decision-making processes within or outside markets. Affect is emotional, not cognitive, so it responds rapidly and automatically. The response, being emotional, need not be rational, and often isn't.

Professor Paul Slovic, a leading authority on cognitive psychology, whose work, along with that of Daniel Kahneman, a Nobel laureate in economics, is central to our look at Affect and heuristics, wrote: "Images, marked by positive and negative affective feelings, guide judgment and decision making."[1] That is, representations of objects or events in people's minds are tagged to varying degrees with positive or negative Affect. A rabid sports fan, for example, will have positive representations for a favored sports team and negative ones for an archrival team. Slovic's paper continued: "People use an Affect heuristic to make judgments. . . . People consult or refer to an 'affective pool' (containing all the positive and negative tags associated with the representations consciously or unconsciously) in the process of making judgments."[2]

We all know that we often develop very intense likes or dislikes that probably taint our judgment. And I'm sure you've found that if someone has a strong political or religious view, it is very hard, if not impossible, to change his or her thinking, no matter how powerful the argument you think you have presented. There is evidence that any such arguments will in fact actually only bolster your interlocutor's view. He may, for example, categorize your argument as a stereotypical response. Similarly, the more we like an investment choice, the stronger the positive Affect we have for it; and the more we dislike a stock or industry, the more negative the Affect it produces on us. And as in the case of political views, further positive news reinforces our positive Affect for a security while negative news reinforces our negative Affect for one we don't like.

Affect plays a central role in what have become known as dual-process theories of our mental processing of information.[3] As the psychologist Seymour Epstein states, individuals understand reality through two interactive parallel processing systems. The rational-analytic system is deliberative and analytical, functioning by way of established rules and evidence (such as mathematics and engineering). The other system, which psychologists have labeled the experiential system, is intuitive and nonverbal. The experiential system draws on information derived from experience and emotional recall and encodes reality into images, metaphors, and narratives to which affective feelings have been attached.[4]

Being emotional, not cognitive, the experiential system is much faster than the rational-analytic system, which may take many days or weeks to gather and put together all the required parts. Notice how quickly a reaction starts to form in our minds if we think we'll have a big investment gain (positive Affect) or we have a wipeout in a favorite stock (negative Affect) or even hear words such as "kidnap" or "drive-by shooting." Affect can be such a powerful emotional pressure that it can insidiously override our training and experience in the marketplace, and, as we'll soon see, it goes a long way toward explaining extreme stock mispricing.

Images and associations are pulled into the conscious mind from past, current, and hoped-for experiences. And the more intensive our positive or negative feelings are, whether about ideas, groups of people, stocks, industries, or markets, the more intensely Affect influences our decisions on them.

Affect may also have an influence on eyewitnesses to an accident or a crime. They are often poor witnesses, and find it difficult to reconstruct events, as they are focused on one emotional detail or another. The Affect system, anchored in emotions, can at times be far from completely rational.

Although analysis is critical to many decision-making circumstances, reliance on Affect and emotions is a quicker, easier, and more efficient way to navigate in a complex, uncertain, and sometimes dangerous world. In periods of great anxiety and uncertainty, it is quite natural for the experiential system, often dominated by Affect, to take over.

A key reason is that Affect often has the power to overwhelm our analytical, rational-analytic memory banks, substituting its independent memory bank of related events and their emotional accompaniments. Easy to use, yes, but sometimes extremely dangerous. Every bubble we looked at in the previous chapter, as we shall see, had Affect at its base.

You may already have guessed that Affect can also be a powerful subliminal force likely to sway an investor's judgment when information is sizable but still incomplete or conflicting and yet a decision must be made. In a strong market investors are often mesmerized by the major gains already made and mouthwatering images of even larger gains ahead. The experiential system easily subdues the more cautious images of the rational-analytic system. In the inevitable panic that follows a bubble, the Affect images change dramatically. We no longer think of enormous gains to be made by holding stellar investments. Now we are forcibly introduced to negative Affect. The Affect system flashes out images of crushing losses ahead. The more the stock falls, the more powerful the negative Affect gets. "Sell, sell," flashes in the mind of most investors before the stocks drop even further. Before long, the image becomes one of total doom ahead.

Affect is by no means limited to the marketplace. Successful marketers of anything from cars to the world of fashion have capitalized on the effects of Affect for decades to manipulate buyers' preferences for their products. Researchers are beginning to study its power in motivating groups to take actions that are sometimes silly, sometimes deadly, in many other areas of behavior, from rioting sports fans to murder. At its darkest there is genocide; dozens of repulsive episodes have taken place since the Holocaust, even though the war crimes trials in Nuremberg in 1945–1946 and the International Court of Justice in The Hague in 1945 laid out rigorous punishments for it. Hatred promulgated by Affect at its extreme can become so deep that the victims are no longer thought of as humans but as predatory animals that must be exterminated in order to survive. Affect can cause behavior to move many standard deviations away from the norm.

Affect can also act very subtly. For example, you think Merck looks good and pharmaceutical stocks are depressed, but there is more information you want to go through. However, you don't have the time to get all the data you need because the stock is moving up. You fall back on Affect, often without knowing it, because it's in sympathy with your gut feeling and reinforces your willingness to make the decision to buy.

Reliance on Affect can mislead us, sometimes very badly. If it were always optimal to follow our affective instincts, there would be no need for the rational-analytic system of thinking to have evolved and become so prominent in human affairs.[5] It's time to move on to some of the deadly shortfalls that Affect bequeaths to markets. The experiential system, provided with psychological rocket fuel from Affect, enhances the powerful images of gains. Affect is potentially more helpful or more dangerous because of its emotional rather than cognitive basis.

Next we'll look at four important forms of Affect, all of which have bloodied investors' portfolios over time: (1) insensitivity to probability, (2) negatively correlated judgments of risk and benefit, (3) the Durability Bias, and (4) Temporal Construal.

1. Insensitivity to Probability

There are a number of key ways in which Affect leads to errors in judgment. The most important is that it causes us to be insensitive to the true probability for investments to increase (or fall) in price while not factoring in the reasons this should happen. When a potential outcome, such as a major gain from a stock purchase, carries sharp and strong affective meaning, the actual probability of that outcome, or changes in the probability due to changing circumstances, will tend to carry very little weight.[6]

Insensitivity to probability is backed by strong research findings.[7] Professors George Loewenstein, Elke Weber, Christopher Hsee, and Ned Welch[8] conducted a fascinating study that showed that if people think they are going to win a state lottery, their bets and their expectations about the chances of winning are likely to be similar whether the probability is 1 in 10,000 or 1 in 10 million. If people feel they are going to win, they can be willing to pay up to 1,000 times more for the same lottery odds! Interestingly, these figures are in line with what speculators paid to buy the hot stock of the day in a stock mania. Loewenstein and his coauthors note that what is going on here is that gamblers are more moved by the possibility, rather than the probability, of a strong positive consequence. The result is that very small probabilities carry great weight.

Another interesting study found that investors apparently did not care what price they paid for an exciting initial public offering (IPO) in a bubble market. The distinguished economist Robert Shiller demonstrated that if an investor wanted to buy a hundred shares of a company (say, at $10), it didn't matter to him if the company had one million shares to sell or, having split just prior to the IPO, five million shares to offer. Shiller found that quintupling the price of the outstanding stock was immaterial to the IPO buyer, who still wanted to buy the same one hundred shares at $10 a share even though they gave him only one-fifth of the previous value, because he was convinced the price would go higher.

Insensitivity to probability is backed by other strong research findings. Yuval Rottenstreich and Christopher Hsee[9] demonstrated that if the potential outcome of a gamble is emotionally powerful, its attractiveness (or unattractiveness) is relatively insensitive to changes in probability as great as from .99 to .01, or 100-fold. *These findings go to the heart of the overvaluation in a bubble. If we have very strong feelings about the pros-*

pects of a stock or another investment, we will sometimes pay 100 times its
real value or more. This finding captures the major reason why stock prices
are driven to astronomical heights during a bubble.

Figure 2-1 shows just how dead-on these findings are. If anything, as we'll see, overvaluations can be even greater than 100 times earnings. From the beginning of 1996 through the peak in March 2000, the NASDAQ 100 made up primarily of the largest dot-com and high-tech stocks increased 717 percent. From the high-water mark of March 2000, the index dropped 83 percent to its October 2002 low, the worst decline of a major U.S. market index since the 89 percent drop in the Dow Jones Industrial Average in the 1929–1932 period. Near the height of the bubble, the NASDAQ 100 had a P/E multiple of over 200 times earnings. Virtually all of the companies in the index had products or services that projected images of rapid growth, often far removed from any realistic chance of being attained.

Two fairly typical examples of the extent of investors' enthusiasm for these stocks follow.

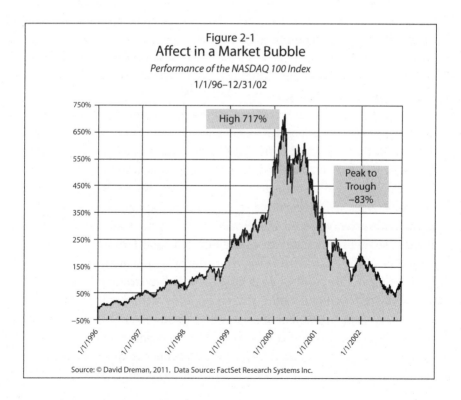

Figure 2-1
Affect in a Market Bubble
Performance of the NASDAQ 100 Index
1/1/96–12/31/02

Source: © David Dreman, 2011. Data Source: FactSet Research Systems Inc.

Example A: America Online (AOL) had a P/E of 200 times trailing earnings in March 2000. The company had shown spectacular earnings growth in the previous six years, and analysts believed the growth rates were likely to accelerate as millions of new customers signed up annually to use its popular online services. Using a standard earnings discount model, I calculated that to justify its then-current price, it would need approximately 18 billion subscribers, or roughly three times the population of the earth. My conclusion at the time was that a large extraterrestrial population needed to be discovered quickly to meet these "modest" growth goals.

Soon after, AOL merged with Time Warner. Much heavier than anticipated competition worldwide, a severe slowdown in online growth, and accounting methods that dramatically overstated earnings and had to be subsequently sharply revised downward, resulting in a major drop in price of the shares of the merged company. From a price of $100 in the first quarter of 2000, the value of the AOL portion of the company fell about 90 percent to its low.

Example B: eToys.com was an exciting new dot-com merchandiser that sold a large variety of toys online. eToys.com's concept was not only to provide shoppers with the largest variety of popular toys available but also to be a substantial time-saver for users of the site. Moreover, users would benefit from discounts that would underprice almost all its other major competitors.

The fact that a number of large competitors already had or were constructing powerful online sites was dismissed by most analysts and investors, as was the fact that eToys.com's discounting policy resulted in large losses for the firm because it did not have the sales volume to receive the large discounts that its competitors did from the major toy manufacturers. At its peak in October 1999, eToys.com had a market value of $10.7 billion, more than triple that of Toys 'R' Us, the largest toy retailer, which had many hundreds of stores nationwide. eToys.com's sales were less than 1 percent of those of Toys 'R' Us. The company, as noted, operated at a loss, whereas Toys 'R' Us had a long record of profitability. eToys.com was also conceived and operated by a middle-level retail executive, and its management depth was limited. More accurately but less kindly, its management was so-so at best.

With no real business plan, the company continued to generate large losses and went into bankruptcy in 2001. All those facts were readily available at the time; however, analysts, money managers, and investors did not process the information because of the very powerful positive affective image the company conveyed, and continued to believe that the stock was an outstanding investment opportunity almost all the way to the funeral. Once again, it seems clear that when positive Affect is in high gear, rational and logical analysis is often overwhelmed by the experiential system.

Although the two stocks had unique individual characteristics, both were part of the NASDAQ Composite Index. Along with many other high-tech and dot-com issues, they were markedly overvalued through this time period. The sensitivity to the *possibility* of a major gain, rather than the *probability* of one, appears to have played an important role in the stupendous overvaluation of dot-com and high-tech stocks in the 1996–2000 dot-com bubble.

Table 2-1, which I originally constructed in November 1999, near the height of the Internet bubble, shows the price-earnings ratios (P/Es) of ten of the most popular Internet stocks at that time. The classic two-tier market of 1971–1974, which focused entirely on large, rapidly growing companies, had an average P/E of 51 for the fifty leading growth stocks at its peak, well above the normal P/E of such growth stocks of 25–35× earnings. After the stocks dropped drastically in the 1973–1974 bear market, they were long held up as the leading example of investors' paying far too much for prospective growth.

Not so in the 1996–2000 dot-com bubble. The price-earnings ratios in Table 2-1 were as high as 1,930 times earnings; the average P/E of the group was an amazing 739. The magnitude of the excesses of this bubble can be gauged from the fact that the average P/E of the ten dot-com companies shown in Table 2-1 was fourteen times as high, on average, as the average P/E of fifty-one of the "Nifty Fifty" stocks of the two-tier market of 1971–1974. The 1996–2000 bubble companies were not small or unknown but had market capitalizations ranging from $1.6 billion to $30.1 billion, larger than the average company in the S&P 500.

We decided to find out what the fundamental value of the stocks in the table really was in October 1999, near the top of the bubble. The analysts' consensus earnings estimates for 1999 were used as the start-

Table 2-1
Footprints of a Mania
The Dot-Com Bubble
1996–2000

Company	10/31/1999 Price	10/31/1999 P/E	PV of discounted future EPS: 15% [1,2]	Price 8/31/2002
eBay	$67.57	1,930	$ 4.75	$56.52
RealNetworks	54.85	1,219	5.31	4.58
Yahoo!	89.53	1,194	10.18	10.29
DoubleClick	70.00	933	6.70	5.63
Priceline.com	60.25	603	8.92	2.35
Amazon.com	70.63	353	17.87	14.94
Lycos[3]	53.38	334	18.87	11.19
Qwest	36.00	327	13.00	3.28
MindSpring[3]	25.69	257	11.80	6.10
E*Trade	23.81	238	10.27	4.34

Average Decline from 11/1999 to 8/31/2002 = −79.1%

1. Earnings are assumed to grow at 50% for the first three years, 25% for the next five years, 20% for the next six years, 15% for another seven years, and 7.5% thereafter.
2. Discount rates are calculated as follows: the 15% rate includes 5.9% on long government bonds plus a 9.1% risk premium.
3. Lycos was purchased on 10/30/00 by Terra Networks SA for 2.15 shares per Lycos share. Mindspring is now Earthlink.

Source: © David Dreman, 2011.

ing point, and then the highest earnings growth rates in U.S. company history were applied for the next twenty-one years for each company in the table, after which the normal earnings growth rate of the S&P 500 was applied. The earnings growth rates attributed to the exciting concept companies were almost farcically high (see the assumptions in Table 2-1), demonstrating that even if earnings had met the almost impossible targets, which almost no company had ever achieved since the founding of the nation, the stocks would still be wildly overpriced.

The stock prices we created in column 3, which showed somewhat lower but still wildly bullish evaluations, were derived by using the discounted earnings of each company. To arrive at these prices, we used a simple earnings discount model, one of the basic methods of valuing a stock's price.*

---

* An earnings discount model takes the analyst's estimate of future earnings for a company well into the future (often thirty years or more) and applies a discount rate to each year's

Compare column 3 with column 1, the then current price of each company. The stocks in column 1 were trading from fourteen times the highest valuations the model gave a company in column 3 to slightly over two times as much on the lowest. Although the prices we gave the column 3 group, based on the hyperexpanding earnings, were preposterously high, the actual company prices in column 1 almost doubled again by March 2000, catapulting the prices of dot-com stocks sharply higher again.

Column 4 of Table 2-1 (the one column added since the 1999 presentation) shows the prices of the stocks on August 31, 2002, after the bubble imploded. The average decline of the group was 79.1 percent. Only one stock, eBay, remains well above the present-value model estimates established in column 3. One stock is a little less than 1 percent above the prices in column 3, while the remaining eight are below these estimates, some very substantially. As noted, an estimated $7 trillion was lost in the bubble in high-tech stocks and the market. As a comparison, the loss from the market's 1987 crash from its peak to its nadir was $1 trillion.

2. Judgments of Risk and Benefit Are Negatively Correlated

Does Affect also blind us to the risk of a security or of our entire portfolio? Our investment teachings clearly state that it doesn't. After all, risk theory has existed for fifty years, and there are untold numbers of antirisk defenses out there to protect risk from attacking our portfolios. The efficient market hypothesis (EMH) and the great preponderance of modern risk theory, used by investors, their advisors, and their mutual funds, believe that risk is solely volatility. Unfortunately, recent work on Affect provides strong evidence that the defenses most people use will not do their job.

EMH argues that the greater the risk taken, the higher the perceived rewards of an investment will be. Affect theory discovered that it doesn't quite work this way. Professors Baruch Fischhoff, Paul Slovic, Sarah Lichtenstein, Stephen Read, and Barbara Coombs[10] found that the judg-

---

earnings composed of the current price of long-term government bonds, then 5.9 percent, and then adds a 9.1 percent risk factor (which the author believed was quite conservative, given the staggering growth projected in markets which were in a very early stage of development and for which almost no attention was paid to future competition or a multitude of other factors that could limit growth over time).

ments of risk and rewards are negatively correlated. That is, the greater the actual risk, the smaller the perceived gain, while the smaller the perceived risk, the greater the perceived gain. In a word, modern risk theory is turned upside down. And research into the role of Affect appears to explain why.

These findings were supported in numerous follow-up papers. Researchers asked subjects how risky various activities were. Repeatedly, subjects answered that for many potentially dangerous or hazardous situations the greater the perceived benefit or reward, the lower the perceived risk. In virtually every case the risk is there but is perceived differently depending on the magnitude of the benefits. Conversely, the lower the perceived reward or benefit, the greater the perceived risk. Researchers, for example, have found that alcoholic beverages and food additives are believed to be low in benefit and high in risk, whereas vaccines, antibiotics, and X-rays tend to be seen as high in benefit and low in risk. In the investment world higher risk is believed to have a close correlation to higher return. This psychological behavior also simply cannot exist according to current investment teachings.

Slovic, MacGregor, Malmfors, and Purchase[11] surveyed members of the British Toxicological Society and found that these experts, too, produced the same inverse relation between judgments of risk and benefit.*[12] The behavioral researchers state that a negative correlation between risk and reward occurs even when the nature of gains or benefits is distinct and qualitatively different from the nature of the risks. What is difficult for investors to understand is that psychologically risk and return appear

---

* As expected, the strength of the experts' affective reactions was found to strongly influence the inverse relation toward the hazardous items being judged. In a second study, these same toxicologists were asked to make a "quick intuitive rating" for each of thirty chemical items (e.g., benzene, aspirin, secondhand cigarette smoke, dioxin in food) on an Affect scale (bad–good). Next, they were asked to judge the degree of risk associated with a very small exposure to the chemical, defined as an exposure that is less than $\frac{1}{100}$ of the exposure level that would begin to cause concern for a regulatory agency. Rationally, because exposure was so low, one might expect these risk judgments to be uniformly low and unvarying, resulting in little or no correlation with the ratings of Affect. Instead, there was a strong correlation across chemicals between Affect and judged risk of a very small exposure. When the Affect rating was strongly negative, judged risk of a very small exposure was high; when Affect was positive, judged risk was small. Almost every respondent (ninety-five out of ninety-seven) answered in this manner.

to often be negatively correlated. In markets we believe that rationally they have to be positively correlated.

A research paper by Ali Alhakami and Paul Slovic[13] indicates that the perceived risk and perceived benefit of an activity (e.g., using pesticides) were linked to the positive or negative Affect associated with the activity. The result implies that the more strongly people like an activity, such as the use of an untested treatment for cancer or the purchase of a dot-com stock, the more they judge the risks to be low and the benefits high. Conversely, the more they dislike activities, such as using coal as a source of energy, drinking alcoholic beverages, or buying stocks with so-so returns, the higher the risk levels they attribute to these.

According to Alhakami and Slovic, this result implies that people base their judgments of the risk and benefits of an activity or a technology not only on what they think about it, *but also on how they feel about it.* If they have an idea or concept they strongly like, they are moved to judge that the risk is low. The more they dislike an idea or concept, the higher they judge the risk. So Affect again enters into the picture, this time allowing our feelings to tamper with and alter our rational decision making and choices on risk. In the realm of finance, Yoav Ganzach[14] found support for concluding that if stocks were perceived as good, they were judged to have higher returns and low risk, whereas if they were perceived as bad, they were judged to be lower in return and higher in risk. However, for familiar stocks, perceived risk and return were positively correlated, rather than being driven by this attitude.

This work is important in explaining the strong role of Affect in the perception of risk in Figure 2-1 and Table 2-1. In both cases the Affect about the investments was very positive. As indicated, it appeared that stocks were priced at many times their real values; in the face of widely followed investment principles, the risk of investing in them was probably overriden by the strong positive Affect for them. Analytical or logical comparisons, which showed how overvalued top NASDAQ stocks were in late 1999 (Table 2-1), failed to change investors' opinions that they were low-risk holdings.

In making their evaluations, swayed by Affect, the analysts probably really did not believe the risk factor was unduly high relative to the expected returns. In my reading of large numbers of analysts' reports near the height of the dot-com bubble, I saw very little analysis of the major risks involved. This point is important in gauging the effectiveness of modern security analysis, and the rational-analytic processes more generally, when emotional influences such as Affect are involved. The risks were often obvious, as in the case of eToys.com and many hundreds of similar stocks of companies that had limited finances, questionable management, and poor business plans but skyrocketing stock prices. Almost all these factors could be checked quickly by any competent researcher but were not, or the information did not register on the researchers. Instead, the great majority of reports discussed the enormous potential returns ahead and detailed why they should occur.

Conversely, in the 1996–2000 bubble, value stocks, which were far less risky by standard valuation yardsticks, had very negative Affect attached to them. As a result, the influence of Affect on most investors at the time made them believe that those stocks were far more risky than their valuation standards would indicate. They were often thought to be significantly more risky than IPOs or dot-com and high-tech stocks, both of which subsequently collapsed. The risk-reward situation had obviously been turned upside down during the dot-com mania. But as we'll see, though a bubble brings these relationships out with far greater clarity, they are always there, opening the road to major opportunities.

When the Internet bubble imploded in the spring of 2000, the supposedly significantly more risky, low-reward value stocks showed stunning positive reappraisals as the carnage in dot-com and other favorites was inflicted. Once again in the investment world, we see a clear case of Affect overpowering the rational-analytic approach, and probably to a degree that has not been observed elsewhere as yet in experiential experiments. Shortly thereafter, more normal evaluations began to be applied again to both dot-com and value stocks, resulting in the reversal, to a major extent, of the valuations during the 1996–2000 bubble.

Unfortunately, before that, the strong influence of Affect on many investors, including large numbers nearing retirement, resulted in enormous losses. The outcome, reported repeatedly in the press, is that millions of people have had to continue to work for extended periods. Introducing findings from the research on Affect appears to provide a plausible explanation of this harmful phenomenon.

Though the linking of strong positive Affect with limited risk in investors' minds, and of negative Affect with high risk, appears far clearer in a bubble environment, it also seems to be present in many other types of market circumstances, as will be discussed. As we saw on page 39, the risk-Affect correlation also has important implications for contemporary risk management and financial theory.

3. The Durability Bias

Another way that Affect tends to skew our assessments in the market arises because we tend to overestimate how long a positive or negative event or earnings surprise will have an impact on a stock and industry or the entire market itself. Professors D. T. Gilbert, E. C. Pinel, T. D. Wilson, S. J. Blumberg, and T. P. Wheatley observed a consistent tendency of market participants to overestimate the length of time a positive or negative Affect would last after experiencing a pleasant or unpleasant event.[15] This effect is called the "Durability Bias."

The finding is important in gauging the overreaction to either a positive or a negative earnings surprise as well as a host of other market positive or negative events. To take one example, oil exploration and development companies plummeted sharply in the spring of 2010, after the BP rig blew up and a major oil spill ensued in the Gulf of Mexico. The prevailing feeling at the time was that no deep drilling would be allowed again in the gulf or other continental waters around the United States for years. Too, the cleanup costs were at the time thought to be prohibitive for both BP and its partners. Within a year, deepwater drilling was allowed again off U.S. shores, and the costs, though high, were manageable by all the firms involved. Some of the stocks originally believed to be the most exposed more than doubled in less than a year.

This finding, as we shall see in Parts III and IV, would seem to be helpful in explaining both the superior performance of "worst" over "best" stocks and the consistent but opposite reaction to surprise events by these two categories.

4. Temporal Construal

Affect leads us to make misjudgments related to time. Events nearer in time are likely to be represented in terms of more concrete and specific detail. Short-term events will include sales and earnings that are higher or lower than expected, and many other expectations that analysts report.[16] Meanwhile, the farther an event occurs in the future, the more probable returns are likely to be represented in terms of a few abstract or general features that contain the perceived essence of the concept of the stock under consideration. This phenomenon is called "Temporal Construal." This Affect characteristic causes investors to extend their views of the prospects of stocks both in and out of favor far into the future. If the future outlook is negative, the results will be reversed.

Affect results in a smoothing effect on the judgment of longer-term prospects. Rather than focusing on dozens of shorter-term inputs—most positive, but some negative—focusing on the *more general thoughts about exciting longer-term prospects tends to result in more favorable forecasts than those made for the short term.*

As a result of a strong positive or negative Affect, a stock, an industry, or the market itself can be priced too high or too low. Professors Trope and Liberman reported that great optimism toward long-term returns might be explained by this Affect characteristic.

Temporal Construal helps explain the consistent outperformance of contrarian investment strategies over time, as well as the major overpricing of technological stocks in bubbles. In the first case (as we shall see in detail in Part IV), investors expect the worst from out-of-favor contrarian stocks and discount their prospects far into the future. In the second case, investors generally extend expectations for concept companies' positive results as they expand their markets rapidly too far into the future. We've now seen a number of instances of just how overvalued such concept stocks can get as investors overestimated the length of time a positive Affect would last for favored stocks such as the dot-com issues in the tech bubbles. Professor Trope and his colleagues have produced a good deal of experimental evidence that documents the difference in the way long-term and short-term estimates are constructed.

A glaring case in point is the expectations before the dot-com bust about Yahoo!'s growth. Yahoo! went public in April 1996 and was the hottest of the hot IPOs through the dot-com bubble.

The stock appreciated 18,000 percent from late July 1996 to its high of $119 (adjusted for stock splits) in January 2000. Investors considered it the Web site extraordinaire, with the potential for almost unlimited growth of advertising, strong revenue streams, and enormous user growth. Yahoo!'s potential growth was considered unequaled.

The company's sales growth in the 1996–2000 period was enormous, rising from $23.8 million to over $1.1 billion (116 percent compounded annual growth over the five-year period). However, earnings did not do quite as well. The company lost money in 1996–1998 before making pennies in earnings per share in 1999 and 2000. It made only a couple of pennies a share for the entire 1996–2000 period on a stock that at its high was, as noted, close to $120. But concept ruled supreme.

In early 2000, Yahoo! had a P/E of 5,938, and most investors expected huge earnings growth in the next ten years—well over 50 percent a year. As good a company as it was, these long-term expectations were wildly overestimated. In the dot-com crash from 2000 to 2002, both a severe reappraisal of its future growth rate and the fact that Yahoo!'s earnings had grown at a far lower rate than the market expected resulted in the stock's dropping 97 percent to its low in early fall of 2001, as the dot-com crash approached its nadir.

Another interesting instance of Temporal Construal can be observed in studies that asked investors to estimate the future performance of their stock portfolios during the 1996–2000 bubble. In 1998, near the height of the bubble, U.S. investors were extremely optimistic about the future returns of stocks. Late that year Paul Slovic, Stephen Johnson, Donald MacGregor, and I were coauthors of a study to pinpoint the expectations of a large number of mutual fund investors for the next ten years. According to our study,[17] when subjects were asked to forecast their average return over the next ten years, investors were highly optimistic, estimating 14 percent annually on average. Stocks have in fact returned about 10 percent over time since the 1920s, so those enthusiastic investors appeared to be anticipating market returns in the decade ahead some 40 percent above those of the past seventy years.

The Implications of Affect on Security Analysis

In this chapter, we have seen how powerful various forms of Affect were in both fueling the bubbles and manias we observed in chapter 1 and then, as circumstances changed, sharply escalating the terror and panic when each bubble imploded. The Affect heuristic is both wondrous and frightening: astounding in its speed, subtlety, and sophistication; frightening in its power to lead us astray. According to Paul Slovic, "It is sobering to contemplate how elusive meaning is, due to its dependence upon Affect."[18]

We should pause for a second to consider the forms of meaning which we take for granted and in which we justify spending immense time and expense to gather information. Will the use of "meaningful information," such as thorough security or market analysis, be in many cases illusionary, since as we'll see, these cases are all too often laced with Affect?

Obviously, it is not going to be easy to protect ourselves from such dangers. That is why the book will introduce disciplines you can follow that will, like a stun gun, stop Affect when it's working against your interests. The real question is whether you can pull the trigger when the time comes. It's harder than it seems. Still, being aware of Affect is a good first step to a better investment strategy.

The Disconnect Between Fundamentals and Price

One of the most notable characteristics of an Affect-induced bubble, as we have seen, is the enormous disconnect between fundamentals and price for analysts, money managers, and other highly trained financial professionals. The standard guidelines used to evaluate a company's outlook are derived from the rational-analytic system.

The CFA Institute and virtually all of the academic training materials teach analysts and money managers to behave in a rational manner and thus to look at all the important fundamentals of a company to determine its price. A bible for this training is Benjamin Graham and David Dodd's *Security Analysis*.[19] A myriad of other books adhere to very similar methods. As we saw earlier, Graham and Dodd use a large number of financial ratios as well as detailed company information to decide on the value of a stock. The standard guidelines used to evaluate a company's outlook sketched out earlier are most often bypassed or short-circuited.

Unfortunately, most professionals—despite their training, the state-of-the-art information available to them, and the best research available—often do no better and sometimes do worse than the average investor. This gives us a good idea of just how strong the forces of Affect actually are.

Insensitivity to probability appears to be the most important Affect characteristic that leads financial professionals to make exactly the same mistakes as the average investor by focusing on a grossly exaggerated view of the values for companies that appear at the time to have almost unlimited growth and profitability. As we've also seen, the finding that judgments of risk and benefit are negatively correlated, the Durability Bias, and Temporal Construal all can knock our portfolios down mercilessly. Affect can turn the playing field upside down. Unfortunately, Affect can take down the professional investor despite his extensive knowledge and training as quickly as it does the individual investor.

Almost no price seemed too high for companies that have already had explosive price appreciation as well as an exciting, if not almost irresistible, story to tell. Strong positive Affect attaches to the image that the dot-com or IPOs issues create instant wealth, and quite likely overwhelms the rational-analytic system, resulting in a major swing away from optimum decision making.

The Consequences for Security Analysis

We should ask if analysts or money managers use any rational evaluation models at all to justify extreme overpricing. While almost all claim they do, the enormous disparity between the maximum price a fundamental model would allow and the substantially higher market prices makes it clear that, as Table 2-1 demonstrated, the models could not in fact be based on accepted valuation techniques.

Looking at the sky-high prices so many analysts paid in recent years, Graham would have shaken his head, although I've heard from some of his still-living contemporaries that the response would have been a little more lively. Graham was ultraconservative on price-earnings and other valuation ratios, normally arguing not to buy a stock with a P/E much above 20, regardless of its outlook, as he believed "Mr. Market," the name he coined for the market, could go to major extremes quickly.

Stocks with average prospects will normally have P/Es of 12 to 15; those with well above average earnings growth prospects will be in a 25-to-35 P/E range; and those with extraordinary growth will be at possibly forty to fifty times earnings. How, then, can we justify the fact that many stocks, recommended by scores of analysts, trade at 100 to 1,000 or more times earnings?

▨ Can Affect Fatally Flaw Security Analysis?

Unfortunately, what comes out clearly is that investment professionals cannot accurately gauge prices in the range of approximately plus or
minus 25 to 35 above or below fundamental value that financial theory
holds a good analyst should, thereby allowing her or him to profit through
buying undervalued or selling overvalued securities respectively. As we
just saw, analysts often missed the proper valuations of Internet and high-
tech stocks by fifty- to 100-fold as evidenced repeatedly in the dot-com
bubble and other tech bubbles since the early 1960s. This created, at least
temporarily, valuations sharply higher than any considered acceptable
that were based on standard security analysis.*

What we see, then, is that positive Affect, in extreme circumstances
such as bubbles overpowers analysts following contemporary security
analysis and raises prices significantly above what long-term valuation
standards will sanction. In a panic, negative Affect results in the opposite
case, reserved for investors who want to sell at any price. Unfortunately, the
very people we depend on most to guide us to safety when a market storm
appears are the first to be swept away when the terrible weather hits.

▨ The Great Escape

The standard guideline used to evaluate a company's outlook is based on
the rational-analytic system. According to the CFA Institute and virtually
all sophisticated academic training in the field, analysts and money managers behave in a rational manner and so look at all the important fundamentals of a company to determine its price, as we discussed earlier. The
bible for this training, as we saw, is normally Graham and Dodd's *Security
Analysis*, or a similar text, as well as hundreds of pages of CFA instruc-
tion, written by highly experienced investment professionals.

Worth repeating is that security analysis can be effective in a range
of approximately plus or minus 25 to 35 above or below fundamental
value. So if a company is undervalued at, say, 10 times earnings, an astute
analyst can buy it and perhaps double his money. However, fundamental

---

*This will be an important point to remember for chapter 7.

analysis cannot work when prices move into outer space. In a bubble, a price-earnings ratio or price-to-cash-flow ratio can go from 10 to 100, or even sometimes to 1,000 or more. A price-to-book-value ratio of 4 can go to 40 or even 400 and so forth. At these levels fundamental security analysis breaks down entirely.

In a bubble or another period of extreme overvaluation, the focus is on grossly exaggerated prospects for a company or an industry that analysts or money managers forecast. Importantly in this situation, standard fundamental analytic tools, such as earnings discount models, which project highly optimistic earnings estimates several dozen years into the future, repeatedly show that the current price of the bubble stock is far too high, as we saw in Table 2-1.

What analysts, along with most people, don't know is that most of the investment rational-analytic standards are often bypassed or short-circuited by Affect as well as by other psychology we will view. Analysts and money managers have enormous difficulty in attempting to work within the rational-analytic system when the experiential system is under full sail. Most professionals do try to get it right, but the force of powerful positive or negative Affect is difficult to cope with, as we now know. I've spoken at half a dozen of the CFA Institute's National Conferences on investor psychology over more than three decades, as well as to many large societies of security analysts and to leading business schools, and I know professionals make a genuine effort to follow their fundamental methods.

Unfortunately, psychology, although widely acknowledged by these groups, is impossible to square with current investment theory, because the latter sits on a foundation solidly built on the rational-analytic approach. When this happens, analysts and money managers abandon this approach all too frequently and shift over to the experiential system, where Affect, in extreme circumstances, as we saw, easily overwhelms our rational-analytic processes.

The bottom line is that no analyst could recommend and no money manager could buy bubble stocks using rational-analytic methods. Analysts and money managers didn't need a financial GPS to calculate how far off course the stocks' pricing was. With this disparity in price, a sextant would have worked just as fine.

The analysts and money managers were hijacked by their expectations, which were heavily weighted by their strong positive Affect for these issues. We should see clearly now that professionals cannot accurately gauge prices in the relatively limited range* that financial theory holds a good analyst should, thereby allowing him to profit through buying undervalued or selling overvalued securities respectively.

Analysts missed the proper valuations, as we saw, by 50 to 100 times on many occasions in bubbles. They created valuation paradigms that justified price-earnings almost exponentially higher than any considered acceptable, employing standard analytical techniques. Does security analysis work using today's rational-analytic methods? Possibly for brief periods of time when the water is tranquil. But don't go out too far: remember, you're paddling a twelve-foot kayak; you're not in a 700-foot ocean liner.

I will be introducing a number of Psychological Guidelines that, if followed, should limit your losses in the psychological traps we will be examining through the course of the book. If they are adhered to, they will protect you from making some of the mistakes most investors are entrapped by. We should also find ways to use these predictable errors to our advantage. Here is the first one.

PSYCHOLOGICAL GUIDELINE 1: Do not abandon the prices projected by careful security analysis, even if they are temporarily far removed from current market prices. Over time the market prices will regress to levels similar to those originally projected.

Next, let's extend our look into other major heuristics or mental shortcuts that we use daily to simplify our lives. Each, although extremely helpful, can also open the door to bias in our investment decisions, resulting in other serious errors that can also be very damaging. Knowing what they are and how they work can help you develop some strong defenses against their excesses.

---

* Approximately + or – 25 percent to 35 percent range above or below fundamental value, as noted previously.

Chapter 3

Treacherous Shortcuts in Decision Making

WHICH IS THE more likely cause of death, being attacked and killed by a shark or getting struck by falling airplane parts?[1] Most people don't have any experience of either, fortunately, but when asked this question they more often than not decide that the shark is the more likely culprit. That's wrong, however. In the United States, death from falling airplane parts is actually thirty times as probable as dying from a shark attack.[2]

What's going on here? Shark attacks, no matter how rare, receive considerable media attention and are horrifically easy to imagine, especially if you've seen the classic movie *Jaws*.[3] But can you recall a media report about falling airplane parts? If any graphic images come to mind, it's likely to be a plane in a cartoon humorously coming apart à la Bugs Bunny. We just don't think about small pieces of airplanes coming off. The images we generally have for airplane failure are of a catastrophic crash that kills passengers rather than anyone on the ground. Lacking firsthand experience of seeing airplane parts falling out of the sky and never having read about the problem, we mentally choose the more available image of shark mayhem as the more likely event.

This is an example of the *availability heuristic,* which leads us to subconsciously give more weight to images that come readily to mind than those that are "fuzzier" to recall.[4] Next, let's look more closely at cognitive heuristics.

Mental Shortcuts

Beginning in the 1970s, researchers began discovering that people adopt an extensive number of such mental shortcuts, or rules of thumb, to make a wide range of day-to-day decisions rather than formally calculating the actual odds of a given outcome. The pioneering work was done by Daniel Kahneman, now of Princeton, and the late Amos Tversky of Stanford. As noted, Kahneman won the Nobel Prize in Economics in 2002 for this work. Tversky would undoubtedly have shared the prize, the recipients of which must be living, had he not died prematurely several years earlier.* These *judgmental heuristics* or *cognitive heuristics* are simplifying strategies we use for managing large amounts of information. They seem to be hardwired into our minds and are thus rather undetectable under ordinary circumstances. Most of us are entirely unaware of them, especially in the heat of action.

Having evolved out of long human experience, these judgmental shortcuts work exceptionally well most of the time, as does the emotional decision making of Affect, and are enormous time-savers.

Consider, for example, what happens as you drive a car down a highway. You concentrate on dozens of mental shortcuts not only to operate the car but also to monitor highway traffic, road signs, and the visibility ahead, as well as the vehicles around you, all the while staying mostly undistracted by the music playing on your iPod and screening out thousands of other distracting and disruptive bits of information. That you can actually do this "almost without thinking" is a tribute to the efficiency of our mental heuristics.

We use such heuristics in dealing with many of our decisions and judgments and tend to become "intuitive statisticians" in the process. We think, for example, that our odds of survival in a crash are better when we are driving at fifty-five miles an hour than at ninety miles an hour, although few of us have ever bothered to check the actual numbers. We

---

* Tversky served on the board of the Dreman Foundation.

readily assess that a professional team is likely to beat an amateur one, assuming that the "amateurs" are not of Olympic quality. And we might expect to get to a city three hundred miles away faster by air than by ground.*

We have an immediate sense of the odds in such situations (or we think we do), using our past experiences to make these assessments quickly. Hundreds of times a day, these heuristics work flawlessly for us.

However, being an "intuitive statistician" has limitations as well as advantages. The simplifying processes that are normally efficient time-savers also lead to systematic mistakes in decision making. Despite what many economists and financial theorists assume, people are not really good intuitive statisticians, and as a result, heuristics are consistently shortchanging investors, even professionals. If I had to pinpoint the one primary error that heuristics cause investors to make, it would be this: they do not calculate odds properly when making investment decisions. The distortions produced by our heuristic calculations are often large and systematic, leading even the savviest investors into blunders of considerable magnitude. In addition, these cognitive biases are locked more firmly into place by group pressures.[5] Our own biases are reinforced by the powerful influence of experts and peer groups we respect, and the pressure for us to follow becomes more compelling.

The research also indicates that even when people are warned of such biases, they appear not to be able to adjust for the effects. So it will take a good deal of concentration and effort on your part to avoid these pitfalls. Doing so begins with becoming familiar with these heuristics. Once their nature is understood, a set of rules can be developed to help monitor your decisions and provide a shield against serious mishaps—perhaps even profit from them instead. But as you'll see, it's much easier said than done, even after people have been made fully aware of them.

▨ The Perils of Availability

Let's start by taking a closer look at the availability heuristic. According to Tversky and Kahneman, it causes us to "assess the frequency of a class or the probability of an event by the ease with which instances or occur-

---

* Writer's gripe: if it is not a United Express flight to a Colorado ski resort, which almost seems to be congenitally late.

rences can be brought to mind."[6] This is why we think deaths by shark attack are more common than deaths from pieces of airplanes falling on people.

The shortcut answers we get this way are accurate most of the time because our minds normally recall most readily events that have occurred frequently. But they can sometimes be strikingly off the mark. We think something is more likely because the prospect is more available in our minds when an event had an especially important meaning—in other words, it had a big impact on our thinking—and had occurred recently.[7] There are two psychological errors involved here. The first of these errors is referred to in the literature as "saliency" and the second as "recency." Saliency leads people to recall distinctly "good" events (or "bad" events) disproportionally to the actual frequency. It's so automatic that we barely recognize that we're doing it.[8] For example, returning to the wilds of nature, the actual chance of being mauled by a grizzly bear at a national park is one or two per million visitors; the death rate is even lower. Casualties from shark attacks are an even smaller percentage of all deaths of swimmers in coastal waters. But because the saliency of an actual attack is so powerful, we wind up thinking such attacks happen more often than they really do. Our memories are heuristically biased to bring scary images to mind more quickly.

I was snorkeling alone in the Bahamas' Exuma National Park several years back, well aware, in the abstract, that the probability of a shark attack was slim. Then a six-hundred-pound bull shark slowly came swimming toward me. As the dorsal fin passed by me inches away, it appeared to have the width of a nuclear submarine. I hoped it knew how unlikely it was to attack as I did. When the shark stopped behind me, my evaluation of attack probabilities skewed sharply higher. Fortunately, the shark didn't have a taste for snorkeler that day—but I was left with a considerable emotional charge that skewed my own calculations of shark attacks for some time to come.

To see recency in action, consider that after disasters, such as floods and earthquakes, purchases of flood and earthquake insurance rise, even though the underlying likelihood of floods and earthquakes hasn't changed. People are led to think these disasters are more likely because they've happened recently.[9] Through such subsconscious mechanisms, recent, salient events often strongly influence decision making in the stock and bond markets that can cause or exacerbate sharp price movements.

One key way in which this occurs is that the recent trend is thought to be the new permanent trend. Take the market when the base rate, meaning the long-term rate of returns of stocks, is trampled under by the case rate, the more recent short-term but sharply higher rate of return stocks are currently generating.* Even though we know that the case rate in most instances does not last and reverts back to the base rate, whether for a stock, a group of stocks, or an industry, our minds cling to a false hope that it won't be so this time. Recency frequently convinces us that the case rate is now the new base rate.

Consider a recent example. Bill Gross, the outstanding head of PIMCO, the largest bond house in the world, and Mohamed El-Erian, its CEO, coined the term "the New Normal" as the economy was put through the shredder in 2007 and 2008. The New Normal anticipated that low earnings and stock prices would be the norm for years into the future because the growth rate of the global economy was altered downward permanently. This chant was widely picked up by both money managers and the media and became the prevailing wisdom about stocks for more than two years.

But the stock market, in its contrarian way, completely ignored the doddering role it was assigned by the experts and started to rally. It had risen more than 100 percent by mid-2011 from its New Normal lows of March 2009. After the market doubled, the New Normal lost much of its luster. This has happened in similar circumstances in the past. Recall the New Era of the 1920s, when stocks roared, or the New Economy during the Internet bubble. I expect we've not heard the last of such clever coinages.

Now consider an even more glaring example. Conventional financial thinking holds that IPOs should be offered at a small discount to its actual value (in the neighborhood of around 10 percent), to ensure that the issue is fully subscribed for.

Figure 3-1 demonstrates the large overpricing of IPOs during the 1996–March 2000 Internet bubble. As the figure indicates, the average IPO was priced at a small premium of 10 percent or less at the first day's closing price for the eight years from 1987 through 1994. Over the next four years, premiums expanded significantly, averaging somewhat under

---

* The base rate's trampling the case rate is also found with other important cognitive heuristics, as we shall see shortly.

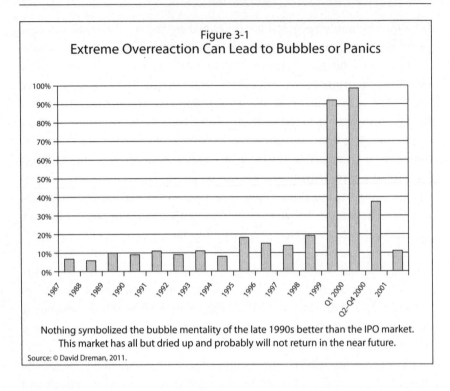

Figure 3-1
Extreme Overreaction Can Lead to Bubbles or Panics

Nothing symbolized the bubble mentality of the late 1990s better than the IPO market.
This market has all but dried up and probably will not return in the near future.

Source: © David Dreman, 2011.

20 percent. Returns of 20 percent in a day are very rare. This major appreciation was by itself enough to attract many investors away from more conventional investments into the far more speculative arena of IPOs. Speculation took over in 1999 and the first three months of 2000, with the average IPO premium rising to a staggering 90 percent, respectively, at the close of the first day's trading. (For those unfamiliar with initial public offerings, this meant that if you were lucky enough to get an IPO at its issue price, you made 90 to 95 percent on average on your investment by the close of the first day of trading.) Moreover, for the first three months of 2000, the peak of the bubble, the average closing price on IPOs of dot-com stocks (not shown in the figure) increased to 135 percent from the original offering price to the close of the first day's trading. IPO valuation premiums thus multiplied ten times or more above the normal premiums over the course of the Internet bubble. The recency and saliency of the enormous price movements resulted in investors vividly recalling the sharp gains these stocks provided while downplaying their considerable risks.

A retrospective analysis indicated that the quality of this group of

IPOs was certainly no better and, judging by the high rate of company failures, probably a good deal worse than IPOs of earlier time periods.

Since the 1960s, as chapter 1 documented, four major technology bubbles have occurred, with the 1996–2000 mania surpassing any in the past in terms of its size, the enormous appreciation, and the magnitude of the eventual crash.

In the bubble of the early 1980s, for example, the Value Line New Issue Survey analyzed a group of proposed IPOs and found that many were start-ups, perhaps 95 percent dream and 5 percent product. The survey also found that quite a few had only one or two full-time employees and some had none. The majority attempted to go public with absolutely no earnings at 20 to 100 times their book value prior to the offering.[10]

In 1994, Professors Jay Ritter of the University of Illinois at Urbana-Champaign and Tim Loughran of the University of Iowa, two of the pioneers in the field of behavioral finance, completed the most comprehensive study of new issues made to date. The study followed the returns of 4,753 IPOs traded on the New York Stock Exchange, the AMEX, and NASDAQ between 1970 and 1990.[11] The average return for IPOs was 5 percent annually, compared with 10.8 percent for the S&P 500. Put another way, investing in the S&P 500 over those twenty-one years would have returned 762 percent versus 179 percent for the IPOs. The far safer stocks of the S&P did more than four times as well!

But perhaps even more telling was that the median five-year return for these almost five thousand initial public offerings was a decline of 39 percent from the original offering price. If an investor couldn't buy the handful of red-hot IPOs that doubled or even tripled on the first trade— and nobody but the largest money managers, hedge funds, mutual funds, and other major investors could—he would lose a good chunk of his original investment.

As in the case of the Value Line study, Loughran and Ritter's results indicate that many IPOs were start-ups, usually high on expectations and low or nonexistent on actual revenues and earnings. They also found that most new issues go public near the top of an IPO market, when the demand is the greatest and the value of the merchandise is at its lowest. Not coincidentally, it is precisely at this time that investors are most excited about stocks with supposedly excellent visibility—further evidence of the strength of recency and saliency.

A 1991 study by Ritter[12] showed that fully 61 percent of IPOs went public in 1983, the peak of the 1977–1983 mania. How many went public in the first five years, when the quality was at its best? Only 6 percent.

A 2011 working paper by Vladimira Ilieva, of the Dreman Foundation, and myself calculated the price of 1,547 IPOs ($2.00 or more in price) that went public between January 1, 1997, near the beginning of the dot-com bubble, and March 10, 2000, its high point. We then measured the drop from the market high to the low price of each issue through December 31, 2002. As Figure 3-2 shows, the average decline from the high to the low price in the dot-com bubble was a startling 97 percent.[13] Finally, the median decline from the IPO offering price was 73 percent higher than the median decline that Ritter and Loughran calculated in this far more severe crash.

Also of interest was that the quality of the IPOs was consistently bad. Of the 1,547 companies in our original sample, only 524 were still listed in mid-2011. The other 66 percent had merged or just plain gone out of business.

Including the work of Ritter and Loughran, we now have an over-forty-year record of how dismal investing in IPOs has actually been. Recency and saliency appear to have played a not-insignificant hand in these

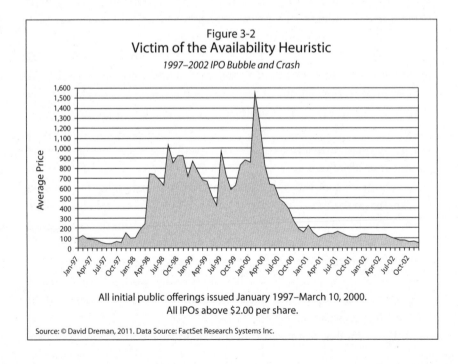

Figure 3-2
Victim of the Availability Heuristic
1997–2002 IPO Bubble and Crash

All initial public offerings issued January 1997–March 10, 2000.
All IPOs above $2.00 per share.

Source: © David Dreman, 2011. Data Source: FactSet Research Systems Inc.

results. Other studies support the findings. H. Nejat Seyhun reported that the market beat a sample of 2,298 IPOs for six years,[14] and Mario Levis showed that a group of British IPOs underperformed the U.K. averages for three years.[15] Further research found that IPO fundamentals fell after the offerings, indicating a deteriorating business picture precisely when investors were most excited by the stock.[16]

Loughran and Ritter (1995) concluded, "Our evidence is consistent with a market where firms take advantage of transitory windows of opportunity by issuing equity when, on average, they are substantially overvalued."[17] That's a gentlemanly way of stating that the real mountains of gold were made not by the investors but by the concept weavers, aka the investment bankers, as they were in bubbles hundreds of years back. It seems the investment bankers have known about heuristical errors for centuries and made very good money exploiting them—too good to want to give their discovery to investors or science.

The strength of the subconscious effect of recent and salient events cannot be exaggerated, as the research above indicates. Whether the pain of the 1996–2000 dot-com bubble takes another few years to forget or not, there is little doubt that a new and powerful IPO bubble is out there with results as predictable as any witnessed in this section. Another Psychological Guideline should prove helpful here.

PSYCHOLOGICAL GUIDELINE 2(a): Don't rely solely on the "case rate." Take into account the "base rate," the prior probabilities of profit or loss. Long-term returns of stocks (the "base rate") are far more likely to be reestablished.

PSYCHOLOGICAL GUIDELINE 2(b): Don't be seduced by recent rates of return (the "case rate") for individual stocks or the market when they deviate sharply from past norms. If returns are particularly high or low, they are likely to be abnormal.

Who's on First?

In the preceding chapter I spent a fair amount of time detailing the power of Affect in manias and crashes. In the current chapter I have so far detailed the errors that can result from indiscriminately following the availability heuristic lures of recency and saliency. Now, someone may ask, how can all three be present in the same bubble or any other investor error? This question brings us close to the state-of-the-art research cognitive psychologists are currently undertaking.

Affect, although not discovered until much later than cognitive heuristics, is considered by many senior researchers to be the driving force behind price movements. But to try to give a more precise answer about the contributions of recency, saliency, and Affect at this time would be like getting us into the famous (and endless) Abbott and Costello skit "Who's on First?" But whatever the relative contributions, we receive strong warnings of imminent danger ahead that we can easily pick up.

Although the final research on the contribution of each of these heuristics may take many years to resolve, by now having a knowledge of each, we can build defenses so we can recognize bubbles and get out while there is still time. Naturally, a similar approach could be adapted if stocks dropped to levels that were far too cheap.

The best defense against recency and saliency, in particular, is to keep your eye on the longer term. Though there is certainly no assured way to put recent or memorable experiences into absolute perspective, it might be helpful during periods of extreme pessimism or optimism to wander back to your library. If the market is tanking, reread the financial periodicals from the last major break. If you can, look up *The Wall Street Journal* of late February 2009, turn to the market section, and read the wailing and sighing by expert after expert, just before the market began one of its sharpest recoveries in history. Similarly, when we have another speculative market, it would not be a bad idea to check the *Journal* again and read the comments made during the 1996–2000 or 2005–2006 bubble. Though rereading the daily press is not a magic elixir, I think it can help.

I will also point out some defensive tips that should help. By themselves, these tips are not going to put your investing strategy on a firm footing. But you may want to add them to the strategies we are going to discuss later. Think of them as useful personal sidearms until we can bring in the heavy artillery, which will defend you from the heuristics we have discussed.

▓ A Picture Is Not Worth a Thousand Words

The second important cognitive bias that Professors Kahneman and Tver-sky identified was the one they labeled "representativeness." What they showed in rigorous experimental studies is that it's a natural human ten-dency to draw analogies and see identical situations—where none exist.

In the market, representativeness might take the form of labeling two companies or two market environments as the same when the actual re-semblance is superficial.[18] Give people a little information, and *click!* they pull out a mental picture they're familiar with, though it may only re-motely represent the truth. The two key ways the representativeness bias leads to miscalculations are that it causes us to give too much emphasis to the similarities between events and does not take into account the actual probability that an event will occur, and that it reduces the importance we give to variables that are actually critical in determining an event's probability.

An example is the aftermath of the 1987 crash. In four trading days the Dow fell 769 points, culminating with the 508-point decline on Black Monday, October 19, 1987. This wiped out almost $1 trillion worth of value. "Is This 1929?" asked the media in bold headlines. Many investors, taking this heuristic shortcut, fled to cash, caught up in a false parallel.

At the time the situations seemed eerily similar. We had not had a stock market crash for fifty-eight years. Generations grew up believing that because a depression had followed the 1929 crash it would always happen this way. A large part of Wall Street's experts, the media, and the investing public agreed. Overlooked was the fact that the two crashes had only the remotest similarity. To start with, 1929 was a special case. The nation had numerous panics and crashes in the nineteenth and early twentieth centuries, without a depression. Crashes or no, the U.S. econ-omy has always bounced back in short order. So crash and depression are not synonymous.

More important, it was apparent even in the spring of 1988 that the economic and investment climate was entirely different. My *Forbes* col-umn of May 2, 1988, noted some of the differences clearly visible at the time. The column stated that although market savants and the media were presenting charts showing the breathtaking similarity of the market postcrash stock movements after 1987 to those of 1929, there was far less to it than met the eye. In 1929, the market rallied smartly after the debacle before beginning a free fall in the spring of 1930, and many experts believed that history would repeat itself fifty-eight years later. However, a chart, unlike a picture, is not always worth a thousand words; sometimes it is just downright misleading.

Bottom line: the economic and investment fundamentals of 1988 were worlds apart from those of 1930. After the 1987 crash, the economy was rolling along at a rate above most estimates precrash and sharply above the recession levels forecasted postcrash, accompanied by earnings far higher than projected in the weeks following the October 19 debacle. The P/E of the S&P 500 was a little over 13 times earnings, down sharply from 20 times just prior to the crash and below the long-term average of 15 to 16. The situation was diametrically different from that after the crash of 1929. Back then, corporate earnings, along with the financial system, collapsed, and unemployment soared.

Thus 1987 was certainly not 1929, and investors who succumbed to the representativeness bias missed an enormous buying opportunity; by July 1997, the market had quadrupled from its low.

A more recent example of the bias at work is the pricing of oil and commodities in the 2007–2008 crash and the early part of the Great Recession through 2010. Since 1992, oil prices have risen fairly steadily, from $20 a barrel to $100 in early 2008. The fundamentals for oil were very sound. World demand had outstripped new supply every year from 1982 through 2007. Even after the economy began to fall apart in late 2008, the demand for oil dropped only 1.1 percent in 2009. Moreover, the cost of finding oil was going up sharply, and the discovery of vast new fields was a dream of the past. The last million-barrels-a-day oil field was found in the late 1970s. Too, with the dramatic industrialization of China, along with that of other underdeveloped economies in the Far East and elsewhere, demand for oil expanded rapidly.

The price of oil shot upward, breaking $100 a barrel in early 2008, and continued its sharp increase, reaching $145 a barrel by mid-2008. Investors were desperately selling financial assets other than government bonds and piling into oil and other commodities through 2007 to the spring of 2008. Then panic took over. Untold numbers of comparisons between the 2008–2009 economy and that of the Great Depression were made. Nothing was safe, not even oil, regardless of its fundamentals.

Within months, oil plummeted from its then high of $145 dollars a barrel to $35, a drop of 76 percent. The price of oil had fallen well below the cost of new discoveries. As markets calmed by mid-2009, oil began to rise again; it reached $95 a barrel by June 2011, approximately 170 percent above its low.

You can see how the effects of cognitive biases combine with those of Affect in this case. The fear of losses contributed to people's putting undue weight on the supposed similarity in the collapse of the oil price between 2008 and the free fall of stock prices after 1929 and failing to rationally recalculate that the demand for oil had actually dropped very modestly and usage would climb significantly with even a moderate economic recovery. When such emotion is mixed with the effects of our biases, it's the equivalent of nuclear fusion in the marketplace.

Was it possible to detect that some stocks and commodities were sharply undervalued, just as we saw they were greatly overvalued during the 1996–2000 bubble? My answer is yes. I wrote a column in early June 2009 stating that oil was enormously undervalued for the reasons noted above.[19] Oil was then trading around $68 and *appreciating* about 40 percent from then to June 2011.

The representativeness heuristic can apply just as forcefully to a company or an industry as to the market as a whole. In 2007–2008, many stocks in a number of excellent industries were swept away by the powerful tides that panicked many people. Not only was the sky falling for banks and financial stocks, but many investors calculated that it was also likely to obliterate very strong industrials with worldwide demand for their products, such as Eaton Corporation and Emerson Electric, which dropped 69 percent and 56 percent, respectively, from their late-2007 highs. As the panic worsened, the more analytic investors sold in droves, too. The prevailing fear was that those companies and myriads of others would show minimal earnings for a decade and that many wouldn't survive at all.

By early March 2009, those dire predictions were seen as a lot of hogwash. Eaton and Emerson would rise 265 percent and 142 percent, respectively, by the end of June 2011, and dozens of more cyclical industries, from heavy equipment to mining to oil drilling, had similar bounce backs. Freeport-McMoRan Copper & Gold shot up 315 percent and United Technologies Corporation 149 percent through the end of June 2011. That was the reality.

Awareness of the representativeness bias leads to another helpful Psychological Guideline:

PSYCHOLOGICAL GUIDELINE 3: Look beyond obvious similarities between a current investment situation and one that appears similar in the past. Consider other important factors that may result in a markedly different outcome.

The Law of Small Numbers

A particular flaw in thinking that falls under the rubric of representativeness is what Amos Tversky and Daniel Kahneman called the "law of small numbers."[20] Examining journals in psychology and education, they found that researchers systematically overstated the importance of findings taken from small samples. The statistically valid "law of large numbers" states that large samples will usually be highly representative of the population from which they are drawn; for example, public opinion polls are fairly accurate because they draw on large and representative groups. The smaller the sample used, however (or the shorter the record), the more likely the findings are to be chance rather than meaningful.

Yet the Tversky and Kahneman study showed that psychological or educational experimenters typically premise their research theories on samples so small that the results have a very high probability of being chance.[21] The psychologists and educators are far too confident in the significance of results based on a few observations or a short period of time, even though they are trained in statistical techniques and are aware of the dangers. This is a very important cognitive error and is often repeated in markets in a wide range of circumstances.

For example, investors regularly flock to mutual funds that are better performing for a year or few years, even though financial researchers have shown that the "hot" funds in one time period are often the poorest performers in another. The final verdict on the most sizzling funds in the 1996–2000 dot-com bubble shows why this decision making can be disastrous. During the bubble, tens of billions of dollars flowed into the Janus Capital Group. Its short-term record was spectacular. The flagship Janus Fund surged 10.3 percent ahead of the rapidly rising S&P 500 in 1998 and 26.1 percent in 1999, just before the bubble burst. Still, over the ten years ending in 2003, despite its hot hand when dot-com stocks were flying, the Janus Fund averaged only an 8.7 percent return, which meant it underperformed the market by 22 percent over the entire time frame, including both the dot-com bubble and the crash afterward.

Even this grim statistic doesn't do justice to the damage wrought by Janus. The Janus Fund's assets were only $9 billion in 1993 but reached $49 billion by March 31, 2000, only weeks after the dot-com market peaked. A large number of its customers arrived too late to enjoy the fabulous returns in the 1990s but were there to get bludgeoned in the ensuing bear market. Needless to say, that crowd received a lot less than the 8.7 percent Janus returned for the decade.

Chasing the hot hand ends in disaster more times than not. Some of Janus's competitors in the hot-stock derby performed just as badly. Fidelity Select Telecommunications Equipment fund beat the S&P by 12.4 percent in 1998 and 45.5 percent in 1999, while the AllianceBernstein Technology Fund bested the index by 34.6 percent and 50.7 percent, respectively, in those two years. In spite of the huge years in which the dot-com stocks trounced the performance of everything else, the Fidelity fund lagged behind the S&P 500 by 6 percent, and the AllianceBernstein fund was about flat, annually, for the ten-year period ending December 31, 2003. During this bubble, investors lost many hundreds of billions of dollars in red-hot tech and Internet mutual funds as well as in the hot stocks themselves. The so-called hot funds, it turned out, could not hold a candle to the long-term records of many conservative blue-chip funds.[22]

The Remarkable Success of Wannabe Gunslingers

Another way in which investors regularly make decisions based on much too small a sample of results is putting way too much faith in "hot" analysts. Investors and the media are continually seduced by "hot" performance, even if it lasts for the briefest of periods. Money managers or analysts who have had one or two sensational stock calls, or technicians who call one major market move correctly, are believed to have established a credible record and can readily find a market following for all eternity.

In fact, it doesn't matter if the adviser was repeatedly wrong beforehand; the name of the game is to get a dramatic prediction out there. A well-timed call can bring huge rewards to a popular newsletter writer. Eugene Lerner, a former finance professor and a market letter writer who headed Disciplined Investment Advisors, speaking of what making a bearish call in a declining market can do, said, "If the market goes down for the next three years you'll be as rich as Crassus. . . . The next time around, everyone will listen to you."[23] With hundreds and hundreds of advisory letters out there, someone has to be right. Again, it's just the odds. We do have lottery winners, despite the fact that many millions of tickets may have to be sold to get one.

Elaine Garzarelli gained near-immortality when she purportedly "called" the 1987 crash. Although, as she was the market strategist for Shearson Lehman, her forecast was never published in a research report nor indeed communicated to the company's clients, she still received widespread recognition and publicity for this call, which was made in a short TV interview on CNBC.

Since this "brilliant call," her record, according to a fellow strategist, "has been somewhat mixed, like most of us."[24] Still, her remark on CNBC that the Dow could drop sharply from its then-5,300 level rocked an already nervous market on July 23, 1996. What had been a 57-point gain for the Dow turned into a 44-point loss, a good deal of which was attributed to her comments. Only a few days earlier, Ms. Garzarelli had predicted that the Dow would rise to 6,400 from its then value of 5,400. Even so, people widely followed her because of "the great call in 1987."

Jim Cramer, the popular CNBC commentator—and an ex–hedge fund manager—whom we met earlier, was one of the most voracious cheerleaders of the high-tech dot-com bubble. In a December 27, 1999, missive he wrote, referring to money managers who refused to buy enormously overpriced dot-com stocks, "The losers better change or they will lose again next year"[25]—this less than three weeks before the dot-com market collapsed.

Shortly thereafter, Don Phillips, then the president and CEO of Morningstar, blasted Cramer for outspokenly playing an active role in reinforcing this enormous bubble, noting in passing that his public recommendations were down 90 percent. *Barron's* followed Cramer's subsequent record and stated that he had underperformed the market for several years after the high-tech bubble. Although Cramer's record is hardly sizzling, the law of averages dictates that some of his recommendations have to go up. Cramer is astute at blowing these recommendations out of proportion and is probably more popular today than ever.

Make a few good calls, and you're a hero for a while and the chips pile up in front of you. Being a wannabe gunslinger may not have kept you alive long in the Old West, but it works just fine with investors and the media today. A new Psychological Guideline is helpful here.

PSYCHOLOGICAL GUIDELINE 4: Don't be influenced by the short-term record or "great" market calls of a money manager, analyst, market timer, or economist, no matter how impressive they are; don't accept cursory economic or investment news without significant substantiation.

Beware of Instant Government Statistics

Sometimes the evidence we accept because of the law of small numbers runs to the absurd. Another good example of the major overreaction this heuristic bias causes is the almost blind faith investors place in Federal Reserve or government economic releases on employment, industrial production, the health of the banking system, the consumer price index, inventories, and dozens of similar statistics.

These reports frequently trigger major stock and bond market reactions, particularly if the news is bad. For example, if unemployment rises one-tenth of 1 percent in a month when it was expected to be unchanged or if industrial production falls slightly more than the experts expected, stock prices can fall, at times sharply. Should this happen? No. "Flash" statistics, more times than not, are nearly worthless. They are the archetypal case of mistaken decision making due to the law of small numbers. Initial economic and Fed figures are revised, often significantly, for weeks or months after their release, as new and more current information flows in. Thus an increase in employment, consumer purchasing, or factory orders can turn into a decrease or a large drop in each as the revised figures appear. These revisions occur with such regularity that you would think investors, particularly the pros, would treat the initial numbers with the skepticism they deserve. Yet too many investors treat as Street gospel all authoritative-sounding releases that they think pinpoint the development of important trends.

Just as irrational is the overreaction to every utterance by Fed Chairman Bernanke or his predecessor, Alan Greenspan, ignoring the fact that they entirely missed the subprime mortgage crisis from 2005 through mid-2007. Still, the market hangs on every new comment of Chairman Bernanke and the chairmen of the twelve regional Federal Reserve Banks, from New York and Philadelphia to Dallas and San Francisco, as it does to other senior Fed or government officials, no matter how offhand or contradictory to one another the comments are, or how mediocre the chairmen's forecasting records have been overall.

Like ancient priests examining chicken entrails to foretell events, many pros scrutinize every remark and act upon it immediately, even though they are often not sure what it is they are acting on. Remember the advice of a world-champion chess player who was asked how to avoid making a bad move. His answer: "Sit on your hands."

But too many investors don't sit on their hands; they dance on tiptoe, ready to flit after the least particle of information as if it were a strongly documented trend. The law of averages indicates that dozens of experts will have excellent records—usually playing popular trends—often for months and sometimes for several years, only to stumble disastrously later. These are the lessons that investors have learned the hard way for centuries, and that have to be relearned with each new supposedly unbeatable market opportunity.

The Disregard of Prior Probabilities

One of the results of the tendency to see similarities between situations is to fail to appreciate the lessons of the past. We neglect to study the outcomes of very similar situations in prior years. These are called "prior probabilities" and logically should be looked at to help to guide present decisions, but our ability to disregard them is truly astonishing.[26] It is another major reason we so often overemphasize the case rate and pay little attention to the base rate.

The tendency to underestimate or ignore prior probabilities in making a decision is undoubtedly one of the most significant problem of intuitive prediction in fields as diverse as financial analysis, accounting, geography, engineering, and military intelligence.[27]

Consider the case of an interesting experiment in which a test was conducted with a group of advanced psychology students.[28] They were given a brief personality write-up of a graduate student that was intended to give them no truly relevant information with which to answer the question they were then going to be asked about him: what subject he was studying. The assessment was said to have been written by a psychologist who had conducted some tests on the subject several years earlier. The analysis not only was outdated but contained no indication of the subject's academic preference. (Note that psychology students are specifically taught that profiles of this sort can be enormously inaccurate.)

Here's what they had to read:

Tom W. is of high intelligence, although lacking in true creativity. He has a need for order and clarity and for neat and tidy systems in which every detail finds its appropriate place. His writing is dull and rather mechanical, occasionally enlivened by somewhat corny puns and flashes of imagination of the sci-fi type. He has a strong drive for competence. He seems to have little feeling and little sympathy for other people, and does not enjoy interacting with others. Self-centered, he nevertheless has a deep moral sense.

Tom W. is currently a graduate student. Please rank the following nine fields of graduate specialization in order of the likelihood that Tom W. is now a student in that field. Let rank one be the most probable choice:

Business Administration
Computer Sciences
Engineering
Humanities and Education
Law
Library Science
Medicine
Physical and Life Sciences
Social Science and Social Work

Given the lack of substantive content, the graduate students should have ignored the analysis entirely and made the only remaining logical choices—by the percentage of graduate students in each field: in other words, the base rate. That information had also been provided to them. It was assumed by the experimenters that the graduate students would realize that those were the real data. They had been taught that for a specific situation, the more unreliable the available sketch, the more one should rely on previously established information—that, to use the language of cognitive psychology, the "case rate" (the profile of subject Tom W.) should not have been conflated with the "base rate" (the known percentage of graduate students enrolled in each field). Did the experiment's group members realize that the base rate was the only accurate data they had? They did not!

The student subjects relied entirely upon the irrelevant profile, deciding that computer sciences and engineering were the two most likely fields Tom W. would enter, even if those fields had relatively few enrollees.

But we shouldn't be too hard on those grad students. Investors in the stock market make similar mistakes all the time, as we've seen, being repeatedly impressed by the case rate, even though the substantiating data for it are usually flimsy at best. Too many buyers of red-hot technology stocks in the dot-com bubble failed to consider that the average price decline in very similar stocks in each previous technology bubble collapse had been about 80 percent—repeat, 80 percent. That was the base rate they should have been taking into account.

Let's make this into another Psychological Guideline:

PSYCHOLOGICAL GUIDELINE 5: The greater the complexity and uncertainty in the market, the less emphasis you should place on the case rate, no matter how spectacular near-term returns are, and the more on the base rate.[29]

■ Regression to the Mean

The previous cognitive biases, stemming from representativeness, buttress one of the most important and consistent sources of investment error. As intuitive statisticians, we do not comprehend the principle of *regression to the mean*. This statistical phenomenon was noted more than a hundred years ago by Sir Francis Galton, a pioneer in eugenics, and is important in avoiding this major market error. Studying the height of men, Galton found that the tallest men usually had shorter sons, while the shortest men usually had taller sons. Since many tall men come from families of average height, they are likely to have children shorter than they are; similarly, short men are likely to have children taller than they are. In both cases, the height of the children was less extreme than the height of the fathers. In other words, the heights of the children regressed to the mean height for the population as a whole.

The study of this phenomenon gave rise to the term "regression." The effects of regression are all around us. In our experience, most outstanding fathers have somewhat disappointing sons or daughters, brilliant wives have duller husbands, people who seem to be ill adjusted often improve, and those considered extraordinarily fortunate eventually have a run of bad luck.[30]

Take the reaction we have to a baseball player's batting average. Although a player may be hitting .300 for the season, his batting will be uneven. He will not get three hits in every ten times at bat. Sometimes he will bat .500 or more, well above his average (or mean); other times he will be lucky to hit .125. Within 162 regular Major League scheduled games, whether the batter hits .125 or .500 in any dozen or so games makes little difference to the average. But rather than realizing that the player's performance over a week or a month can deviate widely from his season's average, we tend to focus only on the immediate past record. The player is said to be in a "hitting streak" or a "slump." Fans, sportscasters, and, unfortunately, the players themselves place too much emphasis on brief periods and forget the long-term average, to which the players will be likely to regress.

Regression occurs in many instances where it is not expected and yet is bound to happen. Israeli Air Force flight instructors were chagrined after they praised a student for a successful execution of a complex maneuver, because it was normally followed by a poorer one the next time. Conversely, when they criticized a bad maneuver, a better one usually followed. What they did not understand was that at the level of training of these student pilots, there was no more consistency in their maneuvers than in the daily batting figures of baseball players. Bad exercises would be followed by well-executed ones and good exercises by bad ones. Their flying regressed to the mean. Good landings were followed by poor ones; skillful gunnery was followed by missing the target and good formation flying by ragged patterns. Correlating the maneuver quality to their remarks, the instructors erroneously concluded that criticism was helpful to learning and praise detrimental, a conclusion universally rejected by learning theory researchers.[31]

How does this work in the stock market? According to the classic work on stock returns of Roger Ibbotson and Rex Sinquefield, then at the University of Chicago,[32] stocks have returned 9.9 percent annually on average (price appreciation and dividends) over the eighty-five years to 2010, against a return of about 5.5 percent for bonds. An earlier study by the Cowles Commission for Research in Economics showed much the same return for stocks going back to the 1880s.

As Figure 3-3 shows, however, the return has been anything but consistent—not unlike the number of hits a .300 career hitter will get in individual games over a few weeks. There have been long periods when stocks have returned more than the 9.9 percent mean. And within each of those periods, there have been times when stocks performed sensationally, rising sometimes 40 percent or more in a year. At other times, they have seemed to free-fall. Stocks, then, although they have a consistent average, also have "streaks" and "slumps."

For investors, the long-term rate of return of common stocks, like the long-term batting average of a ballplayer, is the important thing to remember. However, as intuitive statisticians, we find this very hard to do. *Market history provides a continuous example of our adherence to the belief that deviations from the norm are, in fact, the new norm.*

Investors of 1927 and 1928 or 1995–1999 thought that returns of 25 to 35 percent were in order from that time on, although they diverged far from the mean. In 1930, 1931, 1973, 1974, and 2007–2008, they believed that huge losses were inevitable, although they, too, deviated sharply from the long-term mean, as Figure 3-3 clearly shows. Investors of mid-1982, observing the insipid performance of the Dow Jones Industrial Average (which was lower at the time than in 1965), believed stocks were no longer a viable investment instrument; *Business Week* ran a cover story shortly before the great bull market began in July 1982 entitled "The Death of Equities."[33] By 1987, the Dow had nearly quadrupled. And of course, by the late 1990s Wall Street gurus believed that major bear markets were a thing of the past because the Fed had finally mastered the business cycle. Those optimistic thoughts lasted for a shorter period than the average Reno marriage.

The same scenarios have been enacted at every major market peak and trough. Studies of investment advisers' buying and selling indicate that most experts are closely tied, if not pilloried, to the current market's movement. The prevalent belief is always that extreme returns—whether positive or negative—will persist. The far more likely probability is that they are the outliers on a chart plotting returns and that succeeding prices will regress toward the mean, as Figure 3-3 indicates.

We can lose sight of the relevance of long-term returns by detailed study of a specific trend and intense involvement in it.[34] Even those who are aware of long-term standards cannot always see them clearly because of preoccupation with short-term conditions. The long-term return of the market might be viewed like the average height of men. Just as it is unlikely that abnormally tall men will beget even taller men, it is unlikely that abnormally high returns will follow already high returns for long, if at all.

But because experts in the stock market are no more aware of the principle of regression than anyone else is, each sharp price deviation from past norms is explained by a new, spurious theory.

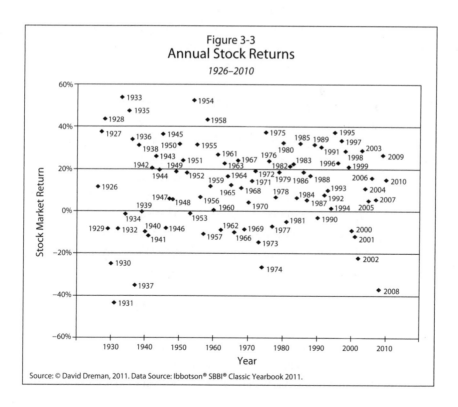

Figure 3-3
Annual Stock Returns
1926–2010

Source: © David Dreman, 2011. Data Source: Ibbotson® SBBI® Classic Yearbook 2011.

▨ The Role of TMI

Another reason we can so easily lose sight of the longer-term truths we should be factoring into our investing choices is the flood of information we must contend with. TMI, the abbreviation for "too much information," became common slang in the early 2000s. Though TMI is often used as a jocular interjection, applied to cases when you've been forced to know more about some person or something inconsequential than you really care to, there's a serious side to TMI: the problem of investor information overload. It's been brought on by the torrent of data available to us today, the processing power of modern computers, and the ubiquitous communication tools we have at our fingertips, and it's no laughing matter.

TMI is anything but new. I'm reminded of the soothsayers' dire warnings to Londoners many months before February 1, 1524. Those expert prognosticators warned, on the basis of massive astrological evidence, that on that day the Thames, that most tranquil of rivers, would suddenly rise hundreds of feet, drowning all who remained in the city. That sent a goodly portion of the city population fleeing weeks before the appointed day, although they soon realized that their prescientific experts were a bit off the mark. The Thames, needless to say, flowed peacefully on within its banks.

The returning population was enraged; many wanted to throw the pack of soothsayers into the river in sacks. The soothsayers, aware of what might happen, huddled together and told the enraged populace that the stars were never wrong, indeed that the flood predicted would take place. But they had made the slightest of errors in their very complex calculations. The flood would occur on February 1, 1624, not February 1, 1524. The good people of London could go home—at least for a while.

What exactly happens when we're confronted with TMI or, to put it in more formal terms, "information overload"?

▨ The Biases Caused by Information Overload

In 1959, the polymath Herbert Simon, winner of the Nobel Prize in Economics, was one of the first academics to rigorously look at information overload. In the simplest formulation, what Simon established was that not only does more information not necessarily bring about better decisions; it can lead to poorer ones. This is because humans cannot process large amounts of information effectively. In Simon's words, "Every human organism lives in an environment that generates millions of bits of new information each second, but the bottleneck of the perceptual apparatus certainly does not admit more than 1,000 bits per second, and possibly much less. We react consciously to only a minute portion of the information that is thrown at us." [35]

And we are biased in the way we do this. Professor Simon notes that this filtering process is not a passive activity "but an active process involving attention to a very small part of the whole and exclusion, from the outset, of almost all that is not within the scope of attention." [36] The key to the bias, he observed, is that when people are bombarded with information they see only the part they are interested in and screen out the rest. More recent research has backed up this finding, including work by Professors Baba Shiv and Alexander Fedorikhin in 1999, [37] as well as Professor Nelson Cowan in a research paper in 2000. [38]

In the context of the stock market (and other trading markets), who suffers most from information overload? It's hard to give the nod to either the professional or the individual investor. The sheer volume of information is nearly unfathomable. Consider just the large number of securities analysts, sometimes twenty or more covering a single company, who must put out research reports and updates, not to mention all the information they must process on related companies, the industry, the market, and other important economic and financial data. Information overload? More like information breakdown. These are people working every day, faced with hundreds, if not thousands, of analytical factors that conventional investment theory insists must be considered, from competition and profit margins across a wide range of product lines to the likelihood that industry and company earnings will rise or fall because of new developments.

This vast, sometimes staggering amount of market information, much of which is complex and contradictory, is nearly impossible to analyze effectively. As we saw in chapter 2, this is an important reason money managers show such poor results over time and only a very small number of analysts and money managers outperform the market. Of course, under these conditions, you can bet that Affect and heuristics are a predictable fallback. (If you very carefully read between the carefully hedged, well-crafted lines of a lot of investment recommendation reports, you may see Affect or a cognitive heuristic peeking out.) This despite the elaborate decision-making process undertaken by highly educated men and women supported by large corporate resources.

I'm afraid we're all just going to have to live with market TMI and information overload, but, as we'll see in Part IV, there are methods that can help us neutralize their negative effects. Let's now look at a few other ways that our brains go wrong in dealing with other heuristic errors.

Doing Heuristic Math

There is yet another powerful heuristic bias stemming from representativeness. This is the intuitive belief that psychological inputs and outputs should be closely correlated. Companies with strong sales growth (the inputs) should be accompanied by rising earnings and profit margins over time (the outputs). We believe that consistent inputs supply greater predictability than inconsistent ones do. Tests, for example, show that people are far more confident that a student is likely to have a B average in the future if he has two Bs rather than an A and a C, although the belief is not statistically valid.[39] To translate this into stock market terms, investors have more confidence in a company that has 10 percent earnings growth that rises consistently year after year than they do in one that has 15 percent growth over the same period but is more volatile, i.e., 18 percent in year 1, 3 percent in year 2, 15 percent in year 3, and so on.[40]

Another direct application of this finding is the manner in which investors equate a good stock with a rising price and a poor stock with a falling one. One of the most common questions analysts, money managers, and brokers are asked is "If the stock is so good, why doesn't it go up?" or "If contrarian strategies are so successful, why aren't they working now?" The answer, of course, is that the value (the input) is often not recognized in the price (the output) for quite some time. Contrarian stocks have outperformed the market for many decades, but that doesn't mean they can't underperform for one year or even a few years—remember the lessons we learned about regression to the mean a couple of sections back. Yet investors too often demand immediate, though incorrect, feedback and can make serious mistakes as a consequence.

Another interesting aspect of this phenomenon is that investors mistakenly tend to place high confidence in extreme inputs or outputs. As we have seen, Internet stocks in the late 1990s were believed to have sensational prospects (the input), confirmed by prices that moved up astronomically (the output). Companies' strong fundamentals in each bubble went hand in hand with sharply rising prices, such as prices for HMO stocks in the mid-1990s or the computer software and medical technology stocks of 1968 and 1973. Extreme correlations between rapidly growing dot-com companies and hockey stick–like stock charts look great, and people are willing to accept them as reliable auguries, but as generations of investors have learned the hard way, they don't last.

The same thinking is applied to each crash and panic. Analysts and money managers pull back the earnings estimates and outlooks (the inputs) as prices (the outputs) drop. Graham and Dodd, astute market clinicians that they were, saw the input-output relationship clearly. They wrote that "an inevitable rule of the market is that the prevalent theory of common stock valuations has developed in rather close conjunction with the change in the level of prices."[41]

As we've seen, demanding immediate success invariably leads to playing the fads or fashions that are currently performing well rather than investing on a solid fundamental basis. An investment course, once plotted, should be given time to work. The immediate investor matching of inputs and outputs serves to repeatedly thwart this goal. The problem is not as simple as it may appear; studies have shown that businessmen and other investors abhor uncertainty.[42] To most people in the marketplace, quick psychological input-output matching is an expected condition of successful investing. Taking advantage of this constantly repeated heuristical error by investors is also a critical part of the strategies to be proposed in Part IV. The consistency of this behavior leads us to our next Psychological Guideline.

PSYCHOLOGICAL GUIDELINE 6: Don't expect that the strategy you adopt will prove a quick success in the market; give it a reasonable time to work out.

Anchoring and Hindsight Biases

Let's briefly look at two other systematic heuristic biases that tend to cause investment errors. They, too, are difficult to correct, since they reinforce the others. The first, known as "anchoring,"[43] is another simplifying heuristic, which sets up a price for a stock that is not far removed from its current trading price as its anchor. In a complex situation, such as the marketplace, we choose some natural starting point where we think the stock is a good buy or a sale and make adjustments from there. The adjustments are typically insufficient. Thus an investor in 1997 who wanted to buy might have thought a price of $91 was too high for Cascade Communications, a leader in PC networking, and $80 was more appropriate. But Cascade Communications was grossly overvalued at $91 and dropped to $22 before recovering modestly. The heuristic process tends to drop the anchors far too close to the stock's current price, and investors don't seem to believe prices can go either much lower if they want to sell or much higher if they want to buy; this often leads to missed opportunities.

The final bias is also interesting. In looking back at past mistakes, researchers have found, people believe that each error could have been seen much more clearly if only they hadn't been wearing dark- or rose-colored glasses. The inevitability of what happened seems obvious in retrospect. *Hindsight bias* seriously impairs proper assessment of past errors and significantly limits what can be learned from experience.[44]

Looking back at the 2007–2008 housing crash, many investors blame themselves because it seems the housing bubble was so obvious. We also knew that the number and variations of derivatives were almost mind-boggling. Some of us saw clear instances of major overleverage in subprime lenders such as NovaStar Financial, New Century Financial Corporation, and many others and acted on them early, at the beginning of 2007.

But what most of us didn't know until after the financial markets began to melt down was the extent of the leverage in the entire financial system, which was multiplied enormously by the increase of specialized obtuse and complex derivatives as well as the intentional enormous replication of poor-quality subprime loans by numbers of banks and investment bankers. Much of this information came out only in late 2009 and 2010, well after the financial debacle, through the actions of House and Senate committees that subpoenaed e-mails and other information from the banks, credit-rating agencies, and investment banks involved. Most investors also did not know how poor the regulation was prior to the bubble that allowed the leverage to get so out of hand, or how enormously overrated subprime mortgages were by Moody's, Standard & Poor's,

and Fitch.* In early 2011, scathing bipartisan reports were released by
the two key Senate commissions: the Wall Street and the Financial Crisis Commission, chaired by Carl Levin (chairman of the Senate Permanent Subcommittee on Investigations); and the Financial Crisis Inquiry
Commission, chaired by Phil Angelides, investigating the debacle. The
reports evidence how risky lending, poor bond assessments by regulatory
and credit-rating agencies, and major conflicts of interest by some of the
Street's largest firms contributed to one of the worst financial disasters in
U.S. history. The commissions wrote scathing reports about the actions
of major financial players from Goldman Sachs to Washington Mutual;
these reports were turned over to the Department of Justice, which is
now investigating the charges, some of which may well be criminal. It
all seems so obvious in hindsight, but, as the above examples show, it is
nightmarishly difficult to see at the time. As a result, we think mistakes
are easy to see and are confident we won't make them again—until we do.
This bias, too, is difficult to handle. Again, that walk to the library may
be as good a solution as any, showing us that mistakes that now seem so
obvious to us were anything but at the time they were made.

Heuristics and Decisional Biases

We have repeatedly seen the seductiveness of current market fashions,
how prudent investors could be swept away by the lure of huge profits
in mania after mania through the centuries. Now, with some knowledge
of availability, representativeness, and the other decisional biases we've
looked at, we can understand why the lure of quick profits has been so
persistent and so influential on both the market population and the expert opinion of the day.

Whatever the fashion, the experts could demonstrate that the performance of a given investment was statistically superior to other less
favored ones in the immediate past and sometimes stayed that way for
fairly long periods (the case rate beats the base rate). Circumstances are
really different this time!

The pattern repeats itself continually. A buyer of canal bonds in the

---

*Mortgage agencies raised their securities quality ratings enormously over where they
should have been; this was an important cause of the financial crisis.

1830s or blue-chip stocks in 1929 could argue that though the instruments were dear, each had been a vastly superior holding in the recent past. Along with the 1929 crash and the Depression came a decade-and-a-half-long passion for government bonds at near-zero interest rates. After a whipping in the markets, investors flock to safety, no matter how little they earn. We repeated the desire for safety by dashing into Treasuries at near-zero interest rates after the crash of 2007–2008 and again in August 2011.

Investing in good-grade common stocks came into vogue in the 1950s and 1960s, and by the end of the latter decade, the superior record of stocks through the postwar era had put investing in bonds into disrepute. *Institutional Investor,* a magazine exceptionally adept at catching the prevailing trends, presented a dinosaur on the cover of its February 1969 issue with the question "Can the Bond Market Survive?" The article continued, "In the long run, the public market for straight debt might become obsolete."[45]

The accumulation of stocks shot up dramatically in the early seventies just as their rates of return were beginning to decrease. Bonds immediately went on to provide better returns than stocks. Professionals tended to play the fashions of the day, whatever they were. One fund manager, at the height of the dot-com bubble, noted the skyrocketing prices of the high-tech and Internet stocks at the time and said that their performance stood out "like a beacon in the night." We all know too well the rocks that beacon led to.

Although market history provides convincing testimony about the ephemeral nature of very high or low returns, generation after generation of investors has been swept up by the prevalent thinking of its day. Each trend has its supporting statistics. The trends have strong affective and heuristic qualities. They are salient and easy to recall and are, of course, confirmed by rising prices. These biases, all of which interact, make it natural to project the prevailing trend well into the future. The common error each time is that although the trend may have lasted for months, sometimes for years, it is not representative and is often far removed from the performance of equities or bonds over longer periods. In hindsight, we can readily identify the errors and wonder why, if they were so obvious, we did not see them earlier.

The major lesson I hope you take away from this chapter is that the information-processing shortcuts we use all the time, though highly efficient in day-to-day situations, systematically work against us in the marketplace. We just are not good information processors in many ways, and the effects of cognitive biases on our decision making are enormous, not only in investing, but in economics, management, and virtually every area of life.

Even so, these findings have been almost completely disregarded by mainstream economics. The prevailing theory of the markets, the efficient-market hypothesis, rejects virtually all of the psychology we've just considered. Instead it posits that investors are rational information processors at almost all times. In order to see just how misleading the tenets of this hypothesis are and how damaging they can be to your investment earnings, let's now take a close look at the hypothesis and the many reasons it should be discarded—or at the least should not govern your own investment decisions.

Part II

The New Dark Ages

with leather patch

Chapter 4

Conquistadors in Tweed Jackets

GOLD WAS ALWAYS on the minds of the Spanish conquistadors of the 1500s. Those freebooting, merciless adventurers heard rumors of an entire city of gold in Peru, ruled by a king who bathed in a golden lake and wore pure gold dust like perfume. They searched and searched for El Dorado and talked of their vision to others. But the city was never found.

Fast-forward some five centuries. Faith and the sword have once more gone in against even more overwhelming odds than those that faced their predecessors centuries ago. The reigning conquistadors are not traditional warriors. To look at them, you'd have thought they were, well, professors, dressed in the armor of academia, often tweed jackets with leather patches covering their elbows. But don't let their conservative attire fool you. They were armed with the most powerful weaponry the investment world had seen to that time—high-level mathematics and statistics, programmed into advanced computers—and their findings were overwhelming. A handful of theorists working at one major university or another across the land (and soon around the globe) came up with a powerful new theory that changed the course not only of Wall Street but of all investment thinking. They had hearts of steel, and their secular and academic faith was no less fervent than the religious zeal of the original conquistadors, while their weaponry terrified all who were foolish enough to challenge it.

I know many disciples of these theorists who would be happy to show you the way to a new El Dorado. They have a mathematical map—and a visionary theory that explains everything about how investors make decisions and markets work. Though they are far too modest to promise cities of gold, they are fervent about owning the key that unlocks the door to the secrets of markets.

Their arguments call to mind Winston Churchill's description of Russia: "a riddle wrapped in a mystery inside an enigma."[1] But to appreciate just how flawed those arguments are, it's important that we first investigate just how they managed to convince so many people of their veracity, because they are indeed both scientific and convincing.

A Revolutionary New Financial Hypothesis

Did the new conquistadors of mathematical analysis actually sweep away the decaying financial culture and replace it with a scientific one, or did something go seriously wrong? Rather than a new Age of Enlightenment, did they bring in a New Dark Age in its place? The historians' Dark Ages, as we know, refer to a period of cultural and economic deterioration. That disruption and decline in Western Europe came after the fall of Rome and lasted to the early part of the Middle Ages. Compared with the highly developed cultures and civilizations of Greece and Rome and the Renaissance era that followed, this period contributed little to the enlightenment of man. Edward Gibbon, in *The History of the Decline and Fall of the Roman Empire*, from his eighteenth-century perspective, expressed his contempt for the "rubbish of the Dark Ages."[2]

I wonder what Mr. Gibbon would think of our day. How, in this time of enormous technological, medical, scientific, and cultural advancement, he might ask, could our thinking powers have gone into such decline? It is certainly not universal, encompassing all parts of our cultural and technological development. Quite the contrary; it is localized in one area of the social sciences: economics.

In the past sixty-five years, the study of economics escaped the cozy confines of the ivory tower and became highly influential. The economic and financial theories economists espoused are now powerful enough to affect the well-being of hundreds of millions of people globally, and they have encouraged us to take a big step back from lessons we learned in the first half of the twentieth century.

A Brief History Lesson

The new conquistadors' bible, the efficient-market hypothesis, or EMH, as it's generally referred to, is the most influential financial theory in generations. In recent decades it leaped out of academia and became the farthest-reaching and most widely followed theory in the world of global finance. Critics protest that its assumptions and much of its research have never been proved. Others go further and state that its premises, as well as thousands of supposedly highly sophisticated mathematical papers supporting it, are rebutted by findings in many sectors of social science—and in the marketplace itself. Still, EMH flourishes, followed by enormous numbers of investors on their own or through the managers of their mutual funds and investment advisers.

How did EMH—and its two close-knit brethren, the capital asset pricing model (CAPM) and modern portfolio theory (MPT)*—become so powerful in the investment world?† How can the teachings influence you, and how have they shaped markets in our time? Just as psychological errors induced by Affect and other cognitive heuristics can be avoided only by gaining an understanding of them, a study of EMH and its shortcomings is essential to protect investors from the harmful fallout it can cause.

The Beginnings of a Powerful New Hypothesis

The revolution began peacefully enough. Louis Bachelier, an outstanding French mathematics student, examined the fluctuations of commodity prices at the turn of the twentieth century in his doctoral dissertation.[3]

---

* Also known as the Markowitz-Sharpe-Lintner-Mossin theory.
† MPT looks to optimize return for a given level of risk. CAPM states that the only way to receive higher returns is to take higher risk; lower risk will result in lower returns.

He concluded that commodity price movement appeared random, that is, without any predictable pattern. Recent price data were of no help in predicting future price fluctuations. His findings were the first contributions to what would become known as the "random walk hypothesis."

Bachelier's work lay dormant for decades until it was rediscovered in 1960. During the 1960s, other researchers started to study stock price movements. One early study showed that randomly chosen series of numbers, when plotted closely together, looked like charts of stock price fluctuations over time.[4] Another study found that stock price movements were remarkably similar to the random movements of minute solid particles, termed "Brownian motion" in physics, after the Scottish botanist Robert Brown, who first observed the phenomenon in 1827.[5]

In the first half of the 1960s, evidence of the random fluctuations of stock prices mounted. Virtually all of the statistical evidence, which was now considerable, buttressed the hypothesis that successive price movements were independent of past price movements.[*]

Essentially, the random walk hypothesis of stock price behavior states that the history of stock price fluctuations and trading volume does not contain any information that will allow the investor to do any better than a buy-and-hold strategy.[6] In short, the odds are strong that you won't beat the averages. The market has "no memory." As with a friend well into his cups whom you are walking to your car, any of his steps will give you no clue of which way he'll lurch next.

Not surprisingly, the theory was not accepted by cheering crowds of those practicing technical analysis, one of the two methods commonly used to determine stock and market values. They make their living, after all, by forecasting stock price movements. *Technical analysis* defines a fairly wide range of techniques, but these are all based on the premise that past information on prices and trading volume gives the sophisticated "expert" a clear picture of what lurks ahead. Unlike *fundamental analysis,* which will be tossed into the arena next, technical analysis attempts to forecast changes in stock prices solely by studying market data, rather than by looking at a company's earnings, finances, and prospects. (The latter is what a fundamental analyst does.)

---

[*] The late Paul Samuelson, a Nobel laureate, contributed one of the most important papers to this subject: "Proof That Properly Anticipated Prices Fluctuate Randomly," *Industrial Management Review* (Spring 1945).

The last thing these grizzled veterans needed to hear from a passel of young, clean-shaven, academic computer geeks was that *their methods didn't work*. If the academics were correct, it meant that technical analysis ought to be abandoned.

Obviously, a major war of ideas was about to break out. The technicians threw in their most sophisticated techniques, ranging from advanced charting formations to support and resistance levels. Most technicians work from dozens of separate patterns of prices and methods, relying on their judgment to use the proper combination for each case. They weren't going down without giving it their best shot, and with the advent of more and more powerful computers, they could produce graphs and charts, data histograms and retrospective analysis as never before.

The Professors Kept A-coming

The academics, though, shot back with their own impressive firepower. Basically two techniques were employed. The first was evidence that showed that stock price movements were random.* A number of detailed studies were made in the early 1960s that, updating the prior research, demonstrated that stock movements were random, and the proof of a "trend" so vital to the technician could not be found. Such tests were performed by Arnold Moore in 1964,[7] Clive Granger and Oskar Morgenstern in 1963,[8] and Eugene Fama in 1965.[9] Fama, for example, in his doctoral dissertation, analyzed the prices of the thirty stocks in the Dow Jones Industrial Average at time intervals varying between one day and two weeks for more than five years. His results firmly supported the random walk hypothesis.

If stock prices are random, no matter what price and volume information you have or how strong a chart may look, the chart is meaningless as a predictive instrument, because the next price move is entirely independent of the preceding one. If a stock has moved up seven days in a row, that has no influence on what it will do on the eighth day. It can trade up or down or be unchanged, just as a coin coming up heads many

---

* The initial work by Bachelier showed that similar movements of commodity prices were thought to be random, as were the particles in Brownian motion. The research did not show that stock prices themselves were random.

times in a row has a fifty-fifty chance of coming up heads again on the next toss.

In extensive testing employing rigorous statistical procedures, only relatively minor departures from randomness in price movements were found from day to day, week to week, and month to month.[10] The central thesis of the technician that markets and stocks display major identifiable trends that may be used to predict future movement stands refuted.

The second argument the technicians used was more difficult to handle. "True," they could say, "randomness might be proved from day to day or for a number of successive weeks or even months, but aren't the measurements unfair? The tests have measured only total price data and indicated randomness. Could there not be useful direction in price changes within the time periods studied, such as hour to hour, that the daily or weekly studies did not pick up? Or trends that could be seen only by using selective data such as price-volume statistics together with Kondratieff waves?"* In effect, the technicians were inviting the academic researchers to test the systems used in technical analysis rather than price movements as a whole, which they proceeded to do—with devastating results. Some of the first tests, for example, were on different "filter" systems, techniques technicians believe indicate a stock is reversing a trend. If a stock was going down, the filter might show the stock was bottoming and a buy order should be put in or the reverse. But the tests showed that after deducting commissions, filters do not lead to higher returns.[11] An investor is as well off with a buy-and-hold strategy or, in layman's terms, simply buying and holding a portfolio. Relative-strength methods, which buy stocks that are performing better for a time, were also tested and provided no better results.[12] The popular Dow Theory in its turn was subjected to scientific scrutiny. Peaks, valleys, support, and resistance levels, although important to technicians, were all shown to have no predictive value. Price action was random after both "sell" and "buy" signals were given.

The computer proved fickle. Though helping the chartist when in

---

*There are hundreds of such indicators. Price volume statistics measure whether stocks are moving up or down on increasing volume. A stock rising on increasing volume is considered bullish, and a stock going down is bearish. Nikolai D. Kondratieff was a brilliant Russian economist who is known for the Kondratieff wave, major self-correcting economic cycles that the European economies seemed to go through approximately every fifty years. After holding a major position under Lenin after the Russian Revolution, he disappeared into the Soviet Gulag system and was never heard from again.

his hands, it was also turned against him. In one such test, a computer program analyzed 548 stocks trading on the New York Stock Exchange over a five-year period, scanning the information to identify any one of thirty-two of the most commonly followed patterns, including "head and shoulders" and "triple tops and bottoms." It was programmed to act on its findings as a chartist would. It would, for example, buy on an upside breakout after a triple top, a strong technical indicator that the stock would go higher; or it would sell after the market had plunged through the support level of a triple bottom, indicating that the stock would drop lower. The computer measured its results, based on these signals, against the performance of the general market. No correlation was found between the buy and sell signals and subsequent price movements. Once again, our old friend the buy-and-hold strategy would have worked just as well.

Price-volume systems met with the same fate. Although this is an important technical tool, the size of neither price nor volume changes appears to have a bearing on the magnitude or direction of the future price; stocks going down on heavy trading may reverse themselves and go up in the next period, as may stocks currently going up on large volume.[13]

All the tests indicated that mechanical rules do not result in returns any better than the simple buy-and-hold strategy.[14] The evidence accumulated is voluminous and strongly supports the random walk hypothesis. With a very minor caveat, some tests have shown a degree of dependence (nonrandom price movements), indicating that a number of marginally profitable trading rules and small filters appear to work consistently. The problem is that the numerous transactions involved in such systems generate substantial commissions, which absorb the expected profit.[15]

In numerous tests, then, no evidence to date has been able to refute the random walk hypothesis. Technicians nonetheless claim that their methods work, and if you look at their examples they certainly appear to. But, as we have seen, their success is actually only chance in accordance with the laws of averages. Also, of course, their methods work much better with hindsight. Technicians, being human, forget their "misses" and remember their "hits." If they were wrong, the cause wasn't the basic technique but its misapplication or the fact that another application or supplementary information was required. Technicians have also claimed that some technical systems work, supported by computer evidence of a correlation over certain periods of time. Undoubtedly this is true, but

when a portion of these results was tested more thoroughly, using different time periods and more extensive price information, the correlation
disappeared, again showing that the results of the systems were based
simply on chance.

When all is said and done, it is impossible to absolutely prove that
the random walk hypothesis never works, for that would mean testing
not only all the hundreds of systems but also the hundreds of thousands
of possible combinations, with the final decision depending on the technician's own interpretation. An enormous number of tests would be required to do this. Technicians can, quite rightly, say that not all systems
have been examined and that in any case their decisions were not based
on any one method but were the outcome of judgment and experience.
Still, from the substantial evidence accumulated, no system of technical
analysis has as yet been found that can put a dent in the random walk
hypothesis.

Even though the academic findings have been strongly refuted,
chartists and other technicians continue to flourish. They disregard the
findings—if they are aware of them—because "their" system is different
and hope their clients also ignore the research. Occasionally they let off
steam at their antagonists, but usually their protests are without factual
support.

When they are not otherwise warning investors to beware, the academics appear to regard technicians with a detached amusement that
some may reserve for witch doctors or primitive soothsayers in bygone
cultures (I won't include astrologers today). This tough and dedicated cult
of financial forecasters has been taking its lumps for many years, not only
from academics but also from the proponents of fundamental analysis.
Some unkind fundamental analysts I have known would go so far as to
propose a new experiment to the academics: a survey would be taken of
shiny suits, frayed collars, and sundry holes in the attire of a sample of
technicians, to be measured against a control sample of other Wall Streeters. They believe the findings would show technicians to be far the worse
for wear and tear, since most tend to follow their own pronouncements.

Even so, many fundamental analysts are part-time dabblers in the
technical mystique. Although fundamental analysis is dominant on Wall
Street, most members of this group at one time or another take a peek "to
see what the charts tell them," probably more often in periods of crisis

but also as a final affirmation of a decision to buy. We find that in spite of the accumulation of evidence for more than five decades on the unproductiveness of technical analysis, it continues to be widely practiced by investors.

The Academic Blitzkrieg Rolls On

Unfortunately for most money managers and analysts, the academics did not rest on their laurels after this one rather clear-cut victory. Beginning in the mid-1960s, a much more ambitious operation was launched when the researchers asked whether fundamental analysis, the gospel of the large majority of Wall Street professionals, is of any use in obtaining above-average returns in the market.

The fundamentalist school believes that the value of a company can be determined through a rigorous analysis of its sales, earnings, dividend prospects, financial strength, and competitive position, and other related measures. Fundamental analysts have been trained in its many complex nuances and applications, in both undergraduate and graduate schools,* and have expanded their knowledge through daily application in their work. Such analysis is used by the great preponderance of mutual funds, bank trust departments, pension funds, and investment advisers, as well as most brokers.

Yet despite their impeccable credentials, the money managers' record has been anything but awe-inspiring over the years. One of the first studies of money managers' results was undertaken by the SEC, which measured the performance of investment companies from the late 1920s to the mid-1930s. The report stated, "It can then be concluded with considerable assurance, that the entire group of management investment companies proper (closed end funds) failed to perform better than an index of leading common stocks, and probably performed worse than the index over the 1927–1935 period."[16] Alfred Cowles, an American economist and businessman who founded the Cowles Commission for Research in Economics Research and its journal, *Econometrica,* ana-

---

* A significant number of academics still believe in, or at least still stay employed, teaching these subjects.

lyzed the performance of investment professionals in 1933 and concluded that stock market money managers do not beat the market. The study was updated in 1944, with the same results.[17]

Numerous scholarly studies of the lackluster performance of money managers were published in the 1960s and 1970s. One of the most exhaustive and devastating studies was by Irwin Friend, Marshall Blume, and Jean Crockett of the Wharton School in 1970.[18] The report was widely read and discussed by both academics and professional investors. One hundred thirty-six funds produced an average return of 10.6 percent annually between January 1960 and June 30, 1968. During the same period the shares on the New York Stock Exchange produced an average return of 12.4 percent annually.

If fundamentalists were perplexed by why their results weren't better, the academics certainly were not. Starting in the mid-1960s, they shifted their research firepower from technical to fundamental analysis. Extensive studies have been made of mutual funds and other professional performance results, the great majority of which subscribe to security analysis. The professors demonstrated once again that the funds and, for that matter, other large accounts of money managers did not outperform the market.[19]

A powerful cast of financial academics led the charge of EMH against the then-conventional wisdom, including the Nobel laureates Marshall Blume, Merton Miller, William Sharpe, and Myron Scholes, as well as distinguished academics such as Professors Eugene Fama and Richard Roll.

Academic analysis proved as unsparing of the fundamental practitioner's sensibilities as of the technician's. Other prevailing beliefs were treated as harshly. No link was found between the widely held belief that higher portfolio turnover led to better performance. Rapid turnover does not improve results but seems to damage them slightly. No relationship was found between performance and sales charges, although mutual funds with higher sales charges often claimed they provided better results.[20] In sum, the reports firmly concluded, mutual funds do not outperform the market.

The results hardly comforted fund managers, who like to represent to clients that they provide superior performance. Mutual fund managers not only underperformed the market but, if we adjust for risk as the academics defined it, often fared worse. At the time, the money managers appeared to be routed as badly as the Inca armies who fled from Francisco Pizarro and his terrifying cannon and cavalry.* But, as we'll see, it's one thing to overthrow the ideology of the native rulers with computer "horses," and another to rule over the theoretical world.

The Efficient-Market Legions Surge Further

As we've seen, the academic investigators proposed a revolutionary new hypothesis that we briefly examined earlier, the efficient-market hypothesis (EMH), which holds that competition between sophisticated, knowledgeable investors keeps stock prices where they should be. This happens because all facts that determine stock prices are analyzed by large numbers of intelligent and rational investors. New information, such as a change in a company's earnings outlook or a dividend cut, is quickly digested and immediately reflected in the stock price. Like it or not, competition by so many market participants, all seeking hidden values, makes stock prices reflect the best estimates of their real worth. Prices may not always be right, but they are unbiased, so if they are wrong, they are just as likely to be too high as too low.

Since meaningful information enters the marketplace unpredictably, prices react in a random manner. This is the real reason that charting and technical analysis do not work. Nobody knows what new data will enter the market, whether they will be positive or negative, or whether they will affect the market as a whole or only a single company.

A key premise of the efficient-market hypothesis is that the market reacts almost instantaneously (and correctly) to new information, so investors *cannot benefit*. To prove this contention, researchers conducted a number of studies that they claimed validated the thesis.

One important study explored the market's understanding of stock splits. In effect, when a stock is split, there is no free lunch—the shareholder still has the same proportionate ownership as before. If naive traders run up the price, said the academics, knowledgeable investors will sell until it is back in line, and market efficiency will be proved. And, said the researchers, this is indeed the case. Tests have confirmed that stock prices after a split was distributed maintained about the same long-term relationship to market movements as before the split.[21]

---

* Horses and cavalry were then unknown in the Americas.

Another study measuring the earnings of 261 large corporations between 1946 and 1966 concluded that all but 10 to 15 percent of the data in the earnings reports were anticipated by the reporting month, indicating the market's awareness of information.[22] Other tests came up with similar results, demonstrating, the professors said, that the market quickly adjusts to inputs.

Did these tests actually prove what they claim and cinch the case that markets react quickly to new information? Remember these and other EMH cornerstones. We'll see shortly whether these tests, along with many others, will boomerang back on the researchers who tossed them so confidently at investors.

The Capital Asset Pricing Model: EMH Victory or Trojan Horse?

With the stock market declared efficient, the theorists could tell investors they should expect only a fair return—that is, a return commensurate with the exact risk of purchasing a particular stock. The capital asset pricing model (CAPM), a younger brother of EMH, comes into play here. Risk (as CAPM defines it) is volatility. The greater the volatility of the security or portfolio, measured against the market, the greater the risk.

The most common quantitative measure of volatility is designated as beta.* It can be the volatility of a mutual fund, a portfolio, or a common stock. To calculate it, a mutual fund, a portfolio, or a stock must be measured against a benchmark, normally a stock index. Stock portfolios of larger-capitalization mutual funds or other similar portfolios are often measured against the S&P 500, which is assigned a beta of 1. If the mutual fund has a higher beta, the academics say, it is more risky than the index. Conversely, a lower beta is considered less risky. Over time, risk and return must always be in line, say the theorists. Securities or portfolios with greater risk should provide larger returns; those with less risk, lower returns. Thus the money manager whose portfolio outperforms the market by 3 percent a year might have a much higher beta for his portfolio. Since the academics assume that there is a direct correlation between risk

---

* Beta is calculated using regression analysis. Nonmathematically, think of beta as a number signifying the relative volatility of a stock compared with the broad market.

(volatility) and return, after adjusting for volatility, the manager who outperforms the market by 3 percent might actually be doing worse than a manager who outperforms by 1 percent. The academics call this measurement risk-adjusted return.

The efficient-market hypothesis, elegant in its simplicity, is intuitively appealing because it explains the single most obvious mystery about investing: how can tens of thousands of intelligent, hardworking professional stock pickers be endlessly outwitted by the market and embarrassed by their selections?

EMH has much wider implications than the random walk hypothesis,* which said only that investors would not benefit from technical analysis. If correct, the new argument tears the heart out of fundamental research. No amount of fundamental analysis, including the exhaustive high-priced studies done by major Wall Street brokerage houses, will give investors an edge. If enough buyers and sellers correctly evaluate new information, under- and overvalued stocks will be rare indeed.[23]

The implications are sweeping. If you're in the market, the theory tells you to buy and hold rather than trade a lot. Trading increases the commissions you pay without increasing your return. The theory also tells you to assume that investors who have outperformed the market in the past were just plain lucky and that you have no reason to believe they will continue to do so.[24]

The semistrong form of EMH contends that no mutual fund, million-dollar-plus money manager, or individual investor, no matter how sophisticated, can beat the market using public information. This is the most widely accepted form of EMH today.

If the "weak form" of EMH, the random walk hypothesis, made some dramatic claims, the "strong form" doubled down. The stronger form claims that no information, including that known by corporate insiders or by specialists trading the company's stock (who have confidential material about unexecuted orders on their books), can help you outperform the market. In the few studies done to date, some evidence has surfaced that both insiders[25] and specialists[26] display an ability to beat the market. However, the strong form of EMH is generally considered too extreme and is not widely accepted.

---

* Later called the weak form of EMH.

Further Academic Backing of EMH

Professor Eugene Fama,* the leading advocate of EMH (*Fortune* magazine once referred to him as the Solomon of stocks), reviewed the literature and development of EMH in December 1991[27] and again in 1998.[28] Fama's reports were thorough, covering hundreds of papers published since his last major review twenty years earlier. The papers strongly supported the semistrong form of EMH.

Despite the tens of thousands of academic papers written about EMH in the last forty-five years, relatively little new research supporting the efficient-market hypothesis has been produced, with two exceptions. Some new studies show daily and weekly predictability in price movements from past movements. But after transaction costs, there is nothing much left to put in your wallet.

A second area of new support for efficient markets, according to Fama, comes from event studies, the study of specific events and how they affect a stock or the market. In the past twenty years, hundreds of such studies have been undertaken. Fama concludes that "on average stock prices adjust quickly to information about investment decisions, dividend changes, changes in capital structure, and corporate-control transactions."[29] He also refers to another large body of research from event studies showing the opposite conclusion: rather than adjusting rapidly to new information, prices adjust slowly and thus inefficiently. Nevertheless, he concludes his review article with this statement: "The cleanest evidence of market-efficiency comes from event studies, especially from event studies on daily returns."[30]

Fama adds in his 1998 paper that market efficiency still survives. He spends considerable time discussing anomalies that challenge the efficacy of EMH, stating that they are chance results. But to do so he must be dismissive of major work, ironically by both other scholars and himself, that has stood for decades. The good professor and a large number of other EMH adherents even tend to deny that anomalies actually exist. We will go into these anomalies in some detail in the chapters ahead.

Since the 1960s, EMH researchers have shown a strong inclination to

---

* As of 2011, he is the Robert R. McCormick Distinguished Service Professor of Finance at the University of Chicago Booth School of Business.

dismiss anomalies by criticizing the methodology of other investigators or on other grounds, as we'll see in chapter 6.*†

The Power of an Idea

Whether EMH, CAPM, and MPT do a good job of describing markets or are pure blather, they have fired the imagination not only of academia but also of Wall Street. Prior to these theories, investment managers and mutual funds were measured on the rates of return their portfolios generated, usually compared with the S&P 500 or the Dow Jones, with no adjustments made for risk. The development of the CAPM resulted in academics' and consultants' putting risk measurements into the formula to determine how well a portfolio performed. If a portfolio earned the market return with higher risk, it was deemed, on a risk-adjusted basis, to have underperformed the market; and if it earned the market return with lower risk, it was deemed to have outperformed the market.

Risk measurement has grown into a multibillion-dollar industry and influences the decisions of countless investors, either directly or through their pension funds. If you buy a mutual fund from Morgan Stanley, Charles Schwab, or virtually any other brokerage firm, as millions do, you might take your cue from a Charles Schwab–recommended list. To rank funds, Schwab and most other mass marketers calculate risk as well as performance. Similar risk measurements are used by consultants who recommend money managers to large pension funds and the large brokerage houses, the latter of which in turn recommend money managers for millions of smaller customers. On the theory that you cannot beat the market over time, more than a trillion dollars has also gone into various forms of index funds.

In the space of twenty pages or so, I have documented the academic dismantlement of the two most important market theories of our day— technical and fundamental analysis—and their replacement, at least in-

---

* In 1992, Professor Fama himself "discovered" that contrarian strategies actually worked, after dismissing them for twenty years because of claimed methodological errors. They were then considered an "anomaly."

† In fact, numerous research studies, including some on contrarian strategies, were dismissed for one methodological cause or another—yet after they were *redone,* correcting for the methodological criticisms, the findings remained valid.

tellectually, by a third. The new theory has swept through the universities and then progressively through the financial press, among individual and corporate investors, and among professionals themselves. On the assumption that it is impossible to outdo the market, many professionals have radically altered their techniques and their concept of risk—a fitting tribute to the power of an idea conceived less than five decades ago.

The theory so pervades professional investing and academia that Michael Jensen, one of the important contributors to its development, stated some years back, "It's dangerously close to the point where no graduate student would dare send off a paper criticizing the hypothesis."[31] At the same time, it is sad, for in accepting the new way, the money manager acknowledges that his or her prime raison d'être—to earn superior returns for the client—is beyond reach.

The spread of the new faith was not unlike the conquest of the vast Inca empire by Pizarro and his 180 conquistadors. Like the conquistadors, the scholars used both faith and the sword to annihilate the pagans' beliefs in the old marketplace. If the true faith was not accepted, why, then there was the sword—the unleashing of volleys of awesome statistics disproving everything the professionals believed. What amazes in retrospect is that the leaders of the new faith subdued millions of investors with a smaller troop than the original conquistadors.

An Achilles' Heel

But it's not time to wave the white flag just yet. The golden age of efficient markets may not be destined to last. If we scrutinize the theory more closely after the chilling market events of more recent times, the elegant hypothesis seems to have more than a few major hitches. The professors assumed that investors were as emotionless and as efficient as the computers they used to generate their theory. They completely omitted any psychology, including the compelling work we looked at in the previous chapters that seems to fuel many of the major investor errors we repeatedly make, from their calculations. This by itself could be a fatal blow to the hypothesis, but, as we shall see in the next two chapters, there are other, even more serious flaws.

Although the efficient-market hypothesis seems to unravel some of the investment knots we have seen, such as why professional investors as a group do not outperform the market, it fails to untie many others. How, for instance, could investors en masse underperform the market for decades? How could the bulk of professional opinion prove so consistently and dramatically wrong at crucial market turning points? Or, if investors are so unfailingly rational, how could euphoria and panic prevail as often as we saw in the past chapters? More specifically, if the market is so efficient, how could the 1996–2002 and 2003–2009 bubble and crashes, two of the most severe in economic history, occur within only a few years of each other, particularly when legions of investment professionals were not only trained in, but carefully followed, efficient-market teachings and invested trillions of dollars according to this contemporary bible?

The truth is that the work of outstanding academics, including several dozen Nobel laureates whose research is the bedrock supporting EMH and MPT, has caused heretofore unheard-of market damage in numerous bubbles during the past twenty-five years.

These revolutionary new ideas that sprouted from financial ivory towers around the world won't give you the odds to beat the market or for that matter even keep you afloat. Many of the basic teachings of EMH have now been conclusively refuted by advanced forms of the same statistical analysis that devastated the investment heathen. Yet contemporary investment practice is built on the belief in efficient markets. Large numbers of investors, though they believe the theory to be bankrupt, don't know where else to turn.

The efficient-market hypothesis is the natural extension of the last two hundred years of economic theory. At last a place was found for economists to take a stand that would once and for all establish that people behaved in the rational manner economists have assumed for centuries. Their laboratories are, of course, the stock markets and other financial markets. Demonstrating that people actually behave rationally in these markets would be almost akin to discovering the holy books of economics.

It is not surprising, then, that the original "evidence" by Fama, Blume, Jensen, Scholes, and others, that markets were efficient, was enthusiastically greeted by economists, perhaps nowhere more than at the University of Chicago, one of the renowned bastions of laissez-faire. Equally logical was that Chicago became the intellectual heart of this dynamic new research.

Market economists threw down the gauntlet. As one academic noted,

"You can see why the idea [of perfectly knowledgeable investors in the stock market] is intriguing. Where else can the economist find the ideal of the perfect market? Here is a place to take a stand if there is such a place."[32] Take a stand they did, although, as we'll see, it is beginning to look more and more like that last stand by General Custer.

So deep was their conviction that these theories would usher in the golden age of markets, if not economics, that they were convinced the statistics would bear them out. But as we'll see next, they do not.

Still, to avoid ensnarement by EMH, you must understand its teachings well. There are no government-required labels to warn you away from the EMH-CAPM-MPT trap; lacking knowledge, you can easily be caught up in it. A flawed investment theory is not market-neutral; it can be destructive to the capital of average and sophisticated investors alike. To find the road to successful investment, we must stay well clear of the theory. That will take something more than looking up imploringly to the heavens.

Where, then, do the real odds of market success lie? Are there any real odds at all? We will examine these questions shortly, but first let's look at why EMH has failed and how its failure affects you as an investor.

Chapter 5

It's Only a Flesh Wound

WHEN I THINK of those defending EMH, a striking image comes to me from the English comedy film *Monty Python and the Holy Grail*. King Arthur and his squire are riding through the forest—well, we hear the sound of horses' hooves, but actually the two are on foot, prancing along through the trees and meadows—when they find their path blocked by the Black Knight, who demands that the king fight to the death to pass. In the ensuing swordfight, King Arthur lops off one of the Black Knight's arms, then the other, but the knight refuses to yield. "You haven't got any arms left," the king points out. "Look!"

"What! Just a flesh wound!" the knight retorts. The battle continues, and King Arthur disposes of both of the knight's legs. Unyielding, reduced to mere head and torso, the knight still won't give in. *"The Black Knight always triumphs!"* he bellows bravely. *"Come back here and take what's coming to you. I'll bite your legs off!"*

As this chapter will show, EMH is in a spot not all that dissimilar, refusing to yield no matter how battered.

Interestingly, the historical reality of England's King Arthur has never been satisfactorily established. It's just not verifiable history. Yet in grand novels, poems, plays, children's books—even the satirical deflating by

Monty Python—his legend is secure. With EMH we have a plethora of data, and it ought to have been simple enough to establish—or refute—the validity of its "legendary" findings by now. Yet, unlike that of King Arthur's tales, the historical basis of EMH has undergone considerable revisionism, and with each updating, the base of its statistical observation has become shakier.

In the previous chapter I described how EMH swept through academia in the 1960s and then took Wall Street by storm. Like George Patton's Third Army roaring through Germany in 1945, the efficient-market hypothesis overwhelmed the obsolescent weapons of Wall Street's technicians and fundamentalists with its seemingly invincible new weaponry of powerful statistical analysis and mathematics. Because academic findings clearly showed that money managers could not outperform the market, a trillion dollars flowed into funds based on various indexes, from the S&P 500 to the Russell 2000.* Owing to the scope of their victory, some academics even expressed concerns that the markets might not continue to be as efficient as the realization spread that money managers and analysts could not beat the market and as a result would probably be laid off. Since these managers and analysts were essential, according to EMH, to keeping markets efficient, too many such layoffs would make them less so. This was a bad dream for those of us in the investment field but, as it turns out, only that. This chapter and the next should demonstrate that it is actually built on sand and will show some of the reasons why. In our journey we will see much of the supposedly powerful statistical documentation of the theory crumble, because either the tools did not do what they claimed or the researchers ignored or downgraded powerful data that refuted their claims.

There is a clear disconnect between real-world results and the predictions of the distinguished academic pioneers who formulated EMH. In this chapter, after we have compiled a solid reference base of major market events that refute EMH's basic premises, we will turn to fundamental flaws in the analysis used to buttress the theory. As we'll see, when the EMH blinders come off, the lessons are noteworthy.

Like the Black Knight's predicament, it isn't going to be pretty, but it will clear your path to future investing success. Just as the Black Knight loses one arm, then the other, then both legs, yet vows to fight on, EMH is

---

* The Russell 2000 Index is the most widely followed small-company index.

going to lose one support after another yet remain—you guessed it—the academic theory that trumps all others.

Now we're going to examine in detail three market events that EMH adherents said could not have happened. With all the financial bloodshed, a few lessons should have been learned, but that was not the case. They are:

1. The 1987 stock market crash
2. The 1998 Long-Term Capital Management debacle
3. The 2006–2008 housing bubble and market crash

1. The 1987 Stock Market Crash

The crash of 1987 was to that time the worst market panic since 1929–1932. The seeds were planted in Chicago in the early 1980s. The Chicago commodity exchanges were eager to expand their business away from wheat, soybeans, cattle futures, livestock, and other commodities. Hungriest of all was the Chicago Mercantile Exchange (the Merc), which had a reputation over the years of cornering markets and performing other high-wire acts that fell on the wrong side of the law. Over its history many attempts had been made to close it down. Scandals abounded, particularly in the onion pit. Onions were one of the major commodities traded, and as a result of the corners, squeezes, and other illegal activities, Congress finally legislated the end of trading in onion futures. The exchange limped along, with a seat in the 1960s and '70s costing only a pittance.

That all changed in the span of a little over a decade. The Chicago exchanges, led by the lowly Merc under its dynamic chairman, Leo Melamed, were transformed from trading grain, cattle futures, and pork bellies to playing a key role in the U.S. stock and bond markets. Behind the radical reorientation of their business activities were a number of major EMH academics. Not coincidentally, most of the professors were at the University of Chicago, one of the strongest bastions of laissez-faire in the country. The academics believed that financial futures gave markets far more liquidity, providing what they thought would be much broader markets and lower trading costs, thereby enhancing markets' efficiency.

The star of the show was the S&P 500 futures, introduced by the Merc in April 1982. Most commodity traders thought it couldn't be done, because futures trading was commonly considered to be a form of gambling. Futures trading, because of its speculative nature, had never been allowed to interact with stock trading. Such a reaction, most investors believed, would result in greater volatility in the stock market. Even leaders in the futures industry believed that was the case. Walter E. Auch, then the chaiman and CEO of the the Chicago Board Options Exchange (CBOE), wrote a letter to the Commodity Futures Trading Commission (CFTC), the country's top commodities regulator, warning of the potential for "sophisticated manipulation and that index futures are a dressed up form of wagering."[1]

The danger was very real. We know that a major cause of the 1929 crash was excessive margin trading at razor-thin margins of 10 percent. In the congressional reforms of the early 1930s, Congress gave the Federal Reserve the power to raise margins on stock purchases, so it could never happen again. And the Fed used this power. Stock margins were never under 50 percent and have been raised in more speculative markets to as high as 100 percent on occasion in the post–World War II period. Even so, margins on stock futures today are much lower than stock margins, normally 5 percent prior to the 1987 crash and now about 7 percent.

Commodity margins were about one-tenth as high as stock margins in 1987, well below the low margins blamed for the 1929 crash, more than wiping out a good part of the congressional reforms regulating margin trading after the 1929 crash. The commodity exchanges had strong academic support from the professors because of the latter's fixation on more liquid markets while entirely disregarding the dangers of very high leverage.

Sharp drops or crashes have often occurred in the past in both commodity and stock markets when margin requirements were too low. So, through the back door of financial futures, aided by powerful believers in EMH, the Merc and the CBOT could buy or short stocks at margins lower than those in effect in 1929. Players on the commodity exchanges—and they included large numbers of Wall Street firms and hedge funds—could leverage their positions almost ten times as high on stock futures as they could when buying stocks themselves. Since stock futures trading was about double the dollar amount of trading on the NYSE, the tail of S&P 500 futures could most definitely wag the dog, the stock market itself. Not to worry, said the professors, ignoring the numerous collapses of commodity markets in the past, it can't happen today. Markets are efficient, and index arbitrage, an offshoot of futures trading, will make them even more so.*

When the Merc applied to the CFTC for permission to trade S&P 500 futures, the exchange, along with powerful academic backing, made a strong case that movements of S&P 500 futures would not initiate movements of stocks in the index. This was a prediction that would cost investors many hundreds of billions of dollars by linking the speculative culture of the commodity exchanges to the far more conservative floor of the New York Stock Exchange.

The Mercantile Exchange knew it had a huge moneymaker in stock futures. It launched a giant promotional campaign featuring the S&P 500 futures, ran full-page ads in *The Wall Street Journal,* and hired celebrities such as Louis Rukeyser, the host of the TV show *Wall Street Week,* to promote the idea, as well as holding heavily attended seminars across the country conducted by some of the best-known EMH theorists to explain the benefit of S&P 500 futures to leading money managers.

The promotion paid off. By the end of 1987, trading in S&P 500 futures alone was over $300 billion a month, about double the $153 billion traded on the NYSE. The CBOE trading of the S&P 100 (a compact version of the S&P 500, limited primarily to the highest market caps in the index) amounted to another $2.4 billion.[2]

From being a center of trading eggs and pork bellies, Chicago had become one of the world's largest financial markets. And the Merc controlled 75 percent of the stock index market.[3] Reflecting the seemingly endless prosperity in its financial instruments division, the value of seats had climbed from a pittance to $190,000 in eleven years.[4]

Then there was index arbitrage (also called program trading), which allowed S&P index funds and scores of other major institutions to buy or sell either the S&P stocks or the S&P futures if the prices of either one got out of line with the other. If, for example, the value of all the stocks in the S&P 500 was at 250 and S&P futures were trading at 252, an alert institutional investor could, using computerized trading, quickly short sell the S&P futures and buy the stocks, locking in a return of 0.8 percent before commissions. When the futures and the S&P index went back to their normal value, the transaction would be reversed. Such a small return seems hardly worth the effort, but if the sums were large, say $100

* For a definition and details, please see text below.

million, if the purchases were on minuscule margin, and if the transactions were repeated many times in a month or two, the profits could be very large.

PORTFOLIO INSURANCE: THE FINAL
COMPONENT OF THE CRASH

Portfolio insurance was a product designed to protect the capital of institutional investors in a down market while giving them all the upside in a rising one. In brief, it was a way to have your cake and eat it too. First of all, it was not insurance at all, although it was slickly marketed as such. It purported to protect an institution's portfolio, if markets went down, by short selling S&P 500 futures. The more the market dropped, the more futures would be sold, progressively lowering the institution's stock exposure to the market.* If the portfolio dropped 3 percent, the computers of Leland O'Brien Rubinstein Associates and other portfolio insurance firms, which licensed their model, would sell futures akin to 10 percent of their portfolio. If the S&P went down another 3 percent, another 10 percent of the futures would be sold. If the S&P subsequently went up 3 percent, the 10 percent futures position would be repurchased and little would be lost, and so on.

If the price of the S&P 500 went down, the futures would be sold, not the stocks of a pension fund, a hedge fund, or any other institution that owned them. Futures were considereded exceptionally liquid, and, markets being totally efficient according to EMH, could be sold in the blink of an eye. According to its adherents, it was a perfect system, said to maximize market gains and protect against losses, supposedly at only a small cost to the owner.

Why? Because the S&P futures had *infinite liquidity.* This is a central belief of efficient marketers and the core concept of portfolio insurance. If markets went down, swarms of sophisticated buyers would come out of the woodwork and immediately buy the futures at lower prices. If the market went still lower, even larger hordes of buyers would be there to scoop up the depressed values. After all, a cardinal EMH belief was that

---

* Shorting S&P 500 futures had the same effect on a portfolio as selling stocks directly and was believed to be much easier to do. If a money manager decided to lower his equity exposure by 10 percent, he could short the S&P futures 10 percent and get the same result.

since markets were entirely rational, increasing numbers of buyers would appear as prices declined. End of discussion.

"Liquidity begets liquidity," the academics chanted. But lo and behold, they turned out to be all wet.

Did portfolio insurance actually protect a portfolio? Well, no. It would lessen the institution's losses if executed well, but it could not prevent them, nor was it designed to do so. Moreover, if a market was quite volatile it might end up costing big, even if prices did not move much, because of the small losses and commissions generated by frequently getting into and out of the market.

The keen-eyed *Barron's* editor Alan Abelson cut through the hype immediately. "It is an exotically labeled version of the small speculator's stop-loss order," he wrote. Under its complex mathematical formulas, it was simply another market-timing device. The previous chapter briefly discussed the uninspiring record of market-timing products, but as with so many others, this one, with the backing of academics steeped in EMH lore, became wildly popular. The consistency of academic thinking on market timing might seem a touch questionable here.

The mathematical calculations for portfolio insurance were based on the Black-Scholes Option Pricing Model, which for sheer complexity possibly rivaled the mathematical formulas designed to launch a space shuttle. Designed by Fischer Black and Nobel laureate Myron Scholes, this method soon became the standard way of pricing stock options. Hayne Leland and Mark Rubinstein, both in the Department of Finance at the University of California at Berkeley, adapted the model to portfolio insurance. Leland was known as the father of portfolio insurance, partly because of an article published in 1980 in the *Journal of Finance,* the most prestigious academic and pro-EMH journal.[5] Behind the awesome mathematics was a disarmingly simple but fallacious idea: you could all but guarantee yourself against downside by eliminating risk when the market dropped, clients were told, while reaping the benefits of a bull market by keeping a larger percentage of the portfolio in stocks.

Major pension and other institutional funds were keen to line up to participate in this sure thing. At one New York investment conference in the summer of 1986, the number of institutional investors who wanted to attend a workshop on portfolio insurance became so large that the workshop was expanded into the entire meeting. "It was madness," said John O'Brien of Leland O'Brien Rubinstein.[6] But it was madness he liked, as his firm was reeling in tens of billions of dollars of institutional assets that it managed. According to the Brady Commission report on the 1987 crash, $60 billion to $90 billion of funds were invested in portfolio insurance programs just prior to the crash.

PREVIOUS WARNINGS IGNORED

Something was wrong. Perhaps it seemed coincidental at first, but the vast growth of index arbitrage, portfolio insurance, and index and stock options didn't do what the efficient-market advocates had assured regulators and the public they would: decrease market volatility. Quite the opposite: there were violent stock market downturns of almost 100 points, first on July 7 and 8, 1986, and then came a minicrash on September 11 and 12 of the same year, followed by another near-collapse in the averages of almost 100 points in late March 1987. Concern began to mount among a number of senior investment professionals, including John Phelan, the president of the New York Stock Exchange. I wrote a column in *Forbes* entitled "Doomsday Machine," with the subtitle *financial index features + program trading* + low margins = potential disaster.* The article, published on March 23, 1987, described in detail how the interaction of index arbitrage and portfolio insurance would cause a crash. Unfortunately, it happened pretty much as described six months later.

Because of the *Forbes* article, I was invited to sit on a panel with some eminent academics, the majority of whom strongly backed portfolio insurance and index arbitrage trading techniques. Also present were three commissioners of the SEC, all believers in efficient markets. The conference was held at the University of Rochester, New York, a bastion of EMH, in June 1987. Almost to a man, the prestigious academics on the panel scoffed when I spoke and stated why I felt a market crash could happen. Some of the great men snickered; others merely yawned politely. Who was a mere Wall Street money manager to debate with professors of their stature?

Worse was in store for the two panelists holding views similar to mine. Robert Shiller, whom we met earlier, was taken to task and practically called a heretic. "With your training, how can you subscribe to such

---

* Another term for index arbitrage.

ridiculous views?" a member of the audience demanded. Jay Patel, then a professor of finance at MIT, received similar treatment. Despite three sharp downturns caused by the violent interactions of index arbitrage and portfolio insurance, those vehicles were not only given a clean bill of health at the meeting but were considered essential to keeping markets efficient. Then the unthinkable happened.

THE CRASH THAT WAS THEORETICALLY IMPOSSIBLE

What surprised me about the 1987 crash was the ferocity of the decline, in spite of what I knew about the dangers of the interaction of portfolio insurance and index arbitrage, as well as the tens of billions of dollars in play. The darkest scenarios I could envision didn't even come close.

Although many explanations were bandied about, there were no major events responsible for this crash, nor was the market wildly over-valued. Sure, there was some concern in the marketplace—there always is—but the anxiety level was below amber. What was disturbing was that a long-overdue correction was distorted into a disaster by the new S&P derivatives, which in times of rapidly falling prices magnified the drop sharply. That's exactly what happened on Black Monday, October 19, 1987. The result? A minor correction in the Dow turned into a 508-point panic for the day. Wow.

The Dow Jones plummeted 22.6 percent on Black Monday alone, a plunge almost twice as large as the percentage drop on Black Tuesday, October 29, 1929. It started on Wednesday morning, October 14, 1987, with the Dow just over 2,500. By noon the next Tuesday, October 20, the Dow was slightly above 1,600, a decline of more than one-third. It was the worst crash in U.S. history to that time. (The 508-point drop on October 19 was only 60 percent of the total decline.)

What created this disaster? Let's look more closely at the role of port-folio insurance and index arbitrage during those five terrifying days. A number of studies on market volatility, which examined index arbitrage and portfolio insurance, had previously been commissioned by the com-modity exchanges after the sharp 100-point drops previously discussed. Those "impartial studies" were performed for the exchanges by con-sultants salivating at the giant commissions the programs were bring-ing them. The studies, like others we will examine later, were flawed, as they covered short and relatively quiet market periods.* (Remember the law of small numbers.) The researchers concluded that the interaction between the two would not affect market volatility. Famous last words.

Who started the selling? Computers, followed by humans in shock. What looks good in the lab can act like nitroglycerin when shaken. Unfortunately, the nitro was shaken. Bam! Crash!

The S&P was down 3 percent on Wednesday, October 14, and the portfolio insurance formula went into action. Leland O'Brien Rubinstein and Wells Fargo began to sell futures by October 14 or 15 as prices fell more than 3 percent. Still the S&P futures stayed at a small premium to the S&P, in line with where they were expected to be.† On Friday, October 16, the S&P 500 Index took a sharp drop of more than 5 percent and the futures went to a minuscule discount to the S&P 500 stocks, of less than two-tenths of 1 percent.

One would think that the EMH gurus running the portfolio insurance money management firms would have been elated with how well their portfolios were performing in a rapid market downturn. The truth was that they were terrified. The liquidity of their catchphrase "Liquidity begets liquidity" was starting to dry up. Buyers of futures were becoming increasingly scarce, and they lowered their bids as the decline in S&P futures increased. EMH theory said that this was impossible, but it was happening. The result was that the portfolio insurers could sell only a small fraction of the S&P futures their formulas called for. By Friday, October 16, with an estimated $60 billion to $90 billion in portfolio insurance and sales far behind the PI formulas required, it would turn into a serious problem if the market went lower the next week. But what if the unimaginable happened, EMH liquidity theory was wrong, and liquidity dried up? The problem would become a nightmare.

The professors at the portfolio insurance firms may or may not have known about another equally devastating problem. Like the British who used the Enigma machines in World War II to decipher the most important German military codes, thus learning exactly what the enemy would do, the major brokerage houses and S&P futures traders also knew almost

---

* The studies were flawed because the time periods were too short and did not cover characteristics of behavior in different market cycles.

† According to EMH, futures cannot fall below the cash price for the same expiration date. For details, see page 114.

precisely how much the portfolio insurance managers still were behind in their futures selling. It wasn't nearly as complex as Enigma to decode. Remember, if the market dropped 3 percent, the insurers were supposed to sell 10 percent of the futures to reduce the equity exposure to the predetermined lower level in order to remain delta neutral (the level of stocks and bonds the formula called for).

The academics turned portfolio insurers made another small error. They didn't count on how cutthroat the brokers and the futures traders who acted for them, as well as other players, could be. After all, that wasn't factored into EMH theory. But everyone in the game knew the portfolio insurance managers were well behind the predetermined selling they were required to do. If the other brokerage houses and traders sold futures en masse or shorted stocks quickly early on Monday, they would get the jump on the portfolio insurers and make jillions buying the futures back at much lower prices. The stage was set.

On Black Monday, October 19, 1987, the impossible happened: liquidity dried up completely. The market opened and began to drop rapidly, with heavy S&P 500 futures selling leading the way, dropping 3.5 percent on the first trade. Every knowledgeable pro was shorting S&P futures. As the futures dropped, computerized program traders (index arbitragers) rushed in, buying the discounted futures at increasingly lower prices and selling stocks, dropping their prices sharply. This forced the portfolio insurers to sell futures even more frantically at increasingly large discounts to the value of the S&P 500 as they fell further and further behind the amount they had to short to protect their clients' portfolios. The death spiral continued. Major investment houses and commodity traders, knowing the desperation of the portfolio insurance managers, continued to short futures ahead of the portfolio insurers. The portfolio insurance managers were forced to sell at any price to realign their portfolios. So utter was the collapse of portfolio insurance that as the market continued to free-fall, the theory blew apart completely. S&P futures traded at such a large discount to the S&P 500 that portfolio insurance managers were forced to sell their clients' stock, which they had never conceived of selling under any circumstances. This pushed the S&P stocks down even further.

This doomsday interaction between portfolio insurance and program trading continued through the day and was strongly reinforced by larger and larger amounts of selling by institutional and individual investors re-acting to the panic and stampeding for the exits. Prices dropped more than ever before in modern times.

The panic had spread like a rampaging forest fire out of the futures pits of Chicago into the stock market itself, where it sharply magnified the impact. The crapshooting spirit of the commodity pits had been injected into the floors of the country's major stock exchanges, with devastating results.

THE IMPOSSIBLE HAPPENS

The S&P 500 was down 20.5 percent at the close on October 19, and the S&P 500 futures dropped 28.6 percent; this left them at a 23.3-point dis-count (10.4 percent) to the S&P 500. According to EMH theory, futures cannot ever fall below the cash price for the same expiration date (in this case the end of December 1987). The reason is simple: when an investor buys a stock or the S&P 500 on margin, he or she has to pay the broker an interest charge to carry it. The interest (about 5 percent at the time) is priced into the S&P 500 futures contract, so it must always be at a pre-mium to the cash price of the S&P itself. This should apply even in a panic if people are rational. If the S&P 500 futures contract goes to a discount, the trader makes an automatic profit by selling the S&P 500 stocks and immediately buying the discounted futures. When the futures contracts expire less than two months later, he pockets his gains.*

But as we saw the S&P 500 futures didn't stay at a premium; they dropped 10.4 percent below the cash price. This gave knowledgeable in-vestors such as index funds and other investment firms with cash an in-credible return. They simply had to buy the future and sell or short sell the S&P 500 stocks instantaneously.

Let's go through the mechanics to see how this was done. Since they had to put only 5 percent down on the futures because of the ri-diculously low margin requirement, they made nearly 228 percent on the money they actually put down in margin, on an absolutely safe, com-pletely hedged investment. When the contract expired in late December 1987, they would sell the S&P stock portfolio at the same time the futures contract expired; this is rudimentary index arbitrage. At expiration of the

---

* See the following example.

futures' contract, the price of the S&P futures, bought at a large discount to the cash price, would rise to the price of the S&P 500 stock index, capturing the full original 10.4 percent discount on the S&P 500 futures.

Take the example of an institution or brokerage firm that bought $10 million of futures for its own account. It would have put up only $500,000 in margin and would come up with $1,137,900 in profit on the contract's expiration, or the 228 percent shown before.* This action makes a mockery of the omnisciently rational investor of EMH theory.

As noted, this is the type of riskless, high-return transaction that EMH theorists state can never happen in an efficient market. Occurring in one of the most widely traded, carefully followed markets in the world, large, riskless profits available to knowledgeable investors are a very serious challenge to EMH. No explanation by the EMH theorists, to my knowledge, has ever been forthcoming. This event also puts an enormous dent in Professors Roll's and Fama's theory of rational crashes, which we'll look at shortly.

As I see it, many of the major pillars supporting the efficient-market hypothesis were destroyed in the 1987 crash. Five should be noted.

1. Liquidity dried up. A crucial assumption of EMH, that there is always sufficient liquidity in markets, was disproved, as the above events indicate. The lack of understanding by the academics and the portfolio insurance managers of liquidity was a primary cause of the 1987 crash.

2. The argument that rational investors keep stock prices in line with their value, another core assumption of EMH, was seriously challenged. When was the market efficient? When professional and other sophisticated investors took the S&P 500 down from 315 to 216 (31 percent) in five trading days or when it recovered all of its losses nineteen months later, with only minor changes in the underlying fundamentals?

3. Another example of glaring market inefficiency was the 28.6 percent drop in prices of S&P 500 futures to the actual 20.5 percent drop in the price of the S&P itself on October 19, allowing savvy investors

---

* This assumes using the closing prices of both the S&P 500 index and the S&P 500 futures. The spread varied throughout the day. The profit is calculated after commissions are included. There were also quite a number of other ways to capture the greater part of the spread.

to make gigantic profits on their capital in two months. The corner-stone of EMH theory states that such actions by rational investors are impossible because of their automaton-like rationality.

4. The EMH offspring, CAPM, states that risk is defined solely as volatility. The only way to lower risk is to lower volatility. But the risk that caused the 1987 crash was not volatility. The panic was caused by a serious lack of liquidity as the futures market dried up, as well as enormous excess margin. Both are measures of risk that are not part of EMH risk theory and therefore are excluded from it. This prodigious flaw in risk measurement is vitally important to your investment decisions. (Solutions will be discussed in chapter 14.)

5. EMH theorists thought that increased leverage would facilitate more efficient markets by strongly encouraging futures trading on stocks at low margins. These academics played an important role by having their recommendation to drastically lower stock future margins about 90 percent below stock margins accepted by the regulators, the SEC, and CFTC. They apparently did not consider that in a major downturn low leverage could unleash massive selling that could cause markets to plummet as they did both in 1929 and again in 1987.

What lessons did EMH theorists, as well as true believers, including then Fed Chairman Greenspan, learn from this crash? As noted, none. The theorists tried to explain away all the causes, although their explanations ranged from skimpy to downright foolish. As a result, the mistakes were repeated and contributed to two more market collapses, as we will see next.

2. The 1998 Long-Term Capital Management Debacle

You'd think that after the 1987 crash EMH would have undergone some serious revisions if not outright rejection by Wall Street analysts, as well as questioning by its adherents. But that didn't happen. By 1998, a new crisis was beginning to reach the boiling point, owing to the actions of a monster hedge fund's investment strategies. The firm was "too big to fail" long before the term became popular. The mixture of EMH theory, the increasing belief in the almost godlike investment capabilities of rising efficient market superstars, and serious amounts of money produced a crisis that was stunning in both its speed and its scope.

Long-Term Capital Management (LTCM) was the world's largest hedge fund. Beginning operations in March 1994, by early 1998 it had acquired assets of more than $100 billion, as well as more than $1 trillion in derivatives. More than fifty of the largest banks and investment banks in the United States and abroad scrambled to do business with it in spite of the almost impossibly tough terms it demanded, concessions that no other hedge fund was given. By 1998, it was the envy of Wall Street, more than quadrupling its original investment in less than four years.

LTCM, led by its chairman, John Meriwether, was considered the crème de la crème for the exceptionally high level of its traders, but mostly because it hired some of the superb efficient-market superstars, led by Robert Merton and Myron Scholes, the latter of whom was instrumental in developing the Black-Scholes model. They shared the Nobel Prize in Economics in 1997. In addition, a group of brilliant Ph.D.s, several of whom were excellent traders, surrounded the two masters. On paper there wasn't another firm with this kind of dazzling cast, as its record from the start seemed to prove.

LTCM concentrated on "relative value" trades in both domestic and global bond markets. If two high-quality bonds, for example, had almost the same maturity but one yielded 25 basis points (one-quarter of 1 percent) more than the other, LTCM would buy the higher-yielding bond and short the lower-yielding one. Or if a highly rated bond in Spain provided a higher yield than one in the United Kingdom, again with nearly the same maturities, the fund would buy the Spanish bond and short the U.K. issue. These were called "paired trades."

The fund was also highly diversified, owning and shorting thousands of issues. Another feature of LTCM's strategy was to buy somewhat riskier and more illiquid bonds in its trades than the ones it shorted to increase the spread. This increased the return on each paired transaction, as less liquid and slightly riskier bonds commanded a somewhat higher yield than bonds with the same risk and liquidity. LTCM believed that this was a low-risk strategy because interest rates tend to rise or fall in sync, so spreads move only a fraction as much as the value of the bonds themselves; LTCM should fare well no matter whether bonds rose or fell or even if the market crashed. One of the academics calculated the risk in a spread transaction at only about 4 percent of owning a bond outright.

The paired-trade strategy that was a good part of LTCM's portfolio was in essence a nickel-and-dime business. Myron Scholes, aside from being an outstanding academician, was also the firm's top marketer. As he explained it, "the fund would be earning a tiny amount on thousands of trades as if it were vacuuming up nickels that nobody else could see."[7] In essence it would be like a giant penny arcade making big money on the volume of nickels and quarters thrown into the wide variety of game machines on the premises.

The confidence so many felt in the strategy was premised on work by Robert Merton, who was considered one of the outstanding experts on risk. He had made major breakthroughs in EMH theory in risk, which eventually earned him the Nobel Prize. Merton was convinced, as were almost all EMH believers, that volatility was the sole measure of risk; this was the bedrock of LTCM's approach. He was equally sure that volatility remained stable over time. If a stock or bond had a certain volatility, it might swing higher or lower temporarily but would always return to its calculated rate. Since that was the case, LTCM could use volatility as its most important tool. If volatility was higher than it should be for the bond bought in a pair trade and lower than normal for the one sold short, it would return in each case to its normal level. The higher the volatility on the bond purchased and the lower the volatility on the bond sold, the greater the added return to the trade when the risk swung back to its normal level. That this assumption was never proved was of no consequence.

The strategy was also premised on the belief that volatility was mathematically predictable. A large amount of testing was done on volatility, as well as the chance that something could go wrong. Using the cardinal Merton principle that volatility did not change, LTCM was convinced that it could calculate precisely the odds of what the best, average, and worst days would return, as well as the odds that the portfolio could take serious or mortal losses. Even worst-case calculations showed that the firm could sail through the most punishing financial hurricanes.

The belief that volatility was mathematically predictable was not held only at LTCM; it was a core belief throughout the Street. The Black-Scholes pricing model was anchored on the predictability of volatility, and trading rooms on Wall Street and in every major financial center globally monitored volatility as if it were the Holy Grail. Every major trading floor was staffed by bright young Ph.D.s who had studied under Fama, Merton, Scholes, or other strong EMH believers, and they didn't question the unproved premise that yesterday's prices were reliable and predictable indicators that would determine today's value. *When Genius Failed*, Roger Lowenstein's first-rate book on Long-Term Capital Management, quotes Peter Rosenthal, LTCM's press spokesman, as glibly stating "Risk is a function of volatility. These things are quantifiable."[8] "Meriwether, Merton, Scholes and Company had no more earnest belief."[9] The LTCM portfolio contained thousands of paired trades with precise data on the volatility and expected return of each.

THE FAIL-SAFE STRATEGY

What the professors and traders didn't focus on was leverage or liquidity. Since they had volatility completely under control and that was the only source of risk, liquidity and leverage did not matter a hoot. So focused were they on volatility, and so strong was their belief that volatility was risk, that leverage and liquidity as independent risk elements were considered inconsequential. They were not even a punctuation mark in the EMH-inspired formulas LTCM used.

The question most often asked by LTCM academics and portfolio managers was how much volatility ("Vol") it took to optimize returns. The answer that almost consistently came back was that the Vol could be raised, with little addition to risk. The leverage went from 20 to 1 to 30 to 1, but Vol, they believed, could still go higher.

The gods continued to smile on Long-Term Capital Management. In 1994, it earned 20 percent; in 1995, its net return was 43 percent. By the spring of 1996, it had $140 billion in assets under management, and its capital had tripled to $3.6 billion. After only two years of operations, its assets were larger than those of Lehman Brothers or Morgan Stanley and were approaching those of the giant Salomon Brothers. In 1996, it earned 41 percent net of fees or $2.1 billion, more than giant blue-chip growth companies such as Walt Disney, McDonald's, and American Express.

But there were other somewhat less appetizing aspects to this sizzling growth. By early 1996, the firm's leverage had, as noted, climbed to 30 to 1. Leverage works well, as we saw, when markets are going up, as they were before the 1929 and 1987 crashes, but when markets go down, it's death. At 30-to-1 leverage LTCM had to lose only 3.3 percent of its market value to have its capital wiped out entirely. Meanwhile, its return on total assets was less than 2.5 percent, before counting its large derivative positions in the many hundreds of billions of dollars. Including those, it was probably less than 1 percent.[10] A ninety-day Treasury bill at that time yielded 4.5 percent, which was approximately 4.5 times LTCM's return on total assets. Almost all of LTCM's return came from levels of leverage that defied gravity.

Then, in mid-1997, the Asian economies began to melt, first Cambodia, then the Philippines, then Malaysia, then South Korea, followed by Singapore and Indonesia. Enormous amounts of stock were dumped. And markets crashed while currencies went into free fall. The Asian Tigers became terrified kitty cats. The contagion spread to South America, Eastern Europe, and Mother Russia.

LTCM determined to make its signature bet in the crisis. Because volatility was very high, the company decided to short sell volatility options not only on the S&P 500 but on major indexes in Europe and other major markets.* Volatility, Merton and the group were certain, would revert to the mean, and this meant that volatility futures would fall sharply. And here the biggest error in volatility measurement LTCM ever made mortally wounded the fund.

Merton was taking an enormous chance. EMH theory, the Black-Scholes model, and Merton's models say only that a stock's volatility is consistent over time. They do not say in *what* time period volatility securities or derivatives will revert to the mean. It's like crossing a river that's four feet deep on average, carrying a fifty-pound backpack: it might be three feet deep in some places and fifteen feet deep in others. Not good survival odds, but precisely the odds Merton the supermathematician had chosen.

In a bad crash or a bear market, would it take six months, twelve months, or even years before volatility went back to its normal level, as Merton and EMH believers fervently believed would occur? The efficient-market theory had no answer for that. How could it have one? The belief appears to have come from an EMH theory, not rigorous testing. But LTCM was leveraged 30 to 1, so the return to normal volatility had to come very soon, because leverage—not recognized by EMH as a risk factor—will gobble capital up almost at the speed of light if the markets

---

* Such options did not exist, and LTCM had to construct and sell customized derivatives to make the transactions.

continue to go against it. Unfortunately, that's exactly what could happen to LTCM. Merton and Scholes were making the same kinds of bets that any desperate amateur deeply out of pocket might make: LTCM could fail on the toss of a coin.

Maybe the gods were not major EMH adherents after all. LTCM's spreads on its paired trades did not narrow; they widened. Through 1998, a flight to safety occurred in almost every sector it was invested in. Remember, the firm was always invested in the riskier, not safer, bonds and was short of the safest bonds. To add to its problem, the volatility indices it short sold skyrocketed as volatility increased. In May, problems with the Asian Tigers flared up again. By early June, the Russian financial system was near collapse. World markets turned down sharply. LTCM was hit even harder because the dash to the safest securities rapidly widened the spreads between its long holdings and its short positions, while volatility increased further.

LTCM reported a loss of 18 percent for the first half of 1998. More important, as its capital dropped, its leverage increased dramatically, making it less and less able to meet margin calls. Then, in August 1998, Russia defaulted on its debt and market fear heightened across the board. LTCM's capital of more than $5 billion near year-end 1997 fell to the hundreds of millions within four months. The two risks not even considered punctuation marks by EMH theorists and by Merton and Scholes—leverage and liquidity—came to the forefront, *just as they had done in the 1987 crash.*

As the markets tumbled, the enormous short positions the firm owned resulted in gigantic losses; the increasing flight to safety continued to cause the more risky bonds it held to drop significantly more than the higher-quality bonds it had shorted in the paired swaps. Too, the volatility swaps that Merton and his team had shorted heavily because they believed Vol was much too high soared higher. Calls for more margin poured in to cover the flood of new losses, and consequently the firm's capital was hemorrhaging rapidly.

As a result of the firm's gigantic margin calls and its inability to sell most major positions because they were very illiquid, the fund's leverage shot up to 100 to 1, which meant that even a 1 percent drop in assets would bankrupt it. But it couldn't sell to protect itself because its positions were gigantic and always less liquid than the positions it sold short. In the good times its capital, enormously magnified by leverage, made it huge profits. But in those brutal markets, selling even a small fraction of any holding would reduce prices sharply (lack of liquidity again). LTCM was doomed!

August was a cruel month for Long-Term Capital Management. It lost $1.9 billion, or 45 percent of its capital. It had $155 billion in assets, with a leverage ratio of 55 times its shrunken capital. Mathematicians calculated that the odds of the losses LTCM incurred in August were so freakish as to be unlikely to occur over many repetitions of the life of the universe.[11]* Its position was untenable. The leverage could not be reduced because of the enormous size of its trades and the complete loss of liquidity. As with subprime bonds almost a decade later, any attempt to sell would see the already wafer-thin markets for the securities it held collapse.

The markets were in a state of near-panic. Meanwhile, LTCM was surrounded by a pack of predators: bankers and brokers who knew that its liquidity and leverage problems would put it under. They began shorting LTCM's positions, well aware that in a forced liquidation, when it was compelled to sell, prices would drop drastically and the bankers could cover their shorts at bargain prices. The parallels between the portfolio insurers in 1987 and LTCM are remarkable. Both were undone by a massive lack of liquidity when it was most needed, in a bear market.

By September 1998, the Federal Reserve Bank of New York, under William McDonough, its talented president, was concerned about the plight of LTCM. Although he had no authority to inspect the books of a hedge fund, LTCM gave the New York Fed permission to do so. What he saw alarmed him. Not only did he see that the collapse of LTCM was imminent; he also realized that the enormous positions in many thousands of holdings, if dumped on the market to sell at any price, could severely disrupt the already badly shaken financial system and possibly lead to disaster. He and his chief aides called numerous meetings with the leaders of the largest banks and investment firms in the United States, as well as important banks abroad that held large LTCM loans against the securities swaps and other holdings of the fund.

An agreement to take over all of LTCM's positions would need the support of amost all of the major banks and investment bankers on Wall Street. In the end, after much haggling, its positions were sold to a con-

---

* Obviously the mathematicians worked for LTCM. With high leverage and poor liquidity, the odds of a disaster of this sort were conservatively millions of times smaller.

sortium of sixteen banks that anted up more than $260 million each. The fund's shareholders saw their investments drop 92 percent in five months. By comparison, over the four-year period that Long-Term Capital Management existed, the S&P 500 had doubled.

Despite this massive failure of EMH, neither of the two Nobel laureates who had championed the fund's strategy questioned the theory. Although Merton admitted that the fund's risk measurements hadn't worked, he stated that the principles it had followed were right. What was needed, he argued, was more sophisticated modeling. He went back to teaching at Harvard and, perhaps ironically, was hired by J. P. Morgan as a risk consultant.

In a speech a year later, Scholes concluded that the change in volatility must be attributed to a permanent change in what investors would pay for the more risky investments LTCM made. This meant that all the theory about volatility that had been used up to then must have changed permanently by events at the time LTCM went down, which is not unlike saying that the weight of the supports necessary to build an expansion bridge of a certain length and width had suddenly and permanently been altered by a sudden change in the laws of physics. Scholes never doubted the efficacy of EMH's supporting volatility theory. Since the permanent changes he discussed were reversed within a few years, his theory may have a few minor holes in it.

Indeed, no questions were raised by EMH supporters generally about LTCM's premises on volatility or whether leverage or liquidity was also a possible risk factor. How could they be?

3. The 2006–2008 Housing Bubble and Market Crash

By now we are all familiar with the housing bubble of the early to mid-2000s. The interactivity of so much of our financial system and the complexity and the unethical practices carried out by far too many of the large institutions involved are well beyond the scope of this work. What can be sketched out briefly is the part EMH theory played in fueling this bubble to the gigantic proportions it reached. This crisis was not dissimilar to the destruction of Long-Term Capital Management but on a colossal scale.

In spite of the 1987 crash and the LTCM debacle, investment institutions still had almost blind faith that volatility was the sole measure of risk. Leverage, although extremely high on subprime and other lower-quality residential mortgage-backed securities (RMBSs),* was of almost no concern to the portfolio managers or the risk-control departments of these institutions, who were all trained in the EMH and CAPM theories of risk. Nor, for that matter, was their liquidity questioned. There were many thousands of series of home mortgages, whose quality varied enormously, from good to very poor. Normally liquidity was low, because each mortgage issue usually contained a number of series of RMBS issues ranging from AAA, the highest rating, to series that were toxic at best. Most required substantial analysis to determine even a rough price range, so dealers' spreads between bids and offers were normally large. Still, volatility was the only risk factor considered, and as housing prices boomed consistently higher, it was very low indeed.

After 2002, leverage began to soar to as high as 35 to 1 to 40 to 1 for some of the mortgage lenders, investment bankers, and hedge funds and up to 30 percent for some of the most aggressive banks. Margin was plentiful and, with cheap rates almost effortless to obtain, it encouraged leverage, much as it had for LTCM or in the 1987 crash. Mortgage originators[†] and mortgage companies almost had the banks throwing money at them.

Finally, banks and investment bankers also financed a large number of innovative, often complex investment companies that owned large holdings of such bonds as well as often extremely obtuse derivatives. Forget that the security for many of the loans was subprime mortgages or that the investment bankers leveraged their capital enormously. The banks' risk-control departments thought all this was fine. After all, near the top of the bubble the volatility of the RMBS portfolios continued to be very low, and they had also learned from Professors Merton, Scholes, and Fama that volatility never changes for long. Risk was in an iron cage, so they could relax and make big money for their firms and themselves.

But despite the assurances of Fed chairmen Alan Greenspan and Ben

---

*Mortgage bonds backed by pools of mortgages, with different credit ratings. The top credit ratings, AAA, AA, and A, are theoretically the most secure and receive their money first in the event of defaults. They also receive lower interest rates. The lower the quality, the higher the risk and the higher the interest rate. These are Standard & Poor's rating scale. The other rating agencies have almost identical scales with minutely different letters—e.g., Moody's uses Aaa instead of AAA.

† Companies, including banks, that originate mortgages and then sell them to investment banks to make into mortgage-backed securities, which they sell off at handsome profits to hedge funds and a large number of different financial institutions.

Bernanke after him, as well as many other experts, that everything was just peachy, the nation's frenetic housing bubble was coming to an end. By late summer 2006, home prices began to drop, and they fell steadily through 2007. By early 2007, the home mortgage market began to disintegrate. Housing prices continued to drop in 2008 to April 2009, accompanied by a flood of homeowners who went into arrears on their mortgages, along with a rising tide of foreclosures. Not surprisingly, the market for mortgage bonds collapsed. Beginning in 2007, liquidity began to freeze, and by 2008 it had dried up almost completely. Residential mortgage-backed securities, which had started turning down in August 2006, collapsed in the following two years. The damage was worse than that caused by any stock market crash in the nation's history. Interesting that Standard & Poor's, which gave AAA ratings to thousands of issues of subprime trash, gave U.S. Treasuries a lower rating in 2011. But that's another story.

Figure 5-1 shows that the supposedly low-volatility ABX-HE-BBB investment mortgage index, rated as investment quality (one of the higher bond ratings), sank into a black hole, dropping almost 98 percent from its July 19, 2006, price to its April 2009 low. To take another example, even AAA mortgage-backed subprime securities, the highest credit rating, fell 70 percent or more during this period.

How could this happen? There are numerous reasons, but most of the damage was once again caused by leverage and lack of liquidity. As we saw, banks, investment banks, hedge funds, and other mortgage buyers were all very highly leveraged.

Table 5-1 illustrates the destruction caused to highly leveraged owners of mortgage-backed securities or any other type of investment, for that matter. The table assumes that the speculator borrows thirty times his capital, in the range of mortgage security borrowing noted a few pages back. If the prices of his RMBS securities dropped only 3.3 percent, his capital would be wiped out entirely. If the bonds dropped 5 percent, he would lose his capital plus an additional 50 percent.

But as we know, housing prices didn't go down 5 percent; they went down 33 percent to their lows in April 2009, and the drop in RMBS securities was significantly higher. If the buyer had owned ABX AAA RMBS subprime securities (the highest rating the agencies gave), on margin, he would have lost 70 percent of his principal to the low. If he had leveraged them thirty times, he would have lost twenty-one times his original investment in margin calls. If he owned the ABX issue we looked at in

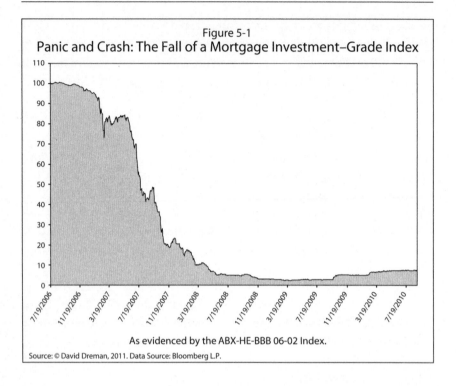

Figure 5-1

Panic and Crash: The Fall of a Mortgage Investment–Grade Index

As evidenced by the ABX-HE-BBB 06-02 Index.

Source: © David Dreman, 2011. Data Source: Bloomberg L.P.

Figure 5-1, he would have lost thirty times his initial investment. To put this into numbers, if an institution had invested $10 million in this bond, leveraging it thirty times, the loss would have been $294 million.

That's why Bear Stearns, Lehman Brothers, and Washington Mutual, all heavily leveraged in toxic bonds, no longer exist. That's also why the Treasury, under Hank Paulson, needed $700 billion of Troubled Assets Relief Program (TARP) funds to bail out the banks and investment bankers. Without that fund, many more would not exist today.

But why couldn't investors just sell the toxic securities? Again, the answer was a complete lack of liquidity. The portfolios normally held a wide variety of mortgage-backed securities with dozens of different pools. Nobody knew what they were really worth. In a bottomless market, why take the risk? Leverage and liquidity targeted mortgage bonds with the devastating power of a nuclear bomb. Thank you again, EMH and CAPM.

Granted, not all mortgage bonds fared quite this badly, but these figures make clear why the massive bailout of financial institutions was undertaken. Whether it was right or wrong to rescue the banks and investment bankers, given the shocking incompetence of many of their senior

Table 5-1 The Devastating Effects of Financial Leverage	
% Drop ABX-HE-BBB 06.02	Drop in Initial Equity Assuming 30:1 leverage
1%	−30%
5%	−150%
10%	−300%
25%	−750%
50%	−1,500%
75%	−2,250%
90%	−2,700%
98%	−2,940%
100%	−3,000%

Source: © David Dreman, 2011.

executives, is a question the reader should answer. But after three severe wipeouts caused by excessive leverage and lack of liquidity, shouldn't they, too, at least have been aware of the enormous danger to the financial system of too much leverage and too little liquidity?

In their defense, I would say only that they were completely wedded to the idea that volatility was the only measure of risk to worry about and therefore did not factor in liquidity, leverage, or other risk factors. This held even though some of the largest of them, including Citigroup, owned a dozen or more mortgage originators (companies that underwrote the mortgages) and clearly knew how bad the product really was. As for Professor Fama and his colleagues, did this experience shake their belief that volatility is the only measure of risk or that the market is efficient? Apparently not. In 2007, with mortgage-backed security prices already dropping rapidly, Fama said in an interview, "The word 'bubble' drives me nuts," and went on to explain why people could trust housing market values. "Housing markets are less liquid, but people are very careful when they buy houses. . . . The bidding process is very detailed."[12] Amen.

▓ Rational Markets Don't Have Bubbles or Crashes

In spite of what we've just seen on bubbles in this chapter and in earlier ones, most EMH believers still deny that bubbles and crashes exist. "I don't even know what a bubble means. These words have become popular. I don't think they have any meaning."[13] That's Professor Fama, trying to defend the central core of the efficient-market hypothesis, that prices are always where they should be. He denies the existence of manias and crashes. Still, bubbles and IPOs present a particularly vexing point to EMH because they seem to defy consistently rational behavior. Fama and other EMH adherents are backed into a corner. EMH has to deny the existence of manias and panics, or it will be pierced by a fatal arrow—not a particularly pleasant way for a popular hypothesis to die. There was only one escape, and Professor Fama, never accused of not being highly intelligent, found it.

He states emphatically that bubbles don't exist. Why? Because rational investors always keep prices where they should be. In the *New Yorker* article, Fama dodges, ducks, or sidesteps the volley of arrows the well-versed financial reporter John Cassidy fires at him. But in doing so he steps into a position even more challenging that to my knowledge has never been examined.

Continuing with EMH logic, if, as Fama says, there are no bubbles or panics, we have to look more closely at the rational investors who perform this extraordinary feat. We already examined this question in some detail in chapter 2* and again briefly in this chapter and found there are no widely followed fundamental analytical methods used by security analysts, money managers, and other rational investors that condone buying stocks at prices anywhere from 10 to 100 times or more normal valuation levels in a bubble. What is apparent from chapter 2 is that analysts and money managers do move away en masse from their analytical methods and pay bizarre prices. By doing so they are not acting with the automaton-like rationality EMH assumes. If they did follow their fundamental training, prices could not reach bubble levels.

EMH believers seem to have put themselves into an untenable position. They state that it is professionals and other sophisticated investors

---

* To review the standard techniques, please go back to chapter 2.

who keep prices where they should be. But as we see, obviously the logic doesn't work. Could it be that once again EMH theory has made a bold assumption about the behavior of sophisticated investors without a shred of evidence that it is correct? A statement that seriously threatens the central premise of EMH theory is that it is highly knowledgeable investors that keep prices where they should be. Perhaps a little more research on how highly sophisticated investors act, rather than how they should act in theory, might prove very helpful.

Have We Learned Anything Yet?

You can now judge how accurate EMH has been in its core assumptions:

- About liquidity
- About leverage
- About the correlation between volatility and returns
- About whether volatility is stable over time
- About rational investment "automatons" always keeping prices right

All the theoretical pillars of EMH and CAPM appear to have been knocked down. We have also seen the enormous damage done to the markets and economy during the long and celebrated reign of EMH.

What now? Should we just walk away from the markets, and forget about investing except under the mattress? EMH has led many millions of people to disastrous investment decisions. But there is a better way. It lies not far ahead of us, now that we are past the Black Knight and rode beyond the worst of the efficient-market forest. There are still major opportunities in the markets, I assure you, if we know how to identify them.

First, though, we need to equip ourselves with stronger armor and new broadswords forged by psychology and the new contrarian strategies. This done, we will learn how to dispose of the EMH dragon for good.

Chapter 6

Efficient Markets and Ptolemaic Epicycles

MY EXPERIENCE AS a *Forbes* columnist for more than thirty years—writing columns that EMH partisans did not take kindly to—gives me the tiniest inkling of what Galileo went through with his scientific work in the early seventeenth century. The great Italian scientist supported the new heliocentric idea of the solar system when a huge majority of philosophers and astronomers still subscribed to the geocentric view, namely, that the earth is the center of the universe. Galileo was forced to recant his views. When he published again, in 1632, he was arrested by the Inquisition, was found "vehemently suspect of heresy," [1] was forced to recant yet again, and spent the rest of his life under house arrest.

The geocentric view, by the way, had an impeccable pedigree going all the way back to the work of Ptolemy, a revered scholar who lived in the second century A.D. in Alexandria, the University of Chicago of its day. He was part of a cosmopolitan elite who had made the Egyptian city a jewel of scholarly activity, and his own outstanding contribution was the Ptolemaic system.

His treatise, using hundreds of years of celestial observations, explained the motion of the sun and planets and provided convenient tables allowing the computation of future or past positions of the planets. The basic premise was that the earth was the center of the universe and the planets, the sun, and the stars orbited around it. The Ptolemaic system was universally accepted by the civilized world for almost 1,600 years, filling a major role in land and sea navigation.

None other than Galileo introduced the telescope to astronomy in 1609. He became the first man to observe the craters of the moon, sunspots, the four large moons of Jupiter, and the rings of Saturn. Far from abandoning the Ptolemaic system, the model became increasingly complex in order to incorporate the new observations. Now the planets and stars moved around one another and around the earth in a combination of circles, epicycles, and eccentrics (large deferent circles—don't ask—around whose centers the epicycles revolved). The result of this hodgepodge was a mind-boggling whirl.

Nonetheless, the Ptolemaic system met two major criteria of a useful scientific hypothesis: it was "predictive" in correctly forecasting where various celestial bodies would be at future points in time, and it was "explanatory" because it codified a system of planetary motion.

It was also entirely wrong.

Which brings us back to EMH. As discussed earlier, EMH and its companions, MPT and CAPM, are based on extensive mathematical analysis. Other critics and I would not dispute this. Apart from the strong evidence of the theory's inaccuracy that we saw in the record of events covered in the preceding chapter, the controversy now moves further to the reason why: the underlying assumptions of EMH, as we'll see, are highly questionable, or have never been tested, or are outright fallacious. Much of the ultrasophisticated mathematical analysis is constructed on these seriously flawed assumptions, which appear to be built on sand. Just as a space launch requires a sophisticated launch pad for a highly complex shuttle to be able to blast off, so highly advanced mathematics requires a solid base to predict market action correctly.

The second important area we'll look at is the mathematical testing itself. Here I think you'll find some surprises. Much of the original EMH testing was flawed, as we saw with volatility theory in the previous chapter, and didn't prove that volatility was the sole or even an important risk factor. Once we've examined these assumptions and their flaws, you'll understand why I liken the continued belief in EMH to the unyielding acceptance of the Ptolemaic system after Galileo had shown that the sun does not revolve around the earth.

Volatility's Last Stand

The preceding chapter showed that EMH assumptions had gone down in flames in the cases of the 1987 market crash, the Long-Term Capital Management debacle (1998), and then the 2007–2008 crash and the steep recession following it. One of the chief culprits was inadequate risk theory, with its focus on volatility to the almost complete exclusion of leverage, liquidity, and other important risk factors. Unlike the Ptolemaic system, EMH hasn't even had reliable predictive power, and it offers no more accurate explanations of market movements than Ptolemy did of planetary motion.

Two questions we should now ask:

1. Why was there an almost obsessive focus on volatility as the sole measure of risk by the academics?
2. Was this focus justified?

Let's look at these questions next.

Much of the previous chapter swirled around volatility. Does greater volatility reward investors with higher returns, and lower volatility with lower returns? From what we've seen in that chapter, the answer is a definite no. In reality, academic research found answers to this question more than three decades ago. Let's look at these answers now.

How did leading EMH academics know that investors measured risk strictly by the volatility of the stock? They didn't, nor did they do any research to find out, other than the original studies of the correlation between volatility and return, whose results were mixed at best. The academics simply declared it as fact. Importantly, this definition of risk was easy to use to build complex computer finance models, and that's what the professors wanted to do. They could then build a simple but elegant theory.

Economists find this view of risk compelling, if not almost obsessional, because it is the way rational man *should* behave according to economic theory. If investors are risk-averse and economists can show this to be so, they have proof of a central concept of economic theory: that man is a rational decision maker. If investors will take greater risks only if they receive higher returns—eureka!—an eight-lane highway opens between investment markets and microeconomic theory. And via this highway, investment markets deliver to economic theory the ultimate payload— proof positive of rational behavior in markets they've searched for more than two centuries. Right or wrong, the idea is too seductive for economists to give up.

As we know, the professors also devised measures to adjust mutual funds' and money managers' performance for the riskiness of their portfolios—measures that, if volatility is not the sole measure of risk, are fallacious. Still, four decades or more later, these are still the key measurement of risk and return used. I might return 15 percent a year and my competitor 30 percent, but if her portfolio was much more volatile than mine, I would have the better risk-adjusted returns.

It turns out it could all come from the Wizard of Oz. But why is that a surprise? Volatility gives the appearance of being a highly sophisticated mathematical formula but was constructed by people looking into a rearview mirror. Volatility takes inputs that seemed to correlate with it in the past and states they will work again in the future. This is not good science. To me it doesn't seem to be much different from a technician relying on past price movements to determine those in the future, an argument the academics almost gleefully disproved, as we saw earlier. However, to protect their volatility theory, they use a similar tactic. I'm sure you've deduced that it's to protect CAPM theory and thereby EMH.

But the critical question is still there: why is volatility the measure of risk, rather than an analysis of a company's financial strength, earnings power, leverage, liquidity, outstanding debt, and dozens of other measures that investment experts in corporate management use? Sure, volatility is alluring to economic types, but what else has it got going for it? Possibly you accept the measures without question. Most people do. But in truth it is faulty.

In the first place, it has been known for decades that there is no correlation between risk, as the academics define it, and return. Higher volatility does not give better results, nor lower volatility worse results.

J. Michael Murphy, in an important but little-read article in *The Journal of Portfolio Management* in the fall of 1977, reviewed the research on risk.[2] Some of the conclusions were startling, at least for EMH and CAPM believers. Murphy cited four studies that indicated that "realized returns often tend to be higher than expected for low-risk securities, and lower than expected for high-risk securities, . . . or that the [risk-reward] relationship was far weaker than expected."[3] He continued, "Other important studies have concluded that there is not necessarily any *stable* long-term relationship between risk and return;[4] that there often may be virtually no relationship between return achieved and risk taken;[5] and that high volatility unit trusts were not compensated by greater returns"[6] (italics in original).[7]

In 1975, a paper by Robert Haugen and James Heins analyzing risk concluded with the statement "The results of our empirical effort do not support the conventional hypothesis that risk (volatility)—systematic or otherwise—generates a special reward."[8] Remember, this research was done in the middle to late 1970s, just as CAPM and the concept of risk-adjusted returns were starting the investment revolution and more than a decade before Nobel Prizes were awarded to its advocates.

The lack of correlation between risk and return was not the only problem troubling academic researchers. More basic was the failure of volatility measures to remain constant over time—the assumption of constancy being central to both CAPM and MPT. Recall that Nobel laureate Robert Merton of Long-Term Capital Management almost believed he could set his watch by it—until its instability played an important role in the firm's implosion. The instability of volatility also played a major role in the collapse of subprime mortgage bonds in 2007–2008, as well as in the 1987–1988 crash, when S&P futures and index volatility shot up enormously, and in the 2000–2002 crash, when dot-com and high-tech stock volatility increased sharply.

The impact of volatility goes far beyond the market itself. CAPM had long been used by corporate managers to determine the attractiveness of new ventures. Because the accepted wisdom holds that companies with higher volatility must pay commensurately higher returns, CEOs of higher-volatility companies might be ultracautious in investing in a new plant unless they are certain they can receive the extra return the investment must yield.

On a broader scale, volatility theory, it seems, resulted in bad business decisions in corporate America for a long time, because "good companies" were told that the markets would always have capital available for their growth. This encouraged them to reduce their liquidity. By the

1980s, economists, notably the EMH pioneer Michael Jensen at Harvard, argued that since EMH always got prices right in the market, the best thing corporate CEOs could do, not just for their companies but for the sake of the economy, was to maximize their stock prices.[9] This would give them easier and cheaper access to the capital markets. The message came out loud and clear: do what's best to get your stock price higher, even if it means compromising on your company's long-term viability and profitability. The theory played a role in the significant decrease in liquidity reserves held by companies during the financial crisis of 2007–2008, which led to a major magnification of the economic downturn. Again we see the type of damage that a flawed theory can wreak.

Beta Rides to Town

Although beta is the most widely used of all volatility measures, a beta that can accurately predict future volatility has eluded researchers since the beginning. The original betas constructed by William Sharpe, John Lintner, and Jan Mossin were shown to have no predictive power; that is, the volatility in one period had little or no correlation with that in the next. A stock could pass from violent fluctuation to lamblike docility.

Since the cornerstone of MPT and an implicit assumption of EMH is that all investors are risk-averse, in the same manner, the absence of a demonstrable beta was a serious problem for the researchers from the beginning. If investors are risk-averse, beta or other risk-volatility measures must have predictive power. That they have not, that there is no correlation between past and future betas, was a major anomaly, a "black hole" in the theory. Without a tenable theory of risk, the efficient-market hypothesis was an endangered species.

Barr Rosenberg, a well-respected researcher, developed a widely used multifactor beta, which included a large number of other inputs besides volatility to measure the risk of specific securities. These multifactor betas were often called "Barr's bionic betas." Unfortunately, they were as hapless as their predecessors. Other betas were experimented with, all with the same result. Future betas of both individual stocks and portfolios were not predictable from their past volatility.

The evidence, for the most part, was kept on the back burner until Eugene Fama put out his own paper on risk and return in 1992. Fama and his coauthor, James MacBeth, had published a paper in 1973 indicating that higher beta led to higher returns.[10] It was one of the instrumental pieces of CAPM. Later, collaborating with Kenneth French, also at the University of Chicago, Fama examined 9,500 stocks from 1963 to 1990.[11] Their conclusion was that a stock's risk, measured by beta, was not a reliable predictor of performance.

Fama and French found that stocks with low betas performed roughly as well as stocks with high betas. Fama stated, "Beta as the sole variable in explaining returns on stocks is dead."[12] Write this on the tombstone: "What we are saying is that over the last 50 years, knowing the volatility of an equity doesn't tell you much about the stock's return."[13] Yes, make it a large stone, maybe even a mausoleum.

An article in *Fortune* on June 1, 1992, concluded, "Beta, say the boys from Chicago, is bogus."[14] The *Chicago Tribune* summed it up well: "Some of its best-known adherents have now become detractors."[15]

If not beta, then what? If risk cannot be measured by volatility, how can it be determined? According to Professor French, "What investors really get paid for is holding dogs."[16] Their study, as we will see, indicated that stocks with the lowest price-to-book-value ratios and lowest P/Es provide the highest returns over time, as do smaller-capitalization companies. Stock returns are more positively related to these measurements than to beta or other similar risk criteria.[17]

Fama added, "One risk factor isn't going to do it." Investors must look beyond beta to a multifactor calculation of risk, which includes some value measurements and other criteria.[18]

Fama, along with Kenneth French, in a paper in 1996, refuted another written by academics who sought to defend beta, stating, in part, "'It' [beta] cannot save the Capital Asset Pricing Model, given the evidence that Beta alone cannot explain expected return."[19]

Buried with this canon of modern finance is modern portfolio theory, as well as a good part of EMH. Fama's new findings rejected much of the academic work of the past, including his own. He said at beta's graveside, "We always knew the world was more complicated."[20] He may have known it, but he did not state the fact for more than two decades. His statement that "beta is dead" was the shot at volatility heard round the financial world.

Although the beta model and thus CAPM were shattered, Fama was not in mourning for long. In 1993, he and French substituted a new theory of risk to take its place, the three-factor model, scarcely a year after beta was buried. A suspicious type might wonder if the new romance had not already been blossoming before the funeral. The formula they introduced included small-capitalization (small-cap) and low-market-to-book-value (value) stocks in addition to beta.* Fama did say that "the three-factor model is not a perfect story." [21] Very true. It was an anomaly the professor found that seemed to give EMH more accurate volatility measurements, although no explanation of why it should be used was given.

As we'll see, EMH urgently needed new measurements that would show some correlation between higher return and higher volatility to save it from extinction. This methodology and reasoning, as we'll soon see, seems to have twisted scientific method into a pretzel to keep the key pillar of EMH from collapsing. As one financial professor, George Frankfurter, put it in discussing the Fama and French findings:

> Modern finance today resembles a Meso-American religion, one in which the high priest not only sacrifices the followers—but even the church itself. The field has been so indoctrinated and dogmatized, that only those who promoted the leading model from the start are allowed to destroy it. [22]

This is not just ivory-tower stuff, as we've seen. Beta and other forms of risk measurement determine how trillions of dollars are invested by pension funds, other institutional investors, and the public. High betas are no-nos, while the money manager who delivers satisfactory returns with a low-beta portfolio is lionized. [23]

Take, for example, Morningstar, the largest service monitoring mutual funds. Although it is an excellent and easily readable source that I refer to often, its concept of risk is problematic. Morningstar's five stars, its top ranking, widely followed and much sought after, uses Fama's three-factor model, which is dubious at best, as part of its risk measurement.

---

* By coincidence, two of the three components have been used in my contrarian strategies for over thirty years.

The Failure of CAPM and Ensuing Volatility Theory

We saw that volatility theory has never worked and has cost most people who relied on it dearly over four decades. However, the researchers are putting together even more problematic risk/volatility hypotheses that almost send chills down my spine. My advice is to avoid it entirely. The next few pages will tell you why.

As we've seen, Professor Fama and many others have abandoned CAPM, the original volatility theory, acknowledging that it has failed, while Nobel laureates such as William Sharpe still dispute this contention.[24] Much as the stream of new findings of celestial motion based on telescopes' improved accuracy destroyed the Ptolemaic system, so, as new, more powerful statistical information poured in that contemporary volatility measures do not work, CAPM and EMH were similarly threatened.

The Flaws in EMH-CAPM Volatility Assumptions

EMH proponents recognize the danger their theory is now facing. For investors to be omnisciently rational, there must be a systematic correlation between risk and return. Without it, EMH goes the way of the brontosaurus. If some investors get more return with the same or lower volatility and others get lower returns over time with the same or higher volatility, as we saw in the previous chapter, this indicates that investors are *not* omnisciently rational, and a dagger is pointed at the heart of EMH and CAPM.

To defend efficient markets, Fama, as we saw, after abandoning CAPM, went to the three-factor model of risk in his 1992 paper, while others have gone on to a plethora of theories, including four- and five-factor risk evaluation models, to show that there is still a correlation between risk and return.

However, this leads to a number of serious errors in the formulation of the new models. These models are built to replace CAPM; but they are built in an identical fashion, that is, they all attempt to show that higher volatility provides higher return and that lower volatility provides lower return. If CAPM could not do this, why should any new model built in an identical manner do so? CAPM was dumped because it didn't work, but its central tenet, that there is a direct correlation between risk and return, is being kept as the core of EMH risk analysis.

So researchers must search for new sets of risk and return variables that will give them the correlation between higher risk and higher return. In effect, they must create a new CAPM (naturally with a new name) that behaves almost exactly as the old one was supposed to behave but didn't. In short, it appears they are attempting to create something along the lines of a financial Stepford wife. But this leads them deeper into the theoretical jungle.

Where can you find these critical new risk variables that will work and give you better results than the old CAPM, which was proved not to work? You can't very well advertise for them in the classifieds of *The New York Times* or *The Wall Street Journal* under "Wanted: new risk factors." And certainly not under "Wanted: financial Stepford wives."

Unfortunately, this is where efficient market researchers are today. Have they subsequently found a way out of the volatility woods? Not exactly. The first problem is that they have presented a grab bag of simple correlations that attempt to show a link between risk and return. This is very dangerous scientific ground. As Milton Friedman warned, "If there is one . . . [correlation] . . . consistent with the available evidence there are always an infinite number that are."[25] Even if the academics found a correlation between volatility and return, which is doubtful from what we have seen, there could be hundreds of others that explain risk and return better.

The first problem researchers have is that they cannot prove that the three-factor, the four-factor, or any other models they put forth actually work rather than simply being chance correlations. As Friedman also noted, one of the basic rules of scientific method is that *correlation is far removed from causation*. There can be innumerable chance correlations for any effect, but without reasonable evidence that one or another is true, they are pure coincidence and likely to go away with time. A humorous example of chance correlation was the Hemline Indicator, which was shown in a well-known Wall Street chart for decades. When fashion dictated that hemlines should be high, in periods such as the 1920s, the 1960s, the 1980s, and the 1990s, markets roared ahead. When hemlines dropped in the 1930s, in the 1940s, and again in the 1970s, markets went lower. According to this tongue-in-cheek hypothesis, the height of hemlines dictated where markets would go. Obviously, few took it seriously.

However, many EMH researchers seem to accept chance correlations as proof, although there is no evidence that a myriad of other variables might also correlate as well as or better than the ones they've selected. No new theory of volatility and return has been discovered that shows a consistent correlation between the two. Still, the EMH researchers continue to struggle to find one. They have scanned thousands of possible financial variables in an attempt to do this, but none has worked consistently.

Not only is this bad science; it is likely to blow up over time because of the lack of critical scientific underpinnings to these correlations. Importantly, Fama, in his 1998 survey of market efficiency, wrote that all of the volatility models tested to date "are incomplete descriptions of average returns."[26] In brief, they do not work consistently. Using these methods, the researchers seemingly entrapped themselves.

Unfortunately, this logic has yet another hurdle to clear. Even if it were true, it is not enough to say that a correlation between risk and return has been discovered or shortly will be. If markets are efficient, the sophisticated investors that supposedly keep prices in line with value must have known about the new correlation generations back, even if the academics didn't. If they did not, how have markets been efficient over the decades? Since there is no evidence that a new proof of volatility has been brought forth or will be, *we have to conclude that EMH risk measurements have not been correct and may have been significantly wrong for decades.* The logical jungle seems to get more impenetrable with each new finding.

But without this volatility correlation EMH goes the way of the Ptolemaic system. It is also remarkably similar to the Ptolemaics working on epicycles and eccentric circles to attempt to save their system. It's sad to see gifted researchers cross over from the bounds of scientific discovery to enter a world of ideologues, some of whom at times appear to be almost zealots.

The Achilles' Heel of EMH

In chapter 4 we saw the supposedly overwhelming evidence that it is impossible to beat the market over time. Let's now look more closely at the original work the researchers did, which "proved" that no investor could beat the markets. I'm sure the results will surprise some of you.

There's no clearer statement of the testament, according to Fama,[27] than his own concise description of efficient markets: if the necessary conditions for market efficiency are present—i.e., information is readily available to enough investors and transaction costs are reasonable—there is no evidence of consistently superior or inferior returns to market participants.

The argument assumes that thousands of analysts, money managers, and other sophisticated investors search out and analyze all available information, constantly keeping prices in line with value.[28] Since the academics claimed that it was difficult to assess how investors analyze information to determine undervalued stocks, tests of this premise focus on whether groups of investors have earned superior returns. The group whose members most frequently serve as guinea pigs is that of mutual fund managers, because information about their decisions and performance is readily available. The research shows that mutual funds do not outperform the major averages, whether risk-adjusted or not, although the risk-adjusted studies that support the efficient-market hypothesis are now certainly open to question.

Flawed Statistics and Kangaroo Courts

The statistics of the original mutual fund researchers in the 1960s and early 1970s failed to turn up above-average performance by investors, thereby contributing the essential evidence to make the EMH case.

But on closer examination, the efficient-market victory vanishes. Studies have demonstrated that the standard risk adjustment tools the researchers used back then were too imprecise to detect even major fund outperformance by money managers of their benchmark average. The statistical tests used made it extremely difficult to show superior manager performance when it existed, because the hurdles that outperforming portfolios had to clear were set far too high. One, for example, showed that using the techniques of Michael Jensen, only one manager of the 115 measured demonstrated superior performance at a 95 percent confidence level, the lowest statistical level normally acceptable.[29]

Even to be flagged on the screen, the manager had to outperform the market by 5.83 percent annually for fourteen years. When we remember that a top manager might beat the market by 1½ or 2 percent a year over that length of time, the returns required by Jensen to pick up managers outperforming the averages were impossibly high. Only a manager in the league of Warren Buffett or John Templeton might make the grade, and certainly not every year. One fund outperformed the market by 2.2 percent a year for twenty years, but according to Jensen's calculations, this superb performance was not statistically significant.[30] "There is very little evidence," Jensen wrote at the time, "that any individual fund was able to do significantly better than that which we expected from mere random chance."[31]

In another academic paper, using standard risk adjustment techniques, the researchers showed that it was not possible, at a 95 percent confidence level, to say that a portfolio that was up more than 90 percent over ten years was better managed than another portfolio that was down 3 percent. It was also noted that "given a reasonable level of annual outperformance and variability (volatility), it takes about seventy years of quarterly data to achieve statistical significance at the 95% confidence level."*

One researcher, in an understatement, noted that the problem lay in weak statistical tools. Corroborating those findings, Lawrence Summers, the former head of the President's Council of Economic Advisors, estimated that it would take 50,000 years' worth of data to disprove the theory to the satisfaction of the stalwarts. Indeed, the EMH performance and risk measurement tools were so weak that it proved impossible to delineate even outstanding performance, which by sheer coincidence was the one thing that would invalidate the hypothesis.[32] Obviously, this important "proof" that managers could not beat the market was put together with seriously inadequate statistics that coincidentally seemed to consistently give outstanding managers the short end of the count.

How, too, could the $63 billion Magellan Fund, for example, with more than a million shareholders and under three separate money managers, outperform the market for well over a decade? Or John Templeton and John Neff, the latter running billions of dollars for the Windsor Fund for more than two decades? How are these stellar results possible with only publicly available information? Is it sheer chance, as EMH adherents

---

* One has to marvel at the manner in which the statistics on superior manager performances were set up.

are forced to claim? Are these simply more on a growing list of "aberrations" (a popular term used for events that cannot be explained by a theory)? If they are, we must look at how many other institutional investors have outperformed, using statistics that can actually detect superior performance, not inadvertently filter it out, as Jensen's methods did.

Why Weren't Failed EMH Performance Measurements Recalculated?

Given this fact, did the supposedly impartial academics correct their work when better statistical techniques were available? Apparently not. In spite of the above and other evidence, the conclusions of Jensen's mutual fund study, although seriously flawed, are still used to support the main premise of efficient markets.

Although Fama, French, and others showed that CAPM risk measurements were valueless, this is only a part of the story. Risk-adjusted and non-risk-adjusted mutual fund performance measurements, in addition to Professor Jensen's, have also been shown to be misleading, because of the weakness of the statistical tools employed. Still they, too, have not been recalculated by EMH defenders to get a fairer picture of how mutual funds have really performed against markets. We have just seen how, as a result of these measurements, outstanding performance was not detected, and this was one of the most powerful "proofs" that EMH used to show that markets were efficient. As noted, the records of most managers who consistently outperformed the market were wiped out by statistical gobbledygook.

The ghosts of beta and other academic risk measurements still walk the night, defending EMH and weeding out any above-average performance not permitted by the theory. These are not the only instances of such tactics being employed by the true believers.

Revenants and errors notwithstanding, superior performance, a death knell for EMH, could not be eliminated by the believers. Next we'll look at some of the ghost busters.

Those Dreadful Anomalies

Another major challenge to EMH is its claim that groups of investors, say, with professional knowledge or skills or methods, have consistently kept prices where they should be.[33] We just saw differently. However, EMH makes an even stronger statement: that *no group of investors or any investment strategy can do better than the market over time.* And here again the trouble starts.

The tenet that managers do not outperform or underperform a market benchmark has a corollary: there is no method or system that consistently can provide higher returns over time. This statement is contradicted by a large body of evidence that some investment strategies consistently do better than the market and others consistently underperform over time. The jury has come in with a unanimous decision on this one: the verdict is solidly against EMH.

As we will see extensively in Part IV, a considerable body of literature demonstrates that contrarian strategies have produced significantly better returns than the market over many decades. The explanation for this explicitly contradicts the central tenet of EMH—that people behave with almost omniscient rationality in markets.

Conversely, the tenet that no group of investors and no strategies should consistently underperform in an efficient market is another rock that EMH flounders on. Below-market performance has been turned in for decades by people who buy favorite stocks, as we will see in detail when we examine contrarian strategies. Another significant underperformance finding, as noted, is the research that shows that IPOs have been dogs in the marketplace for forty years.[34] So overperformance and underperformance for long periods—neither of which, EMH states, is possible—show up on both sides of the anomaly coin.

The anomalies show no sign of going away after four decades of counterchallenges; rather, they have been gaining in strength in the last few years, as dozens of articles have examined contrarian effects. The most important anomaly—contrarian strategies that beat the averages over extended periods—was as we saw documented by Professors Fama and French in 1992.[35] Their own data contradict the contention that efficient markets have held up well. And the claims that these strategies are more risky have never been documented. The body of contradictory findings above challenges believers to either retract much of the theory or explain how such events can happen.

Another Challenge to Market Efficiency

Another major premise of EMH is the hypothesis that all new information is analyzed almost immediately and accurately reflected in stock prices, thus preventing investors from beating the market. Burton Malkiel, the author of *A Random Walk Down Wall Street,* now in its tenth edition, wrote in an article reviewing the evidence on efficient markets in 2005, "In my view, equity prices adjust to new information without delay, and, as a result, no arbitrage opportunities exist that would achieve above average returns, without accepting above average risk."[36] But do equity prices really adjust to new information "without delay"? This statement has been hard-core EMH for more than forty years and has been cited by almost every scholar in the field. True prices often react to new information about a stock, but where is the proof that they react to it correctly?

There is none. In a series of studies we are about to examine, we'll often find that the researchers mistakenly take any market reaction to new information as the correct one. A number of these studies also make it clear that the initial market reactions are wrong. You will also see this predictable reaction to earnings surprise over thirty-eight years in chapter 9, where the first reaction repeatedly is not the correct one. It is also demonstrated in papers by Ray Ball and Philip Brown (1968)[37] and Victor Bernard and Jacob Thomas (1990)[38] and noted by Eugene Fama in his 1998 survey of EMH literature.[39]

The fact that Professor Fama finds these latter researchers' findings to be "robust" is particularly interesting, as they directly dispute the important assumption of efficient markets that new information is immediately and correctly reflected in stock prices. Here again we see a vital pillar of EMH begin to rock because an essential assumption of the theory was never tested by its proponents in a thorough manner. *Stocks were tested merely for a reaction to new information, not for the correct reaction to the information.* There are many dozens of potential prices a stock can reach on news; how do we know which one is correct? It's almost equivalent to saying that if a man can jog he's capable of winning the 100-meter sprint at the Olympic Games.

The Tortuous Path to Market Efficiency

To give you a fuller grasp of the depth—or lack thereof—of the testing that was used to back up this argument, let's look at other research performed in the past few decades that supposedly left no doubt of how quickly and accurately investors interpreted market information.

Bolting the Barn Door After the Mare Gallops Off

The landmark 1969 study to show that prices adjust to new information rapidly was done by four outstanding researchers of EMH—Eugene Fama, Lawrence Fisher, Michael Jensen, and Richard Roll (hereafter, FFJR collectively).

The researchers examined all stock splits on the New York Stock Exchange from 1926 through 1960.[40] The results the investigators arrived at, using extremely sophisticated statistical techniques for the time, indicated that stock prices do not move up after splits, as investors have digested all the positive information beforehand. The authors concluded that their work provides strong support for the hypothesis that the market is efficient. In truth, this, like most of the other experiments in this category, is a rather simplistic experiment of market efficiency, as it involves a very basic test of understanding uncomplicated, readily available information, hardly on a par with the complex decisions involving thousands of interacting variables that are called for in more normal investment analysis, such as that we saw in chapters 2 and 3. But to move on.

This study has been cited in hundreds of academic papers and has been taught to hundreds of thousands of graduate students as one of the major research works upholding market efficiency. However, the study is seriously flawed. *The researchers knowingly measured a time period months after the information was released to gauge its effect on the market, rather than measuring at the time when the information was made public.* It's not a little like locking the barn door after the mare has galloped away.

The information enters the market at the time of the split announcement, most often two to four months before the split is distributed to the company's shareholders. The earlier time is when the measurement should commence to see if the news resulted in a rise in stock prices as a result of the split, as it does for earnings surprises, dividend increases or decreases, or other announcements that can have a major impact on stock prices.

Sadly, this information was unavailable, so the researchers measured from the month in which the stock split was actually distributed, a period when the information had been out for two to four months, and reported that no extra return was made from that point onward. Naturally, their measurements of stock movement at that point were meaningless, as the market had already digested the news from two to four months before and the informational content was already fully reflected in the stock prices.

In *Contrarian Investment Strategies: The Next Generation,* I analyzed the chart the researchers provided from the examination; it was obvious that the steepest run-up after the announcements of splits came in the two-to-four-month period immediately after the announcement. In fact, the average extra monthly return for the four months in which the splits are announced is almost double the above-market returns in the previous twenty-six months.[41]

This raises a difficult problem for the researchers. What the chart appears to show, assuming that the majority of split announcements occurred two to four months prior to the stock distribution, is that the stocks may indeed have provided above-average returns after the announcement date. The positive adjustment to the splits, then, appears not to have been immediate but to have taken place for some months after the split's announcement.

If this is the case, the researchers' argument is invalid. The most logical conclusion is that the stocks continued to rise as a group for an extended period after the split announcement, which is exactly opposite to what the paper concluded.

The academics do, as noted, explain several times in the paper that the announcement date was not in their database.* Perhaps this was fortunate for them. *If it were possible to place the split at the correct point, as the above analysis indicates, the conclusion would have been very different, the evidence helping to prove the tenet that markets react to new*

---

* Except for a sample of only 52 of 904 splits, or less than 6 percent, which the authors say support their case.

information in an inefficient, not an efficient, manner, which would certainly help to question the overall efficiency of markets.

Three decades later, in 1996, the research was replicated by David Ikenberry, Graeme Rankine, and Earl Stice,[42] who examined 1,275 two-for-one stock splits from 1975 to 1990 on the New York Stock Exchange and the AMEX. They observed excess returns of 3.4 percent after the split announcement and 7.9 percent for the first year after, followed by higher average returns in the three-year period following the split.

Hemang Desai and Prem Jain (1997) found higher returns of 7 percent to 12 percent in the twelve months following a stock split.[43] These results flatly contradicted FFJR's 1969 paper, again providing evidence that markets react to new information in an inefficient, not an efficient, manner. The above findings are in line with our analysis.

Professor Fama, in his 1998 survey of EMH research, ignores the fact that the critical FFJR 1969 findings have been strongly refuted, and that the glaring flaw in the methodology has been identified. Instead, he seemingly questions the other researchers' findings, noting that the time periods of the studies are different, as well as some of their other minor methodology. *In doing so, it appears, he is attempting to deflect the fact that the critical focus of the FFJR paper—to determine whether the market responds almost immediately to the announcement of a stock split—was flubbed.* That the time periods were different is entirely irrelevant to this work. It was a smooth maneuver; since the point of the original study was to find out whether stock splits have an immediate impact on prices, he has sidestepped the raison d'être of the 1969 study and ducked the fact that the later findings seem to disprove the FFJR research. Some spinmeisters might want to study such thinking, which seems classic to their field.

Without the FFMR paper and other similar research, which also has significant problems, the critical tenet of EMH—that investors process information quickly and correctly—collapses completely.

As noted, the FFJR study is considered by many as one of the strongest and best-known research supporting EMH.

More Leaks in the EMH Dreadnought

There's nothing like really taking a close look at the original data. I mean really close, if you want to see what a researcher is doing. So let's look at other studies that claim that the market adjusts quickly to new information. The first was performed by Ray Ball and Philip Brown in 1968.[44] The two investigators examined the normal rates of return from 1946 to 1966 for 261 firms. They divided the stocks into two groups, those whose earnings in a given year increased relative to the market and those whose earnings decreased. The performance was measured after each year-end. They found that stocks whose earnings increased outperformed the market, while those that decreased underperformed the market. The researchers concluded that the stock prices had already anticipated most of the news of earnings announcements.

The theorists overlooked one simple fact that is well known to most investors: companies normally report quarterly, not annually. The SEC has for many years required public companies to disclose this financial information within ninety days. Furthermore, even back then, analysts provided research reports on how companies were faring, most often containing full-year earnings estimates, often supplemented by press releases from company spokesmen. Still, Ball and Brown stated that investors correctly judged the prospects of companies and thus determined the movement of their stock prices when they actually had the information on hand to do so. Again the question comes up of how aware the researchers are of practical market information, such as reporting and research. To conclude that the market is efficient from this rather obvious and again simple finding is stretching the point.

Another supposedly awesome bit of evidence to support the hypothesis was a study by Myron Scholes in 1972.[45] Scholes analyzed the effect of secondary offerings of stock and concluded that, on average, a stock declined 1 or 2 percent when such an offering was made. The largest declines resulted from the sale of stock by corporations or corporate officers. He also stated that the full price effects of a secondary are reflected in six days. He concluded that since the SEC does not require the identification of the seller until six days after the offering, the market anticipates the informational content of the secondary and is therefore efficient. Here again is a sweeping conclusion based on nominal price movements over a short period of time.

Secondary offerings normally bring stock prices down temporarily; this is almost a platitude. What is important is whether the stocks are brought down appropriately. How do they perform relative to the market three, six, or twelve months later? Too, many brokers disclose beforehand who the sellers are. To state that the market anticipates this information because the SEC does not require it is a chancy conclusion. Often this information is provided anyway.

Another study examined how quickly markets integrate new information into stock prices. The research considered how companies react to the announcement of merger and tender offers. Fama, in his 1991 review of efficient markets, stated:

> [I]n mergers and tender offers, the average increase in stock prices of target firms in the three days around the announcement is more than 15%. Since the average daily return on stocks is only about .04% (10% per year divided by 250 trading days), different ways of measuring expected returns have little effect on the inference that target shares have large abnormal returns in the days around merger and tender announcements.[46]

Again this appears to be a wee break with reality. Merger and tender offers are almost always made at a higher price, sometimes significantly higher than the price before the offer.

That stock prices go up 15 percent on average over the three days around the announcement of an IPO certainly is not proof that markets are efficient. Again, as seen earlier in this chapter, highly regarded EMH theorists make a major mistake in assuming that just because stocks respond to new information, they are responding correctly to it. Often the bids for both mergers and tender offers are raised as company management demands and frequently receives higher prices (particularly with hostile takeovers). The stocks also often trade at a discount to the proposed offering price for an extended period of time.

The 15 percent that stocks appreciate around the date of the initial announcement of an offer is half of the approximately 30 percent total increase that shareholders received on average, for periods ranging from a few weeks to a couple of months before or after the offer was consummated, according to other studies.[47] Even allowing for the occasional offer that is dropped, the first tender price appears far too low. The market again seems to be incorrect in its initial pricing of tender offers and mergers.

No evidence is provided that the initial reaction to the news is the correct one, as prices far too frequently move up from the trading levels following the announcements. This premise spawned a generation of risk arbitrageurs who have made enormous returns on their capital. The study is somewhat unsophisticated in its knowledge of mergers and acquisitions, and from the evidence available it appears that markets are inefficient rather than efficient when measuring initial offerings relative to the final takeover price.

To use a chess analogy, it's like concluding that if I move a chess piece after a move by the current world chess champion, the fact that I pushed the piece at all puts me on his level of play. Once again the theory: any price movement is the correct price movement. Nonsensical, yes; a nice daydream, yes; but also the essence of the weak "proofs" of EMH we are looking at.

Other Evidence Against Efficiency

Our case further strengthens with other evidence that efficiency is quite a bit rarer than the theorists admit. The evidence that markets do not adjust quickly to new information keeps mounting. Roni Michaely, Richard Thaler (one of the pioneers of behavioral finance), and Kent Womack studied the subject in 1994.[48] The three researchers measured how stocks behaved after a dividend cut or increase during the 1964–1988 period. The average stock underperformed the market by 11 percent in the year after the announcement of a dividend cut, and by 15.3 percent for the three-year period. It outperformed by 7.5 percent in the year following a dividend increase, and by 24.8 percent for the three years afterward. This study indicates again that markets do not adjust to new information quickly.

A number of other studies have shown that the market is slow to digest new information. Several researchers have found that when a company reports an earnings surprise (that is, a figure above or below the consensus of analysts' forecasts), prices move up when the surprise is positive and down when it is negative for the next three quarters.[49] Jeffery Abarbanell and Victor Bernard, as will be noted in chapter 9, have shown that analysts don't adjust their earnings estimates quickly after past mistakes.[50] The "buy-and-hold" contrarian strategies presented in chapters 11 and 12[51] demonstrated that "worst" stocks with earnings surprises continued to outperform and "best" stocks to underperform the market for periods of up to nine months. These findings that markets are slow to react fully to information, rather than reacting instantaneously, appear to shoot another arrow through EMH.

Finally, Robert Shiller argues that if markets were efficient, when we look back at history, stock prices at a given time should be related to prices that we can say are "rational."[52] To find out if this is true, he looked back at prices that would be considered rational in light of the dividends subsequently paid. The study covers the 1871–1979 period.

The rational index Shiller created after the fact follows a smooth, stable path, whereas the actual market index veers sharply above or below it for extended periods, displaying substantial volatility. Shiller concluded, "[S]tock price volatility over the past century appear[s] to be far too high . . . to be attributed to new information about future real dividends."[53] In short, markets over that long term did not respond accurately to information but rather moved far higher or lower than was warranted.

A Black Hole in EMH Theory

Recall that adherents of EMH believe that knowledgeable investors keep prices where they should be. Unfortunately, this does not appear to be true; and if it is not true, then the most important axiom of the hypothesis is gone.

One of the key questions efficient-market adherents have not examined is how professional investors keep prices in line with values. What methods do they use to do so? It's doubtful that this question has ever been explained by EMH believers, and is anything other than a critical theoretical assumption. Perhaps this is due to the fact that academics have little understanding of the tools and models knowledgeable investors employ. In chapter 2, we looked at some of the important fundamental methods used to train analysts and money managers, including the use of numerous stock market evaluation techniques and ratios. These methods, if followed, should prevent them from buying stocks that are enormously overpriced.

If they do buy bubble stocks or other highly overpriced stocks, as actually occurs frequently, they are walking away from their years of experience and training and the valuation methods they have used repeatedly through their careers. Such actions would not be considered rational and should not happen. However, they do occur repeatedly during bubbles or periods of skyrocketing prices, as does selling excellent companies that have been knocked down sharply in periods of panic.

Importantly, the errors are made, as noted, by the very professional and knowledgeable investors that EMH states keeps markets efficient. If they can't keep prices at correct levels, how do markets stay efficient? The answer, obviously, is that they don't. That is the real reason bubbles happen so frequently and go to prices that are often astronomical before they are dashed down in the ensuing panic.

I know, these seem to be very peculiar rational investors. Since we are in an EMH chapter, I will only refer in passing to the psychology we learned in Part I, which can play into this otherwise unfathomable behavior.

The Black Swans of EMH

The history of science teaches us that, given capable, intelligent people, large errors normally do not occur in the development of a hypothesis but rather occur in the assumptions upon which the work is based. Powerful statistical techniques without realistic assumptions take on a life of their own. As bad currency drives out good, more than five decades of bad constructs in finance and economics have driven out good science, leaving few useful contributions for the enormous effort expended.

To be fair, the concept of efficient markets has come under attack even by financial academics. Edward Saunders, Jr., using the work of Karl Popper, one of the important theorists on scientific method in the last half of the twentieth century, criticizes the scientific approach of EMH.[54] Popper stated in a famous analogy that to prove the theory that all swans are white, the researchers should not concentrate their efforts on searching for more white swans. On the contrary, they should search for black swans, because finding even one would destroy the theory.[55] EMH researchers have not followed Popper's teachings. The black swans of EMH are the ever-increasing number of major anomalies outside the theory's explanatory range. Not only have EMH researchers continued to search for more white swans, but they have put together an unrelenting campaign to exterminate black swans—the anomalies that cannot exist if EMH is correct.

A Leap of Faith

Even if the studies claiming that markets are efficient were not problematic, there is a much more serious question about them that was raised in chapter 4. The scientific findings were far too modest to justify the researchers' all-encompassing, revolutionary conclusions. What proof did the researchers have that the markets respond not only immediately but correctly to new information? None. They accepted market reaction to uncomplicated information as proof positive not simply of reaction but of the correct price reaction to the event. The investigators never attempted to test investors' ability to interpret far more complex financial and economic data, such as we've viewed throughout the text.

The pattern is common not only to EMH studies but to most areas of mathematical economics. The researchers are very rigorous in their statistical analysis but extremely liberal, if not specious, in their interpretation of broader issues. We saw this in their presentation of the studies that attempted to prove that markets are efficient. The work looked at obvious examples of news affecting markets. These findings, which one could call "slivers of efficiency," led the researchers by quantum leaps to much broader conclusions. If markets can understand the impact of relatively simple news of mergers or secondary offerings, the reasoning goes, they must be equally capable of gathering and correctly interpreting complex data about companies; industries; economic, monetary, and financial conditions; and the market itself.[56]

One must marvel at the boldness of these scholars to build an all-encompassing theory on such flimsy evidence. It is an enormous leap of faith from these simple findings to the conclusion that the market correctly interprets all information, no matter how complex, such as that contained in a bubble or panic, correctly and almost instantaneously. That is like saying that if my daughter, when she was six, could count to a hundred without difficulty, she should also be able to comprehend the theory of relativity—though I'm sure that if asked back then, she would have readily given me an answer, as she did to anything else, but somehow I think it would have missed the mark.

Unfortunately, when put to the test, the canons of EMH resound like a string of stunning military defeats. None of the risk measurements that the academics credit to rational investors have stood the test of time; here, it seems, we have a financial epicycle. The risk-return paradigm must exist, or EMH will be remembered in history much like the Ptolemaic system, a theory widely popular for a long time that ultimately failed and was discarded.

We have also examined in some depth the three key assumptions of the efficient-market hypothesis.* The three have been discredited by both the relative weakness of and errors in the supposed "proofs," as well as very strong evidence that disputes the efficiency hypothesis.

Finally, as we've previously established, there is the major problem with the EMH assumption that investors can interpret vast amounts of data. Findings in cognitive psychology and other psychological disciplines demonstrate that this assumption is not accurate. To use another chess analogy, although hundreds of millions of people play the game, there are only a score of grand masters and only one world champion. If people are not equally adept at interpreting the complex world of the chessboard, can they be any more equal at understanding the more complex and significantly more emotional world of markets?

Ultimately, what chapters 5 and 6 seem to declare to EMH, CAPM, and MPT advocates is the equivalent of "Sorry, it turns out that the sun does not revolve around the earth. Try to accept it."

Epilogue to Part II: The Crisis of Modern Economics

How strong is the support for EMH today? A first thought might be that it is very strong, given the thousands of articles still written by scholars in some of the world's most prestigious financial and economic journals and its widespread use in the investment world. Yet from what we've seen, this revolutionary theory seems to have been built on the flimsiest of foundations—unkind critics might say a house of cards. As we saw, one of the most important pillars of the hypothesis—the theory of the rational measurement of risk—was simply a questionable assumption of financial academics, which was necessary to bind investment theory to economics. Yet for EMH to be correct, it was essential that investors measure risk in

---

* The belief that investors cannot consistently beat the market, that markets respond to new information quickly and accurately, and that experienced and knowledgeable investors keep prices where they should be.

this way. The academics willed it to be true. And they continue to do so today, although it almost boggles the mind that some of the world's finest economists have trapped themselves in such a logically indefensible position.

The most important reason researchers failed so badly on risk measurement is the manner in which EMH and most other economic investigators conduct their research. Since World War II the social sciences have attempted to become as rigorous as the physical sciences. No discipline has put more effort into this goal than economics. Starting more than sixty years ago, economists held out high hopes that through mathematics they could make the dismal science as predictable as Albert Einstein's theory of relativity or Johannes Kepler's laws of planetary motion. Nobel laureate Paul Samuelson, then a young professor of economics at MIT, was the first to integrate the techniques of differential equations, which had met with such success in physics, into a structured approach that could be used to study virtually any economic problem.

The key assumption was rationality: for a firm it meant maximizing profits; for an individual, maximizing his or her economic desires. Rational behavior is the bedrock of Samuelson's work. This dubious platform allowed economists to merrily build the most complex mathematical models. Economics could now be converted into a precise physical science.

A PACT WITH MEPHISTOPHELES

It would be unfair to say that economists and efficient-market adherents are unaware of the simplicity and vulnerability of their assumptions. The premise of economic rationality is one that has perplexed economic theorists for a long time. The assumption was derived in the golden age of rationalism in the eighteenth and early nineteenth centuries.

Absolute rationality has all but been discarded in philosophy and the social sciences. It's commonly accepted that although people often act rationally, there are also many times when they don't. Market and economic history strongly supports the findings of the behavioral experts.

Why, then, do most economists persist in using an outmoded concept of human behavior as the cornerstone of their theory? Many agree that the concept of rationality, so central to EMH, is problematic. Still they strongly defend its usefulness; as one book stated decades ago, "To introduce a more realistic assumption would make economic theory very difficult."[57]

Economic theory and later financial theory have been caught on the horns of this dilemma for many decades. Should they espouse realistic assumptions, and if so, what should these be? Or should the assumptions, although acknowledged to be unrealistic, allow extensive analysis, however flawed in terms of practical value? It's difficult to construct economic theory on numerous behavioral or other assumptions, even if they're realistic. Rationality gives economists one simple and unwavering assumption to build upon; however, the construct is often seriously flawed.

Paul Samuelson, as noted, was the pioneer in using highly sophisticated mathematics to solve economic problems. A new economic age had begun. The goal was to make economics as predictable as physics or other physical sciences. The findings of economic theory would be as precise as measuring the exact expansion of steel on a bridge of a given length as the temperature rose. The only solid platform upon which the higher math could be built was the bedrock of rationality. Integrating sociological or psychological theories could result in a number of possible starting points, with new ones added over time, and it would be impossible to anchor complex mathematical formulas on a changing behavioral platform. No, the most practical solution, to most economists, was to use the assumption of consistent rationality, even if it was often incorrect.

As a result, the great majority of economic research gravitated in that direction, despite the warnings of some of the important economic thinkers of the past. John Maynard Keynes, for example, was trained as a mathematician but refused to build his classic theory on unrealistic assumptions. Like his teacher, the great Victorian economist Alfred Marshall, Keynes believed that economics was a branch of logic, not a pseudo–natural science. Marshall himself wrote that most economic phenomena do not lend themselves to mathematical equations and warned against the danger of falling into the trap of overemphasizing the economic elements that could be most easily quantified.

The Samuelson revolution, with its emphasis on complex quantification parroting the physical sciences, came to totally dominate economics in the postwar period. Mathematics, which pre-Samuelson was a valuable but subordinate aid to reality-based assumptions, now rules economics. Good ideas are often ignored by economists simply because they are not written down in pages of highly complex statistical formulas or don't employ equations using most of the letters of the Greek alphabet. The vast amount of research published in the academic journals contains minuscule additions to economic thinking but is dressed in sophisticated mathematical models. Bad ideas planted in deep math tend to endure, even when the assumptions are questionable and evidence strongly contradicts the conclusions. As Nobel laureate Paul Krugman noted, "As I see it, the economic profession went astray because economists, as a group, mistook beauty, clad in impressive-looking mathematics, for truth." [58]

Economic ideas and principles once understood by educated readers are now unfathomable to all but the most highly trained mathematical researchers. This would be well and good if economics had achieved the predictability of a physical science. But without realistic assumptions, the dismal science has been broken down rather than been rejuvenated by mathematics. Nobel laureate Joseph Stiglitz, in his 2001 Nobel Prize lecture, spoke to this point in discussing the inadequacy of preferred economic models: "[With one model] I only varied one assumption— the assumption concerning perfect information—and in ways which seemed highly plausible. . . . [As a result] we succeeded in showing not only that the standard theory was not robust. . . . Changing only the one assumption . . . had drastic consequences, [to the theory] but also indicated that an alternative robust paradigm with great explanatory power could be constructed." [59]

In the wake of the financial crisis and the Great Recession, the flaws in economics and EMH have taken on new urgency as millions of people are asking how the economy could have gone so wrong. The questioning is coming not only from major economists and the large numbers of unemployed but from *The Wall Street Journal* and other bastions of laissez-faire. [60]

Most economists, including the world's most powerful central bankers, had believed for decades that people were rational enough and the markets smooth enough that the whole economy could be reduced to "a handful of equations." The equations are assembled into mathematical models that attempt to mimic multilevel economic behavior from Washington to Berlin to Beijing. But, as we see, they didn't work. Instead we are still suffering through the worst financial crisis in modern history. It is certainly not about efficient-market theory alone that the questions are being asked.

The questioning has gone on for decades. As John Cassidy pointed out in an excellent article in *The New Yorker,* complex new mathematical theories, such as those of Robert Lucas, Jr., a Nobel Prize winner from the University of Chicago, while causing a generation of novice economists to build ever more complex models, have been discredited, with no agreement on what should replace them.

Lucas's work concluded that the Federal Reserve should not actively guide the economy but only increase the money supply at a constant rate.[61] The research came under sharp theoretical attack, again because at the core of Lucas's complex mathematical formulas were untenable simple assumptions such as that supply always equals demand in all markets. (If this were true, we could not have unemployment; the supply of workers would never exceed the demand for them.) Once the supply/demand assumption is dropped, few of Lucas's conclusions hold up. Commenting on the impracticality of Lucas's work, Joseph Stiglitz, then the chairman of the president's Council of Economic Advisors, said, "You can't begin with the assumption of full employment when the President is worried about jobs—not only this President, but any President."[62]

Economics, traditionally one of the most important of the social sciences, has suffered a self-inflicted decline. Not all in the profession are unaware of this. In 1996, the Nobel Prize in Economics was awarded to two men: William Vickrey, an emeritus professor at Columbia University (for a research paper in 1961), and James Mirrlees, a professor at Cambridge University. Although the popular press extolled Vickrey's contribution as breaking fresh intellectual ground in fields as diverse as tax policy and government bond auctions, the professor denied the hyperbole. He said, "[It's] one of my digressions into abstract economics. . . . At best it's of minor significance in terms of human welfare."[63] When interviewed, he talked instead about unrelated work he had done, which he considered far more important. Complicated statistical analysis is no different in the investment arena, nor should it be, since it's another branch of economics. Simple assumptions are usually necessary as a platform for abstruse statistical methods. More complex assumptions, although far more descriptive of the real world, do not allow the development of the mathematical analysis that the researchers desire or the academic journals will publish.

Given the simple assumption of rationality, researchers in the best tradition of the Samuelson Revolution can merrily take off to examine how the totally rational investor will approach markets. They can then use the most complex differential equations or other mathematical methodology to discover new results. Whether the assumptions have the remotest connection to reality is irrelevant. Who cares?

Thomas Kuhn, in his classic work *The Structure of Scientific Revolutions,*[64] takes a tolerant approach to the problem of paradigm change. It is essential, Kuhn wrote, for scientists to have a paradigm from which to work. A paradigm is the body of theory the scientific community in a field accepts and works within.

"Paradigms gain their status," Kuhn argued, "because they are more successful than their competitors in solving a few problems that the group of practitioners has come to recognize as acute."[65] Thus, EMH, in the early years, provided an explanation of prices fluctuating randomly and why technicians could not consistently outperform markets.

Kuhn also noted that "normal science does not aim at novelties of fact or theory, and when successful finds none."[66] As a paradigm becomes widely accepted, its tools and methods become more deeply rooted in the solution of problems. The accepted tools for broadening the efficient-market paradigm were beta and MPT.

The goal of normal science is not to question the reigning paradigm but to explain the world as viewed through it. Anomalies that contradict the basic tenets of the paradigm are a serious challenge to it. A paradigm must be able to explain the anomalies, or it will eventually be abandoned for a new one that provides explanations that the first one cannot.

Thus scientists naturally defend their paradigm. They prefer to believe that all swans are white and do not search for black ones. If scientists find black swans—the anomalies to EMH are such an example—they try to explain them within the theory. A change in a paradigm is a nerve-racking and difficult period with much acrimony.*

Its adherents have a vested interest in upholding the validity of the old paradigm, because all their knowledge, experience, and recognition are tied to it. Rejecting their paradigm is often equivalent in a literal sense to rejecting their religion. Kuhn writes that many older scientists will never give up the current paradigm; others will accept parts of it and try to integrate the old with the new. Usually, it takes a new generation of re-

---

* Change undermines their basic approach. EMH and other such economic axioms allow them to proceed in the manner they know best. They are, after all, trained far more thoroughly in statistical method than in behavioral finance.

searchers to completely accept a new paradigm. As Paul Samuelson once put it, "Scientific progress is advanced funeral by funeral."

And here is a key about why EMH still has so many adherents. Kuhn also brings up a critical point: scientists will never abandon a paradigm, no matter how harsh the criticism, unless they have a more compelling one to take its place that will solve most of the problems the old one could not. It is not surprising, then, that even with the major challenges put to EMH, the hypothesis has not been abandoned. Even though its central tenets have been destroyed empirically, it lives on. Thus, when CAPM was destroyed, the deans of efficient markets stated that there were new measures of risk standing patiently in the wings, with others waiting to be discovered. Or when contrarian value methods were shown to outperform the market, efficient-market researchers claimed that they were riskier. EMH is following the precise course of scientific discovery that Kuhn predicted.

In Part IV, a new paradigm of market behavior will be offered, based on much we have learned about predictable investor psychology and with strong empirical evidence to back its assumptions. The good news for investors is that it leads to methods that have consistently outperformed markets over time. The bad news is that it is likely to go through an academic Dante's Inferno for years, perhaps decades, if Kuhn is correct.

Kuhn also noted that not only is new research not rejected, but its adherents have at times been punished. Thus Giordano Bruno, a Renaissance poet and philosopher, was burned at the stake, and Galileo, as we saw, was imprisoned. The fact that EMH researchers seem intolerant of work that opposes their theory is certainly predicted by the history of scientific discovery. Not surprisingly, there is no forum for dissenting thought, as the academic journals normally do not publish work they consider at odds with their paradigm, including that of knowledgeable Wall Streeters and psychologists.

Too, EMH adherents are not above attacking research that disagrees with their beliefs. In the early 1980s, for example, both *Barron's* and *Forbes* ran feature stories questioning the efficacy of EMH. The result was an onslaught of critical letters from hundreds of academics that lasted for months. The most common theme was: how could the magazines dare to challenge the work of the distinguished researchers?

Another disagreeable characteristic of changes in paradigms, demonstrated again with EMH, is the researchers' use of a number of methods to make the black swans go away. Any criticism of EMH research is met either by silence, if it is not published in major financial or economic journals, or by dismissal on methodological grounds, as was the case with contrarian strategies until the evidence became too strong. EMH researchers then stated the strategies must be more risky, although they have not yet found a reason why.

If black swans cannot be ignored, they are attacked. A favorite charge of senior academics defending EMH is data mining, that is, mining only the data you want. This charge, of course, is not used against EMH researchers, who, as we have seen, are now desperately trying to find a risk-reward formula that actually works, although their data mining appears to be on a scale worthy of giant mining concerns such as Rio Tinto or BHP Billiton. Another of their favorite techniques is to criticize methodological flaws, almost down to the misplacement of a semicolon. EMH believers have fortunately never made such errors.

But the black swans refuse to swim away. They are hatched by many causes, from the shattered assumptions of EMH risk theory to the widespread evidence of investor overreaction to the enormous mispricing in both bubbles and crashes. EMH believers summarily dismiss two different but opposite anomalies—investor overreaction and underreaction—glibly stating that since there is significant evidence on the two, one offsets the other.* This is questionable science, since they are two separate anomalies that the researchers cannot explain. Eliminating two separate bodies of evidence because they show opposite results is like stating that $1 + 1 = 0$.

These, then, are some of the hurdles nonbelievers must jump. Some of us have been through this routine numerous times. I turned in my first paper on the superior results of low-P/E strategies in 1977. It was never sent out to a referee, because the editor obviously believed it to be heretical. Only when several of the deans of EMH came out with very similar research fifteen or more years later was it recognized, the credit, of course, going to several of the deans who had originally dismissed such work. Perhaps even worse, the academic journals are, in effect, in the pockets of the major EMH researchers. To publish in the major journals, you must be a true believer or at least a reasonable compromiser. The journals, of course, can make or break the careers of most academics.

---

* Eugene Fama, 1998 review mentioned previously (see page 140).

Recall Popper's statement that only one black swan would be sufficient to kill a theory. Unfortunately for the theorists, there are too many paddling around in the EMH pond to become an endangered species.

This, then, is the dark side of EMH. But to put it into context, it is not very different from the protest and rancor when any established body of knowledge is threatened by inexplicable facts, and dissenters, at least to my knowledge, are not burned at the stake.

If I have been somewhat hard on EMH, it is because I cannot accept the manner in which its case has been built, or the widespread damage that its core ideas have brought to markets and, through them, to many millions of people. Although I do not believe the hypothesis, I certainly respect the arduous experimental efforts made by the many researchers in the area. They have finally brought the long-overdue winds of change to Wall Street. Investors who are really interested in how the market works must appreciate these university researchers. Much of the research was necessarily tedious, dull, and time-consuming, but it was essential in building the foundation of a new investment structure.

Without the thorough measurement of technical and fundamental performance records, Wall Street would have continued in the old, unsuccessful, often disastrous ways, with no impetus toward change. Although it's obvious that I believe EMH is transitory, it did start the winds of change blowing.

Armed with the knowledge of the power of psychology to influence our investment decisions, as well as the discovery that the most widely followed investment theory of our time will not help us but work against us, we are now ready to begin to examine strategies that have worked and will continue to work in the difficult markets we currently face.

Part III

Flawed Forecasting and
Poor Investment Returns

Chapter 7

Wall Street's Addiction to Forecasting

Maybe you remember when American folk songs were prominent, or you discovered them on your own and just liked what you heard. You are likely, then, to have heard the name of Woody Guthrie. (And everyone knows his anthem, "This Land Is Your Land.") He came out of hard times in Oklahoma during the Great Depression, and his songs celebrated the nation's down and out. His 1939 song "The Ballad of Pretty Boy Floyd" included the line "Some will rob you with a six-gun, and some with a fountain pen,"[1] a biting reference to the millions of people who were losing their farms and homes to the foreclosing banks of the time. Now substitute computer spreadsheets for a fountain pen, perhaps with an added stanza or two for some contemporary wrinkles such as collateralized debt obligations, credit default swaps, toxic assets, and exotics, and the lyrics ring true today.

The national debate on whether there should be more or less regulation and government spending rolls on, with no consensus in sight. It seems that lately, economists can't agree about much. (See page 155 for more on this.) At any rate, it's pretty obvious what we're all wondering: how did the experts ever get us into such a mess?

By this time you might feel a little as though you've just come off basic training on Parris Island or running the New York Marathon. We've moved at a brisk pace through some of the important details of why an understanding of investors' psychology and the intellectual clash over efficient markets is essential to give you the edge when you go into the market wars.

We've detailed the formidable conceptional obstacle course that each presents but that you can come through with flying colors: investor psychology, because it can give you an understanding of how to protect and enhance your savings; efficient-market theory, because, though a failing hypothesis, it can provide deadly results if you're not aware of the ways it can strike. I hope that the two opening sections have provided you with at least a bare-bones understanding of their importance for what comes next in our psychological investor program.

In this chapter we will begin to lay out why contemporary investment theory has proved so disappointing over time. It's not because, as the EMH theorists assume, we are rational automatons, but quite the opposite, because we are human and succumb to human errors—errors that standard investment theory does not take account of.

Psychology and Major Investment Errors

Over the last fifty years or so, cognitive psychology has moved in a strikingly different direction from economics theorizing. While economists were embracing a conceptually useful reduction—rational man—psychologists were out to establish an increasingly complex picture of how humans processed information. Spurred by rapid advances in cognitive psychology, sociology, and related fields from the 1980s on, psychologists looked more and more at what differentiated the human mind from machine-based computer logic.

Even as computers seemed to become capable of mimicking aspects of human cogitation, the fact remains that no computer can rival the human mind for its overall capabilities. However, our mental processes, as we have seen, do not work with the flawless logic of computers, so psychologists have investigated the limits of expert knowledge and information handling. What they found was the often subliminal reasons why even experts fail—and why the rest of us aren't going to do much better.

Scores of studies have made it clear that experts' failure extends far beyond the investment scene. It's a basic problem in human information-processing capabilities. Current work indicates that our brains are serial or sequential processors of data that can handle information reliably in a linear manner—that is, we can move from one point to the next in a logical sequence. In building a model ship or a space shuttle, there is a defined sequence of procedures. Each step, no matter how complex the technology, advances from the preceding step to the next step until completion.

The type of problem that proved so difficult to professionals is quite different, however; here configural (or interactive) reasoning, rather than linear thinking, is required. In a configural reasoning problem, the decision maker's interpretation of a piece of information changes depending on how he or she evaluates other inputs. Take the case of a security analyst: when two companies have the same trend of earnings, the emphasis placed on growth rates will be weighed quite differently depending on the outlooks for their industries, revenue growth, profit margins, and returns on capital, and the host of analytical criteria we looked at previously. The analyst's evaluation will also be tempered by changes in the state of the economy, the interest rate level, and the companies' competitive environment. Thus, to be successful, analysts must be adept at configural processing; they must integrate and weigh scores of diverse factors, and, if one factor changes, they must reweigh the whole assessment.

As with juggling, each factor is another ball in the air, increasing the difficulty of the process. Are professionals, in or out of the investment field, capable of the intricate analysis their methods demand? We have seen how difficult this task is and why so many people unconsciously turn to experiential reasoning instead of the rational-analytical methods that are prescribed.

A special technique was designed, using a statistical test called analysis of variance, or ANOVA, to evaluate experts' configural capabilities. In one such study, nine radiologists were given a highly configural problem: deciding whether a gastric ulcer was malignant.[2] To make a proper diagnosis, a radiologist must work from seven major cues either present or absent in an X-ray. These can combine to form fifty-seven possible combinations. Experienced gastroenterologists indicated that a completely accurate diagnosis can be made only by configurally examining the combinations formed by the seven original cues.[3]

Although the diagnosis requires a high level of configural processing, the researchers found that in actual practice, it accounted for a small part of all decisions, some 3 percent. More than 90 percent came from serially adding up the individual symptoms.

A similar problem is deciding whether a psychiatric inpatient is to be allowed to leave the hospital for short periods. The hospital staff has to consider six primary cues that can be present or absent (for example, does the patient have a drinking problem?) and sixty-four possible interactions. In another study, nurses, social workers, and psychologists showed little evidence of configural thinking, although it was essential to reaching the optimum solution.[4] In a third study, thirteen clinical psychologists and sixteen advanced graduate students attempted to determine whether the symptoms of 861 patients were neurotic or psychotic, a highly configural task. The results were in line with the first two examples.[5]

Curious as to what he would find in the stock market, Paul Slovic tested the importance of configural (or interactive) reasoning in the decisions of market professionals. In one study he provided thirteen stockbrokers and five graduate students in finance with eight important financial inputs—the trend of earnings per share, profit margins, outlook for near-term profits, and so on—that they considered significant in analyzing companies. They had to think configurally to find the optimum solution. As it turned out, however, configural reasoning, on average, accounted for only 4 percent of the decisions made—results roughly equivalent to those of the radiologists and psychologists.

Moreover, what the brokers said about how they analyzed the various inputs differed significantly from what they did.[6] For example, a broker who said that the most important trend was earnings per share might actually have placed greater emphasis on near-term prospects. Finally, the more experienced the brokers, the less accurate their assessment of their own scales of weighting appeared to be. All in all, the evidence indicates that most people are weak configural processors, in or out of the marketplace. So it turns out that human minds—as I'm sure you've suspected—are not hardwired anything like the way computers are.

Information-Processing Vulnerabilities

As we saw in our first look at information processing in chapter 3, Herbert Simon more than fifty years ago wrote extensively on information overload. Under certain conditions, *experts err predictably and often*; in fields as far apart as psychology, engineering, publishing, and even soil sampling, all of them make the same kinds of mistakes. The conditions for such errors are as fertile in the stock market as anywhere.

I briefly mentioned that the vast storehouse of data about companies, industries, and the economy mandated by current investment methods may not give the professional investor an extra "edge." When information-processing requirements are large and complex analysis is necessary to integrate it, the rational system, which is deliberative and analytical, is often subtly overridden without the professional's knowledge by the experiential system. Inferential processing delicately bypasses our rational data banks. As we've seen, ingesting large amounts of investment information can lead to worse rather than better decisions because the Affect working with other cognitive heuristics, such as representativeness and availability, takes over.

In the next chapter, you'll see that forecasting, the heart of security analysis, which selects stocks precisely by the methods we are questioning, misses the mark time and again. We'll also see that the favorite stocks and industries of large groups of professional investors have fared worse than the averages for many decades. This is the primary reason for the subpar performance of professionals over time that was witnessed by the efficient-market researchers in Part II, rather than the EMH myth of rational automatons who make flawless decisions that keep markets efficient.

To outdo the market, then, we must first have a good idea of the forces that victimize even the pros. Once those forces are understood, investors can build defenses and find routes to skirt the pitfalls.

How Much Is Too Much?

Under conditions of complexity and uncertainty, experts demand as much information as possible to assist them in their decision making.

Seems logical. Naturally, there is tremendous demand for such incremental information on the Street because investors believe that the increased dosage gives them a shot at the big money. But, as I have indicated earlier, that information "edge" may not help you. A large number of studies show rather conclusively that giving an expert more information doesn't do much to improve his judgment.[7]

In a study of what appears to be a favored class of human guinea pigs, clinical psychologists were given background information on a large number of cases and asked what they thought their chances were of being right on each one. As the amount of information increased, the diagnosticians' confidence rose dramatically, but their accuracy continued to be low. At a low level of information, they estimated that they would be correct 33 percent of the time; their accuracy was actually 26 percent. When the information was increased fourfold, they expected to be correct in 53 percent of the cases; in fact, they were right 28 percent of the time, an increase of only 2 percentage points.

Interestingly, the finding seems universal: only a marginal improvement in accuracy occurs as increasing amounts of new information are heaped on. The same results were obtained using racetrack handicappers. Eight veteran handicappers were progressively given five to forty pieces of the information they considered important in picking winners. One study showed that their confidence rose directly with the amount of information received, but the number of winners, alas, did not.[8]

As the studies demonstrate, people in situations of uncertainty are generally overconfident on the basis of the information available to them, believing they are right much more often than they are. One of the earliest demonstrations of overconfidence involved the predictive power of interviews. Many people think a short interview is sufficient for making reasonable predictions about a person's behavior. Analysts, for example, frequently gauge company managers through meetings lasting less than an hour. Extensive research indicates that such judgments are often wrong. One interesting example took place at the Harvard Business School. The school thought that by interviewing candidates beforehand, it could recruit students who would earn higher grades. In fact, the candidates selected that way did worse than students accepted on their academic credentials alone. Nevertheless, superficial impressions are hard to shake and often dominate behavior.

Overconfidence, according to cognitive psychologists, has many implications. A number of studies indicate that when a problem is relatively simple to diagnose, experts are realistic about their ability to solve it. When the problem becomes more complex, however, and the solution depends on a number of hard-to-quantify factors, they became overconfident of their ability to reach a solution (accuracy 61 percent). If the task is impossible—for example, distinguishing European from American handwriting—they became "superoverconfident" (accuracy 51 percent).[9]

A large number of other studies demonstrate that people are consistently overconfident when forming strong impressions from limited knowledge. Lawyers, for example, tend to overestimate their chances of winning in court. If both sides in a court case are asked who will win, each will say its chances of winning are greater than 50 percent.[10] Studies of clinical psychologists,[11] physicians,[12] engineers,[13] negotiators,[14] and security analysts[15] have all shown they are far too confident in the accuracy of their predictions. Clinical psychologists, for instance, believed their diagnosis was accurate 90 percent of the time, when in fact it was correct in only 50 percent of cases. As one observer said of expert prediction, "[It] is often wrong but rarely in doubt."

The same overconfidence occurs when experienced writers or academics working on books or research papers estimate the time of completion. The estimates are invariably overconfident; the books and papers are completed months or years behind schedule, and sometimes they are not completed at all.

Studies in cognitive psychology also indicate that people are overconfident that their forecasts will be correct. The typical result is that respondents are correct in only 80 percent of the cases when they describe themselves as 99 percent sure[16]—not what you'd exactly want in a stress test or another health-critical test result.

The question becomes even more interesting when experts are compared with laypeople. A number of studies show that when the predictability of a problem is reasonably high, the experts are generally more accurate than laypeople. Expert bridge players, for example, proved much more capable of assessing the odds of winning a particular hand than average players.[17] When predictability is very low, however, experts are more prone to overconfidence than novices. When experts predict highly complex situations—for example, the future of troubled European Union countries such as Portugal and Greece, the impact of religious fundamentalists on foreign policy in the Middle East, or the movement of the stock market—they usually demonstrate overconfidence. Because of the richness of information available to them, they believe they have the advantage in their area of expertise. Laypeople with a very limited understanding of the subject, on the other hand, are normally more conservative in their judgments.[18]

Overconfident experts are legion on the investment scene. Wall Street places immense faith in detailed analysis by its experts. In-depth research houses turn out thousands upon thousands of reports, each running to a hundred pages or more and sprinkled with dozens of tables and charts. They set up Washington and international listening posts to catch the slightest whiff of change in government policies or economic conditions abroad. The latest turn here, now being investigated by the SEC, is to hire former corporate executives from major companies they follow to give them "the real scoop" on "what's going on" inside. Scores of conferences are naturally called to provide money managers with this penetrating understanding. All too often they have proved to be "wrong in depth," as one skeptic put it.

The more detailed the level of knowledge, the more effective the expert is considered to be. Despite widespread concerns from 2005 through 2007, major bankers and investment bankers, including Citigroup, Lehman Brothers, and Goldman Sachs, stated emphatically that there was no sign of a bubble in the housing market. They continued to sell subprime toxic waste, including part of their own inventory, by the tens of billions of dollars to their own clients, until the subprime markets completely dried up in mid-2007. To survive, many were forced to ask for a bailout, which was organized by Hank Paulson, the Treasury secretary and ex-CEO of Goldman Sachs. As with the clinical psychologists and the handicappers, the information available had little to do with accurately predicting the outcome.

The inferior investment performance we've seen, as well as more that we will look at next, was based on just such detailed research. To quote a disillusioned money manager of the early 1970s, "You pick the top [research] house on the Street and the second top house on the Street—they all built tremendous reputation, research-in-depth, but they killed their clients."[19] Nothing much has changed.

I offer a Psychological Guideline for investing that is applicable in almost any other field of endeavor:

PSYCHOLOGICAL GUIDELINE 7: Respect the difficulty of working with a mass of information. Few of us can use it successfully. In-depth information does not translate into in-depth profits.

I hope it is becoming apparent that configural relationships are extremely complex. Stock market investors are dealing not with twenty-four or forty-eight relevant interactions but with an astronomical number. As we have already seen, far fewer inputs can overtax the configural or interactive judgment of experts. Because most Wall Street experts, like those elsewhere, are unaware of these psychological findings, they remain convinced that their problems can be handled if only those few extra facts are available. They overload with information, which doesn't help their thinking but makes them more confident and therefore more vulnerable to making serious errors. The difficulty of configural reasoning is unfortunately almost unknown by both investors and EMH theorists.

Overconfidence Takes a Bow

As we saw earlier, the phenomenon of overconfidence seems to be both an Affect and a cognitive bias. In other words, the mind is probably designed to extract as much information as possible from whatever is available. The filtering process, as we saw in chapter 3, is anything but a passive process that provides a good representation of the real world. Rather, we actively exclude information "that is not in the scope of our attention." [20] It thus provides only a small part of the total necessary to build an accurate forecast in uncertain conditions.

Evaluating stocks is no different. Under conditions of anxiety and uncertainty, with a vast interacting web of partial information, it becomes a giant Rorschach test. The investor sees any pattern he or she wishes. In fact, according to recent research in configural processing, investors can find patterns that aren't there—a phenomenon called illusory correlation.

Trained psychologists, for example, were given background information on psychotics and were also given drawings allegedly made by them but actually prepared by the researchers. With remarkable consistency, the psychologists saw in the drawings the cues that they expected to see: muscular figures drawn by men worried about their masculinity or big eyes by suspicious people. But not only were those characteristics not stressed in the drawings; in many cases they were less pronounced than usual.[21] Because the psychologists focused on the anticipated aberrations, they missed important correlations that were actually present.[22]

Investors attempt to simplify and rationalize complexity that seems at times impenetrable. Often they notice facts that are simply coincidental and think they have found correlations. If they buy the stock in the "correlation" and it goes up, they will continue to invest in it through many a loss. The market thus provides an excellent field for illusory correlation. The head-and-shoulders formation on a chart cuts through thousands of disparate facts that the chartist believes no one can analyze; buying growth stocks simplifies an otherwise bewildering range of investment alternatives. Such methods, which seemed to work in the past, are pervasive on Wall Street. The EMH theorists' search for the correlation between volatility and returns that the theory demands seems to be another example. The problem is that some of the correlations are illusory and others are chance. Trusting in them begets error. A chartist may have summed it up most appropriately: "If I hadn't made money some of the time, I would have acquired market wisdom quicker."

Which brings us to the next Psychological Guideline, one that may at first glance appear simple but is important and will prove harder to follow than you may think!

PSYCHOLOGICAL GUIDELINE 8: Don't make an investment decision based on correlations. All correlations in the market, whether real or illusory, will shift and soon disappear.

This is important for the investor: if analysts are generally optimistic, there will be a large number of disappointments created not by events but by initially seeing the company or industry through rose-colored glasses.

The late Amos Tversky, a pioneer in cognitive psychology, researched expert overoptimism and overconfidence in the stock market. According to Tversky, "In one study, analysts were asked such questions as what is the probability that the price of a given stock will exceed $X by a given date. On average, analysts were 80% confident but only 60% accurate in their assessments."[23] The study was repeated numerous times.

In other studies, analysts were asked for their high and low estimates of the price of a stock. The high estimate was to be a number they were

95 percent sure the actual price would fall below; the low estimate was the price they were 95 percent sure the stock would remain above. Thus, the high and low estimates should have included 90 percent of the cases, which is to say that if the analysts were realistic and unbiased, the number of price movements above and below this range would be 10 percent. In fact, the estimates missed the range 35 percent of the time, or three and a half times as often as estimated.

Tversky went on to note that "rather than operating on rational expectations"—with total logic, unaffected by behavior, as efficient-market theory assumes investors do—"people are commonly biased in several directions: they are optimistic; they overestimate the chances that they will succeed, and they overestimate their degree of knowledge, in the sense that their confidence far exceeds their 'hit rate.'"[24]

Tversky was queried about overconfidence at an investment behavioral conference in 1995 that I attended and also spoke at. The questioner asked what he thought of the fact that analysts were not very good at forecasting future earnings. He responded, in part, "From the standpoint of the behavioral phenomena . . . analysts should be more skeptical of their ability to predict [earnings] than they usually are. Time and time again, we learn that our confidence is misplaced, and our overconfidence leads to bad decisions, *so recognizing our limited ability to predict the future is an important lesson to learn*" (italics mine).[25]

He was asked at the same conference if analysts and other professional investors learn from their experiences. He replied that "unfortunately cognitive illusions are not easily unlearned. . . . The fact that in the real world people have not learned to eliminate . . . overconfidence speaks for itself."[26]

I'm afraid we're overconfident that we can overcome our tendency to be overconfident by simply recognizing that we tend to be overconfident. It's just not that simple, alas.

Analysts' Consistent Overoptimism

Given what we just saw, how optimistic do you think analysts' earnings estimates are? Jennifer Francis and Donna Philbrick studied analysts' estimates for some 918 stocks from the Value Line Investment Survey for the 1987–1989 period.[27] Value Line is well known on the Street for near-consensus forecasts. The researchers found that analysts were optimistic in their forecasts by 9 percent annually, on average. Again, remembering the devastating effect of even a small miss on high-octane stocks, these are very large odds against investors looking for ultraprecise earnings estimates.

The overoptimism of analysts is brought out even more clearly by I/B/E/S, the largest earnings-forecasting service, which monitors quarterly consensus forecasts on more than seven thousand domestic companies. Despite these allowable quarterly estimate changes, analysts tend to be optimistic, according to I/B/E/S. What seems apparent is that analysts do not sufficiently revise their optimistically biased forecasts in the first half of the year and then almost triple the size of their revisions, usually downward, in the second half. Even so, their forecasts of earnings are still too high at year-end.

A study that Eric Lufkin[28] of Morgan Stanley and I collaborated on for my *Forbes* column some years back (January 26, 1998) provided further evidence of analysts' overoptimism. I updated the study to the end of 2006 in Table 7-1. The study measures analysts' and economists' estimates against the actual S&P reported earnings from 1988 to 2006, a nineteen-year period, which saw more than its share of bubbles and crashes, as well as economic booms and recessions. Analysts make "bottom-up" estimates; that is, they look at all the important fundamentals of a company and then make their estimate for a stock. They forecast company by company and then the companies are added up, with the proper weighting in the S&P 500 index for each, to arrive at a forecast. Economists, on the other hand, make "top-down forecasts"; that is, they look at the economy and then decide how their overall forecasts will trickle down to individual company estimates. A glance across each year shows the percentage increase or decrease in earnings the analysts forecast in column 2, those the economists forecast in column 3, and the actual increase or decrease in earnings that the S&P 500 showed for the year in column 4.

What is striking is how overly optimistic the estimates by both analysts and economists actually are. To be fair, let's look at analysts' and economists' estimates over the entire nineteen years of the study and then compare them with the actual earnings of the S&P 500. As Table 7-1 shows, the average estimate for analysts was a 21 percent increase in earnings, the average for economists was 18 percent, and the actual earn-

Table 7-1
Taking Advantage of Overreaction
Analysts' and Economists' Earnings Growth Estimates for the S&P 500, 1988–2006

Year*	Analysts	Economists	Actual
1988	30%	15%	36%
1989	10%	4%	−4%
1990	14%	12%	−7%
1991	2%	7%	−25%
1992	38%	49%	20%
1993	23%	36%	15%
1994	39%	29%	39%
1995	11%	5%	11%
1996	18%	12%	14%
1997	20%	5%	3%
1998	14%	14%	−5%
1999	28%	15%	28%
2000	8%	7%	4%
2001	17%	19%	−51%
2002	57%	50%	15%
2003	44%	39%	72%
2004	19%	10%	20%
2005	8%	11%	19%
2006	−2%	0%	17%
Average	21%	18%	12%
Average Annual Percentage Error*	81%	53%	

*Estimates made in January each year.

Source: © David Dreman, 2011. Data Sources: I/B/E/S and Thomson First Call.

ings increase for the S&P was 12 percent. As column 3 demonstrates, economists—supposedly charter members of the "dismal science"—made earnings forecasts that were overoptimistic by an astounding 53 percent (over S&P reported earnings) annually on average over the nineteen-year period. Could anything be worse? Why, yes: analysts were overoptimistic by 81 percent annually on average over that time, an enormously high miss. The study evidence: earnings forecasting is neither an art nor a science but a lethal financial virus.

What makes analysts so optimistic? The subject is anything but academic because it is precisely this undue optimism that induces many people, including large numbers of pros, to buy stocks they recommend. As we have seen in the recent examples and will see more thoroughly in the chapters ahead, unwarranted optimism exacts a fearful price. A Psychological Guideline is again in order:

PSYCHOLOGICAL GUIDELINE 9: Analysts' forecasts are usually overly optimistic. Make the appropriate downward adjustment to your earnings estimate.

Now, there are people with outstanding gifts for abstract reasoning who can cut through enormously complex situations. Every field has its William Miller or Bill Gross. But such people are rare. It seems, then, that the information-processing capabilities and the standards of abstract reasoning required by current investment methods are too complicated for the majority of us, professional or amateur, to use accurately.

A Surefire Way to Lose Money

At this point, you might be wondering if I'm exaggerating the problems of decision making and forecasting in the stock market. The answer, I think, can be found by considering the favorite investments of market professionals over time.

Consider a large international conference of institutional investors held at the New York Hilton in February 1968. Hundreds of delegates were polled about the stock that would show outstanding appreciation that year. The favorite was University Computing, the highest-octane performer of the day. From a price of $443, it dropped 88 percent in less than twelve months. At an *Institutional Investor* conference in the winter of 1972, the airlines were expected to perform the best for the balance of the year. Then, within 1 percent of their highs, their stocks fell 50 percent that year in the face of a sharply rising market. The conference the following year voted them a group to avoid. In another conference, in 1999, a large group of professionals polled picked Enron as the outstanding performer for the next twelve months. We all know what happened to that hot stock.

Are those results simply chance? In an earlier book, *The New Contrarian Investment Strategy* (1982), I included fifty-two surveys of how the favorite stocks of large numbers of professional investors had fared over the fifty-one-year period between 1929 and 1980. The number of professionals participating ranged from twenty-five to several thousand. The median was well over a hundred. Wherever possible, the professionals' choices were measured against the S&P 500 for the next twelve months.*

Eighteen of the studies measured the performance of five or more stocks the experts picked as their favorites.[29] Diversifying into a number of stocks, instead of one or two, will reduce the element of chance. Yet the eighteen portfolios chosen underperformed the market on sixteen occasions! This meant, in effect, that when a client received professional advice about those stocks, they would underperform the market almost nine times out of ten. Flipping a coin would give you a fifty-fifty chance of beating the market.

The other thirty-four samples did little better. Overall, the favorite stocks and industries of large groups of money managers and analysts did worse than the market on forty of fifty-two occasions, or 77 percent of the time.

But those surveys, although extending over fifty years, ended in 1980. Has expert stock picking improved since then? *The Wall Street Journal* conducted a poll on whether the choices of four well-known professionals could outperform the market each year between 1986 and 1993. At the end of the year, four pros gave their five favorite picks for the next year to John Dorfman, the editor of the financial section, who reviewed them twelve months later, eliminating the two lowest performers and adding two fresh experts. In sixteen of thirty-two cases, the portfolios underperformed the market—a somewhat better result than in the past, but no better than the toss of a coin.[30] †

Table 7-2 gives the results of all such surveys that I found through 1993. As the table shows, only 25 percent of the surveys of the experts' "best" stocks outperformed the market. The findings startled me. Though I knew that experts make mistakes, I didn't know that the magnitude of the errors was as striking or as consistent as the results make evident.

But some of the studies go back to the 1920s, and the last one ends in 1993. Has stock picking improved since then? After all, in the past fifteen years, the performance of professional investors has been more carefully

---

* Several studies used different averages and time periods.

† I was one of the experts for six years. Over that period, I used the contrarian strategies we will look at, and my portfolios outperformed the market in five of the six years I participated, from 1987 to 1992, with a combined gain of 156 percent versus 120 percent for the market.

Table 7-2
Experts' Forecasts of Favorite Stocks and Industries

Time Span	Source of Surveys	Total Surveys	Percent of Surveys Underperforming Market in Next Year
1929–32	Cowles Surveys	3	100
1953–76	Trusts and Estates	21	67
1967–69	Financial Analysts Journal	1	100
1967–72	California Business	7	71
1969–73	Institutional Investor	7	100
1973	BusinessWeek	2	50
1974	Seminar (Edson Gould)	2	100
1974	Callan Associates	4	100
1974–76	Mueller Surveys	4	75
1980	Financial World "All-Stars"	1	100
1986–93	The Wall Street Journal	8	50
Total number of surveys		60	
Percent of professional surveys *underperforming* **the market**			75

Note: Dividends excluded in all comparisons.
Source: © David Dreman, 2011. Reprinted from *Contrarian Investment Strategies: The Next Generation.*

scrutinized than ever before. As we saw in chapters 1 and 2, money managers as a group have not outperformed the market. Another study done by Advisor Perspectives for the ten years ending December 31, 2007, analyzed how stocks in the S&P domestic indices performed against the S&P benchmark index. As Table 7-3 shows, using one of the S&P indices as a benchmark, the S&P indices outperformed the stocks in six of the nine sectors and tied once.

In only one case, the S&P 500/Citigroup Growth, did the mutual funds significantly outperform the S&P index. In brief, the averages beat the money managers two-thirds of the time over the ten-year period.

Finally, for the five years ending in 2009, the S&P 500 Index outperformed 60.8 percent of actively managed large-cap U.S. equity funds, the S&P MidCap 400 index outperformed 77.2 percent of midcap funds, and the S&P Small-Cap 600 index outperformed 66.6 percent of small-cap funds.

The studies now in place as a group for more than seventy-five years clearly demonstrate just how badly money managers and analysts under-

Index	Annualized Performance %	Index Performance Rank	Index Outperformance Versus Active Managers %	Abbreviation
S&P Mid-Cap 400	11.2	1	78	MC (Mid Core)
S&P Mid-Cap 400 Growth	11.1	2	72	MG (Mid Growth)
S&P Mid-Cap 400 Value	11.1	3	70	MV (Mid Value)
S&P Small-Cap 600 Value	9.0	4	53	SV (Small Value)
S&P Small-Cap 600	9.0	5	61	SC (Small Core)
S&P Small-Cap 600 Growth	8.2	6	50	SG (Small Growth)
S&P 500/Citigroup Value	6.6	7	46	LV (Large Value)
S&P 500	5.9	8	60	LC (Large Core)
S&P 500/Citigroup Growth	4.8	9	35	LG (Large Growth)

Table 7-3
Ten Years Ended 2007

Note: S&P growth and value index returns use the Barra methodology from 1998–2005 and the Citigroup methodology for 2006–2007.

Source: © Copyright 2009, Advisor Perspectives, Inc.

performed the market. They also clearly demonstrate that professional investors, in the large majority of cases, were tugged toward the popular stocks of the day, usually near their peaks, and, like most investors, steered away from unpopular, underpriced issues, as the subsequent year's market action indicated. Also interesting is that one industry—technology—was favored over the years, although there were dozens to choose from. And it was favored so unsuccessfully! Experts' advice, in these surveys at least, clearly led investors to overpriced issues and away from the better values.

What can we make of these results? The number of samples seems far too large for the outcome to be simply chance. The evidence indicates a surprisingly high level of error among professionals in choosing stocks and portfolios over six and a half decades.

The failure rate among financial professionals, at times approaching 90 percent, indicates not only that errors are made but that under uncertain conditions there must be systematic and predictable forces working against unwary investors.

Yet again, such evidence is obviously incompatible with the central assumption of the efficient-market hypothesis.[31] Far more important is the practical implication of what we have just seen, another plausible explanation of why fundamental methods often don't work. Investment theory demands too much from people as configural and information processors. Under conditions of information overload, both within and outside markets, our mental tachometers surge far above the red line. When this happens, we no longer process information reliably. Our confidence rises as our input of information increases, but our decisions do not improve. This leads to another Psychological Guideline.

PSYCHOLOGICAL GUIDELINE 10: Tread carefully with current investment methods. Our limitations in processing complex information prevent their successful use by most of us.

Though it is probably true that experts do as poorly under other complex circumstances, market professionals unfortunately work in a gold-fish bowl. In no other profession I am aware of is the outcome of decisions so easily measurable.

In examining the stock-picking record of money managers and other market pros, a critical question is: how accurate are analysts' earnings estimates? Those are the key elements underlying stock selections and the heart of investing as it is practiced today. That's the question to be examined next. The results of some very thorough studies on the accuracy of the top security analysts, the cream of the crop, will surprise you.

Chapter 8

How Big a Long Shot Will You Play?

IN THE EARLY 1970s, when I was an analyst, nothing was online. Nada. Zilch. Today, the analysts at major brokerage houses have immediate access to competitors' reports, estimate changes, and volumes of other information. There is exponentially more information available now than back then. It's like moving from a hand-cranked telephone to the latest iPhone. Yet in spite of the information revolution, there is every reason to believe, as we'll soon see, that earnings estimate errors remain enormously high, much too high to be of any use in determining the intrinsic value of most stocks. It isn't a matter of my colleagues in the industry not giving their all, either. Rather, as you undoubtedly know, iPhone-equipped or not, forecasting is far from an exact science. The weather forecaster who sends you out for a sunny day only to leave you drenched in an afternoon shower has more in common with a Wall Street security analyst than you might think.

If you're like me, you'll occasionally take a chance at winning a reasonable poker pot. But more generally, how big a long shot will people play? When analysts like an idea, it can be off the chart. As we saw in chapter 2, if players think they are going to win, they'll readily pay the same price for a lottery ticket whether the odds are 10,000 to 1 or 10 million to 1 against winning. As we also saw, the possibility of winning, rather than the probability of doing so, can cause very low odds to carry great weight, even when the probabilities against the players are increased by 1,000 times.

Are those people daft? Maybe a little, but, as we have seen, many investors have played with the same odds in every bubble and mania that we've looked at. They also play with odds that are against them—certainly not as spectacular but still high—in far more tranquil markets. Why do they do it so consistently?

If you watch an early-morning market show on CNBC or Bloomberg or read *The Wall Street Journal* to start the day, you have undoubtedly noticed that the anchors or reporters attentively listen to or write about the advice of a collection of well-dressed men and women who seem to know everything about the markets. In this chapter, we'll examine the reliability of the advice of this chic group who happen to be security analysts. Breaking news in the financial media is often an analyst's raising or lowering his or her earnings estimates of a stock or industry. Upgrades or downgrades are listened to carefully, even when we don't know a company's name or industry. Changes in analysts' estimates on major companies are showstoppers that freeze people in their tracks. If the downgrade or upgrade is major, it can move the stock and its industry noticeably.

The people whom the media cover so attentively consider themselves to be hardheaded realists, not pointy-headed theoreticians. They're immersed in the reality of daily market action, not writing math equations and running computer simulations, and they are confident that they are offering analytically tried-and-true expert advice to investors. Fair enough. Let's put them to the test and track their actual performance. Their estimates and recommendations are the crucial factor the majority of investors look at when deciding what stocks to buy, hold, or sell. It's time for us to analyze if CNBC, Bloomberg, or other media are giving us any more consistently accurate information than the Weather Channel.

◼ Forecasting Follies 1: Predicting Company Earnings

Although they don't agree on many issues, Wall Streeters and financial academics concur that company earnings are the major determinants of stock prices. Modern security analysis centers on predicting stock movements from precise earnings estimates. As a result, major brokerage houses still have eight-figure research budgets and hire top analysts to provide accurate estimates. The largest bank trust departments, mutual funds, hedge funds, and money managers demand the "best" because of the hundreds of millions of dollars in commissions they command.

Several decades ago, *Institutional Investor* magazine formalized the process of determining the "best" analysts. Each year the magazine selects an "All-Star" team made up of the "top" analysts in all the important industries—biotech, computers, telecommunications, pharmaceuticals, and chemicals—after polling hundreds of financial institutions. There are first, second, and third teams, as well as runners-up for each industry. The magazine portrays the team on its cover each year, often dressed in football uniforms with the brokerage firm's name on each star's jersey. The competition to make the teams is fierce, as we'll see later in this chapter.

If a brokerage firm can boast a number of All-Stars, its profitability ratchets up accordingly. Some years back, the managing partners and the director of research of a large brokerage house decided to let one of their analysts go. The office executioner was on his way to inform the analyst when the research director came running down the corridor, grabbed his arm, and, gasping for breath, said, "Wait . . . we can't do it . . . he just made the second team."

Salary scales, as you may guess, are in the stratosphere. Experienced analysts make between $700,000 and $800,000 a year; standouts receive more. Then there is the million-dollar-a-year club, which includes several dozen of the Street's outstanding oracles. Incomewise, they are in a class with popular entertainers and professional athletes.

Some analysts earn in the eight figures, exceeding the pay of a number of CEOs of Fortune 500 companies. Jack Grubman, the once highly regarded telecommunications analyst, jumped ship from PaineWebber to Salomon Brothers in the mid-1990s. The price was a two-year contract with annual pay of $2.5 million. The salary was so high that his research colleagues jokingly referred to underwritings of the firm being offered to its clients in "Grubman units" of $2.5 million each. Needless to say, Wall Streeters often accord top analysts the same hero worship that teenagers reserve for rock stars and film heroes.

The hero worship diminished sometime after the dot-com collapse in 2002, when SEC and state investigations of major analysts produced disturbing results. In late April 2003, the SEC and New York State regulators released thousands of documents that showed that the traditional rules of the Street had been violated, and the "Chinese Walls" supposedly keeping bankers from influencing the work of security analysts came tumbling down. Although the investigations focused on two of Wall Street's most highly paid and powerful analysts, Jack Grubman of Salomon Smith Barney* and Henry Blodget of Merrill Lynch, it rapidly expanded to many dozens of other analysts. E-mails and other documents showed that many analysts had been pressured into giving favorable ratings to weak companies, a good number of which were wobbly Internet firms with almost no business plans, revenues, or viable platforms. Because underwriting IPOs had become so profitable during the dot-com bubble in the late 1990s, the pressure to serve major corporate clients rather than retail clients was overwhelming. In the mad scramble to bring in billions of dollars of investment banking fees from IPOs, analysts spoke in double-talk. Publicly they heaped praise on shaky companies they followed, rating them as strong or even "screaming" buys. In e-mails to investment banking clients they mocked the same firms, calling them "pigs," "junk," "crap," and much worse. A distinct pecking order existed. Retail clients were encouraged by the analyst to buy these poor-quality issues, often at a substantial premium from where they were issued, while institutional investors were sometimes tipped off to stay well clear. Henry Blodget had a buy recommendation out on GoTo, a dot-com stock. When an institutional heavy hitter asked him what he liked about the company, Blodget flippantly replied that there was "nuthin" interesting about the issue except for the large investment banking fees Merrill was getting.[1] Bad as it was, this game was only penny ante for some of the more serious analysts.

Jack Grubman was among the masters. Grubman was always negative on AT&T, but Citigroup CEO Sandy Weill "asked" him to take a fresh look at his rating of the company, which he had previously never recommended. "Asked," in this case, implied funneling millions of extra

---

* Now a subsidiary of Citigroup.

bonus dollars to Grubman if he went along. Rumor at the time had it that AT&T's chairman would not let Citigroup participate in a major forthcoming underwriting unless Grubman, who carried enormous weight in the communications sector, upgraded the stock. Grubman, under Weill's watchful eye, upgraded the stock to a buy near its peak in 1999. Shortly thereafter, Citigroup earned $63 million in underwriting fees when AT&T spun off its wireless unit.

By 2002, all this had changed. Mom-and-pop investors were being clobbered on WorldCom and other telecom stocks that Grubman insisted on rating highly as markets collapsed. Suspicion rose that he was aiding Citigroup's investment banking efforts, particularly with the scandal-ridden WorldCom, which generated very large investment banking fees as it continued a major acquisition program. Citigroup was estimated to have made $1 billion in fees generated by Grubman from its investment banking subsidiaries, while shareholders lost $2 *trillion* in the telecom scandal alone.[2]

(Grubman resigned under suspicion in August 2002. He received $30 million in severance pay from Citigroup's brokerage subsidiary, and by mutual agreement, Citi continued to pay his legal bills.)

In the ensuing settlement with Eliot Spitzer, the New York State attorney general, Citigroup and ten other banks settled charges of conflicts of interest for $1.4 billion. Four hundred million dollars of that amount came from Citigroup. In a separate settlement with Spitzer and the SEC, Grubman was banned from the securities business for life, as was Henry Blodget. Ironically—or perhaps not—almost all of the surviving brokerage and investment banking firms were bailed out by TARP in 2008 with taxpayer funds that came in part from retail investors including, by then, the struggling "moms and pops" who bought the bad analysts' recommendations.

It's amazing how quickly we forget. By the mid-2000s, our trust in analysts' forecasting abilities had been completely restored. Needless to say, "the elite," selected by *Institutional Investor* from over 15,000 analysts across the country, are sensational stock pickers.

Aren't they?

Financial World measured the analysts' results some years back.[3] The article stated, "It was not an easy task. Most brokerage houses were reluctant to release the batting averages of their superstars."[4] In many cases, the results were obtained from outside sources, such as major clients, and then "only grudgingly." After months of digging, the magazine came up with the recommendations of twenty superstars. The conclusion: "Heroes were few and far between—during the period in question, the market rose 14.1%. If you had purchased or sold 132 stocks they recommended when they told you to, your gain would have been only 9.3%," some 34 percent worse than selecting stocks by flipping coins. The magazine added, "Of the hundred and thirty-two stocks the superstars recommended, only 42, or just ⅓, beat the S&P 500." A large institutional buyer of research summed it up: "In hot markets the analysts . . . get brave at just the wrong time and cautious just at the wrong time. It's uncanny when they say one thing and start doing the opposite."[5]

In addition to superstars, professional investors rely on earnings forecasting services such as I/B/E/S, Zacks, Investment Research, and First Call, which have online features that give the pros instant revisions of estimates. First Call provides a service that also gives money managers, as well as competing analysts, all analysts' reports immediately upon their release. Many of the reports deal with forecast changes. More than 1,000 companies are covered.

The requirement for precise earnings estimates has been increasing in recent years. Missing the analysts' estimates by pennies can send a stock's price down sharply. Better-than-expected earnings can send prices soaring. How good, then, are the estimates? We've already seen that the performance of the *Institutional Investor*'s "All-Stars" has been anything but inspiring. But that was for only a one-year period. Nobody's perfect, after all. Was it just a onetime slip? A fluke? Or do we see a black swan gliding slowly across the waters toward us? This answer will be important to the investment strategies considered in the chapters ahead.

▇ Forecasting Follies 2: The Long-Term Record

Updating the work in *The New Contrarian Investment Strategy,* as well as a number of articles in *Forbes* and elsewhere,[6] I did a study in collaboration with Michael Berry of James Madison University on analysts' surprises— how much their forecasts missed actual earnings forecasts—that was published in *Financial Analysts Journal* in May–June 1995.[7] It examined brokerage analysts' quarterly forecasts of earnings as compared with earnings actually reported between 1973 and 1991, which I subsequently updated to 2010. Estimates for the quarter were almost always made in the previous three months, and analysts could revise their estimates up to two weeks before the end of the quarter. In all, 216,576 consensus forecasts[8] were used, and we required at least four separate analysts' estimates before including a stock in the study.[9] Larger companies, such as Microsoft or Apple, might have as many as thirty or forty estimates. More than 1,500 New York Stock Exchange, NASDAQ, and AMEX companies were included, and on average, there were about 1,000 companies in the sample. The study was, to my knowledge, the most comprehensive on analyst forecasting to date.[10]

How do analysts do at this game, where even slight errors can result in instant wipeouts? A glance at Figure 8-1 tells all. The results are startling: analysts' estimates were sharply and consistently off the mark, even though they were made less than three months before the end of the quarter for which actual earnings were reported. The average error for the sample was a whopping 40 percent annually. Again, this was no small sample; it included more than 800,000 individual analysts' estimates.

Interestingly, these large errors are occurring in the midst of the in-

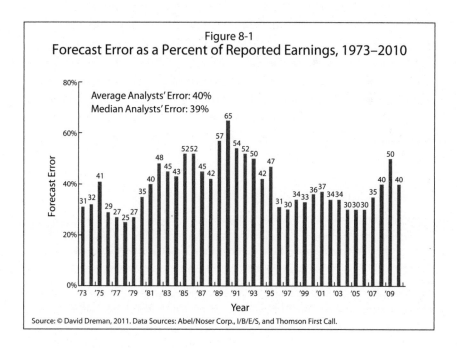

Figure 8-1
Forecast Error as a Percent of Reported Earnings, 1973–2010

Source: © David Dreman, 2011. Data Sources: Abel/Noser Corp., I/B/E/S, and Thomson First Call.

formation revolution. Yet in spite of this fact, estimated errors remain enormously high—much too high to be of any use in determining the real value of most stocks. Yes, the margin of error simply swamps any chance of accurately determining earnings!

Since many market professionals believe that a forecast error of even plus or minus 3 percent is large enough to trigger a major price movement, what did an average miss of 54 percent in 1991 or an average error of 40 percent over the past thirty-eight years do? When we look at sharp price drops on sizzling stocks after analysts' misses of only a few percent, it becomes apparent that even small estimate errors can be dangerous to your investment health. Yet that is precisely how the game is played on the Street by analysts, large mutual funds, pension funds, and other institutional investors, and swallowed by average investors.

You might wonder whether the results are skewed by a few large errors. To check for that kind of skew, we measured earnings surprises four different ways.[11] In all cases, errors were high. What about surprises from companies that report small or nominal earnings? A miss of the same amount would obviously result in a higher percentage error for companies reporting very small earnings per share compared to those reporting much higher earnings per share. If, for example, the estimate was $1.00 and the company actually reported 93 cents, the miss would be 7.5 percent. But if the estimate was 10 cents and the company reported only 3 cents, the miss would be 233 percent.*

No matter how we analyzed it, the slightest error in the earnings forecast had a disproportionate effect on the fortunes of a company's stock, irrespective of other measures of the company's soundness or management performance.

---

* To measure this effect, we analyzed a subset of the stocks in Figure 8-1 that eliminated all companies that reported earnings in the plus or minus 10-cent range to prevent large percentage errors in this group from distorting the study. The problem is that many of the fastest-growing small companies report earnings of 30 to 50 cents a share annually, which could translate into 7.5 to 12.5 cents quarterly. Large companies in this range were also eliminated. Even with this ultraconservative method, the average forecast error was 20.5 percent on average, more than quadruple the size that market pros believe could set off a major price reaction.

■ Forecasting Follies 3: Missing the Consensus Forecast

I'm sure that many readers know only too well what happens when a stock misses the consensus forecast by much. E*Trade, a former dot-com favorite, tumbled 42 percent in late April 2009, when earnings came in a little more than 4 percent below estimates. Akomai Technologies dropped 19 percent in July 2009, when earnings came in 2 percent below forecast. Symantec fell 14 percent in July 2009, when reported earnings were 4 percent under estimates. But this was not a one-way street; Amazon.com rose 33 percent in October 2009, when earnings came in 36 percent above forecast. All this occurred in a market that went up over 20 percent that year.

Earnings surprises, as you would suspect, have had a major impact on stocks over time. During the Internet bubble, 3Com tumbled 45 percent when analysts' forecasts missed reported earnings by a scant 1 percent in 1997. Sun Microsystems dropped 30 percent on a 6 percent shortfall. On May 30, 1997, Intel announced that its earnings for the June quarter would be sharply higher than in the corresponding 1996 quarter; however, they would be below the analysts' consensus forecast by 3 percent. This caused a price drop of 26 points, or 16 percent, on the opening, which reverberated first through technology stocks and then through the market as a whole. The result was that the S&P 500 lost $87 billion in minutes. People who relied on the estimates got clobbered—to say the least.

Again, one must ask if there are exceptions. How good is this dedicated and hardworking group at its members' vocation? As we just saw, earnings surprises of even a few percentage points can trigger major price reactions. Current investment practice demands estimates that are very close to—or dead-on—reported results. Normally, the higher the valuation of a stock, the more important the precision is. As noted, Street-smart pros normally expect reported earnings to be within a 3 percent range of the consensus estimate—and many demand better.

Is this doable? Look at Figure 8-2. We used our large database of 216,576 consensus estimates. To utilize a stock, we required at least four analysts' estimates on it, bringing the total to 866,000 individual estimates at a minimum. Since a large number of stocks have more estimates—Apple, for example, has forty—I estimate that the total number of analysts participating in the estimates was well over one million for the thirty-eight years to the end of 2010.

Figure 8-2 summarizes our findings. We gave the analysts more leeway than most give themselves, widening the forecasting range from 3 percent to 5 percent to consider an estimate a miss. Even so, the results are devastating to believers in precise forecasts. The distribution of estimates clearly refutes their value to investors. Less than 30 percent of estimates were in the plus or minus 5 percent range of reported earnings that most pros deem absolutely essential. Using the plus or minus 10 percent error band, which many professional investors would argue is far too large, we found that only 47 percent of the consensus forecasts could be called accurate in the quarter. More than 53 percent missed this more lenient minimum range. Worse yet, only 58 percent of the consensus forecasts were within the plus or minus 15 percent band—a level that almost all Wall Streeters would call too high for any quarter.

Of what value are estimates that seriously miss the mark more than 50 percent or 70 percent of the time? After the horror stories precipitated when forecasts were off even minutely, the answer seems to be—not much. We have seen that estimates carefully prepared only three months in advance, by well-paid and diligent analysts, are notoriously inaccurate.

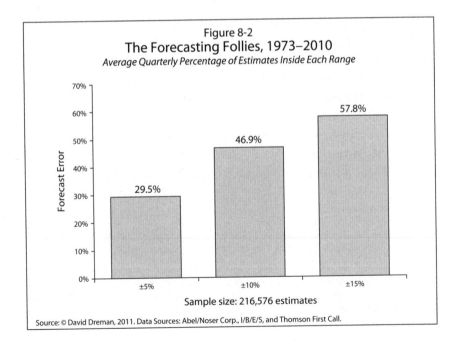

Figure 8-2
The Forecasting Follies, 1973–2010
Average Quarterly Percentage of Estimates Inside Each Range

Sample size: 216,576 estimates

Source: © David Dreman, 2011. Data Sources: Abel/Noser Corp., I/B/E/S, and Thomson First Call.

To complicate matters, many stocks sell not on today's earnings but on expected earnings years into the future. The analysts' chances of being on the money with their forecasts are not much higher than the chance of winning a major trifecta. Current investment practices seem to demand a precision that is impossible to deliver. Putting your money on these estimates means you are making a bet with the odds heavily against you. A Psychological Guideline is in order here.

PSYCHOLOGICAL GUIDELINE 11: The probability of achieving precise earnings estimates over time is minuscule. Do not use them as the major reason to buy or sell a stock.

Forecasting Follies 4: Industry Forecasts

"But maybe there's a reason for this," believers in their forecasting prowess might argue. "Analysts may not be able to hit the broad side of a barn overall, but that's because there are a lot of volatile industries out there that are impossible to forecast accurately. You can make good estimates where it counts, in stable, growing industries where appreciation is almost inevitable."

That's a plausible statement. We fed it into our computer, which digested the database and spat out the answer a few minutes later. We divided the same analysts' consensus estimates into twenty-four industry groups* and then measured the accuracy for each. The results are shown in Table 8-1. The industry error rates were smaller than those for forecasting individual companies but still almost six times as high as the 5 percent accuracy level most analysts consider too lenient. The average error was 28 percent and the median 26 percent. We also found that over the entire time period, almost 40 percent of all industries had analyst forecast

---

* The original study by Eric Lufkin covered the 1973–1996 period. Lufkin used a government industry classification system that was discontinued in the late 1990s. The industry taxonomy developed by Standard and Poor's (S&P) and Morgan Stanley Capital International (MSCI), called Global Industry Classification Standard (GICS), classifies industries more accurately for financial use. Historical data under the GICS system are available starting in the mid-1990s. However, Lufkin's results showed even higher industry forecast errors over that period, indicating that industry forecast errors over a thirty-eight-year period were large.

Table 8-1
Analyst Forecast Error by Industry Group, 1997–2010

24 Industry Groups
Average Industry Group Error: 28%
Median Industry Group Error: 26%

Industry	% Error	Industry	% Error
Automobiles and components	45%	Materials	33%
Banks	26%	Media	49%
Capital goods	23%	Pharmaceuticals, biotechnology, and	
Commercial and professional services	24%	life sciences	31%
Consumer durables and apparel	26%	Real estate	13%
Consumer services	27%	Retailing	26%
Diversified financials	20%	Semiconductors and semiconductor	
Energy	35%	equipment	34%
Food and staples retailing	23%	Software and services	31%
Food, beverage, and tobacco	22%	Technology, hardware, and equipment	35%
Health care equipment and services	21%	Telecommunication services	35%
Household and personal products	16%	Transportation	29%
Insurance	24%	Utilities	26%

Source: © David Dreman, 2011. Data Sources: Abel/Noser Corp., I/B/E/S, and Thomson First Call.

errors larger than 30 percent annually, while almost 10 percent of industries showed surprises larger than 40 percent.

As the chart shows, analysts' errors occurred indiscriminately across industries. Errors are almost as high for industries that are supposed to have clearly definable prospects, or "visibility," years into the future, such as computers or pharmaceuticals, as they are for industries where the outlooks are considered murky, such as autos or materials. This result is so consistent that we should call it a Psychological Guideline.

PSYCHOLOGICAL GUIDELINE 12: There are no highly predictable industries in which you can count on analysts' forecasts. Relying on their estimates will lead to trouble.

The high-visibility, high-growth industries have as many errors as the others. The fact that analysts miss the mark consistently in supposedly high-visibility industries—and give much higher valuations—suggests that those industries are often overpriced.

Finally, let's settle one remaining item of business regarding analysts' forecasts. Are they less accurate in a boom period or a recession, when earnings are presumably more difficult to calculate? Could this difference be a possible reason why their forecasts are not any better?

Forecasting Follies 5: Analysts' Forecasts in Booms and Busts

Our 1973–2010 study covered seven periods of business expansion and six periods of recession. If you think about it, you might expect to see analysts' forecasts too high in periods of recession, because earnings are dropping sharply, owing to economic factors that are impossible for analysts to predict. Conversely, in periods of expansion, estimates might be too low, as business is actually much better than economists and company managements anticipate. This certainly seems plausible and at first glance provides a partial explanation for the battered analysts' records. Unfortunately, it just ain't so, as Table 8-2 shows.

The table is broken into three columns: All Surprises, which is the average of all positive and negative surprises through the study; Positive Surprises; and Negative Surprises.[12] The surprises are shown for each period of business expansion or recession. The bottom row shows the average of all consensus forecasts for periods of both expansion and recession. The average surprise for expansionary periods, 39.2 percent, is little different from the average surprise through the entire period, 39.3 percent, or the average surprise of 43.9 percent in recessionary periods. Moreover, the averages of positive surprises in expansions and recessions are also very similar, 23.3 percent versus 26.0 percent, as are negative surprises, –66.0 percent versus –70.0 percent.

The statistical analysis demonstrates that economic conditions do not seem to magnify analysts' errors. They are about as frequent in periods of expansion or recession as they are at other times. What did come out clearly is that analysts are always optimistic; their forecasts are too optimistic in periods of recession, and this optimism doesn't decrease in periods of economic recovery or in more normal times. This last finding is not new. A number of research papers have been devoted to the subject of analyst optimism, as chapter 7 showed, and, with the exception of one that used far too short a period of time, all have come up with the same conclusion.[13] This is an important finding for the investor: if analysts are

Table 8-2
Analysts' Forecast Errors in Expansions and Recessions, 1973–2010

	All Surprises (Absolute value)	Positive Surprises	Negative Surprises
Expansions	39.2%	23.3%	−66.0%
Recessions	43.9%	26.0%	−70.0%
Full Sample (1973–2010)	39.3%	23.8%	−65.1%

All figures are average surprises.
Surprise = (Actual − Forecast) / |Actual|, in percent

Source: © David Dreman, 2011. Data Sources: Abel/Noser Corp., I/B/E/S, and Thomson First Call.

generally optimistic, there will be a large number of disappointments created not by events but by initially seeing the company or industry through rose-colored glasses, as we saw in chapter 7.

Forecasting Follies 6: What Does It All Mean?

We have found that large analyst forecast errors have been unacceptably high for a very long time. An error rate of 40 percent is frightful—much too high to be used by money managers or individual investors for selecting stocks. Remember, stock pickers believe they can fine-tune estimates well within a 3 percent range. But the studies show that the average error is more than thirteen times this size. Error rates of 10 to 15 percent make it impossible to distinguish growth stocks (with earnings increasing at a 20 percent clip) from average companies (with earnings growth of 7 percent) or even from also-rans (with earnings expanding at 4 percent). What, then, do error rates approaching 40 percent do?

Dropping companies with small earnings per share to avoid large percentage errors does not eliminate the problem; the error rate is still over 20 percent. Worse yet, analysts often err. Figure 8-2 showed that only 30 percent of consensus analysts' estimates fell within the 5 percent range of reported earnings. Remember, too, that many analysts think this range is too wide. Missing the 5 percent range would spell big trouble for stock pickers relying on precision estimates.

Unfortunately, the problems do not end here. Forecasting by industry was just as bad; the current studies to 2010 (and an earlier study between 1973 and 1996; see footnote, page 195) showed error rates almost indistinguishable between industries with supposedly excellent visibility, for which investors pay top dollar, and those considered to have dull prospects. If earnings estimates are not precise enough to weed out the also-rans from the real growth stocks, the question naturally arises why anyone would pay enormous premiums for "high-visibility" companies.

Finally, we have seen two additional problems with analysts' forecasts. First, the error rates are not due to the business cycle. Analysts' forecast errors are high in all stages of the cycle. Second, and more important, analysts have a strong optimistic bias in their forecasts. Not only are their errors high, but there is a consistent tendency to overestimate earnings. This is deadly when you pay a premium price for a stock. The towering forecast errors combined with analysts' optimism result in a high probability of disaster. As we saw, even a slight "miss" for stocks with supposedly excellent visibility has unleashed waves of selling, taking the prices down five or even ten times the percentage miss of the forecasting error itself.

The size and frequency of the forecasting errors call into question many important methods of choosing stocks that rely on finely tuned estimates running years into the future. Yet accurate earnings estimates are essential to most of the stock valuation methods we looked at in chapter 2. The intrinsic value theory, formulated by John Burr Williams, is based on forecasting earnings, cash flow, or dividends, often two decades or more ahead. The growth and momentum schools of investing also require finely calibrated, precise estimates many years into the future to justify the prices they pay for stocks. The higher the multiple, the greater the visibility of earnings demanded.

If the average forecast error is 40 percent annually, the chance of hitting a bull's-eye on an estimate ten years out seems extremely slim. Two important questions might be asked at this point. The first is whether efficient-market theorists and androidlike analysis keep prices where they should be by flawlessly processing key information accurately. The charts just presented indicate that the information input by analysts to make their estimates is anything but correctly processed. Given the results we've viewed, if serious errors are repeatedly made with the vital analytical inputs, what keeps markets efficient? Second, analysts do not learn from their errors, as we've seen for periods exceeding thirty years. Rational investors should adjust almost immediately to keep markets efficient. Why is this not done? Unfortunatley, a gaggle of black swans has landed in this chapter, detailing forecast errors that once again must be labeled "anomalies" to protect EMH. Which brings us to another Psychological Guideline.

PSYCHOLOGICAL GUIDELINE 13: Most current security analysis requires a precision in analysts' estimates that is impossible to provide. Avoid methods that demand this level of accuracy.

Forecasting Follies 7: Hey, I'm Special

What can we make of these results? If the evidence is so strong, why aren't more investors, particularly the pros, aware of it, and why don't they incorporate it into their methods, rather than quick-marching into an ambush? Why do Wall Streeters blithely overlook these findings as mere curiosities—simple statistics that affect others but not them? Many pros believe that their own analysis is different—that they themselves will hit the mark time and again with pinpoint accuracy. If they happen to miss, why, it was a simple slip, or else the company misled them. More thorough research would have prevented the error. It won't happen again.

Let's examine why this mentality is prevalent in the face of overwhelming evidence to the contrary. It should be an interesting drama in several acts. The show has a terrific cast of experts from many fields, the action is compelling, and there's a heartwarming (perhaps make that "portfolio-warming") lesson for the audience.

Forecasting Follies 8: Some Causes of Forecasting Errors

As we just saw, investors either ignore or are not impressed by the statistical destruction of forecasting, even though the devastation has been thorough and spans decades. There are a number of reasons, some economic, some psychological, why investors who depend on finely calibrated forecasts are likely to end up with egg on their face. Two academics, John Cragg and Burton Malkiel (the latter of whom we met briefly in chapter 6), did an early analysis of long-term estimates, published in the *Journal of Finance*.[14] They examined the earnings projections of groups of security analysts at four highly respected investment organizations, including two New York City banks' trust departments, a mutual fund, and an investment advisory firm. These organizations made one- to five-year estimates for 185 companies. The researchers found that most analysts' estimates were simply linear extrapolations of current trends with low correlations between actual and predicted earnings.

Despite the vast amount of additional information now available to analysts, say Cragg and Malkiel, and their frequent company visits, estimates are still projected as a continuation of past trends. "The remarkable conclusion of the present study is that the careful estimates of security analysts . . . performed little better than those of past company growth rates."

The researchers found that analysts could have done better with their five-year estimates by simply assuming that earnings would continue to expand near the long-term rate of 4 percent annually.[15]

Yet another important research finding indicates the fallibility of relying on earnings forecasts. Oxford Professor Ian Little, in a 1962 paper appropriately titled "Higgledy Piggledy Growth," revealed that the future of a large number of British companies could not be predicted from recent earnings trends.[16] Little's work proved uncomfortable to both EMH theoreticians and EMH practitioners, who promptly criticized its methodology. Little good-naturedly accepted the criticism and carefully redid the work, but the outcome was the same: earnings appeared to follow a random walk of their own, with past and future rates showing virtually no correlation, and recent trends (so important to security analysis in projecting earnings) provided no indication of the future course.[17]

A number of studies reach the same conclusion:[18] changes in the earnings of U.S. companies fluctuate randomly over time.

Richard Brealey, for example, examined the percentage changes of earnings of 711 U.S. industrial companies between 1945 and 1964. He, too, found that trends were not sustained but actually demonstrated a slight tendency toward reversal. The only exception was companies with the steadiest rates of earnings growth, and even their correlations were only mildly positive.[19]

Juxtaposing the second set of studies with the first provides part of the explanation of why analysts' forecasting errors are so high. If analysts extrapolate past earnings trends into the future, as Cragg and Malkiel have shown, and earnings do follow a random walk, as Little and Brealey demonstrated, one would expect sizable errors. *And large forecast errors are what we have found consistently.*

Thus, once again and from quite another tack, we see the precariousness of attempting to place major emphasis on earnings forecasts. Which calls for another Psychological Guideline:

PSYCHOLOGICAL GUIDELINE 14: It is impossible, in a dynamic economy with continually changing political, economic, industrial, and competitive conditions, to use the past to estimate the future.

There are several other economic reasons that can cause earnings forecasts to be off base. One is what the Harvard economist Richard Zeckhauser calls "the big bath theory." In a paper that he wrote with Jay Patel of Boston University and François Degeorge of the HEC School of Management in Paris, the researchers provided evidence that many companies try to manage earnings by attempting to show consistent, gradual improvements.[20] Analysts have an appetite for steady growth, and that is what management tries to serve up. When the managers can't do it, they take a "big bath," writing off everything they can, perhaps even more than is necessary (accounting again), in order to produce a steady progression of earnings after the bath. The big bath could be another unpredictable effect that throws analysts' forecasts off.

Reviewing the evidence makes it appear that forecasting is far more art than science and, like the creative fields, has few masters. Apart from highly talented exceptions, people simply cannot predict the future with any reliability, as the figures starkly tell us.

BEHAVIORAL FINANCE: CAREER PRESSURES ON ANALYSTS' RECOMMENDATIONS

There are some substantive factors that affect analysts directly, the most important being career pressures (behavioral finance labels this as a part of agency theory*). These can result in forecasts that stray markedly. After surveying the major brokerage houses some years back, John Dorfman, then editor of the market section of *The Wall Street Journal*, whom we met earlier, provided a list of what determines an analyst's bonus, normally a substantial part of his or her salary.[21] In Dorfman's words, "Investors might be surprised by what *doesn't* go into calculating analysts' bonuses. Accuracy of profit estimates? That's almost never a direct factor. . . . Performance of stocks that the analyst likes or hates? . . . It is rarely given major weight." *The ranking of seven factors determining an analyst's compensation places "accuracy of forecasts" dead last.*

What is most important is how the analyst is rated by the brokerage firm's sales force. That was precisely the same pressure on analysts seen earlier during the Internet bubble, which led many into a serious conflict of interest with part of their clientele.

Many firms conduct a formal poll of the sales force, which ranks the analysts primarily on how much commission business they can drum up. At Raymond James, the sales force's ratings accounted for 50 percent of the analysts' bonuses. Top executives also review a printout of how much business is done in the analysts' stocks. The report is called "stock done" for short. PaineWebber† kept careful records of what percentage of trades it handled in every stock, and its market share in stocks it provides research for compared with market share of competitors. Michael Culp, then the director of Prudential Securities,‡ instituted a rule requiring his analysts to make 110 contacts a month—but, he added quickly, most of his analysts were not affected, because they were already making 135. Another firm ranks analysts' recommendations when calculating their bonuses. A buy recommendation is worth 130 points, a sell recommendation only 60, because sell recommendations don't generate nearly as much business as buy recommendations; no points are added for accu-

---

* Agency theory describes a relationship in which one party, called the principal, delegates work to another, called the agent. The theory states that different parties involved in a given situation with the same given goal will have different motivations and that these different motivations can be manifested in divergent ways. The behavior of Jack Grubman, Henry Blodget, and other analysts we viewed earlier during the Internet bubble was another aspect of agency theory.
† Now a subsidiary of UBS.
‡ Now a part of Wachovia Securities.

racy.[22] We also have seen where this road led in the earlier section on the marketing of dot-com stocks.

Making the *Institutional Investor* All-Star Team, according to *The Wall Street Journal* list, ranks second. Having an analyst on "the Team," as we've seen, results in big commissions for the firm. Even as he denied the importance of the *Institutional Investor* poll, one research director said, "Most of the guys know they'll be visiting for *I-I* in the spring." That is, the analyst will be making the annual pilgrimage to visit institutional clients, implicitly lobbying for their vote to fame and fortune. "I'm a lonely guy in March and April, shortly before the balloting," he continued.

Do you find these remarks disturbing? The analysts' behavior is certainly better than it was during the dot-com bubble, but the temptations not to put out sell reports and the rewards for putting out as many buy recommendations as possible are high. Most investors directly or indirectly put their savings into the hands of research analysts whose forecasts are the cornerstones of their recommendations. But the forecasts are a trivial factor or even a nonevent in determining their compensation. Unfortunately, that's always been the name of the game. The key question for the investor is whether an analyst is giving you his best recommendations or, given his compensation, which is based upon maximizing his commissions generated, recommending what is likely to sell the most. Obviously, this is impossible to pinpoint. But there is a good Psychological Guideline that will help:

PSYCHOLOGICAL GUIDELINE 15: If you're interested in an analyst's recommendation, get all of his reports for at least the last three to five years and see how they've done. If they haven't done well or he can't provide them, move on.

There are yet other direct pressures on analysts. An important one, well known on the Street, is the fear of issuing sell recommendations. Sell recommendations are only a small fraction of the buys. A company that the analyst issues a sell recommendation on will often ban him from further contact. If he issues a sell recommendation on the entire industry, he may receive an industry blackball, which virtually excludes him from talking to any important executives. If the analyst is an expert in the industry and it represents the main part of his intellectual property, he is facing major career damage by pressing the sell button.

Recommending a sell, even when the analyst proves to be dead-on, can be costly. In the late 1980s, an analyst at Janney Montgomery Scott issued a sell recommendation on one of the Atlantic City casinos owned by Donald Trump. Trump went bananas and insisted that the analyst be fired for his lack of knowledge. Shortly thereafter, he was fired—but naturally, said the brokerage firm, "for other reasons." The analyst proved right, and the casino went into Chapter 11 bankruptcy. Out of a job, he won the equivalent of a few years' salary from an arbitration panel. But he was never rewarded for his excellent call and, in fact, suffered because of it.

Another analyst was banned from an analysts' meeting of the then high-flying Boston Chicken (later named Boston Market). His offense: he had issued a sell recommendation on the company. "We don't want you here," Boston Chicken's CFO told him. "We don't want you to confuse yourself with the facts."[23] The facts were that Boston Chicken filed for Chapter 11 bankruptcy not long afterward. A number of studies indicate that analysts issue five or six times as many buy as sell recommendations.[24] Obviously, career pressures have an impact on the buy-sell-hold rating.

Many companies retaliate when analysts write negative reports on them. The retribution can take many forms. One analyst at Prudential Securities wrote a number of negative reports about Citicorp in 1992. Frustrated that Prudential could not become the lead underwriter in some asset-backed bond deals, a Prudential investment banker went to Citicorp and was told that the reason was the analyst. The same analyst, a year later, criticized Banc One and its complex derivative holdings, which eventually cost it hundreds of millions of dollars in write-offs. Banc One stopped its bond trading with Prudential. By coincidence, the analyst left the firm shortly thereafter. At Kidder Peabody an analyst repeatedly recommended the sale of NationsBank (now Bank of America). The bank stopped all stock and bond trading for its trust accounts with Kidder.[25]

For analysts at brokerage firms that are also large underwriters, the pressure is even greater. Negative reports are a major no-no. Bell South officials were unhappy about the comments of a Salomon Brothers analyst who stated that its management was inefficient and ranked it sixth out of the seven regional Bells. Salomon, the bond powerhouse, was excluded from the lucrative lead-manager role in a large Bell South issue. In late 1994, Conseco fired Merrill Lynch as its lead underwriter in a big bond offering shortly after its analyst downgraded Conseco's stock. Smith Barney, according to sources, believes it lost a chance to be part of the underwriting group of Owens-Corning Fiberglas after one of its analysts wrote a negative report on the company.[26]

Just how heavy career pressures can be for analysts working for major underwriting firms if they recommend a sale is shown in an academic study. The work examined 250 analyst reports from investment banking houses, matching them up with 250 from brokerage firms that did not conduct investment banking. The conclusion: investment banking house brokers issued 25 percent more buy recommendations and a remarkable 46 percent fewer sell recommendations.[27]

What is apparent from the above circumstances and those we saw earlier is that an analyst's most important responsibility is to be a good marketer of the brokerage firm. The analyst must tell a good story, not one that is necessarily right. The bottom line is commissions. A good marketer and a good forecaster are different animals. We have already seen one example of the "All-Stars" significantly underperforming the market with their picks. Another example is that major money managers, to whom the All-Stars devote the bulk of their attention, consistently do worse than the averages.

Analysts of necessity use disingenuous gradations that actually mean sell, such as underweight, lighten up, fully valued, overvalued, source of funds, swap and hold, or even strong hold. Peter Siris, a former analyst at UBS Securities, summed it up well several decades ago: "There's a game out there. Most people aren't fooled by what analysts have to say . . . because they know in a lot of cases they're shills. But those poor [small] investors—somebody ought to tell them."[28] *You've been warned!*

Even if brokerage firms don't focus on accurate estimates, however, analysts are not punished for producing them. And although firms may be pressured by their underwriting clients not to make sell recommendations on their stocks, to my knowledge an analyst has never been reprimanded for writing a highly optimistic report on them.

▦ Forecasting Follies 9: Psychological Influences on Decisions

In the preceding chapter, we saw that expert forecasts were sharply off the mark in many fields besides the stock market. Within the market, the analyst traveling with a laptop can run spreadsheets, check stock quotes, receive faxes, even tap into voluminous databases. At home base, his data input capabilities increase enormously. As one Morgan analyst stated, extracting useful information from the forty-nine databases the bank subscribes to is like finding a needle in a haystack. "The more data you get, the less information you have," he groaned.[29] His intuition coincides with the psychological findings. Increased information, as was demonstrated, does not lead to increased accuracy. A large number of studies in cognitive psychology indicate that human judgment is often predictably incorrect. Nor is overconfidence unique to analysts. People in situations of uncertainty are generally overconfident on the basis of the information available to them; they usually believe they are right much more often than they are.

These findings apply to many other fields. A classic analysis of cognitive psychologists found that it was impossible to predict which psychologists would be good diagnosticians. Further, there were no mechanical forecasting models that could be continuously used to improve judgment. The study concluded that the only way to resolve the problem was to look at the record of the diagnostician over a substantial period of time.

Researchers have also shown that people can maintain a high degree of confidence in their answers, even when they know the "hit rate" is not very high. The phenomenon has been called the "illusion of validity," as noted before briefly.[30] This also helps explain the belief that analysts can pinpoint their estimates despite the strong evidence to the contrary. People make confident predictions from incomplete and fallible data. There are excellent lessons here for the stock forecaster.

Forecasting Follies 10: Mr. Inside and Mr. Outside

Daniel Kahneman, who for several decades was a coauthor of many important scholarly pieces with Amos Tversky, wrote on this subject in collaboration with Dan Lovallo.[31]

Forecasters are "excessively prone" to treating each problem as unique, paying no attention to history. Cognitive psychologists note that there are two distinct methods of forecasting. The first is called the "inside view." This method is the one overwhelmingly used to forecast earnings estimates and stock prices. The analyst or stock forecaster focuses entirely on the stock and related aspects such as growth rates, market share, product development, the general market, the economic outlook, and a host of other variables.

The "outside view," on the other hand, ignores the multitude of factors that go into making the individual forecast and focuses instead on the group of cases believed to be most similar. In the case of earnings estimates, for example, it would zero in on how accurate earnings forecasts have been overall or how accurate they have been for a specific industry or for the company itself in deciding how precisely the analyst can estimate and the reliance that can be placed on the forecast.

If stock market forecasters are to succeed using the inside view, they must capture the critical elements of the future. The outside view, in contrast, is essentially statistical and comparative and does not attempt to read the future in any detail.

Kahneman relates a story to demonstrate the difference. In the mid-1970s, he was involved with a group of experts in developing a curriculum on judgment and decision making under uncertainty for high schools in Israel. When the team had been in operation for a year and had made some significant progress, discussion turned to how long it would take to complete the project. Everyone in the group, including Kahneman, gave an estimate. The forecasts ranged from eighteen to thirty months. Kahneman then asked one of his colleagues, an expert in curriculum development, to think of similar projects he was familiar with at a parallel stage in time and development. "How long did it take them from that point to complete their projects?" he asked.

After a long pause the expert replied with obvious discomfort that, first of all, about 40 percent of the projects had never been completed. Of the balance, he said, "I cannot think of any that was completed in less than seven years, nor any that took more than ten." Kahneman then asked if there were any factors that made this team superior in attempting the task. None, said the expert. "Indeed we are slightly below average in terms of our resources and our potential." As experienced as he was with the outside view, the curriculum development expert was just as susceptible to the inside view.*

As is now apparent, the inside and outside views draw on dramati-

---

* Kahneman also noted that it took eight more years after that discussion to complete the project.

cally different sources of information, and the processes are poles apart. The outside view ignores the innumerable details of the project on hand (the cornerstone of analysis using the inside view) and makes no attempt to forecast the outcome of the project into the future. Instead, it focuses on the statistics of projects similar to the one being undertaken to determine the odds of success or failure. The basic difference is that with the outside view, the problem is treated not as unique but as an instance of a number of similar problems. The outside view could be applied to a large number of the problems we've seen, including curriculum building, medical and psychiatric or legal diagnosis, and forecasting earnings or future stock prices.

According to Kahneman, "It should be obvious that when both methods are applied with intelligence and skill the outside view is much more likely to yield a realistic estimate. In general, the future of long and complex undertakings is simply not foreseeable in detail." The number of possible outcomes when dozens or hundreds of factors interact in the marketplace is, for all practical purposes, infinite. Even if one could foresee each of the possibilities, the probability of any particular scenario is negligible. Yet this is precisely what analysts are trying to accomplish with a single, precise prediction.

Forecasting Follies 11: The Forecasters' Curse

Let's return to our analytical friends and look at their chances of success in terms of the inside view. As Table 8-3 makes clear, the probability of their being correct on their forecasts over any but the shortest periods of time is extremely low, and this means that the chances of making money consistently using precise forecasts are almost negligible.

As we saw earlier, the Street demands forecasts normally within a range of plus or minus 3 percent. Table 8-3, taken from our previous analysts' forecasting study, shows how slim the probability of getting estimates within even the wider 5 percent range actually is. Remember, only 30 percent of forecasts made this target in any one quarter.

The table shows the chance of an analyst's hitting the target for one quarter, four quarters, ten quarters, and twenty quarters; for all earnings surprises in column 1, negative surprises in column 2, and positive surprises in column 3. It is not reassuring. The odds against the investor

	Table 8-3 The Chances of a Stock Surviving Without a 5% Earnings Surprise, 1973–2010		
	Any Surprise	**Negative Surprise**	**Positive Surprise**
1 Quarter	30%	66%	62%
4 Quarters	1/132	1/5	1/7
10 Quarters	1/199,000	1/62	1/113
20 Quarters	1/40 billion	1/3,800	1/12,800

Source: © David Dreman, 2011. Data Sources: Abel/Noser Corp., I/B/E/S, and Thomson First Call.

who relies on fine-tuned earnings estimates are staggering. There is only a 1-in-132 chance that the analysts' consensus forecast will be within 5 percent for any four consecutive quarters. Going longer makes the odds dramatically worse. For any ten consecutive quarters, the odds of fine-tuning the estimates for a company within this range fall to 1 in 199,000, and for twenty consecutive quarters, they fall to 1 in 40 billion. We stopped our calculation of estimates there, as the odds would have been likely to go up to the trillions twenty years out. Yet those are exactly the forecasting techniques most good investors on the Street use—and, oh yes, what the EMH theorists say keeps the market efficient. Both are guilty of significant error: For the practitioners it is not wanting to believe the odds are so high against forecasting. For the theorists it is not having an inkling of how badly one of the chief tools of security analysis performs. The bell tolls for both groups.

To put this all into perspective, *your probability of being the big winner of the New York State Lottery is more than 777 times as great as your probability of pinpointing earnings every quarter for the next five years.* Few people would put a couple of bucks into a lottery against odds like those, but millions of investors will play them in the marketplace for big stakes anytime.

Some folks will say, "Who cares if earnings come in above estimates? In fact, I'll applaud." Fair enough. So we asked: what are the chances that you will avoid a 5 percent negative surprise for ten to twenty consecutive quarters? The answer is "Very poor." The investor has only a 1-in-5 chance of *not* getting a negative earnings surprise 5 percent below the consensus forecast after only four quarters. After ten quarters, the chance of not receiving at least one crippling earnings surprise goes down to 1 in 62, and after twenty quarters, it is 1 in 3,800.

Yet, as we have also seen, forecasts often have to go out a decade or more to justify the high prices at which many growth companies are trading. If the odds are staggeringly high against being precise for five years, what are they for ten or fifteen? Many extremely pricey growth stocks must make their forecasts for ten- or fifteen-year periods in order to justify their current prices.

Think about it: should anyone not on something want to play against these odds? Yet, as we know, relying on accurate estimates is the way most people play the investment game. Investors who understand these prohibitive odds will obviously want to go with them if there is a way to do it, which is exactly what we'll look at in the next section.

What we see here is a classic case of using the inside rather than the outside view. Evidence such as the above strongly supports Kahneman's statement that the outside view is much more likely to yield realistic results. Yet, as Kahneman states, "The inside view is overwhelmingly preferred in forecasting."

In the marketplace, the outside view does not give the stock investor the same confidence that he is in control and can use his expertise to power through to above-average returns. Nor does it provide much excitement or good "war stories," which most clients like. It is used far less frequently than the inside view, although we have seen in the previous chapter that index funds, which are structured entirely on the outside view, easily beat most mutual funds over time. The superior returns from contrarian strategies also come from the outside view, as we'll see in the next section.

Another Psychological Guideline is appropriate here:

PSYCHOLOGICAL GUIDELINE 16: The outside view normally provides superior returns over time. To maximize your returns, purchase investments that provide you with this approach.

Looking at the figures above, someone might ask, "Why?" The answer is again psychological. The natural way a decision maker approaches a problem is to focus all of his or her knowledge on the task, concentrating particularly on its unique features. Kahneman noted that a general observation of overconfidence is that even when forecasters are aware of findings such as the foregoing, they will still use the inside approach, disregarding the outside view, regardless of how strong its statistical documentation is.

Often, the relevance of the outside view is explicitly denied. Analysts and money managers I have talked to about high error rates repeatedly shrug them off. In sum, they ignore the record of forecasting because they have been taught and believe that investment theory, when executed properly, will yield the precise results that they require. Analysts and money managers seem unable to recognize the problems inherent in forecasting.

This situation is not unique to Wall Street. Indeed, the relevance of the statistical calculations inherent in the outside view is usually explicitly denied. Doctors and lawyers often argue against allying statistical odds to particular cases. Sometimes their preference for the inside view is couched in almost moral terms. Thus, the professional will say, "My client [or patient] is not a statistic; his case is unique." Many disciplines implicitly teach their practitioners that the inside view is the only professional way to come to grips with the unique problems they will meet. The outside view is rejected as a crude analogy from instances that are only superficially similar.

Not to pay enormous prices for the skyrocketing earnings estimates of a company such as Google, on the cutting edge of Internet technology, many analysts would argue, is vastly unfair to current shareholders and potential buyers. Ironically, rapid technology change, accompanied by rapierlike earnings growth, makes the forecasting process even more difficult than it is for more mundane companies.

Forecasting Follies 12: Analysts' Overconfidence

The forecasting pond is getting crowded. Let's conclude with some recent examples in case you think that in the 2000s we turned a corner to a better understanding of the problems.

Large optimistic errors appear to be a way of life with corporate capital spending, particularly when new technologies or other projects where the firm is in an unfamiliar situation are involved. A Rand Corporation study some years back examined the cost of new types of plants in the energy field.[32] The norm was that actual construction costs were double the initial estimates, and 80 percent of the projects failed to gain their projected market share.

A psychological study examining the cause of this type of failure concluded that most companies demanded a worst-case scenario for a capital spending project. "But the worst case forecasts are almost always too optimistic. When managers look at the downside, they generally describe a mildly pessimistic future rather than the worst possible future."[33]

Overoptimism often results from differences in estimates made from the inside rather than the outside view. A clear-cut example is demonstrated by the behavior of large banks, investment bankers, the Federal Reserve, and the Treasury throughout the financial crisis almost until the end. As the financial system began to unravel in late 2006 and early 2007, dozens of reassuring statements were made by these large institutions that they would emerge with little damage. Those utterances were supported by Fed Chairman Bernanke, Treasury Secretary Paulson, and dozens of other senior officials.

On the outside, thousands of stories on the housing bubble and many of its excesses appeared in the media, by many astute observers, including Paul Krugman, a Nobel laureate in economics, and Gretchen Morgenson, a Pulitzer Prize winner with *The New York Times,* up to two years before the bubble popped. They were ignored or shrugged off by both the Fed and senior government officials.

Through 2007 and 2008, as conditions worsened, the banks and investment banks continued to be inordinately optimistic about the value of their toxic mortgage portfolios. They were substantially underreserving their losses to the spring of 2008, even though the subprime mortgage origination industry and many hedge funds had already collapsed several months before, with many dozens wiped out entirely. Only when banks and investment bankers realized their survival was at stake did reality break through, and enormous write-downs of these holdings took place. By then, of course, it was far too late.

Here is a good Psychological Guideline to train yourself to follow.

PSYCHOLOGICAL GUIDELINE 17: Be realistic about the downside of an investment; expect the worst case to be much more severe than you anticipated.

In this chapter, we have looked at the striking errors in analysts' forecasts, errors so large that they render the majority of current investment methods inoperable. We have also seen that even though high error rates have been recognized for decades, neither analysts nor the investors who religiously depend on them have altered their methods in any way.

The problem is not unique to analysts or market forecasters. We have also seen how pervasive it is in many professions where information is hard to analyze, as well as how difficult the problem is to recognize, let alone change. Finally, we have found overoptimism to be a strong component of expert forecasts, both within and outside the stock market.

Now the question is: what can we do about it? The answer is that we need to move on to a better investing paradigm that does not rely primarily or exclusively on the efficient-market hypothesis or on the forecasts and estimates of company earnings from securities analysts. On the contrary, there is a better way.

Chapter 9

Nasty Surprises and Neuroeconomics

HISTORY IS REPLETE with unheeded alarm bells and dreadful surprises. Almost a hundred years ago, in 1915, the German embassy took out an ad in *The New York Times*. It warned U.S. citizens that they risked torpedo attacks on Allied passenger ships. The United States had not yet entered World War I. (In fact, President Woodrow Wilson would successfully run for reelection on the slogan "He kept us out of war.") Yet when the British ocean liner *Lusitania* left New York bound for Liverpool, many American passengers were on board, along with 173 tons of rifle ammunition and shells for the British army. A German submarine attacked the ship off the south coast of Ireland, causing the loss of 1,198 passengers and crew, including 114 Americans. Although the ship was a legitimate target under international law, many Americans were outraged at the "surprise," and public sentiment began to tilt against Germany. Two years later, the United States was in the war on the side of the British.

Twenty-six years later, the United States was surprised again. This time it was Pearl Harbor. The Japanese sneak attack on the military naval base in Hawaii catapulted the United States into World War II. Decades later, the evidence is fairly conclusive that in 1941 there were plenty of warning signs of what the Japanese navy intended. (Interestingly, it seems that many U.S. military leaders felt that the "inferior" Japanese people could never pull off such an attack.) That surprise also galvanized and unified a nation still reeling from the Great Depression and the widespread fears of civil strive, anarchy, and communism.

Knowing history, some twenty-three years later President Lyndon Johnson informed the American public of yet another complete surprise. To whip up support for a major escalation of the Vietnam War, in 1964 he greatly exaggerated the report of an attack on a U.S. destroyer in the Gulf of Tonkin. North Vietnamese torpedo boats had supposedly attacked the USS *Maddox* without provocation or cause. (Few knew at the time that the previous day the South Korean navy, under U.S. direction, had carried out clandestine raids on nearby North Vietnamese islands or that the destroyer had been on an intelligence mission.) Reacting to the announcement, Congress immediately handed the president the sweeping powers he requested and a blank check for the war.

Not unexpectedly, Congress's "buyer's remorse" at the actions it authorized would rival that of any investor caught up in a very nasty market surprise. Patriotic emotions had again swept aside more reasoned considerations—yes, shades of Affect—and had momentous consequences. As history bears out, warning signs may not be seen clearly during the moment, but nasty political surprises can almost predictably lead to overreactions by officeholders and the general public alike.

In the markets, investors also react to surprise in a fairly predictable way. In the 2000s alone, the collapse of Enron in 2000–2001, followed by that of WorldCom in 2002 and then Bernie Madoff in 2008, soured millions on stocks. The distrust has been heightened by the flash crash of May 6, 2010, in which the Dow Jones Industrials dropped more than 600 points in minutes and the intraday swing was over 1,000 points, the second largest in market history. At the time of this writing the SEC and CFTC still have not taken appropriate action to prevent another flash crash from occurring; their inaction has further disillusioned investors and resulted in a flood of cash pouring out of stocks into Treasury bonds at almost zero yields.

That's what surprises do on Wall Street. They continually change our outlook on owning bonds or stocks or gold. Within the stock market they do the same for companies' earnings outlooks—and thus inevitably their stock prices. The market is always adjusting to surprises or anticipating them or discounting them: the standard fare of investment news you hear or read every day. The key players, of course, in initiating a market surprise are the analysts we met in the previous chapter, the men and women who predict what will happen *barring any surprise.* Ironically, here we have a self-fulfilling prophecy. It's their pinpoint forecasts, which are rarely met, that create the majority of earnings surprises on stocks.

After covering the many aspects and systematic patterns of surprise in this chapter's first section, the last part of the chapter will introduce a relatively new field of science dubbed "neuroeconomics," which breaks down some traditional boundaries. This field combines research from neuroscience, psychology, and economics to analyze how people make decisions. It catalogs the inner activity of the brain using advanced monitoring technology to spot what actually happens when we evaluate decisions, categorize risks and rewards, and interact with other people. In short, one of its aspects is an objective, biologically based extension and confirmation of important findings in cognitive psychology. The results are often surprising!

Surprise and the Market

Time to think twice about that stock purchase? Possibly. But far more important, maybe it's time to reconsider the whole mechanism of surprises, not simply from an anecdotal perspective but from a solid statistical basis. Yes, negative surprises have enormous influence on us, both as citizens and as investors. But there is the other and far more upbeat side of the coin: positive surprises put spring in our step and add heft to our portfolios. In this chapter we will look at earnings surprises. Although, as we just saw, they occur frequently, they don't necessarily have to be anxiety-producing events. Quite the opposite; if you know what you're looking for, they can bring up some very cheery days. We'll see that earnings surprises have a consistent and predictable effect on stock prices that you can use to your advantage.

Specifically, they have a dramatically different impact on stocks that people like as contrasted to those people don't like. Importantly, the new and rapidly growing field of neuroeconomics uses brain scans to study some of our major emotional reactions to surprise, providing a solid explanation of what we shall see. And understanding the nature of surprises provides a high-probability method of beating the market.

Surprise: No Price Is Too High for Growth

At times, no price seems too high for aggressive growth stocks or IPOs. Investors repeatedly pay through the nose and just as repeatedly get stung. Nevertheless, as we've seen, strong psychological forces compel people to buy sizzling issues and then prevent them from analyzing where they went wrong.

The pattern is, not unexpectedly, repeated for larger companies. Investors believe they can forecast the prospects for both exciting and unexciting stocks well into the future. They have high hopes for "best" stocks and high confidence that their expectations will be met. Similarly, they have low expectations for stocks that appear to have lackluster or poor prospects but again high confidence that their estimates will be dead-on. The previous chapter showed just how dead-on such forecasts actually are.

Companies with the best prospects, fastest growth rates, and most exciting concepts normally trade at a high price relative to earnings (P/E), high price to cash flow (P/CF), and high price to book value (P/BV), and invariably provide low or no dividend yields. Conversely, stocks with poor outlooks trade at low price to earnings, price to cash flow, or price to book value and usually have higher dividend yields.*

Often, the disparity between what investors will pay for a favored stock and one badly out of favor is immense, as chapters 1 and 2 showed. Investors, for example, happily shelled out 100 times more for each dollar earned by the Internet wunderkind eToys.com, shortly before it went to dot-com heaven, than for a dollar earned by boring old JPMorgan Chase. Investors pay such price differentials because of their confidence in their ability to pinpoint the future. Let's look at what happens when—surprise!—their forecasts miss the mark.

---

*For information on where to find price-earnings, price-to-book-value, and price-to-cash-flow ratios and dividend yields of companies, please turn to page 320 in chapter 12.

▨ Surprise: What Our Studies Revealed

To find out how stocks react when analysts err, I did a number of studies in collaboration with Drs. Eric Lufkin, Vladimira Ilieva, Nelson Woodard, Mitchell Stern, and Michael Berry over time, the latest one for the thirty-eight years ending with 2010.[1] To be consistent, we worked with exactly the same analysts' consensus forecasts that were used to calculate analysts' errors in the preceding chapter.

We wanted to measure a number of factors important to investors. First, what do analysts' forecasting errors do to stock prices? Second—and as important—do earnings surprises have the same impact on favored as on unfavored stocks? Stocks trading in outer space are there because of analysts' confidence in their future—possibly mixed with a wee dose of overoptimism. Did they react the same way to earnings surprises as to stocks that are in the investor doghouse? Third, we wished to examine just how accurate investors expect analysts' forecasts to be. To help resolve this, we measured how even tiny surprises affect a stock's price by considering any amount over one penny a share a surprise.

To answer the three questions, we analyzed the stocks strictly according to how exciting or dull investors believed their prospects were, using three different value measures: the price-to-earnings, price-to-cash-flow, and price-to-book-value ratios. The higher the three ratios, the more enticing the stock is to an investor and the more he or she is willing to pay. Conversely, the lower the three ratios, the more unpopular the stock. We divided the stocks in all of the quarters in our 1973–2010 study into three groups strictly by how they ranked by each of these three value measures. The 20 percent of stocks that had the highest P/Es, for example, were placed in the top P/E group (called a quintile), the next 60 percent in the middle group, and the lowest 20 percent in the bottom quintile. We did this for all three value measures. The portfolios were reassembled on this basis for every quarter in the study. We then calculated the effect of surprises on each group of stocks beginning in the first quarter of 1973 and ending in the fourth quarter of 2010, a thirty-eight-year period in all.[2]

The study used the 1,500 largest companies in the Compustat database with fiscal years ending in March, June, September, and December.[3] Approximately 750 to 1,000 large companies were used in each of the 152 quarters of the study.

▉ Surprise: What the Historical Record Shows

Next we set a yardstick to gauge the result of market surprises. The surprises are measured against the analyst consensus forecast, the average estimate of the group of analysts following each stock, as described in the preceding chapter. A surprise is measured against actual earnings, so it doesn't matter whether the earnings are up or down. If a company reports a loss of 80 cents a share, as an example, and the Street expected a loss of one dollar a share, then it would be considered a positive surprise of 20 cents divided by the 80 cents reported, or 25 percent.

Do surprises affect favored and unfavored stocks in the same way? To find out, we'll look at all surprises, the combined effect of positive and negative surprises on the favorite stocks—the highest quintile—the middle quintiles, and the out-of-favor stocks—the lowest quintile. The results are shown in Figures 9-1, 9-2, and 9-3. In each case, the 20 percent of stocks most out of favor by one of the three value measures—price to earnings (9-1), price to cash flow (9-2), and price to book value (9-3)—

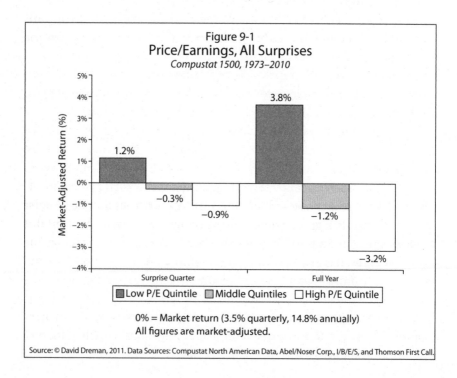

Figure 9-1
Price/Earnings, All Surprises
Compustat 1500, 1973–2010

0% = Market return (3.5% quarterly, 14.8% annually)
All figures are market-adjusted.

Source: © David Dreman, 2011. Data Sources: Compustat North American Data, Abel/Noser Corp., I/B/E/S, and Thomson First Call.

are depicted by the dark bar, the 60 percent of stocks in the middle groups by gray, and the most favored 20% by white.[4] The charts calculate the return above or below the market's for each of the 152 quarters of the study.

The market return* is set at 0 in the center of the vertical axis of the chart. The surprise return must be added to the market return in each period to get the total return. If a bar shows a 1 percent positive return on the left, for example, it means that the stock did 1 percent better than the market over the average three-month return of the study. The market provided a 3.5 percent return on average, quarterly, so the total quarterly return would be 4.5 percent (the market return plus 1 percent or 4.5 percent for the average quarter throughout the study). If the stock did 1 percent better for the full year, it would return 14.8 percent, as shown in the chart, plus an additional 1 percent, or 15.8 percent for the full year on average, annually, throughout the entire study. If it was a 3 percent negative quarterly return, it did 3 percent worse than the market. This type of chart lets you easily appraise how surprise affects each group of stocks.

The figures show the effect of an earnings surprise, measured in the quarter in which earnings were actually reported—which is always the quarter following that in which the earnings surprise took place. We will call this latter quarter the "surprise quarter." The left-hand group of bars shows the effect of the surprise in the quarter it was announced, while the right-hand group represents the effect after one year.

A glance at each of the charts shows that all surprises (positive and negative combined) helped unpopular stocks and hurt popular ones. Looking first at price-earnings ratios in Figure 9-1, we see that all surprises to unpopular stocks returned 1.2 percent above the market's return in the surprise quarter over the life of the study, about a third more than the market.

What's more, beyond the surprise quarter, the beneficial or lethal effect of a surprise increased for the full year. All surprises for out-of-favor stocks (the low-P/E group) returned an average 3.8 percent above market each year. This is 26 percent annually above the market return over the life of the study. It is also triple their outperformance in the surprise quarter itself. By contrast, as the figure shows, favorite stocks, in this case the 20 percent of stocks with the highest P/E multiples, had a return almost 1 percent below the market in the quarter, which widened to 3.2 percent

---

* The market return appears at the bottom of each chart.

annually on average for the entire study, some 25 percent under the market return.

Surprise, as we might expect, did not seem to have much effect on the 60 percent of stocks that make up the middle grouping. These stocks are not normally over- or undervalued much. As Figure 9-1 shows, the stocks were down by less than one-third of 1 percent in the surprise quarter. A year after the surprise there was a small negative (−1.2 percent) effect.

However, the difference in the effects of all surprises on "best" and "worst" stocks was large and increased over time. "Worst" stocks outperformed "best" stocks by 2.1 percent in the surprise quarter, then steadily rose to 7.0 percent (or approximately 50 percent of the market return) in each year of the study.

To summarize, Figure 9-1 reveals that earnings surprises did not affect the returns of the various P/E groups the same way. Surprise significantly benefits unfavored low-P/E stocks and works against the high-P/E group, while it has a nominal effect on stocks in the middle group. Is there any difference in how surprise affects stocks ranked by the other value measures?

Surprise: Toute la Différence

Figure 9-2 looks at the effects of all surprises on stocks measured by price to cash flow. The chart is nearly identical to Figure 9-1 for the surprise quarter and the full year. The lowest-price-to-cash-flow group again strongly outperformed the market in both cases. Similarly, the favorite stocks, the 20 percent of highest-price-to-cash-flow issues, significantly underperformed the average in both periods, while the middle group was almost unaffected by surprises. By this value measurement, surprises in analysts' forecasts once again work powerfully in favor of the most unwanted group and against the most highly regarded stocks.

Figure 9-3 demonstrates the effects of all surprises measured by price to book value. Remember, the higher the price-to-book-value ratio, the more popular a stock is, and the lower this ratio, the less popular the stock is. Again, the results are similar. Favorite stocks underperformed in the surprise quarter (−0.7 percent) and did even worse for the full year (−2.8 percent). Unpopular stocks outperformed in the quarter (+0.7 percent) and took off nicely over the full year (+2.9 percent above market).

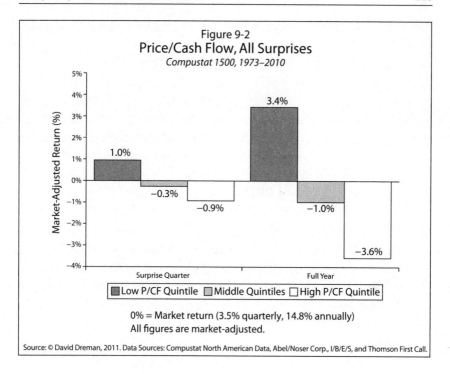

Figure 9-2
Price/Cash Flow, All Surprises
Compustat 1500, 1973–2010

0% = Market return (3.5% quarterly, 14.8% annually)
All figures are market-adjusted.

Source: © David Dreman, 2011. Data Sources: Compustat North American Data, Abel/Noser Corp., I/B/E/S, and Thomson First Call.

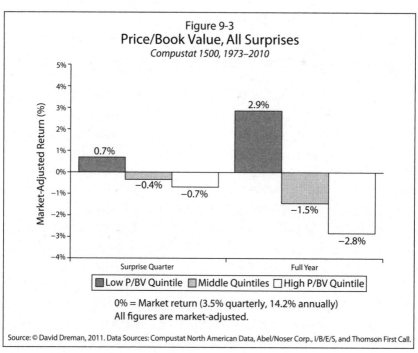

Figure 9-3
Price/Book Value, All Surprises
Compustat 1500, 1973–2010

0% = Market return (3.5% quarterly, 14.2% annually)
All figures are market-adjusted.

Source: © David Dreman, 2011. Data Sources: Compustat North American Data, Abel/Noser Corp., I/B/E/S, and Thomson First Call.

Again, the middle 60 percent of stocks were far less affected by earnings surprises.

What is remarkable is not only that out-of-favor stocks outperformed by all three measures but how similar the performance was regardless of the value measure we chose. We thus begin to see a path to making money in the stock market. Earnings surprises, whether positive or negative, affect favored and out-of-favor stocks very differently. Surprise consistently results in above-average performance for out-of-favor stocks and below-average performance for favored stocks. Has the lightbulb gone on? We can find illumination in this Psychological Guideline.

PSYCHOLOGICAL GUIDELINE 18: Earnings surprises help the performance of out-of-favor stocks, while affecting the returns of favorites negatively. The difference in returns is significant. To enhance portfolio performance, you should take advantage of the high rate of analysts' forecast error by selecting out-of-favor stocks.

Conversely, buying favorites will cost you money. How much money? A look at the magnitude of the surprise effect is sobering, as I'll demonstrate shortly.

▓ The Effects of Positive Surprises

In the preceding section we looked at all surprises, both positive and negative combined, for three of the major fundamental yardsticks, the price-to-earnings, price-to-cash-flow, and price-to-book-value ratios. In this section we will separate the surprises and look first at how positive surprises—higher-than-expected earnings—effect each of the above fundamentals.

Examine Figure 9-4. It shows the effects of positive surprises on stocks in our high, low, and middle groupings, by P/E. As you can see, positive surprises galvanize the lowest 20 percent of stocks. In the surprise quarter, they outperform the market average by 2.6 percent, or 75 percent. For the full year, the lowest P/E quintile charges ahead of the market by a remarkable 6.7 percent annually on average through the 1973–2010 period, returning 21.5 percent. Think about that for a moment. Since the mid-1920s, stocks have returned about 9.9 percent annually.[5] Owning out-of-

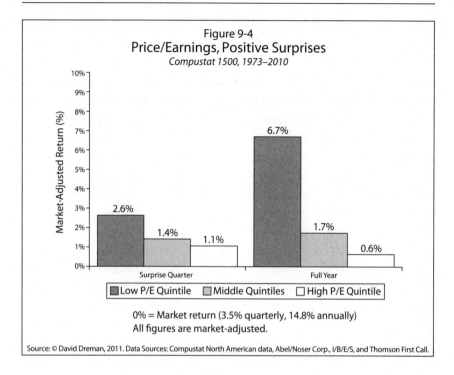

Figure 9-4
Price/Earnings, Positive Surprises
Compustat 1500, 1973–2010

0% = Market return (3.5% quarterly, 14.8% annually)
All figures are market-adjusted.

Source: © David Dreman, 2011. Data Sources: Compustat North American data, Abel/Noser Corp., I/B/E/S, and Thomson First Call.

favor stocks that have positive surprises will fetch you almost double the broad market return over time. We'll look at the reasons for this astonishing increase in return shortly.

Positive surprises also have a noticeable but more subdued effect on stocks in the middle quintiles. The middle group outperformed the market by 1.4 percent in the same quarter. But the above-market return stayed the same for the remaining nine months. The stocks don't continue to appreciate steadily. The price impact due to positive surprises is moderate, probably because they are the least under- or overvalued.

Finally, positive surprises have far less effect on favorite stocks. Stocks that experience positive surprises outperform the market by 1.1 percent in the surprise quarter. The "best" stocks don't keep improving, however, as do those in the low-P/E group. Rather, they lose about half of their small gain over the next nine months.

Although not shown, the lowest 20 percent of stocks ranked by price to cash flow or price to book value are remarkably similar. Both sharply outperformed the market for the surprise quarter and for the full year and routed the most favored stocks for the two periods. The result for the

60 percent of stocks in the middle quintiles is close to those of the other middle groups in the previous charts.

Why do positive surprises for "best" stocks cause only a moderate rise in the surprise quarter? Since analysts and investors alike believe that they can judge precisely which stocks will be the real winners in the years ahead, a positive surprise does little more than confirm their expectations. It's no great shakes—the top companies are expected to have rapidly growing revenues, market share, and earnings. By the end of the year, therefore, the effect of the surprise is minuscule. As we'll soon see, some recent neuroeconomic findings seem to explain why there are these various reactions to surprise by the favored, out-of-favor, and middle groups.

Investors react very differently to positive surprises for out-of-favor companies, no matter which of the three value yardsticks we measure them by. Those stocks moved into the lowest category precisely because they were expected to continue to be dullards. They are the dogs of the investment world and investors believe they deserve minimal valuations. A positive earnings surprise for a stock in this group is an event. Investors sit up and take notice. Maybe, they think, these companies are not as bad as analysts and investors believed. The prices of out-of-favor stocks, therefore, do not just move up in the quarter of the surprise and then drop back again, as do those of the favorites. Instead, they continue to move steadily higher relative to the market in the year following the surprise.

We have seen three distinctly different reactions to earnings surprises by the high, low, and middle stock groups using three of the most important value measurements. However, as with the weather, not all days can be sunny and not all news can be good. Negative surprises, which normally send chills down investors' spines, are the other side of the coin we need to examine.

The Effects of Negative Surprises

Figures 9-5 and 9-6 show the effect of negative surprise on the "best," "worst," and middle groups by price to cash flow and price to earnings. Out-of-favor stocks again win in a breeze. Let's start by looking at price to cash flow (Figure 9-5). Negative surprises in analysts' forecasts have a minimal impact on the lowest 20 percent of stocks in the surprise quarter, and as a result this group falls below the market by only ³⁄₁₀ of 1 percent. Moreover, the market shrugs off the surprise by the end of the year, with the lowest-price-to-cash-flow group outperforming the market by 1.3 percent. (The results for price to book value are similar but are not shown here.)

Negative surprises are like water off a duck's back for this out-of-favor group. Investors have low expectations for what they consider lackluster or bad stocks, and when these stocks do disappoint, few eyebrows are raised. The bottom line is that a negative surprise is not much of an event in the surprise quarter and is a nonevent in the nine months following.

Consider the "best" companies, however. Investors expect only glowing results for these stocks. After all, they confidently—*overconfidently*— believe that they can divine the future of a "good" stock with precision. These stocks are not supposed to disappoint; people pay top dollar for them for exactly this reason. So when a negative surprise arrives, the results are devastating.

Figure 9-5 shows how the "best" stocks, by price-to-cash-flow ratio, reacted to negative earnings surprises. In the quarter in which investors

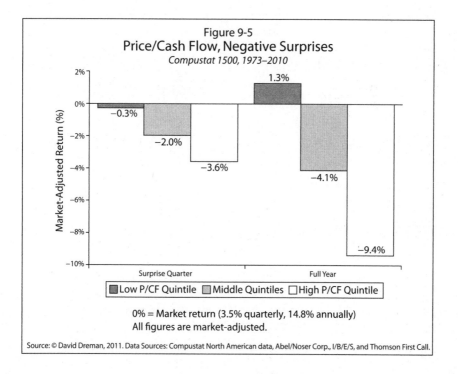

Figure 9-5
Price/Cash Flow, Negative Surprises
Compustat 1500, 1973–2010

Low P/CF Quintile   Middle Quintiles   High P/CF Quintile

0% = Market return (3.5% quarterly, 14.8% annually)
All figures are market-adjusted.

Source: © David Dreman, 2011. Data Sources: Compustat North American data, Abel/Noser Corp., I/B/E/S, and Thomson First Call.

received the news, the stocks underperformed the market by a startling 3.6 percent on average. They did 12 times as poorly as the lowest-price-to-cash-flow group when receiving "bad" surprises. Worse yet, whereas the most out-of-favor stocks outperformed the market slightly in the next nine months, the favorites continued to drop. At the end of the year, they were 9.4 percent under the average. Favorite stocks with negative surprises underperformed the market's return of 14.8 percent by a shocking 64 percent annually, on average, over the thirty-eight years of the study. As Figure 9-5 also shows, the lowest-price-to-cash-flow group outperformed the highest by a remarkable 10.7 percent in years when both groups suffered negative surprises.

Figure 9-6, which measures negative surprises by price-earnings ratio, shows similar results. Negative surprises on the highest 20 percent of P/Es cause the stocks to drop sharply in the surprise quarter; this drop is followed by a larger decline in the next nine months.

What do we make of numbers like these? It's apparent that investors are shaken when companies they expect to excel disappoint. The disappointment does not have to be large. You may remember that we pur-

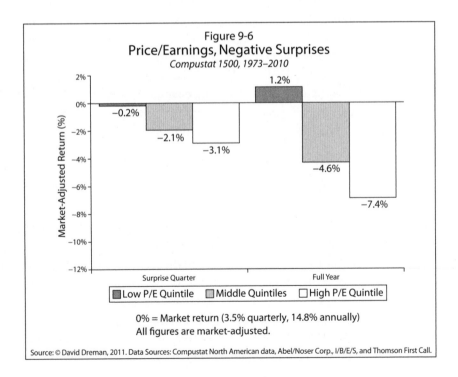

Figure 9-6
Price/Earnings, Negative Surprises
Compustat 1500, 1973–2010

0% = Market return (3.5% quarterly, 14.8% annually)
All figures are market-adjusted.

Source: © David Dreman, 2011. Data Sources: Compustat North American data, Abel/Noser Corp., I/B/E/S, and Thomson First Call.

posely used a very small analyst forecast error—one cent and over—to see how precise estimates have to be. From the major declines of high-visibility stocks on even nominal forecast errors, it's obvious that the pinpoint accuracy demanded of earnings forecasts should not play a major role in valuing a stock. Yet, as we have seen, it's at the heart of security analysis practiced today. A pilot would not use a GPS in his plane that could only get him accurately to within some hundreds of miles of his destination, yet he is quite comfortable using a financial GPS that does just that.

We saw in the previous chapter (Table 8-3) that the probability of avoiding a negative surprise of more than 5 percent was 1 in 62 for ten quarters and 1 in 3,800 for twenty quarters. The current study indicates that investors' tolerance for negative surprises on popular stocks is much lower than this. Considering the devastating effects of negative surprises on favorite stocks, these are odds no rational person should want to face.

Too, we saw in the preceding chapter that analysts are, on the whole, overoptimistic in their forecasts. The combination of analysts' noted overoptimism and their large forecast errors—in one landmark study the error was 9 percent annually—is lethal to buyers of favorite stocks.[6]

Finally, Figures 9-5 and 9-6 show the expected: negative surprises have more effect on the 60 percent of stocks in the middle group than on the lowest-price-to-cash-flow stocks but far less than on the highest-price-to-cash-flow group for both the surprise quarter and the year. But this is mostly offset by their outperformance with positive surprises. Figures 9-1, 9-2, and 9-3 show very similar results. All the findings behind the charts in this chapter are statistically significant.[7]

The Effects of Event Triggers

Regardless of which valuation method was used, when earnings of out-of-favor stocks came in above analysts' forecasts, they shot out the lights. Just as apparent was the sharp underperformance of the winners, the top 20 percent of stocks, as measured by the price-to-earnings or price-to-cash-flow ratio when analysts' estimates were too optimistic.

What the study shows, then, is that the overvaluation of "best" stocks and the undervaluation of "worst" stocks are often driven to extremes. That brings us quite naturally to the next Psychological Guideline.

PSYCHOLOGICAL GUIDELINE 19: Positive and negative surprises affect "best" and "worst" stocks in a diametrically opposite manner.

People are far too confident of their ability to predict complex outcomes in the future. This has been shown to be true in many fields from medicine and law to building new plant facilities. The stock market, with its thousands of continually shifting company, industry, economic, and political events, certainly ranks among the most formidable areas in which to make forecasts.

Good or bad news, which occurs frequently in markets, results in diametrically opposite movements of "best" and "worst" stocks. When we recall that money managers are considered "stars" if they can outperform markets by 2 percent or 3 percent annually over a five-year period, the 3.4 percent annual outperformance of the "worst" stocks after all surprises, as measured by price to cash flow (shown in Figure 9-2, with similar results in Figures 9-1 and 9-3), coupled with the 3.6 percent underperformance of the "best," or 7.0 percent total outperformance of low-P/E over high-P/E stocks, is enormous. The disparity, of course, is firmly anchored in investors' overconfidence in pinpointing future events. We thus see that *earnings surprises have an enormous, predictable, and systematic influence on stock prices.*

Looking carefully at the charts, we can also see that earnings surprises cause two distinct categories of price reactions in both "best" and "worst" stocks. I'll call the first an "event trigger" and the second, which will be discussed shortly, a "reinforcing event."

I define an event trigger as unexpected negative news about a stock believed to have excellent prospects, or unexpectedly positive news about a stock believed to have a mediocre outlook. As a result of the event trigger, people look at the two categories of stocks very differently. They take off their dark or rose-colored glasses. They now evaluate the companies more realistically, and the reappraisal results in a major price change to correct the market's previous overreaction.

THE FIRST EVENT TRIGGER

There are two types of event triggers. The first is a negative surprise for a favored company, which will drive its stock price down. The second is a positive surprise for an unfavored stock, which pushes its price much higher. The event trigger initiates the process of perceptual change among investors, which can continue for a long time. As has been shown, the process goes on beyond the quarter in which the surprise is reported and through the year following the surprise. In the next section, we'll see that it actually continues for much longer periods.

Event triggers can result from surprises other than earnings. A non-earnings surprise might be the FDA's approval of an important new drug or its denial of further testing. Winning or losing a landmark tobacco case would be another. New technology that suddenly makes a semiconductor obsolete would be a third. There could be hundreds of such surprises, any one of which could have a sharp and lasting impact on a stock's price. Although the idea has not yet been tested, observation suggests that the impact of such surprises on stock prices would be similar to the impact earnings surprises have on the best, worst, and middle groups.

Event triggers are, however, most frequently earnings surprises. The first type of event trigger is a negative surprise on a highly regarded company. An example is the free fall in the price of Amgen, the world's largest independent biotech medical company, which has a strong product line for the management of cancers and other serious diseases. Its major products were Aranesp and Epogen to treat anemia in cancer patients. The company added another promising drug for cancer, Vectibix, in 2006. Amgen showed outstanding earnings growth from 2002 through 2005, and the stock price moved from $57 in early 2005 to $86 later that year owing to its earnings, strong product line, and promising pipeline of potential new drugs. Analysts continued to increase their earnings forecasts for the stock.

Then the roof fell in. In late 2006, the company, in attempting to further expand its market for Aranesp, found that the mortality rate, always a concern with this drug, was slightly higher in a new study than in previous ones. Significant concern was expressed by leading oncologists, and recommendations were made to decrease the allowable dosage or possibly ban the drug entirely, which shocked both analysts and investors. Earnings estimates were cut well below the prior exuberant forecasts for a number of quarters, and the stock was downgraded by many on the Street. The price of Amgen plummeted 54 percent by March 2008.

The doomsday scenario analysts painted did not turn out to be nearly as bad as thought. The FDA mandated additional warnings on Arenesp's labeling and moderate downward adjustments in dosages were made, but the drug continued to be a major profit center. Earnings growth began to accelerate in 2008 and was up again in 2009. But the luster was gone. By the fall of 2010, Amgen was no longer considered a "favorite stock." Trading at a P/E of 10×, it was now relegated to the "worst-stocks" category.

The event trigger resulted in a major reassessment of the company by investors. As we saw, investors systematically overrate the future of favored companies. When a negative earnings surprise occurs to a favored stock, accompanied by serious downbeat news, people are shaken by the realization that this could happen to a "best" stock. Their reaction is to sell—fast—sending the prices down, often dramatically. Even when the bad news proved to be not nearly as severe as originally anticipated and the company, in fact, came near to meeting its original earnings targets, the memory of the unpleasant experience lingered. Though many "best" companies bounce back, their stock underperformance continues for some time.

THE SECOND EVENT TRIGGER

Investors do not expect positive surprises from companies they consider to have poor outlooks. When such surprises happen, people begin a process of perceptual change. The stocks are reevaluated more positively, and they outperform the market significantly, largely because of the original undervaluations.

The second type of event trigger is a positive surprise—or a series of positive surprises—for an out-of-favor stock. Take the example of Reynolds American. The company is the second largest cigarette tobacco producer in the United States and was as out of favor as a stock can be.

Through a number of acquisitions, including Conwood Smokeless Tobacco, Reynolds increased its revenues significantly in an industry in which consumption is dropping each year. Reynolds stated publicly that it could increase its profits substantially by consolidating its operations in North Carolina, thereby eliminating well over a billion dollars of expenses and excess plants. The company did exactly that. Beginning with its March 2004 quarter, it produced a string of large earnings surprises, which pushed the stock up 154 percent, including its high 6 percent dividend (a return we can only dream of today) in mid-2007. Investors who bought this stock—and naturally more than a few wouldn't—did very well.

*An Earnings Surprise for a Stock Is Reinforced
by Additional Earnings Surprises*

Investors' perceptions about a company, an industry, or the market itself often do not change with a single positive or negative surprise. Jeffery Abarbanell and Victor Bernard of the University of Michigan, for example, have studied analysts' estimates and found they are slow to adjust to earnings surprises. Whether the estimate was too high or too low, analysts do not revise it accurately immediately but take as long as three quarters after the surprise to do so.[8] When a forecast is too high, it continues to be high for the next nine months, and when it is too low, it continues to be low for the next three quarters.

As Abarbanell and Bernard put it, analysts "underreact to recent earnings reports." This underreaction generates new surprises, which reinforce investors' changing opinion of a company. If, for example, investors are taken aback by a negative earnings surprise on a favorite stock and more negative surprises occur in the following quarters (as a result of analysts' not revising their earnings estimates down enough), people's increasingly poor reappraisal of the company pushes the stock even lower. The event trigger continues over a number of quarters, as we have seen in the various annual quarterly and annual surprise charts. The same is true for a series of positive surprises on an out-of-favor company.[9]

The Effects of Reinforcing Events

The second category of earnings surprises is what I call a "reinforcing event." Rather than changing investors' perceptions about a stock, these surprises reinforce the current beliefs about the company. Since they do, they should have much less impact on stock prices. Reinforcing events are defined as positive surprises on favored stocks *or* negative surprises on out-of-favor stocks. A positive surprise on a favored stock reinforces the previous perception that this is an excellent company. Good companies should do well; if they have positive surprises, it is only to be expected.

Microsoft is the world's largest developer and manufacturer of software and has a major stake in computer equipment. The company is a classic example of a favorite stock experiencing a reinforcing event. In late 2003, "Mr. Softy," as it's sometimes called, racked up good growth in both the consumer and the small and medium-sized business markets. It beat estimates handily in late 2003 and early 2004. However, within only a few months the stock was down about 14 percent, and two years later in mid-2006 it was still down about 13 percent, well behind the market. Again a premier company at a premier P/E showed so-so returns even with very positive earnings surprises.

Boeing was an example of a reinforcing event on an out-of-favor stock several years back. The company hit a rough patch with a machinists' strike and charges related to its 747 and 787 programs, as well as continued woes caused by the global economic downturn that put pressure on its vital commercial airline markets. After missing estimates on the downside four quarters in a row, starting in June 2008, it dropped into the most out-of-favor group, bottoming at $29 per share in March 2009. But it came back strongly, rising over 165 percent by April 2010. Not a bad return from a company whose earnings continued to disappoint!

Figure 9-7 shows how different the impact of earnings surprises is on event triggers and reinforcing events for the surprise quarter (on the left), as well as for the full year (on the right). The figure uses price-earnings ratios to measure the surprise effect, but using price-to-cash-flow or price-to-book-value ratios results in very similar comparisons. The two types of event triggers (negative surprises on favored stocks and positive surprises on out-of-favor stocks) have substantially more impact on stock prices than reinforcing events (positive surprises on favored and negative surprises on out-of-favor issues).

Look first at the event triggers in Figure 9-7, the first two adjoining columns on the left side of the chart, for both the quarter and the year. We see for the event trigger that, adding them together for the average quarter, the total price impact is 5.7 percent (+2.6 percent and –3.1 percent, removing the signs) in the surprise quarter. By contrast, adding the reinforcing events together (the last two adjoining columns on the right side of the quarterly chart) results in a much smaller surprise impact: 1.3 percent (1.1 percent and –0.2 percent) for the same quarter. For the full year, we also see that the size of the event triggers more than doubles, resulting in a total impact of 14.1 percent. This is because, as we saw, positive surprises for out-of-favor stocks and negative surprises for favored stocks are much larger for the full year than for the surprise quarter alone. *Reinforcing events, on the other hand, have a negligible 0.6 percent impact on prices after one year.*

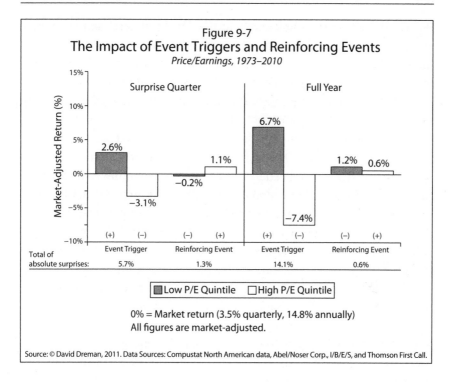

Figure 9-7
The Impact of Event Triggers and Reinforcing Events
Price/Earnings, 1973–2010

0% = Market return (3.5% quarterly, 14.8% annually)
All figures are market-adjusted.

Source: © David Dreman, 2011. Data Sources: Compustat North American data, Abel/Noser Corp., I/B/E/S, and Thomson First Call.

Figure 9-7 demonstrates not only two distinct classes of surprises, event triggers and reinforcing events, but the fact that their response to unanticipated good and bad news is remarkably different. Event triggers result in a perceptual change, which continues through the end of the year and has a major impact on stock prices.

The effect of reinforcing events on prices, on the other hand, is minor by the end of the twelve months following the surprise.

Neuroeconomics and the Market

Neuroeconomics is an important new discipline within economics. Major contributors to this rapidly growing field have written about a significant amount of new research work that appears to strongly support the hypothesis that at least a part of the earnings surprise findings, particularly event triggers and reinforcing events, can be attributed to relatively new research in this field: specifically, the four different types of surprise we saw in Figure 9-7.

We do not need to be experts in biology, chemistry, and neuropsychology to understand the powerful answers that this new discipline gives for why all four kinds of surprises play out the way they do. Fortunately, understanding the interactions themselves is much simpler.

Let's start with dopamine, a chemical naturally released by the body that is commonly associated with the pleasure systems of brain chemistry. It provides feelings of enjoyment and reinforcement, which motivate a person to undertake certain activities. Dopamine, a neural transmitter, transmits nerve impulses, which are released by naturally rewarding experiences such as food, sex, certain drugs, and the neural stimuli associated with them. Of the brain's approximately 100 billion neurons, only about one-thousandth of 1 percent produce dopamine. But this minuscule group has a major effect on how your brain makes certain choices, including investment decisions. It also plays a major role in both alcohol and drug abuse. As Jason Zweig, a respected columnist and author, wrote in *Your Money and Your Brain,* alcohol, marijuana, cocaine, morphine, and amphetamines all seem to be related to the release of dopamine. "All hook their users by affecting in a variety of ways the trigger zones for dopamine in the brain."[10] A hit of cocaine, for example, tells the brain to release dopamine about fifteen times as fast as normal, indicating that it may somehow help transmit the euphoric kick of the drug. "Dopamine spreads its fingers all over the brain," says a neuroscientist, Antoine Bechara of the University of Southern California, of this process.[11] When the dopamine neurons are lit up, they send gushers of energy throughout the brain that make and put decisions into actions. Ironically, *the brain patterns look almost identical when dopamine is quickly activated after the inhalation of cocaine and when an investor is excited by an investment decision he has just made.*[12]

Dopamine is more than simply a rush on its own. An investor must know more: that there's a sizable reward in taking a given action. He must also take the required actions that he thinks will capture the reward.

Next, let's look at the role of dopamine in the various forms of earnings surprises examined. Dopamine neurons are released by rewarding events that are better than predicted, remain uninfluenced by events that are as good as predicted, and are depressed by events that are worse than predicted. This, it appears, is the key reason why effects of the four forms of earnings surprises we just examined have been so consistent over time. Remember: the possibility that the event trigger and the reinforcing events are not random is about 1,000 to 1. If the link between neuroeconomics and earnings surprises stands—and the evidence certainly points that way—this might forge a strong bond between predictable and repetitive economic events and neuroeconomic and Affect findings. These correlations, given the high odds that event triggers and reinforcing events are not pure chance, are highly probable. If this is the case, the similarity of findings in neuroeconomic experiments to those on earnings surprise presents a fascinating topic of research. If the current experiments do show a tie between the two, neuroeconomics as a major economic research tool will certainly become far more important.

Let's briefly look at neuroeconomics research that appears to explain the four categories of classes of earnings surprises, which, as we know, divide into two distinct categories, event triggers and reinforcing events. The researchers Wolfram Schultz of the University of Cambridge (Department of Physiology, Development and Neuroscience), Read Montague at Baylor College of Medicine, and Peter Dayan at University College London have made a number of important research findings about dopamine and reward. They discovered that getting what you anticipated produces no dopamine rush, sending out electromechanical pulses at their resting rate of about three bursts per second. Even though a reward is expected to make investors enthusiastic, it does not. This is almost precisely what we see with the high-P/E phenomenon with positive surprises and negative surprises on out-of-favor stocks with reinforcing events. The reward—in this case a positive surprise on a favored stock—is actually more than investors expected, but the reaction is almost nebulous and sometimes negative. This may also explain why drug addicts require larger hits to get the same high and why investors require larger earnings hits on "best stocks to see their prices move higher."

To neuroeconomists, the two event triggers would be the real surprises. They are major unexpected events. According to a research study by Pammi Chandrasekhar, C. Monica Capra, Sara Moore, Charles Noussair, and Gregory Berns,[13] higher-than-expected rewards are unanticipated and as a result release dopamine. Looking at event triggers shows that a positive earnings surprise for an unfavored stock is also unanticipated by investors holding or interested in the stock. They are likely to experience "rejoice" or elation when their stock shows a positive earnings surprise, and their brains release dopamine.

Research findings on monkeys also show strong results for unanticipated positive surprises. (I apologize to readers who might be offended by the comparison of monkeys to humans. In my defense I can only point out that monkeys, chimpanzees, and pigeons scored higher on some of these neuropsychology tests than did people.)

Schultz studied the brains of monkeys and found that when dopamine comes as the result of a surprise the dopamine neurons fire more strongly and for a longer time than for a reward that was anticipated beforehand.[14] This research, although only now being tested on event triggers, appears to support the unanticipated positive surprise on low-P/E stocks in the event trigger. When investors receive unexpectedly higher earnings on out-of-favor stocks, their dopamine is also likely to fire up almost instantaneously and strongly—Schultz's studies show from three to forty times a second. In Schultz's words, "This kind of positive reinforcement creates a special kind of attention dedicated to rewards. Rewards are what keep you coming back for more." [15] Schultz and Anthony Dickinson, in the 2000 *Annual Review of Neuroscience*, wrote, "In summary, the reward responses depend on the difference between the occurrence and the prediction of reward (dopamine response = reward occurred − reward predicted)." [16]

Chandrasekhar and colleagues' results suggest that activation of a neural network consisting of the rostral anterior cingulate, left hippocampus, left ventral striatum, and brainstem/midbrain is correlated with rejoicing.[17] Don't worry, this is not a test; it's merely here to show how complex these neural interactions can be. Similarly, the second event trigger, a negative surprise on a favorite stock, might cause regret and disappointment. In this case another neural network, the cortical network, is activated. Neuroeconomists can measure the two classes of surprises by using functional magnetic resonance imaging (fMRI). This network activates the degree of regret.[18]

Schultz, Montague, and Dayan also found that if rewards we expect don't pan out, dopamine dries up.[19] Dopamine neurons activate when people spot a signal that the reward is coming, but if it doesn't come, they will instantly stop firing. The brain is thus deprived of its expected shot of dopamine, and disappointment sets in. This is similar to the reaction we see in the earnings surprise on a favored stock that has a negative surprise (an event trigger). Schultz and Dickinson also observed that omitted rewards induce opposite changes in dopamine neurons compared with unpredicted rewards. If a predicted reward fails to occur, dopamine neurons are depressed at the time the reward would have occurred. This suggests a form of error coding that is compatible with the idea that the error directly controls learning about the prediction.[20] The fact that there is no positive reward, but a negative consequence, for each security in the best-stock negative-surprise portfolio quite possibly is responsible for the significant, immediate, and then continuing drop in price. As we have seen, both the positive and the negative effects last for at least four quarters.

Reinforcing events, the two other classes of earnings surprises we noted—a positive surprise on a favored company and a negative surprise on an out-of-favor stock—do not seem to have much impact on our neuroprocessing or, for that matter, in the marketplace, from what the neuropsychologists report in related studies. For example, winning a bet when it is highly probable evokes less rejoicing than winning a bet when the outlook was unlikely. Similarly, losing a bet when the outcome is probable evokes less regret than losing a bet when the outlook is improbable. Chandrasekhar and colleagues indicate that the degree of regret or rejoicing correlates with the perceived probabilities of winning or losing. The higher the expectation of winning, the lower the amount of rejoicing; and the lower the expectation of winning, the higher the amount of rejoicing. Also noted was that different brain regions exhibited activation that increased with the levels both of regret and rejoicing. The authors conclude, "Our results suggest that distinct but overlapping networks are involved in the experiences of regret and joy."[21] What seems apparent from this analysis is that expected positive earnings surprises for favorite stocks result in only a small amount of rejoicing. The same is likely of regret for negative surprises on out-of-favor stocks.

Figure 9-8 demonstrates that this is exactly what happens with the stocks we have labeled as reinforcing events.* Also of interest is the difference in the size of event triggers and reinforcing events, as the neuroeconomists' work would suggest. The event trigger's impact on stock prices is about four times as much as that of reinforcing events in the quarter of the surprise, and almost twenty-four times as much after one year (removing signs on both). The chart is statistically significant at the 0.1 percent level; this means that there is only a 1-in-1,000 possibility that it could be sheer chance. For the investor it clearly provides some robust neuroeconom-

---

* The event triggers in Figure 9-8 are added together and the signs are removed. The same is done for reinforcing events.

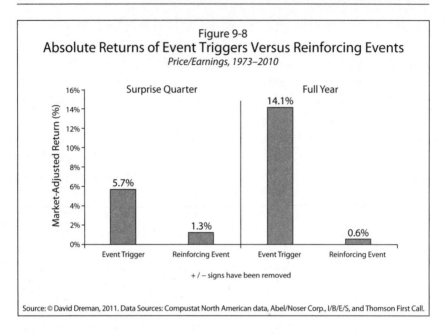

Figure 9-8
Absolute Returns of Event Triggers Versus Reinforcing Events
Price/Earnings, 1973–2010

Source: © David Dreman, 2011. Data Sources: Compustat North American data, Abel/Noser Corp., I/B/E/S, and Thomson First Call.

ics findings that appear to strongly support the purchase of out-of-favor stocks.

The Effects of Surprise over Time

We have seen the results of surprises on "best" and "worst" stocks for up to one year after the surprise is announced. Are there lingering effects beyond that? Figure 9-9, which measures the performance of the "best" and "worst" groups of stocks by P/E ratios for five-year periods following an earnings surprise, using a buy-and-hold strategy, provides the answer.* The figure indicates that the lowest-P/E group showing positive earnings surprises (low-P/E positive) outperformed the market in all twenty quarters after the surprises and recorded an above-market return of 30.3 percent for the five-year period. Conversely, the highest-P/E group receiving negative surprises (high-P/E negative) underperformed in every quarter for the following five years, lagging behind the

---

* Five-year periods were calculated for each three consecutive three-month periods since the commencement of the study and then averaged. There were 132 different periods in the study.

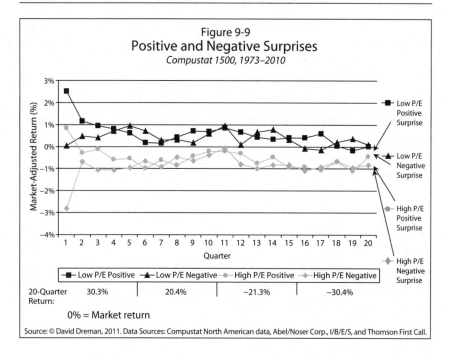

Figure 9-9
Positive and Negative Surprises
Compustat 1500, 1973–2010

Legend	
—■— Low P/E Positive	—▲— Low P/E Negative	—●— High P/E Positive	—◆— High P/E Negative

| 20-Quarter Return: | 30.3% | 20.4% | −21.3% | −30.4% |

0% = Market return

Source: © David Dreman, 2011. Data Sources: Compustat North American data, Abel/Noser Corp., I/B/E/S, and Thomson First Call.

market by 30.4 percent for the full period. As we can see, the differential between the two groups continued to increase significantly through the five years measured.

Is the entire difference in performance between the two types of event triggers caused by earnings surprises? Did the original surprises change investors' perceptions permanently? These questions are impossible to answer statistically at this time. We do know that investors were far too confident of their prognostications for both "best" and "worst" stocks; consequently, "best" stocks were significantly overvalued and "worst" stocks were undervalued. When the dark or rose-colored glasses were removed, perhaps they were swapped for each other. As was also noted earlier, not one but a series of surprises may occur, some in later quarters, including surprises other than analysts' forecast errors, that continue to reinforce the price reevaluations.

What we can say, however, is that the enormous market outperformance by the low-P/E and other low-value groups* and the underper-

---

* As well as similar outperformances by price-to-cash-flow and price-to-book-value groups, which are not shown.

formance by the highest quintile in each value group indicate that there certainly had to be an event or a series of events that changed investors' perceptions of what were "best" and "worst" stocks.

We also see the effects of reinforcing events. "Worst" stocks with negative surprises (low-P/E negative) consistently outperformed after the surprise quarter and for the next nineteen quarters, while "best" stocks with positive surprises (high-P/E positive) just as consistently underperformed. Although the differences are not as large as for "best" and "worst" stocks that experienced an event trigger in the surprise quarter, they are still major. "Best" stocks underperformed the market by 21.3 percent in the full five-year periods, while "worst" stocks outperformed by 20.4 percent. (The results for the two other value measures, price to cash flow and price to book value, are again similar.)

The middle group is not shown. However, the long-term findings differ little from those at the end of the first year. Surprise has a major effect only in the quarter in which the news is announced. After that the stocks perform in line with the market. Overall, positive and negative surprises almost cancel each other out, and this is pretty much what we should expect, since being in the middle group shows that the stocks are not overvalued or undervalued by much.

A Surprising Opportunity

Psychological Guideline 18 positioned us in out-of-favor stocks to take advantage of analysts' forecast errors and other surprises. We can now go further in delineating the effect of surprises, which will prove an essential tool for the strategies to be outlined shortly. Psychological Guideline 20 summarizes our findings on surprise.

PSYCHOLOGICAL GUIDELINE 20(a): Surprises, as a group, improve the performance of out-of-favor stocks, while impairing the performance of favorites.

PSYCHOLOGICAL GUIDELINE 20(b): Positive surprises result in major appreciation for out-of-favor stocks, while having minimal impact on favorites.

PSYCHOLOGICAL GUIDELINE 20(c): Negative surprises result in major drops in the price of favorites, while having virtually no impact on out-of-favor stocks.

PSYCHOLOGICAL GUIDELINE 20(d): The effect of an earnings surprise continues for an extended period of time.

In this chapter, we have examined the role of surprises and have found that they consistently favor stocks that investors believe have poor outlooks and just as consistently work against those believed to be la crème. Because of the frequency of earnings surprises demonstrated in the preceding chapter, we know they are a powerful force acting to reverse previous over- or undervaluations of stocks.

Just how important surprises and the resulting changes in investors expectations are in developing powerful investment strategies will be shown in the next chapter. With our probabilities of winning moving increasingly higher, it's almost time to roll up our sleeves and sit down at a table in the investment casino. Now, what sort of odds would you care to have?

Part IV

Market Overreaction:
The New Investment Paradigm

Chapter 10

A Powerful Contrarian Approach to Profits

Only die-hard New Yorkers or sports masochists—I guess I fall into the latter category—rooted for the New York Giants in Super Bowl XLII. The bookies put the odds at an enormous 17 points favoring the New England Patriots. This meant that if you wanted to bet on the Patriots and collect, they would have to win over the Giants by more than two touchdowns and a field goal. So confident were the public and the experts that this would not happen that *The Boston Globe* had already begun preselling a book on Amazon.com. It was entitled *19–0: The Historic Champion Season of New England's Unbeatable Patriots*. To be released immediately after the inevitable win.

The fans and sportscasters believed it was a mismatch of almost historic proportions. The Giants, underdogs by far entering the playoffs, thought otherwise and made it through to the championship round. In February 2008, a TV audience estimated at more than 50 million saw a hard-fought game. When it was over and the artificial dust had cleared on Super Bowl XLII, the Giants had beaten the mighty Patriots. It took a Giants touchdown in the last thirty-five seconds of play to seal the Patriots' fate, but that's what happened, and it sent the stunned fans into a state of shock.

How could the most powerful football team in decades be reduced to such an ignoble outcome? Many money managers and other professional investors, immaculately dressed in their Paul Stuart suits and Ferragamo ties, sitting in their well-appointed offices, flanked by the latest and most powerful market technology of the day, must wonder the same thing: how can they perform so dismally when they buy the top research and investment advice?

It must be a real puzzle to them.

But . . . are the stocks the experts like really the ones to buy? We have seen that the answer is a strong no. The favorite stocks of analysts and money managers are consistently punished by earnings surprises, while the stocks nobody loves or wants just as consistently benefit from surprises. Investors' enthusiasm often causes popular stocks to become overpriced, while the lack of it dumps them into the bargain basement. Earnings and other surprises result in a reevaluation of both groups and more realistic pricing.

This is certainly a large, critical piece of the puzzle, but how do we fit it into a practical investment strategy? After all, we're not just trying to analyze market dynamics; we're seeking to learn patterns of how to profit from them. For a change, rather than trying to build a deductive case, I'm going to put the answer right out on the table for your inspection. While I'm at it, let's identify the core of this proven investment approach and make the next Psychological Guideline.

PSYCHOLOGICAL GUIDELINE 21: Favored stocks underperform the market, while out-of-favor companies outperform the market, *but the reappraisal often happens slowly, even glacially.*

This reevaluation process, heavily influenced by the new psychological findings of Affect and neuroeconomics, is the key to large and consistent profits in the marketplace. From the dawn of markets, people's reaction to "best" and "worst" investments has been consistent and predictable. And here we come to the bottom line for the practical reader: investors' behavior is so predictable in this respect that the average reader can take advantage of it. There are proven yet uncomplicated contrarian strategies that should allow you to outperform the market handily, with relatively little risk.

In this part we will present a new paradigm (or model) of investing that will both utilize the state-of-the-art psychology we viewed in Part I and combine it with investment methods based on it that have proved highly successful over many decades. The methods also rely on us to disregard some of the conventional teachings we have received about how we should evaluate stocks, bonds, or other investments. But they are anything but bugle blasts ordering you to follow the new knowledge blindly. Each has been proved over time either by psychology or by superior investment performance.

Sounds a little heady, doesn't it? Now let's start at the beginning and see exactly what's behind these assertions. We'll begin with a bit of discussion to reveal the elemental structure, function, and statistical justifications of five major variations on the contrarian strategies, each highly successful to date. Using this key, you'll see how the pieces of the puzzle rapidly fall into place—although I'm afraid it won't get you a discount on one of those Paul Stuart suits or Ferragamo ties. The five important strategies are:

1. Low-price-to-earnings strategy
2. Low-price-to-cash-flow strategy
3. Low-price-to-book-value strategy
4. High-yield strategy
5. Low-price-to-industry strategy

Each of these strategies has a number of subcategories to allow you to custom-tailor it to your own requirements. Strategy 5, a very new and different type of contrarian strategy, will be introduced in chapter 12.

The Investment World Turned Upside Down

What seemed apparent from our review of experts' forecasts is that the companies they liked the best tended to be the wrong ones to buy. Therefore, let's ask another question: should you avoid the stocks the experts and the crowd are pursuing and pursue the ones they are avoiding? The answer, as we shall see, is an unqualified yes.

And we can document the consistent success of this investment strategy going back almost eighty years, a strategy that dramatically opposes conventional wisdom—a prime reason it works.

For the findings show that companies the market expects the best future for, as measured by the price-to-earnings, price-to-cash-flow, price-to-book-value, high-yield, and low-price-to-industry strategies, have consistently done the worst, while the stocks believed to have the most dismal future have always done the best. The strategy is not without an element of black humor. In fact, to the true believers at the shrines of efficient markets or other contemporary investment methods, the approach may appear to be a form of Satan worship: the "best" investments turn out bad, and the "worst" ones turn out good.

However, the findings are not in the least magical and don't contain even a trace of voodoo. Most investors do not recognize the immense difficulty of predicting earnings and economic events, and when forecasting methods fail, a predictable reaction occurs. *Here we confront the main irony: one of the most obvious and consistent variables that can be harnessed into a workable investment strategy is the continual overreaction of people to companies they consider to have excellent or mundane prospects.* This works just as surely with investors today as it has worked with investors in any market in the past.

■ The Boot Hills of Concept Stocks

In order to make evaluations of "best" stocks, forecasts extending growth well into the future must be made with extreme accuracy. As we saw in chapter 8, the reliability of these forecasts is ridiculously low. We also know that when the earnings of a favored company fall below the forecast, the earnings surprise, even if it is minute, has a devastating effect on its stock prices. Not surprisingly, investment strategies *based on precise estimates* have performed erratically, to say the least. There is a Boot Hill full of Internet names from the 1996–2000 dot-com bubble, as well as a Boot Hill containing similar stocks from earlier bubbles and another one of "must-own" concept stocks to be bought at any price.

The term "best," used by so many professional and individual investors, also filters out the inherent risk of the situation. Conversely, the lowest-visibility stocks have been shown to be significantly underpriced and, when they have positive surprises, are subject to sharp upward reappraisals. As we saw in chapter 2, inherent risk is understated for high-expectation situations; it is often exaggerated, sometimes dramatically, for low-expectation stocks. This puts the master key of the book into our hands—and explains why the investment strategies that we'll examine work remarkably well over time.

The Success of Low-P/E Strategies: The Early Evidence

Beginning in the 1960s, researchers began to wonder if visibility—the crucial pillar of modern security analysis—was actually as solid as generally believed. The original studies were done with price-earnings ratios because of their ready availability in the early databases. One of the first of those researchers asked, "How accurate is the P/E ratio as a measure of subsequent market performance?"

Francis Nicholson, then with the Provident National Bank, was the interrogator. In one comprehensive study done in 1968 that measured the relative performance of high- versus low-P/E stocks, he analyzed

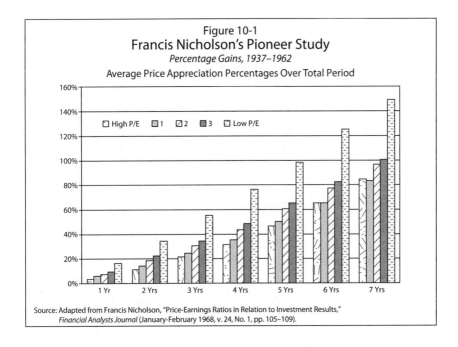

Figure 10-1
Francis Nicholson's Pioneer Study
Percentage Gains, 1937–1962
Average Price Appreciation Percentages Over Total Period

Source: Adapted from Francis Nicholson, "Price-Earnings Ratios in Relation to Investment Results," *Financial Analysts Journal* (January-February 1968, v. 24, No. 1, pp. 105–109).

189 companies of trust-company quality in eighteen industries over the twenty-six years 1937–1962.[1] The results are given in Figure 10-1.

Nicholson divided the stocks into five equal-sized groups according to their P/E rankings. These quintiles were rearranged by their P/E rankings for periods of one to seven years. When the quintiles were recast annually on the basis of new P/E information, the stocks most out of favor showed a 16 percent annual rate of appreciation over the total time span. Conversely, switching in the highest P/Es on the same basis resulted in only a 3 percent annual appreciation over the period. Although the performance discrepancies were reduced with longer holding periods, even after the original portfolios were held for seven years, the lowest 20 percent did almost twice as well as the highest.

With remarkable consistency, investors misjudged subsequent performance. The results are completely uniform. The most favored stocks (quintile 1) sharply underperformed the other groups, while the least popular (quintile 5) showed the best results. The second most popular quintile had the second worst performance, while the second most unpopular quintile had the second best results.

Benjamin Graham's *The Intelligent Investor* cites a second study, this one involving the thirty stocks in the Dow Jones Industrial Average (Table 10-1). The performance of the ten lowest- and ten highest-P/E stocks in the group and of the combined thirty stocks in the industrial average was measured over set periods between 1937 and 1969. In each time span, the low P/Es did better than the market and the high P/Es did worse.

Table 10-1
Average Annual Percentage Gain or Loss
On Dow Jones Industrial Average
1937–1969

Period	10 Low-Multiple Issues	10 High-Multiple Issues	30DJIA Stocks
1937–42	−2.2%	−10.0%	−6.3%
1943–47	17.3%	8.3%	14.9%
1948–52	16.4%	4.6%	9.9%
1953–57	20.9%	10.0%	13.7%
1958–62	10.2%	−3.3%	3.6%
1963–69	8.0%	4.6%	4.0%

Source: Benjamin Graham, The Intelligent Investor, 4th ed., p. 80. Copyright © 1973 by Harper & Row Publishers, Inc. Reprinted by permission of HarperCollins Publishers, Inc.

The study also calculated the results of investing $10,000 in either the high- or low-multiple groups in the Dow Jones Industrial Average in 1937 and switching every five years into the highest P/Es (in the first case) and the lowest P/Es (in the latter). Ten thousand dollars invested in the lowest P/Es this way in 1937 would have increased to $66,866 by the end of 1962. Invested in the highest P/Es, the $10,000 would have appreciated to only $25,437. Finally, $10,000 invested in the stocks of the Dow Jones Industrial Average would have grown to $35,600 by 1962. (Some thirty-five years later, Graham's findings were reintroduced as a hot new investment strategy, "The Dogs of the Dow.")

A number of other studies in the 1960s came up with similar findings. The conclusion of these studies, of course, is that low-P/E stocks were distinctly superior investments over an almost thirty-year period. But theories, like sacred cows, die hard, so these findings created little stir at the time.[2]

The Days of Disbelief

If the low-P/E results were analyzed at all, they were criticized. For one thing, the growth school has always had a major following among investors. Many institutional investors could not bring themselves to believe the efficacy of the findings. After all, like the studies that discredited earnings forecasts, these findings did seem, cavalierly, to toss aside our years of practice (or perhaps brainwashing) to the contrary. When I published a paper in early 1976 summarizing some of the previous research, a number of professionals told me that such information was history: "Markets of the 1970s are very different."

The low-P/E researchers were onto something, but the efficient-market hypothesis was rapidly ascending, and the work was mainly ignored. After all, in the late 1960s, our financial friends in academia were tightening the final nuts and bolts of the formidable efficient-market hypothesis. According to this academic-launched dreadnought, such results simply could not exist—whether they did or not. And that was that!

Further EMH criticism asserted that low-P/E stocks were systematically riskier (in the parlance, had higher betas) and therefore ought to provide higher returns. We have already looked closely at the failure of risk measures that the EMH academics used in chapters 5 and 6.

However, even in science fact has little chance against entrenched belief. For the coup de grâce, methodological criticisms of the studies were wheeled into action. They were mostly hairsplitting and not convincing—at least to me. But recall Einstein's dictum "It is the theory that describes what we can observe." Those findings could not exist if the dreadnought was to proceed merrily along annihilating traditional investment practice.

Buying low-P/E stocks appeared successful in studies of past performance. As a practical matter, it had worked for me—no small inducement to belief. Consequently, I updated several studies that I had used first in *Psychology and the Stock Market* (1977) and second in *Contrarian Investment Strategy* (1979). The low-P/E findings were still robust.[3]

My findings once again showed the clear-cut advantage of a low-P/E strategy. The study covered the two-tier market of 1971–1972, the bear market of 1973–1974 (the worst in the postwar period up to then), and the subsequent recovery. It did not matter whether investors started near a market top or a market bottom; superior returns were provided in any phase of the market cycle.

Through the 1980s to the mid-1990s, I completed (with various collaborators) half a dozen separate studies on low-P/E strategies, most of which were published in *Forbes*.* One study measured the 1,800 largest companies on the Compustat tapes between 1963 and 1985. The lowest-P/E quintile returned 20.7 percent annually against 10.4 percent for the highest.[4] Another divided the 6,000 stocks on the Compustat tapes into five equal groups according to their market size, for twenty-one years ending in 1989. Each group then was divided again into five subgroups according to P/E rankings. The low-P/E groups handily outperformed the high-P/E groups for all market sizes, ranging from the smallest, at around $50 million in market value, to the largest, at nearly $6 billion.[5]

Another study measured how low price to cash flow performed for the twenty-two years ending March 31, 1985, using 750 large companies. The results are shown in Table 10-2. The stocks were again separated into five equal groups and ranked each year according to the ratio of price to cash flow.[6] As the chart shows, the most out-of-favor stocks—lowest price to cash flow—almost doubled the annual performance of the favorites through this extensive period.[7]

---

* In addition to one academic study in *Financial Analysts Journal* in collaboration with Mike Berry.

Table 10-2 Contrarian Cash Flow						
In the long term—over the last 22 years, April 1, 1963–March 31, 1985—investors who gauged value by cash flow instead of, say, earnings alone would have fared well.				Over the last seven years—January 1, 1978–March 31, 1985 —a particularly strong market period—the practice would also have worked well.		
Price to Cash Flow by Group	Total Return	Appreciation	Dividend	Price to Cash Flow by Group	Total Return	Appreciation	Dividend
Lowest	**20.1%**	**14.6%**	**5.5%**	**Lowest**	**27.4%**	**21.0%**	**6.4%**
Second lowest	14.3	8.0	6.3	Second lowest	20.1	12.2	7.9
Middle	8.7	3.2	5.5	Middle	17.4	11.4	6.0
Second highest	8.0	3.8	4.2	Second highest	19.4	15.3	4.1
Highest	10.7	8.2	2.5	Highest	16.5	14.2	2.3

Source: *Forbes*, June 16, 1986.

But what of some of the past criticisms? Were any of them still valid?[8] Our experimental design adjusted for those criticisms and still provided the results shown above.

All this has been reconfirmed by other research in the late 1970s and early 1980s. Three carefully prepared studies by the late Sanjoy Basu* came up with similar results.[9] In his study, published in the *Journal of Finance* in June 1977, Basu used a database of 1,400 firms from the New York Stock Exchange between August 1956 and August 1971. He took 750 companies that had year-ends of December 31 and turned over the portfolios annually, using prices on April 1 of the following year. As in most of the previous studies, he divided the stocks into quintiles according to P/E rankings. The results (again using total return) are shown in Table 10-3.

Basu found, as we did, that the low-P/E stocks provided superior returns and were also somewhat less risky. In his words, "However, contrary to capital market theory, the higher returns on the low P/E portfolios were not associated with higher levels of systematic risk; the systematic risks of portfolios D and E [the lowest] were lower than those for A, A*, and B [the highest]."[10] This and subsequent work, updated and adjusted for previous criticisms through the mid-1980s, thus added many links to

---

*I had the privilege of knowing and briefly working with Basu in the mid-1980s before his premature death shortly thereafter. We worked on the original concept of industry-relative contrarian strategies used in this book. Before he died, he ran off a test that indicated we were on the right track.

a chain extending over seventy years, documenting the superior performance of low-P/E issues.

Table 10-3
Performance of Stocks According to P/E Ranking
April 1957–March 1971

P/E Quintile	Average Annual Return (%)	Beta (Systematic risk)
A (highest)	9.3	1.1121
A*	9.6	1.0579
B	9.3	1.0387
C	11.7	0.9678
D	13.6	0.9401
E (lowest)	16.3	0.9866

A = highest P/E quintile
A* = highest P/E quintile, excluding stocks with negative earnings

Source: Sanjoy Basu, "Investment Performance of Common Stocks in Relation to Their Price/Earnings Ratio: A Test of the Efficient Market Hypothesis," *Journal of Finance,* 32 (June 1977): p. 67.

Whatever Took So Long?

Given the weight of the evidence, you'd think that contrarian value approaches would have captured the imagination (and wallets) of investors long ago. By the 1990s, perhaps we should have been looking back at the golden age, when only a handful of pioneers reaped the rewards and only the favored few knew what a powerful tool these strategies were. But that's not the case. Even today, in 2011, contrarians are a distinct minority—and, remarkably, are likely to remain so.

One reason for the situation is historical. You'll remember how EMH swept the land and banished the heathens from Wall Street. As the new orthodoxy, EMH had everything to gain from a long and prosperous reign—not to mention a good deal to lose if competing ideas shouldered their way onto the Street. That, of course, is as much innate human psychology as any of the other crowd reactions we will examine.

In the late 1970s and through most of the 1980s, our work did not stand tall with efficient-market advocates, particularly those residing at the high shrine of market fundamentalism, the University of Chicago. As a leading heretic, I often experienced the wrath of the true believers. My work came under sharp attack, and my *Forbes* columns even had the distinction of being assigned to classes of students to hammer apart. On several occasions my unfortunate editors had sets of 10 or more letters attacking the work, letters which they on occasion good-naturedly published.

With the publication of my books and additional articles, the barrage intensified. Letters attacked every part of the findings, saving some choice remarks for the author. None found any statistical fault with the work, but they questioned the Neanderthal beliefs of a writer who couldn't understand the overwhelming sweep and beauty of efficient-market thinking.

When I submitted a paper reporting the findings to the *Financial Analysts Journal* in 1977, it was not accepted or rejected but left in some purgatory reserved for ideas that don't fit the prevailing paradigm.

The low-P/E anomaly was large enough to continue to attract attention from academia and Wall Street. Academics also dismissed the work using their old standby, risk measurement. Low-P/E stocks might provide higher returns, but they were far more risky, said the critics: rational investors accepted the higher risk only by demanding higher returns. Unfortunately, that, too, turned out to be not quite accurate.

The Great Discovery

Through the 1980s, Wall Street became increasingly interested in contrarian investment strategies. With continuing improvements in databases, confirmation that these strategies worked grew stronger and stronger.

The tide continued to gain strength. Dennis Stattman and Barr Rosenberg, Kenneth Reid, and Ronald Lanstein, for example, found that low price to book value outperformed high price to book value and the market.[11] At the same time, the evidence mounted that beta had no value as a predictor of stock prices. Though the economic fundamentalists attempted to rationalize away their existence for almost three decades, those exasperating black swans just did not have the good manners to fly away. That low-P/E strategies worked and volatility didn't work was a death knell for efficient markets.

What was a poor apostle of this new religion to do? Since neither of these results could be denied, the answer, of course, was to be the first to discover them. That is exactly what Eugene Fama, the apostle of efficient markets, did. In the 1990s, academics firmly planted their own flag on the newfound world of contrarian strategies.

In a revolutionary paper that thrust boldly thirty years into the past, Professor Fama discovered precisely what Nicholson, other researchers of the 1960s, Sanjoy Basu, Stattman, Rosenberg and colleagues, and I had found in the 1970s and '80s: that contrarian strategies worked. Worse yet, as we saw in chapter 6, beta didn't work. The three decades of stating that contrarian strategies provided better returns because they were riskier were swept away, as we saw, by the discovery that beta, the risk measure the apostle and his disciples used, was valueless.

To be fair, Fama and French[12] do reference Basu, Stattman, and Rosenberg and colleagues in passing, as well as Ray Ball,[13] who argued that low- P/E is a catchall for all risk that cannot be explicitly separated or even found. Still, Ball's explanation was widely accepted by efficient marketers for years.

The reasoning in Ball's paper is not unlike the phlogiston theory of heat popular in the eighteenth century. According to the theory, some elements are more combustible than others because they contain more phlogiston, while others are less so because they contain smaller amounts. Phlogiston was supposedly weightless and odorless, and could not be detected; nevertheless, it was there. How else could combustion occur? (Or how could low-P/E strategies beat the market if they were not risky, regardless of the fact that said risk could not be detected?) Circular and fallacious reasoning, yes, but Ball, Fama, et al. used precisely this logic to defend EMH. In both cases, the theorists defended themselves against phenomena they cannot explain through the creation of ingenious fudge factors. (The efficient-market hypothesis, as we have seen, has a grab bag full of these defenses.)

The landmark 1992 paper by Eugene Fama and his coauthor Kenneth French showed that the lowest price-to-book-value ratios, lowest price-to-earnings ratios, and small-capitalization stocks provide the highest returns over time.[14] Figure 10-2 provides Fama and French's price-to-book-value results. The sample used an average of 2,300 companies annually from the Compustat North America database. Stock returns are shown in quintiles by price-to-book-value ratios (P/BV), which are recast annually. The highest-price-to-book-value stocks are in column 3 and the lowest, or most unpopular, in column 1. As the figure indicates, low price to book value (20.5 percent) provides more than double the annual re-

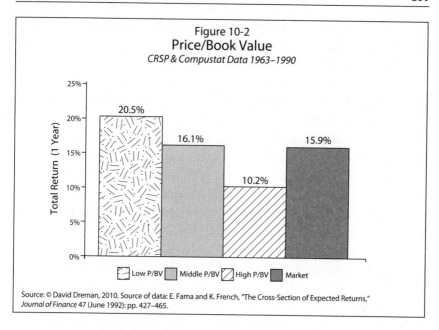

Figure 10-2
Price/Book Value
CRSP & Compustat Data 1963–1990

Source: © David Dreman, 2010. Source of data: E. Fama and K. French, "The Cross-Section of Expected Returns," *Journal of Finance* 47 (June 1992): pp. 427–465.

turn of high P/BV for the entire sample through the life of the study. Low P/BV outperforms the market by 4.6 percent annually on average, while high P/BV underperforms by 5.7 percent.

Fama downplayed the low-P/E effect in an interview, saying the reason low-P/E stocks do well is that so many of them are the same stocks as are in the price-to-book-value sample. One could say precisely the opposite and be just as correct. As *Fortune* concluded, "Some might call that academic hairsplitting." [15] Since Fama had resisted the low-P/E effect for almost thirty years, another not unreasonable conclusion is that it may be a symptom of academic face-saving.

Let's go back briefly to Basu's Table 10-3. In the last column he adjusted his table for risk (beta) and found that volatility was actually lower for low-P/E stocks than for higher P/Es. EMH theory states definitively that low-P/E betas, or risk, must be higher than those of higher-P/E stocks. This has to be the case because these out-of-favor stocks provide higher returns than high-P/E stocks. Remember, the crucial premise of the capital asset pricing model, Fama and colleagues' three-factor model, and all the other EMH risk-return models we saw in chapter 6 is based on the professors' emphatic pronouncement that *higher returns can be achieved only by taking greater risk* (volatility), which we left them still trying to find proof for in that chapter.

But to move on. The blessing of contrarian strategies by the high priests at Chicago now allowed the investment world to eat what had been forbidden fruit. Value strategies were looked at with new reverence, and value indexes were introduced by Standard & Poor's, Frank Russell, and scads of other consultants. Fortified by Professor Fama's findings, other researchers now found the courage to spring boldly into the past.

In "Contrarian Investment, Extrapolation, and Risk," Josef Lakonishok, Andrei Shleifer, and Robert Vishny measured the performance of the three important value strategies we've looked at and came up with similar results.[16] These pesky contrarian strategies, then, have proved watertight for a lot longer than the efficient-market hypothesis. In fact, they have been getting stronger with each passing year.

The good news for you is that this wave of discoveries provides strong evidence that there are consistent, high-odds ways to beat the market. The methods also protect your capital in a bear market, as I'll demonstrate shortly. It sounds a little like having your cake and eating it, too, but there are strong reasons why these strategies continue to work for disciplined investors. (That's why I've included Psychological Guidelines—all based on investors' psychological failings—throughout the text as a critical reminder.)

▮ The Last Nail

As we have seen, there are a number of contrarian strategies besides low P/E that work just fine. Low price-to-cash-flow and low price-to-book-value ratios are both potent tools for beating the market. Some of my more recent work demonstrates that buying stocks with high dividend yields has been successful in outperforming the averages, as has buying the stocks with the lowest P/Es in any industry (the industry-relative strategy). Beating the market isn't easy. According to Vanguard's John C. Bogle, whom we met earlier, only about 10 percent of managers are able to accomplish this in any ten-year period. But someone may ask a pointed question here: "True, you might say the numbers on low-P/E returns are impressive going back to the 1930s and up to 1990, but a lot of water has flowed under the bridge since then. How have contrarian strategies done in more recent times?"

The answer is "Just fine," as we'll see next, and in much more detail in the investment strategy section of the next chapter. All five contrarian strategies we looked at outperformed the market in the 1970–2010 period, which saw the two worst market downturns in our history other than 1929–1932.

Figure 10-3 shows how effective contrarian value strategies have been for the forty-one years ending December 31, 2010. The study measures the Compustat 1500. Four separate value measures were used: low P/E, low price to book value, low price to cash flow, and highest yield. The stocks were divided into quintiles according to these four criteria, and the results were calculated annually throughout the study. The chart shows the returns against market using each of these strategies for this forty-one-year period. The methodology is almost identical to that explained for my chart shown earlier.

Value strategies work with a vengeance! All four outperform the aver-

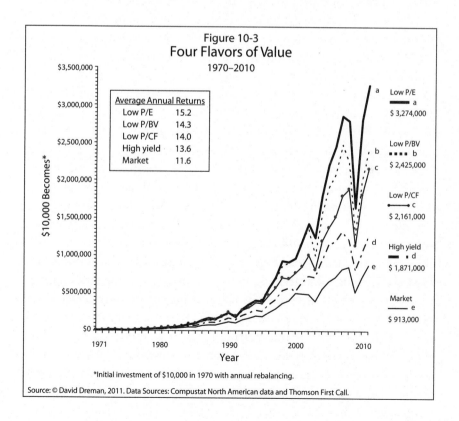

Figure 10-3
Four Flavors of Value
1970–2010

Average Annual Returns	
Low P/E	15.2
Low P/BV	14.3
Low P/CF	14.0
High yield	13.6
Market	11.6

Low P/E — a $ 3,274,000
Low P/BV ■■■■ b $ 2,425,000
Low P/CF ●——● c $ 2,161,000
High yield ■ ▪ d $ 1,871,000
Market —— e $ 913,000

*Initial investment of $10,000 in 1970 with annual rebalancing.

Source: © David Dreman, 2011. Data Sources: Compustat North American data and Thomson First Call.

age, and the returns of three of the strategies are outstanding. Ten thousand dollars invested in the bottom 20 percent of P/Es in the Compustat 1500 in 1970 would now be worth $3,274,000 at the end of December 2010 (all figures assume reinvestment of dividends), about four times the market's cumulative value of $913,000 for investing the same $10,000 for the entire period. Looking at it another way, *$10,000 in 1970 increased 327-fold!*

Low price to book value, a favorite of Benjamin Graham, trailed low P/E but was ahead of the other two strategies for the period and almost triple the return for the market over these four decades. Low price to cash flow, taken from the statistics available from Compustat (thus excluding all the high-octane adjustments claimed to soup up performance), also worked just fine.

The returns shown in the small box near the top of the chart are worth looking at. After both the dot-com crash and the meltdown of 2007–2008, the average annual return over this forty-one-year period was 15.2 percent for low P/E, more than 14 percent for low price to book value, and 14.0 percent for low price to cash flow. This compares with a long-term rate of return for common stocks of 9.9 percent since the mid-1920s. *Contrarian strategies outperformed the long-term rate of return of common stocks, 37 to 54 percent, through this forty-one-year period.* I think we can safely say the sky is not falling on these strategies in spite of the horrendous markets of the the last decade.

Next let's move on to the high-yield investment strategy. This value method is a little different from the other three. Normally, high dividend yields are found in utilities and other industry groups, which are not expected to have rapid appreciation. On the opposite side of the scale, stocks that pay small dividends or none at all are usually found in rapidly growing industries. Instead of paying dividends, companies hold the money back to finance growth. There has always been a good deal of controversy about whether stocks with high dividend yields even come close to the appreciation of the averages.

The answer is surprising. Although trailing the other three value measures, high-yield stocks outdistanced the market by 105 percent (all strategies include reinvested dividends). Ironically, though large numbers of investors buy large dividend payers for income, this method is probably most suitable for tax-free accounts. In a high tax bracket, the performance advantage over the market will decline fairly significantly, because a large part of the return is dividends, which go to Uncle Sam.

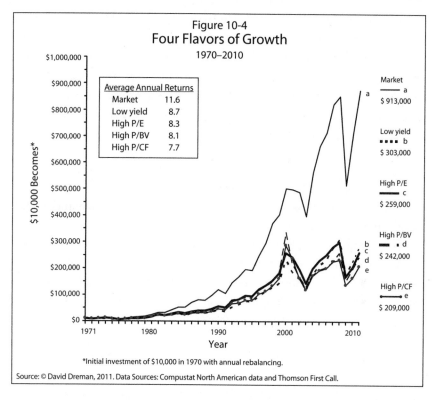

Figure 10-4
Four Flavors of Growth
1970–2010

Average Annual Returns	
Market	11.6
Low yield	8.7
High P/E	8.3
High P/BV	8.1
High P/CF	7.7

Market
—— a
$ 913,000

Low yield
▪▪▪▪ b
$ 303,000

High P/E
—— c
$ 259,000

High P/BV
▪▪ ▪ d
$ 242,000

High P/CF
●——● e
$ 209,000

*Initial investment of $10,000 in 1970 with annual rebalancing.

Source: © David Dreman, 2011. Data Sources: Compustat North American data and Thomson First Call.

Another reasonable question is: how did the favored stocks perform by the same yardsticks? Badly. Regardless of which measure I used, none of the favorites came close to beating the market over the forty-one-year period. Ten thousand dollars invested in the highest-P/E group would have been worth $259,000 at the end of 2010, less than 30 percent of the $913,000 ending value of the market. The same amount invested in highest-price-to-book-value stocks grew to only $242,000, and invested in the highest-price-to-cash flow category, it grew to $209,000: 27 percent and 23 percent of the cumulative market return, respectively. Unexpectedly, the best performer in the "best sector" was the low-yield, no-yield group, which accumulated a dismal 33 percent of the market's value at the end of 2010.

Strikingly, then, *four of the most commonly used valuation ratios when applied to out-of-favor stocks resulted in their all significantly outperforming the market, while the same four metrics, when applied to favored stocks, resulted in their all significantly underperforming the market over the length of the study.*

Unhappily for believers in growth, the long-term drubbing does not stop here. Although there is constant debate in the financial press and the investment media, as well as in Morningstar and other advisory services, about whether value or growth performs better over time, the results of this study are clear-cut. First, contrarian strategies outperform growth strategies regardless of the metric chosen. Next, the margin of outperformance over time is enormous. Low-P/E stocks outperform their high-P/E brethren by close to thirteenfold. Ten thousand dollars initially invested in these stocks in 1970 became $3,274,000, versus the $259,000 invested in high-P/E stocks at the same time. Similarly, $10,000 invested in low-price-to-book-value stocks would have grown to $2,425,000 against the $242,000 that the initial $10,000 would have increased to in high-price-to-book-value stocks. The comparisons of price to cash flow are similar. It's clear that contrarian strategies outperform favored stocks by a country mile. What is also demonstrated is that contrarian strategies have performed very well, *increasing initial capital by up to 327 times, from 1970 through 2010, and this after the worst market downturn since the Great Depression.*

But the story is still not over. Most investors want more than just to increase their nest egg in a rising market. Just as important, they would like to keep it intact when the bear growls. We've seen the intensity of this goal after the 2007–2008 bear market. Morningstar, Lipper, and the Forbes Annual Mutual Funds Survey, among others, rank mutual funds on how they have performed through several bear markets.

To find out how our contrarian strategies worked in down markets, we took the returns of the value stocks in each of the four categories for all fifty-two down quarters in the study and averaged them. As Figure 10-5a shows, the value strategies all did better than the market average in the down markets through the same period (1970–2010). While the market dropped 7.6 percent in the average down quarter, low-P/E, low-price-to-cash-flow, and low-price-to-book-value stocks all fell less, as the figure shows. The best performers, as you might expect, were the high-yield stocks, declining only 3.8 percent, or half as much as the market.

As you have also probably guessed, the high-P/E, high-P/CF, high-P/BV, and low-yield stocks were hit hard. As Figure 10-5b shows, all four strategies were down more than the market average, dropping between 9.5 percent and 10.8 percent and significantly more than the low-value

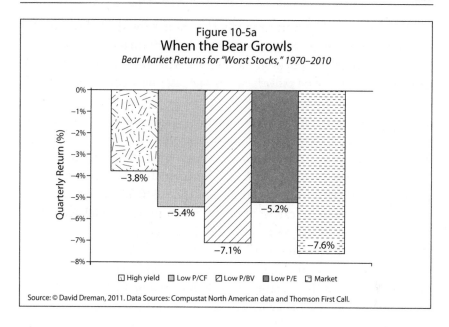

Figure 10-5a
When the Bear Growls
Bear Market Returns for "Worst Stocks," 1970–2010

□ High yield   ▨ Low P/CF   ▨ Low P/BV   ▨ Low P/E   ▨ Market

Source: © David Dreman, 2011. Data Sources: Compustat North American data and Thomson First Call.

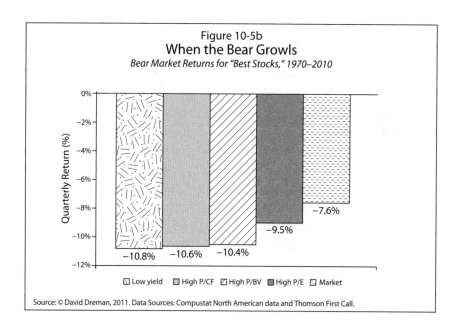

Figure 10-5b
When the Bear Growls
Bear Market Returns for "Best Stocks," 1970–2010

□ Low yield   ▨ High P/CF   ▨ High P/BV   ▨ High P/E   ▨ Market

Source: © David Dreman, 2011. Data Sources: Compustat North American data and Thomson First Call.

metrics* versus a 7.6 percent drop for the market. Value stocks, then, not only provide higher returns in a rising market but also star on the defense. The value strategies originally presented by Ben Graham and other market pioneers played out at least as well as, and perhaps better than, they would have imagined.

Obviously, very few individuals can or need to hold funds in stocks for this period of time. But for those institutions, pension funds, and other long-term buyers who are once again fleeing stocks to buy Treasuries and other bonds at tiny yields, it's a proven strategy that, when folks stop running away from stocks, they should definitely consider.

▓ Summing It All Up

The consistency of these studies is truly remarkable. Over almost every period measured, the stocks considered to have the best prospects fared significantly worse than the contrarian stocks, using the same criteria. This leads us to another Psychological Guideline:

PSYCHOLOGICAL GUIDELINE 22: Buy solid companies currently out of market favor, as measured by their low-price-to-earnings, low-price-to-cash-flow, or low-price-to-book-value ratios or by their high yields.

You might wonder: if these strategies do so well, why doesn't everyone use them? This lands us smack in the realm of investor psychology (or behavioral finance, as it is now called by economists).

Though the statistics drag us toward the value camp, our emotions just as surely tug us the other way. People are captivated by exciting new concepts. The lure of hitting a home run on a hot new idea, as chapter 2 made clear, overwhelms caution. The sizzle and glitz of an initial public offering such as LinkedIn, the Facebook of the professional world, which was issued at $45 and went to $122.70 the same day in May 2011, when it traded at a P/E of 548 times and price-to-book-value ratio of 134 times, or a RealD, in late May 2011 trading at a P/E of 170, are just too great.[17]

---

* A word of caution on performance figures. All are simply averages of performance of the favored stock and contrarian metric results in down quarters throughout the study. Contrarian stocks will not outperform in every down quarter, nor will growth strategies underperform in every one. The same is true for all the charts in this chapter.

Though these are extreme examples of investor evaluation run amok, they show why value strategies have worked so well over the years. People pay for concept, whether in the absurd cases of LinkedIn or RealD or in consistently overpricing the trendy industries of the day. Investors just as surely want to stay well away from companies whose outlooks seem poor.

The favored stocks, on the other hand, present the best visibility money can buy. How, then, can one recommend such a reversal of course? The psychological consistency of the error is remarkable. There are, of course, strong stocks that justify their price-earnings ratios and others that deserve the slimmest of multiples. But, as the evidence indicates, the "best" are relatively few in number, and the chances of recognizing them are very small.

Contrarian strategies succeed because investors don't know their limitations as forecasters. As long as investors believe they can pinpoint the future of favored and out-of-favor stocks, you should be able to make good returns on contrarian strategies. Human nature being what it is, this edge should continue for a few years longer—unless contrarians have a few million new readers sooner. (I'm sure my publisher and I would be delighted to deal with that problem, though.)

We have seen how consistently contrarian strategies have worked for investors over the years. The good news for you is that this wave of discoveries in new psychology and in contrarian strategies is harmonious. This is in strong contrast to EMH and MPT, where psychology exposes their basic assumptions. The research data of stock performance over the years provide strong evidence that there are consistent high-odds ways to beat the market. Next let's extend the explanation to how we can use these strategies to both survive in and crank up our returns in the difficult markets we are likely to face.

Chapter 11

Profiting from
Investors' Overreactions

IN THE PRECEDING CHAPTER we surveyed the four important contrarian strategies that will let us not only survive but be successful in today's markets, and we've seen the spectacular results they provide over time if used properly. In this chapter we'll introduce a new investment hypothesis that seems to explain markets and investors' behavior, as well as risk, far better than does EMH. Now, how can we put its findings to work?

Disproving an old hypothesis and bringing out a new one in its place is always difficult for the proponents of the new one. Though advocates won't be burned at the stake or be under house arrest for the rest of their days, you can be sure that their work will be scrutinized by legions of graduate students all attempting to find even the slightest flaw, down to the punctuation marks. The old theory is the security blanket for the reputations and work of distinguished academics who have devoted their lives to researching, expanding, and broadening the ideas of the accepted hypothesis, the large number who have been taught its efficacy, and the many thousands who work with it almost daily in the investment field because they believe in its validity, as well as the millions of people who depend on its findings to improve their portfolios' results.

Whether the new challenger in the field works or not has almost no significance to the believers in the prevailing theory—at least for the first fifty years or so. But for the reader there's a very different possibility. You don't have to stand on a soapbox and declare that you're a contrarian. All that's required is to reinvest your capital according to the contrarian strategies laid out and withdraw the gains when the time is right.

From the previous chapters, you know that our new hypothesis is built on a considerable amount of evidence in hand and a substantial amount of investigation already carried out. But it remains what it is declared to be, a hypothesis.

That is why research continues and why we cannot "close the books" on investing strategies or portfolio approaches. Even though the results have been so encouraging along the way, more work lies ahead to open up new paths and strategies and to more closely link the contrarian findings to the powerful psychology that is responsible for them.

We've come a long way on the major causes of investment misfires in today's markets. Very few investors will be successful in the contemporary environment without an understanding of how to handle these pitfalls. Now, with this knowledge of what we face, we are ready to move on to the rewards, which, if we stay within the guidelines of our new psychological knowledge, are there for the taking.

Sadly for many, this is the investment world we must deal with today. But as we know, it is often in times of turmoil that new ideas are looked at through new eyes and are accepted. Far from doom and gloom, I believe, we'll see major opportunities ahead. But to reach them, it is important to know what we are fighting and the tactics that will give us the highest probabilities of success.

▓ Section I: The Investor Overreaction Hypothesis

We have seen throughout this book that investors overreact to events and then correct their original reactions by causing major reversals in stock prices. In chapters 1 and 2, we repeatedly saw the enormous swings from frenzied overoptimism in bubbles and manias to the inevitable panic, when prices were often brutally knocked down by as much as 80 to 90 percent. Affect, sometimes accompanied by other cognitive heuristics, stands out as the most likely psychological force causing this investor behavior. But it is not only in manias, contagion, and panics that these predictable overreactions take place.

We see them consistently in far more normal market settings. Take the behavior of earnings surprises described in chapter 9. The "best" stocks, those with the most promising prospects by various yardsticks from high P/E to high price to book value to high price to cash flow, always underperform significantly as a group when they have earnings surprises. Similarly, the "worst" stocks, in terms of the same benchmarks, almost always outperform. The amount of both under- and overperformance is large, about 7 percent a year, which is 70 percent of the average 9.9 percent annual return on stocks since the mid-1920s.

An important cause of the consistent underperformance of the "best" stocks comes from investors' and analysts' overoptimism about their ability to pinpoint earnings, even though the empirical evidence shows emphatically that it can't be done. This overoptimism and the focus on predictable growth, both manifestations of Affect, are the most important components of security analysis in our times and are growing more important each year. Forget Graham and Dodd, who concentrated on a wide range of fundamentals and financial ratios and would completely reject the narrow focus of analysts today. Most of us either directly or indirectly still follow these newer analytical guidelines, unsuccessful as they have proved to be in recent decades.

In the preceding chapter we saw how out-of-favor stocks have sharply outperformed the favorites for many decades. Statistics by Kenneth French, often Eugene Fama's coauthor, on his Web site indicate that this outperformance has taken place in every decade since the 1940s.* As Figures 10-3 and 10-4 showed, an investor who purchased $10,000 in low-P/E stocks in 1970 would have thirteen times the money of someone who purchased $10,000 of the high-P/E index at the same time. Yet a study by Mark Peterson, then of Deutsche Bank, indicates that only about 3 percent of stocks held by equity mutual fund investors are contrarian holdings.[1]

Again, the answer is Affect. We inherently like the "best" stocks or

---

*The Kenneth French site is http://mba.tuck.dartmouth.edu/pages/faculty/ken.french/data_library.html.

industries and stay well away from the "worst." It doesn't matter if we've made the same error dozens of times; the influence of Affect is too strong not to influence our decision-making processes. Affect is very easy to detect in the case of a bubble or a mania—after the fact, of course. But it can also act very subtly when most people select "best" over "worst" stocks or when they ignore the evidence that earnings surprises favor "worst," not "best," stocks. If we look at mental disorders, we find that it's easier for a psychiatrist to diagnose severe paranoia or schizophrenia than to identify neurosis, in which people's behavior often seems normal. The situation is similar with Affect; it's far easier to look at the effects of manias and bubbles than to see the influence of Affect in more normal markets, where price fluctuations are far more moderate. But the data indicate that Affect has a robust effect in these cases, too.

The evidence of consistent and predictable overreactions to events through this book, some new, some discovered over recent decades, led me to the investor overreaction hypothesis, which I introduced in the original edition of *Contrarian Investment Strategy* in 1979. Although the term "overreaction" is almost as old as markets themselves, I developed a testable hypothesis. At that time there were only a handful of anomalies to test, notably the superior performance of out-of-favor stocks and the consistently better performance of lower-rated bonds. Both anomalies had shown superior results for many decades. Sanjoy Basu,[2] in 1977, and behavioral finance pioneers Werner De Bondt and Richard Thaler refer to investor overreaction in their 1985 paper,[3] but limit it primarily to the performance of "best" and "worst" stocks. A stronger version of this hypothesis, reinforced by new psychological discoveries in both Affect and neuroeconomics, is presented here. The number of anomalies in which overreaction takes place has jumped manyfold in the intervening decades.

THE INVESTOR OVERREACTION HYPOTHESIS DEFINED

The investor overreaction hypothesis (IOH) states that investors overreact to certain events in a consistent and predictable manner.

This is based on the psychological forces we examined in detail in the research findings in Part I and the new biologically demonstrated discoveries of neuroeconomics, as discussed in chapter 9.

Three central predictions of IOH are:

1. Investors will consistently overvalue favored stocks and undervalue out-of-favor stocks.
2. Investors will find themselves overoptimistic on the forecasts of "best" stocks and too pessimistic on those of "worst" stocks over time. As a result, earnings surprises tend to favor "worst" stocks as a group in a predictable and consistent manner.
3. Over time both favored and out-of-favor stocks will regress to the mean because of earnings surprises and other fundamental factors, which will result in the underperformance of the "best" stocks while those considered "worst" will outperform.

These predictions are borne out in the market history that we have examined in detail earlier. Unfortunately, we won't run out of good illustrations anytime soon. Let's look at a few more that are in line with IOH-predicted investor behavior.

Investors extrapolate positive or negative outlooks well into the future, pushing the prices of favored stocks to excessive premiums and those of out-of-favor stocks to deep discounts. (The performance of "best" and "worst" stocks can be directly compared, of course, but "best" and "worst" investments can also be instruments other than stocks, and "best" might be in a different market from "worst.")[4] In 1980 and again in 2009 through August 2011, for example, "best" investments included gold—which peaked at $850 an ounce in 1980 before regaining this high again in 2008 and moving up to $1,892 in August 2011—and "worst" included tax-exempt municipal bonds, yielding as high as 15 percent as bond prices plummeted. Premiums or discounts on favored or out-of-favor investments can be substantial and last for long periods of time.

Similar reactions have been noted since the early 1900s with lower-rated bonds, which provide higher returns after adjustments for default levels over time. Such consistent above- or below-average returns are also likely to exist in other financial markets.

The investor overreaction hypothesis states that it is far safer to project a continuation of investor overreaction based on what we know psychologically, backed by the robust findings we have reviewed, than to attempt to project the visibility of the stocks or other investments themselves.

TWELVE KEY PREDICTIONS OF THE INVESTOR OVERREACTION HYPOTHESIS (IOH)

Here's a full list of the predictions based on the IOH:

1a. Absolute contrarian strategies provide superior returns over time.

1b. Out-of-favor stocks, as valued by at least three different major fundamental measurements—low price-to-earnings, low price-to-cash-flow, and low price-to-book-value ratios—will outperform the market as a group over longer periods of time, normally five to ten years or more.

1c. Favored stocks, as measured by high price-to-earnings, high price-to-cash-flow, and high price-to-book-value ratios, will underperform the market over the same time periods.

1d. Out-of-favor stocks should significantly outperform favorites over the same time periods.

2a. Relative contrarian strategies provide superior returns over time. (For details of this strategy, please refer to chapter 12, "Contrarian Strategies Within Industries," page 310.)

2b. The out-of-favor stocks in each industry will outperform the market over longer periods of time, normally from four to six years.

2c. The favored stocks in each industry will underperform the market over the same time periods.

2d. The out-of-favor stocks in each industry should outperform the favorites in each industry over the same time periods.

3. Favored stocks as a group are overvalued and out-of-favor stocks undervalued. Over time both groups will regress to the mean because of earnings surprises and other fundamental factors, which will result in the underperformance of the "best" stocks, while those considered "worst" will outperform, as both move toward a more average valuation.

4a. IOH posits that the outperformance of out-of-favor stocks and the underperformance of favorites is caused primarily by behavioral influences (Affect, cognitive heuristics, neuroeconomics, and other psychological variables).

4b. The role of Affect applies on an industry-relative basis for most and least favored stocks, as it does to stocks on an absolute basis.

5. There are two distinct categories of earnings surprises:
   a. Event triggers—significant positive surprises on the lowest-valued group of stocks and major negative surprises on the highest-valued group. Both result in a consequential impact on the categories' price movement.
   b. Reinforcing events—negative surprises in the lowest-valued group and positive surprises in the highest-valued group. Both have small relative impacts on stock movements.
6a. Surprise will normally have a much smaller impact on the 60 percent of stocks in the three middle quintiles, which are less over- or undervalued using the fundamental value criteria previously noted.
6b. Even without the occurrence of an event trigger, the "best" and "worst" investments regress toward the market average over time, with the "best" stocks underperforming the "worst" ones, whether high price-to-book-value, high price-to-earnings, or high price-to-cash-flow ratio is considered, as chapter 9 demonstrated.
7. A significant part of current investment theory is dependent on accurate forecasting. The IOH predicts that:
   a. Analysts' and economists' consensus forecasts are overoptimistic over time.
   b. Analysts' consensus forecasts on individual stocks will show substantial errors over time, resulting in significant mispricing of stocks on an almost continual basis.
   c. Analysts' consensus forecasts on industries will also show substantial errors over time, resulting in significant mispricing of stocks on an almost continual basis.
8. Investor overoptimism occurs regularly in a number of important market activities, including:
   a. IPOs.
   b. Analysts' and economists' overoptimistic earnings estimates.
9. The overreaction occurs prior to the event trigger or other factors that lead to a reevaluation of the "best" and "worst" stocks. After the event trigger other reevaluation forces occur that continue the reversion to the mean. "Worst" stocks continue their rise in price and "best" stocks their fall for a period of years.
10. The overreaction-versus-underreaction debate in current financial

theory is actually about the two parts of the same process, as find-ings demonstrate.[5]*

11. Because mispricing of securities is constant, markets are continu-ally readjusting securities values. Stock and other financial markets are thus never in equilibrium, contrary to the teachings of EMH and most economic theory.

12. The efficient-market risk hypothesis is questionable,[6] and there is no robust evidence that greater volatility results in higher returns or lower volatility results in lower returns.

To recap, our five contrarian strategies, which are all in accordance with the assumptions of the investor overreaction hypothesis, are:

1. Low-price-to-earnings strategy
2. Low-price-to-cash-flow strategy
3. Low-price-to-book-value strategy
4. High-yield strategy
5. Low-price-to-industry strategy

THE PSYCHOLOGICAL CHOICE: EMH OR IOH?

The efficient-market risk theory and a good part of economic theory are built on the unproved assumption of almost omniscient investor ratio-nality dating from the eighteenth century. As we know, the assumption disregards recent major psychological findings as well as other behav-ioral work over at least the last century. The efficient-market hypothesis has not worked and cannot work for this reason. By contrast, the robust psychological finding that investors frequently overreact supports the investor overreaction hypothesis.

Because the investor overreaction hypothesis is based on psychologi-cal principles, it is also likely to apply in other fields where risk and uncer-tainty exist. The current empirical evidence of the findings supporting the IOH is significant. It is expected that with time the list of such evidence

---

*For information documenting these findings, please see "Investor Overreaction: Evi-dence That Its Basis Is Psychological," David N. Dreman and Eric A. Lufkin, which can be found at www.signallake.com/innovation/DremanLufkin2000.pdf.

should grow considerably. A part of the evidence used to build the IOH was considered to be a series of aberrations by efficient-market believers and dismissed as anomalies.

CRITICAL IMPLICATIONS OF IOH

1. The fact that "best" and "worst" stocks continue to exist in all markets indicates that constant rational pricing, though a cherished EMH concept, has never existed. The investor overreaction hypothesis rejects EMH teaching and conclusions as they are currently presented almost en masse.

2. In many instances IOH is diametrically opposite in its assumptions and conclusions to EMH, and IOH reaches very different conclusions from EMH given the same facts. As we'll soon see, a very different and hopefully improved method for measuring risk will be put forth. In the 1987 crash, for example, the investor overreaction hypothesis would have cautioned against the interaction of index arbitrage and portfolio insurance that led to a lethal market overreaction and the devastating panic that followed. One of IOH's goals is to decrease the causes of major market overreactions and their sometimes devastating consequences. High levels of leverage and liquidity have a long-standing record of creating serious downturns, often accompanied by panic. IOH would thus caution against high leverage and massive illiquidity, because of the dangers of a major overreaction. EMH risk theory ignores them entirely, because, under its assumptions, the only risk is volatility, although, as we saw in chapter 5, this situation resulted in three major panics and crashes.

3. Unlike EMH and general economic theory, the IOH does not accept the belief that equilibrium in markets has ever existed or will exist. In a dynamic, continually changing global economy, thousands of new political, economic, investment, and company-related inputs come up almost instantaneously and are immediately integrated into the marketplace. Decision making, as a result, is always changing, and this makes equilibrium as elusive as finding the Fountain of Youth.

4. The IOH attempts to see the world as it is, not in the idealistic manner that all too many economists have adopted using the rationality assumption. By comparison, the IOH has built its assumptions on

recent well-proved findings of human behavior, and its conclusions are supported by strong statistical findings that investors do behave in the manner that the IOH predicts. It may fall short of a ten commandments for contrarians, but remember, all twelve predictions of the IOH have been confirmed to a high level of statistical probability in the studies reviewed in chapters 9 and 10.

▓ Section II. Four Contrarian Strategies Derived from the IOH

Next we are going to discuss how to use contrarian strategies to boost portfolio results using the findings we have just garnered from the investor overreaction hypothesis. It's important to understand that with ideas, just as with a college course, it's not the amount of information we cram into our brains that does any good but how we apply critical thinking to the subject matter.

MORE RECENT CONTRARIAN PERFORMANCE

You are certainly entitled to ask if these contrarian strategies or any others still work in this new, sometimes alien, investment world, where many of the rules seem to have been washed away. The answer is a definite yes, as Figures 11-1 and 11-2 demonstrate. They cover a very short but explosive period of time, including the bursting of the dot-com bubble in the 2000–2002 period, followed almost immediately by the housing bubble, the ensuing financial crisis, and the market rebound in 2009.

   This time was anything but a cakewalk, but out-of-favor stocks appear to have weathered the storms much better than favored stocks. The chart shows that $10,000 invested in any of the four contrarian strategies from 2000 through 2010 would have outperformed the market through this period. Low-P/E stocks provided the highest return, 11.7 percent annually versus 5.6 percent for the market in what is becoming known as the "lost decade." The three other metrics, low price-to-cash flow, low price-to-book value, and high yield, also outperformed the average, again the Compustat 1500. All four metrics of favored stocks again underperformed the market and all but the low yield had negative returns. The best was low yield, at 2.4 percent annually. The worst were high price-to-cash flow (–2.9 percent annually) and high price-to-book value (–3.0 percent

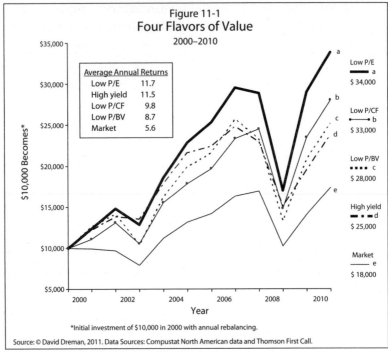

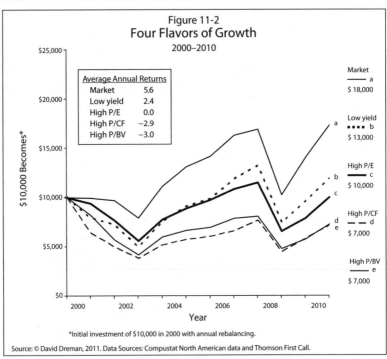

annually). The differences in performance between "best" and "worst" stocks were large. Both low P/E and low price-to-book value returned 11.7 percent more than their higher growth counterparts.

CONSTRUCTING YOUR PORTFOLIO

How, then, can you build a portfolio that should outdistance the market while providing better protection when the bear growls? And, since a good sell discipline is one of the hardest things to develop, what guidelines should you use? The guidelines I'll add in this chapter and the next, including several new ones based on the 2007–2008 market collapse, though certainly not guaranteed to get you out at the top (if you know of any that are, please write), have a high probability of success.

But before figuring out when to sell to protect your profits, let's figure out what to buy. Fortunately, there are four proven ways to do this.

CONTRARIAN STRATEGY 1:
LOW-PRICE-TO-EARNINGS STRATEGY

The low-P/E strategy is the oldest and best documented of all the contrarian strategies and the one most used by market professionals today. Although there are many ways to calculate a P/E ratio, the most common is to take reported earnings for a company (before nonrecurring gains or losses) for the last twelve months and then divide them into the stock price. The strategy has outperformed in both up and down markets since the mid-1930s and probably will for a good deal longer.

Figure 11-3 shows the returns of the low-P/E strategy for the forty-one years ending December 31, 2010, using the 1,500 largest companies on the Compustat database.[7] The return the investor receives each year is broken down into its two basic components: capital appreciation and dividends.

The stocks are sorted in the usual manner into five equal groups in each quarter of the study, strictly according to their P/E rankings, and the returns are annualized.[8]

Figure 11-3 once again demonstrates the superior performance of the low-P/E group. Over the forty-one years of the study, the bottom P/E group averaged a return of 15.2 percent annually, compared with 11.6 percent for the market (the last set of bars on the right) and 8.3 per-

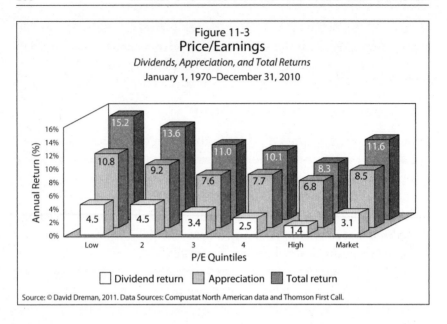

Figure 11-3
Price/Earnings
Dividends, Appreciation, and Total Returns
January 1, 1970–December 31, 2010

Source: © David Dreman, 2011. Data Sources: Compustat North American data and Thomson First Call.

cent for the highest-P/E group. The lowest P/Es beat the highest P/Es by 6.9 percent a year, almost doubling the annual return over this forty-one-year study. If you're putting money away for your retirement fund, this performance differential becomes enormous over time, as Figures 10-3 and 10-4 indicated.

Looking at Figure 11-3 again, you'll see that these stocks also provided higher dividend yields. As the figure also reveals, the low-P/E group yielded 4.5 percent over the life of the study, compared with 3.2 percent for the market and only 1.4 percent for the highest-P/E group. The dividend return advantage of "worst" over "best" stocks was 3.1 percent annually. On a $10,000 investment over forty-one years, the difference in ending portfolio value between the 4.5 percent yield and the 1.4 percent yield portfolios would be $43,098.

But look at the appreciation column in Figure 11-3. Something is way out of whack here. The experts say that the "best" stocks, in this case those with the highest P/Es, should have the largest appreciation. But that's not the case. They have the lowest appreciation, while the investment doggies, the low P/Es, have the highest. All the money that goes into capital expansion for the "best" stocks does not reflect itself in top-gun performance. The down-and-outers once again outstrip the top tier. Low-P/E stocks

Table 11-1				
Price/Earnings				
Buy-and-Hold Annual Returns				
January 1, 1970–December 31, 2010				
P/E Quintile	2 Years	3 Years	5 Years	8 Years
Low P/E	15.5%	14.3%	15.2%	15.2%
High P/E	9.9%	9.2%	9.4%	10.3%
Market	13.3%	11.9%	12.0%	12.7%

Source: © David Dreman, 2011. Data Sources: Compustat North American data and Thomson First Call.

provide the best of both worlds: higher yield and better appreciation, something that conventional wisdom states shouldn't happen.

The higher dividend returns, incidentally, help prop up the prices of cheap stocks in bear markets, one of the important reasons why low-P/E and other contrarian strategies outperform in bad times.

If you don't like to trade much, contrarian strategies are for you. Returns stay high with little or no portfolio turnover. Table 11-1 shows how buying stocks in the lowest P/E quintile and holding them for periods of two to eight years over the 1970–2010 period would have done. As a glance at the table shows, the results are rather remarkable. The low-P/E portfolios still provided by far the highest annual returns for the five-year period (15.2 percent), sharply outdistancing the highest-P/E group (9.4 percent), and the market (12.0 percent) The low-P/E returns stayed well above the market and high-P/E returns for both the three- and the five-year periods as well as for eight years.

It's surprising that the returns stayed as high as they did for so long. This indicates that the undervaluation of low-P/E stocks is very marked. Holding the lowest 20 percent of stocks for nine years (not shown) still provides above-market returns for the low-P/E group, with virtually no deterioration of performance from year 1. For high-P/E stocks, the overvaluation is just as significant (not shown). Even after five years, they continue to display much lower returns than the market.

Another advantage of low-P/E and other contrarian strategies is that they don't require a lot of work to be effective. As we just saw, rebalancing low-P/E portfolios annually with large-sized companies results in far-above-market returns. However, you could rebalance far less frequently. This is a low-intensity strategy with high-intensity results. You don't have to spend much time agonizing over the stocks you pick and monitoring or interpreting every company, industry, or economic squiggle to divine all-important information. Just select your portfolio (we'll look at how to do this shortly) and put it on automatic pilot. You'll save annoyance, not to mention taxes, commissions, and transaction costs, this way. At the same time, you'll outdistance the market by a comfortable margin, and as you know, few money managers can do that. The point of the chart is not to get you to hold a portfolio intact into eternity but to show that our normal work ethic of constantly being busy to be successful is not useful but often counterproductive in investing.

Though I wouldn't buy a portfolio and hold it without looking at it for eight years, Table 11-1 (a large sample of stocks over the last forty-one years) demonstrates that you can make big bucks in the market by positioning yourself carefully at the beginning and fine-tuning moderately thereafter.

CONTRARIAN STRATEGY 2:
LOW-PRICE-TO-CASH-FLOW STRATEGY

Let's now look more specifically at another important contrarian strategy, selecting stocks by price-to-cash flow. Cash flow is normally defined as

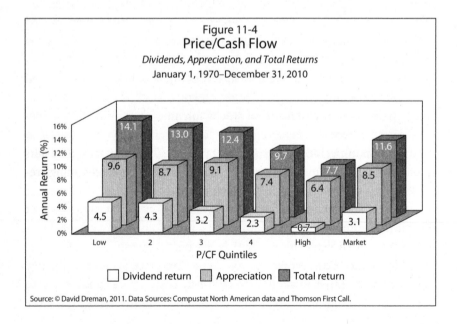

Figure 11-4
Price/Cash Flow
Dividends, Appreciation, and Total Returns
January 1, 1970–December 31, 2010

Source: © David Dreman, 2011. Data Sources: Compustat North American data and Thomson First Call.

after-tax earnings, with depreciation and other noncash charges added back. Cash flow is regarded by many analysts as more important than earnings in evaluating a company, because management can reduce apparent earnings by setting up reserves or taking write-offs or increase them by not taking adequate depreciation or other necessary charges. Although these entries do not show in earnings, they do read loud and clear in the statement of cash flow, which the Federal Accounting Standards Board (FASB) has required companies to issue since mid-1988.

All this was changed by new methods of manipulation by companies such as Enron and WorldCom. In the late 1990s, Enron, employing great skill, borrowed money from Citigroup and other banks and showed it, through complex but fraudulently recorded transactions, as cash flow. After Enron collapsed and its auditor, Arthur Andersen, facing criminal charges, voluntarily surrendered its license to practice, the banks paid billions of dollars in damages for their role in the scam. WorldCom improperly accounted for more than $3.8 billion of expenses, dramatically overstating its earnings. In short, if the scammers are good enough, even cash flow can bite you unless you can trust the company. Figure 11-4 provides the results of low price to cash flow.

CONTRARIAN STRATEGY 3:
LOW-PRICE-TO-BOOK-VALUE STRATEGY

Price-to-book value was a favorite tool of Benjamin Graham and other earlier value analysts,[9] and Figure 11-5 gives the results of each. The sample, the time period, and the methodology are identical to those used for price-to-earnings. Looking again at Figure 11-4, price-to-cash flow, and Figure 11-5, price-to-book value, you can see the superior performance of the "worst" stocks, the lowest 20 percent of price-to-cash flow or price-to-book value, over the top 20 percent. The similarity of results is remarkable. The low-P/E strategy is somewhat more rewarding, returning 15.2 percent annually for the forty-one years of the study versus 14.3 percent for low price-to-book value and 14.1 percent for low price-to-cash flow.

But all three value strategies handily beat the market and sharply outperform the "best" stocks in each case. Once again, we see the key ingredients of outperformance: low price-to-cash flow and low price to book value have significantly higher dividends than the market and more

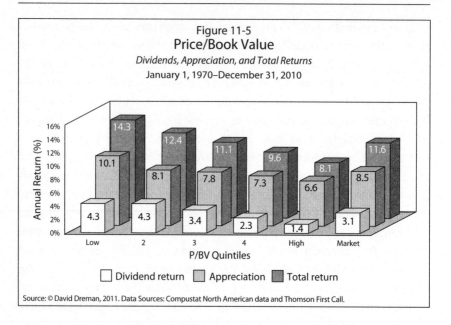

Figure 11-5
Price/Book Value
Dividends, Appreciation, and Total Returns
January 1, 1970–December 31, 2010

Source: © David Dreman, 2011. Data Sources: Compustat North American data and Thomson First Call.

than triple the dividend of the "best" stocks in each category, providing a good contribution to total return. Too, look at the appreciation of the low-price-to-cash-flow and low-price-to-book-value groups. By this measurement, both groups handily outperform not only the most favored stocks but also the market. The accepted reason for buying "best" stocks, much higher appreciation, is thus shown to be fallacious.

Figures 11-3, 11-4, and 11-5 again demonstrate that contrarian stocks give you the best of both worlds: higher appreciation and higher dividends. The bottom quintile provides dividend returns three times as large as the highest-P/E quintile, another easy win for out-of-favor stocks.

Figures 11-3, 11-4, and 11-5 demonstrate that the conventional wisdom of setting radically different investment goals for conservative and aggressive investors is simply one more investment myth. Which brings us to another important investment Psychological Guideline:

PSYCHOLOGICAL GUIDELINE 23: Don't speculate on highly priced concept stocks to make above-average returns. The blue-chip stocks that widows and orphans traditionally choose normally outperform the riskier stocks recommended for more aggressive businessmen or -women.

Stocks classified as "businessman's risk" by many brokerage firms, because of their low dividends and high price-to-book-value ratios, often turn out to be losers. As a group, they consistently underperform the market. A better term might be "businessman's folly." Figures 11-3, 11-4, and 11-5 go far to disprove the concept of "businessman's risk" for buying stocks. It still might be an "all-American" concept, but it is far less widespread today, touted primarily by brokers, who pick up more in commissions.

The strategy of buying the lowest 20 percent of stocks by either price to book value or price to cash flow, as we have seen, holds up through both bull and bear markets. Buying and holding portfolios of the lowest-price-to-cash flow and lowest-price-to-book-value stocks without any change in their composition for periods of two, three, five, and eight years (not shown) provide returns very similar to those of buying and holding the lowest-P/E portfolio (Table 11-1). Investing in these two groups results in returns well above the market's and sharply higher than the favored stocks in each group for every period up to eight years.[10] The "best" stocks continue to underperform for these extended periods.

Again we see that you don't have to watch the market like a gunslinger, ready to slap leather at any new piece of information. Relax; you'll probably make far more by taking your time. And there is the collateral reward of not shooting yourself in the foot by moving quickly and incorrectly, as is often the case with the pros.

The final reward, and one of the most important, of the buy-and-hold approach, as indicated with low-P/E or the other low-price-to-value strategies, is that lower transaction costs and taxes can result in a substantial increase in your capital over time. Transaction costs are often not recognized by investors but can add up, particularly on less liquid stocks. What these three low-price-to-value strategies can do for you over time, then, is provide returns high enough that only a minimum of trading is required, thereby reducing, perhaps substantially, these costs and enhancing your portfolio returns. This leads us to another helpful Psychological Guideline:

PSYCHOLOGICAL GUIDELINE 24: Avoid unnecessary trading. The costs can lower your returns over time. Buy and hold strategies provide well-above-market returns for years and are an excellent means of lowering turnover and thereby significantly reducing taxes and excess transaction costs.

The three major strategies show markedly superior returns for "worst" stocks while avoiding extra trading costs. Finally, since yield is a very important factor for many readers, let's look at the high-yield strategy.

CONTRARIAN STRATEGY 4: HIGH-YIELD STRATEGY

Figure 11-6 provides the annual returns of high-yield strategies. The method and period used are the same as those for the previous three strategies. As the chart indicates, however, high-yielding dividend strategies perform somewhat differently from the previous contrarian strategies. The highest-yielding stocks outperform the market by 0.9 percent and the stocks with low or no yield by 4.0 percent annually.

However, the composition of the returns is different. More than half of the 12.5 percent annual return of the highest-yielding group comes from the yield itself. Moreover, appreciation, at 6.0 percent annually over the forty-one-year period, is lower than for any of the other "worst" groupings or for the market. Buying stocks with high dividend yields beats the market but provides lower total returns than the previous three contrarian strategies.

Once again a buy-and-hold strategy works well for the lowest-price-to-dividend group. Not only do you continue to beat the market over time with this method, but your returns actually increase with a longer holding period.* The average yield, as shown in Figure 11-6, was 6.5 percent annually through the study. Also of note is that the dividend rate increases with time and may yet surprise us again as recessionary conditions slacken.

For investors who require income, this appears to be a far better strategy over time than owning bonds. If interest rates spike up, bond prices will go down sharply. The price of a thirty-year bond, for example, will drop 12 percent for every 1 percent increase in interest rates. With the wide fluctuations of interest rates in recent decades, the bond market has actually been almost as volatile as the stock market. Buying high-yielding stocks makes good sense for the yield-conscious investor. Dividends go up over time; interest payments on bonds do not. Yes, we are in a highly abnormal period today, with short Treasuries yielding almost nothing. But, as chapter 14 will detail, this is likely to be another bad trap for investors.

High-yielding stocks also provide you with the best protection in

---

* With dividends reinvested.

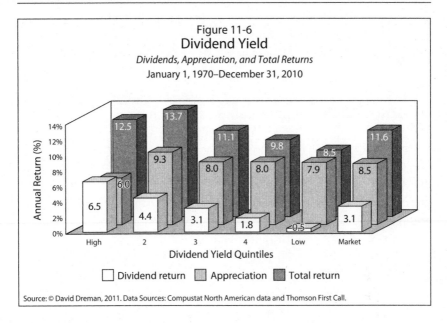

Figure 11-6
Dividend Yield
Dividends, Appreciation, and Total Returns
January 1, 1970–December 31, 2010

Source: © David Dreman, 2011. Data Sources: Compustat North American data and Thomson First Call.

most bear markets, as we saw in Figure 10-5a. These stocks give the dividend-oriented investor more protection of principal on the downside and often provide both rising dividend income and capital appreciation; the latter occurs only rarely with long bonds.* However, this strategy does not always work, as we know all too well from the horrific bear markets, such as 2007 and 2008, followed by 2009–2010, when the dividends of many high-yielding stocks were cut to the bone and people traded even relatively secure dividend income for the absolute, albeit temporary, security of Treasuries. Fortunately, a bear market of this magnitude and severity occurs only once in generations.

Is this strategy for everyone? I don't think so. It works best for people who need a constant source of income. Naturally, unless you hold the stocks in a tax-free account, the income is taxable. And in a tax-free account an investor is far better off using one of the three other contrarian strategies—depending of course on immediate income requirements—which, as we saw in Figures 11-3, 11-4, and 11-5, provide significantly higher returns over time than the high-yield strategy.

Value, then, in the form of contrarian strategies, is the closest thing

---

*For a more detailed discussion of how stocks fare against bonds over time, please see chapter 14.

there is to a strategy for all seasons in the stock market. Now for some application guidelines that will help you implement various contrarian strategies.

Section III. Contrarian Strategies in Action

1. CONTRARIAN STOCK SELECTION: THE A-B-C RULES

The initial problem confronting all investors is how to select individual stocks and the number of stocks to hold in their portfolio. A few simple guidelines have proved their worth over the years:

A. Buy only contrarian stocks because of their superior performance characteristics.
B. Invest equally in thirty to forty stocks, diversified among fifteen or more industries (if your assets are of sufficient size).

Diversification is essential. The returns of individual issues vary widely, so it is dangerous to rely on only a few companies or industries. By spreading the risk, you have a much better chance of performing in line with the out-of-favor quintiles shown above, rather than substantially above or below that level.[11]

C. Buy medium- or large-sized stocks listed on the New York Stock Exchange or only larger companies on NASDAQ or the AMEX.

Such companies, upon which the studies have been based, are usually subject to less accounting gimmickry than smaller ones, and this difference provides some added measure of protection. Accounting, as we have seen, is a devilishly tricky subject and has taken a heavy toll on investors, sophisticates as well as novices.

Larger- and medium-sized companies provide investors another advantage: they are more in the public eye. A turnaround in the fortunes of Ford (which occurred in 2009) is far more noticeable than a change in the fortunes of some publicly owned steak restaurant franchise buried, say, in the sand and wind of Death Valley. Finally, larger companies have more "staying power"; their failure rate is substantially lower than that of smaller and start-up companies.[12]

2. SHOULD WE ABANDON SECURITY ANALYSIS ENTIRELY?

As we have seen, selecting stocks by their contrarian characteristics and placing no reliance on security analysis has given better-than-average returns over long periods of time. Should we, then, consider abandoning security analysis entirely? The evidence we've seen certainly shows that it doesn't help much. However, I would not go quite this far (and not just because I've been thoroughly steeped in the doctrines of the Old Church). I believe parts of it can be valuable within a contrarian framework.

Contrarian methods eliminate or downgrade those aspects of traditional analysis, such as forecasting, that have been shown to be consistently error-prone. By recognizing the limitations of security analysis, you can, I believe, apply it to achieve even better results within the contrarian approach. However, for a lot of you, a well-diversified contrarian index fund built on the principles in this book would be a solid way to invest. Unfortunately, there are very few out there to choose from. Our firm manages a series of contrarian index funds from large cap to midcap to small cap.* Why there are so few baffles me. Over thirty years, contrarian performance has sharply outperformed the market and the various index funds out there, from small to mid to large. It's an idea whose time has come, but it does require a pretty careful reading of the funds' prospectuses as well as a thorough watch over their portfolios to make sure the fellers are actually managing the money the way they say they are.

In the next sections, I'll attempt to show you how five fundamental indicators can be used to supplement the A-B-C Rules of contrarian selection we just looked at. Following this analysis, we'll examine other contrarian methods that do not depend on security evaluation. These, too, should provide above-average market results. After reviewing the various methods, you can choose which suits you best.

3. FIVE SELECTION INDICATORS

In my own application of the low-P/E approach, I select from the bottom 20 percent of stocks according to P/E. The lowest quintiles provide plenty of scope for applying the ancillary indicators that follow.

---

* The Dreman Market Overreaction Fund.

If, after what you've seen, you are brave enough to dabble in security analysis, here are the indicators I consider most helpful:

Indicator 1. A strong financial position. This card is essential in today's market, where liquidity is hard to find. This is easily determinable for a company from information contained within its financial statements. (The definitions of the appropriate ratios—current assets versus current liabilities, debt as a percentage of capital structure, interest coverage, and so on—can all be found in any textbook on finance, as well as in material provided free of charge by some of the major brokerage houses.)*

A strong financial position will enable a company to sail unimpaired through periods of operating difficulties, which contrarian companies sometimes experience. Financial strength is also important in deciding whether a company's dividends can be maintained or increased. And of course in a liquidity crisis, such as the one that we have just gone through and that continues to linger, it is often the difference between survival and insolvency. Mercifully, serious crises of this sort occur only every century or so, or did. In any case, companies with financial strength not only survive but often prosper in such times. Look no farther than Warren Buffett's Berkshire Hathaway.

Indicator 2. As many favorable operating and financial ratios as possible. This helps ensure that there are no structural flaws in the company. Again, the definitions of such ratios can be found in standard financial textbooks.

Indicator 3. A higher rate of earnings growth than the S&P 500 in the immediate past and the likelihood that it will not plummet in the near future. Such estimates are an attempt not to pinpoint earnings but only to indicate their general direction. Remember that we are dealing with stocks in the bottom quintile, for which only the worst is expected. Unlike those who use conventional forecasting methods, we do not require precise earnings estimates; we need merely note their direction and only for short periods, usually about a year or so.

In my initial contrarian work, I was more of a purist on this subject.

---

* Martin S. Fridson's book *Financial Statement Analysis* (New York: Wiley, 2002) provides a brief introduction to corporate accounting and outlines most of the important financial ratios the average investor would require.

I thought: since contrarian strategies worked at least in part because of analysts' errors, why bother with forecasting at all? Some rather harsh experiences have caused me to modify this position.

If, for example, the Street estimates that a company's earnings are likely to be down for some time, I would not rush in to buy, no matter how positive my indicators appear to be. Often, as we've seen, analysts are overoptimistic. All too frequently, an estimated moderate decline in earnings turns into a drop off a cliff. This was the case with many of the financial stocks, from Citigroup to Wachovia to AIG, in 2007–2008, when the analysts were making estimates of relatively small declines in earnings, but those companies' income had actually fallen off the cliff.

The important distinction between forecasting the general direction of earnings and trying to derive precise earnings estimates is that the former method is far simpler and the probability that it will succeed much higher.

Indicator 4. Earnings estimates should always lean to the conservative side. This ties in with Graham and Dodd's margin of safety principle, even more so after our frightening trip through the lands of overoptimistic analysts. Sometimes you don't need a pencil to recalibrate estimates to lower, more realistic levels; you need a large excavator to drop them down into their proper subterranean place. Remember, too, that by relying on general directional forecasts and keeping them ultraconservative, you are reducing the chance of error even further. If you do this and the company still looks as though its earnings will grow more quickly than the S&P for a year or so, you may have a potentially rewarding investment.

Indicator 5. An above-average dividend yield, which the company can sustain and increase. This indicator depends on Indicators 1 through 4 being favorable. We have seen that conventional thinking about dividends is far off the mark. High-yield strategies also outperform the market. In practice, I have found that Indicator 5 improves performance when used in conjunction with the primary rules of buying contrarian stocks.

Now that we have looked at five indicators that should prove helpful regardless of the contrarian strategy we use, I'll turn briefly to another matter. A question I'm frequently asked is "What is the best approach to contrarian investing? Is it better to select one method, such as price to earnings or price to book value, and focus solely on it?" For me, the answer is no. Though you can certainly select one strategy and run with it successfully, once again I favor a more eclectic approach. Our money management firm uses the low-P/E method as its core strategy but also utilizes the other three contrarian strategies extensively. Investment opportunities vary, and often you can find exceptional value with one method that does not show up as clearly with another.

Low P/E is probably the most accessible of the four contrarian strategies, because the information on P/E ratios is available daily in the financial section of any large newspaper, next to a stock's price. The information is also updated quarterly, as are price-to-cash flow and price-to-book value. Though price-to-dividend information is also nearly instantaneous, it is a secondary strategy because of the superior returns of the first three contrarian methods. However, it, too, has its moments in the sun, as we shall see.

4. CONTRARIAN STRATEGIES IN ACTION

To the Front

It's time to move into the trenches to see how contrarian decisions are made under fire. I'll draw on past recommendations I've made in my *Forbes* column and to the clients of our investment counseling firm, as well as examples from the Dreman High Opportunity Mutual Fund, which I manage. Though one can be accused of telling "war stories," remembering only the victories while conveniently forgetting the setbacks (not to mention the routs), I think that it helps to present practical examples of how the A-B-C Rules and five indicators often had clear-cut results—not only with 20/20 hindsight but at the time. Our first stop will be a couple of examples of how we've selected low-P/E stocks.

Using the Low-Price-to-Earnings Strategy

Altria Group

I recommended Altria Group ($49), the parent of Kraft Foods as well as Philip Morris, in *Forbes* in late September 2004. Here was a classic value stock and one that was heartily disliked by a good part of the public because of its ownership of Philip Morris, the nation's largest cigarette manufacturer, which at the time was undergoing several large class action suits. After carefully researching the class actions, we came to the decision that the cases, although generating major headlines about potentially devastating losses, were unlikely to cause serious damage to Altria with its rock-solid financial position and enormous cash flow.*

This was the kind of stock that Benjamin Graham might have dreamed of. First, its P/E and price-to-cash-flow ratio were extremely low in 2003, at the time 10× and 9×, respectively. Moreover, it yielded 6 percent back then and had raised its dividend almost every year since the 1930s. Indicators 1, 2, and 5 were almost off the charts. But there was more.

Although Altria was under heavy legal and media assault, all the lawsuits were against the U.S. tobacco subsidiary (Philip Morris USA). When we added up the combined operations of Altria, their value, by what we considered conservative accounting, came to roughly $105 a share, with Philip Morris's domestic value about $45, or 43 percent of our estimate of the value of the total operation. So great were the unfounded fears of the enormous size of the legal settlements that the company was trading at a larger than 60 percent discount to its real worth. Moreover, the U.S. Supreme Court was growing concerned about the size of the punitive damage awards to plaintiffs above actual damages claimed, sometimes reaching ten or even a hundred times the damage claims themselves. The Court's concern was the size of damage awards across the board.

Our analysis was extremely thorough, particularly examining the potential for bankruptcy, which appeared very far-fetched. The Supreme Court dramatically lowered the amount that could be paid above actual damages and also tightened the rules significantly on class actions, another major benefit to Philip Morris. By March 2008, the share price more than doubled in value, including dividends.

Apache Corporation

With the demand for oil outstripping new supply since 1982 and the last million-barrel-a-day field found in Kazakhstan in 1979, oil prices had moved up fairly steadily over time until late 2008. One of the most prom-

---

* As a manager, one has a fiduciary obligation to bring one's clients the best legitimate opportunities available. The client makes the decision on the moral question of whether to own tobacco, alcohol, or defense stocks and so on.

ising industries, if oil prices rose, was the large exploration and development companies that have large oil and reserves, a good portion of them domestically. Similarly, they would perform worse than the large integrated companies, such as Exxon Mobil, Royal Dutch/Shell, or BP, if prices came down. I recommended the purchase of Apache in *Forbes* on July 25, 2005, at $65, when it was at a P/E of 11×, significantly below that of the market.

At the time Apache was cash rich and held major reserves. The company was rapidly increasing its spending on finding new oil and gas. Its programs in discovering major new oil in recent years, in relatively safer areas of the globe, had proved very successful.

The company spent its exploration money wisely, and its reserves grew handsomely. By the end of 2007, its price was up 70 percent from the time of the *Forbes* recommendation, in a market that was starting to turn down sharply. Apache was also strong, as measured by the first three indicators, and met all its objectives in a so-so market.

In 2008, the worst market collapse since 1929–1932, Apache was hit hard; with the price of oil plummeting, the stock fell to a low of $51 in early 2009 but rebounded sharply beginning in the spring of 2009. Oil prices spiked up again to $110 a barrel in the winter of 2011, and Apache shot back to $130. It has also taken advantage of a major opportunity.

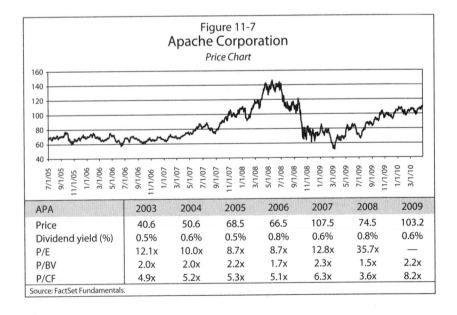

Figure 11-7
Apache Corporation
Price Chart

APA	2003	2004	2005	2006	2007	2008	2009
Price	40.6	50.6	68.5	66.5	107.5	74.5	103.2
Dividend yield (%)	0.5%	0.6%	0.5%	0.8%	0.6%	0.8%	0.6%
P/E	12.1x	10.0x	8.7x	8.7x	12.8x	35.7x	—
P/BV	2.0x	2.0x	2.2x	1.7x	2.3x	1.5x	2.2x
P/CF	4.9x	5.2x	5.3x	5.1x	6.3x	3.6x	8.2x

Source: FactSet Fundamentals.

During the BP oil spill in the summer of 2010, it was able to buy major additional reserves from BP valued at $7 billion in fields in Canada and Egypt, as well as the Permian Basin, at what were considered to be bargain prices.

Apache was a good example of buying strong value and holding on to it through a disastrous market, because the basic reasons for doing so had not changed—that is, unless you believed another Great Depression was on our doorstep. (See Figure 11-7.)

Using the Low-Price-to-Cash-Flow Strategy

BHP Billiton

Low price to cash flow, as Figure 11-3 demonstrated, has also provided well-above-average returns over time. Price to cash flow is often a more useful measure than earnings when a company has large noncash expenses, such as depreciation in bad years.* If you try to buy normally low-P/E cyclical stocks in a recession, when the earnings of such companies tumble, the P/Es can get very high. This happened to BHP Billiton, one of the world's largest natural resource producers, which I recommended in *Forbes* in February 2009, at $48. Although the company had relatively strong finances, its earnings began to collapse as the worldwide recession almost brought the purchase of most natural resources to a screeching halt in the last months of 2008. BHP's earnings dropped 62 percent, from their record high of $5.11 in fiscal 2008 (ended June 30) to $2.11 in fiscal 2009, and the company's cash flow also dropped about 50 percent, but with its strong cash flow in prior years and its financial strength this was more than adequate to cover the company's requirements.

Once again stories were spun out in the financial pages, and sometimes on front pages, of how major industrial firms and mines might take years to recover. Apparently forgotten was that BHP was one of the lowest-cost producers of natural resources globally. With the mild recovery, earnings and cash flow bounced back strongly in 2010, in line with where they had been in its second best year, 2007. By December 2010,

---

* Although these charges are reflected in earnings, they do not show in cash flow. Granted, the depreciation must be made up eventually; but it gives breathing space if the company needs it to meet payments in financially difficult years.

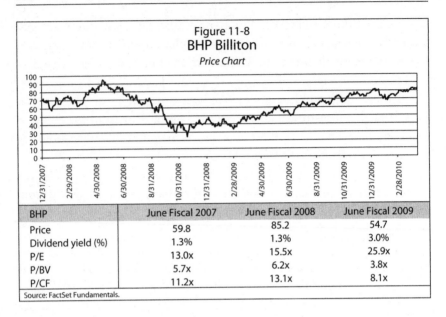

Figure 11-8
BHP Billiton
Price Chart

BHP	June Fiscal 2007	June Fiscal 2008	June Fiscal 2009
Price	59.8	85.2	54.7
Dividend yield (%)	1.3%	1.3%	3.0%
P/E	13.0x	15.5x	25.9x
P/BV	5.7x	6.2x	3.8x
P/CF	11.2x	13.1x	8.1x

Source: FactSet Fundamentals.

BHP, trading at $93, had almost doubled from the price at which I had recommended it in *Forbes*. So strong was its cash flow that it raised its dividend rate 50 percent in 2008 and another 17 percent in 2009. That BHP increased its dividend at all, rather than markedly, indicated management's confidence that the company was rock solid because of its financial strength, despite the sometimes frightened comments by both analysts and the press. (See Figure 11-8.)

And a Strikeout!

Fannie Mae

Fannie Mae, a blue chip for generations, appeared to be a cheap stock trading at $37 near the end of 2007, when it was recommended. The company had had above-average earnings growth for decades. True, the mortgage market for subprime and other riskier mortgages was dropping rapidly, the company had been running at a loss for several quarters, and there were slick roads ahead, but Fannie had been through numerous bad housing markets since it was founded by the Roosevelt administration in 1938. The company and its somewhat smaller counterpart, Freddie Mac, had much tighter credit standards than the banks, the S&Ls, and the investment banks. An examination of their default ratios confirmed that over time their credit standards had been much higher for buyers to qualify for mortgages, and their default ratios had been much lower. The stock was purchased because it had a strong mandate, a protected business model, and historically good earnings growth, as well as a low P/E ratio.

What was not known at the time or in subsequent interviews with senior management, including the chairman of the board, was that the pastoral landscape the executives painted verbally was far removed from the facts. Under severe pressure from both the Democrats, led by Congressman Barney Frank, and the Bush administration, led by James B. Lockhart III, the head of the Federal Housing Finance Agency (FHFA), which regulated Fannie and Freddie, enormous political pressure was put on Fannie and Freddie. They were repeatedly threatened with the loss of their vital low-cost financing if they didn't make increasingly larger amounts of mortgages available to lower-income groups.

In the spring of 2008, both Treasury Secretary Hank Paulson and New York Fed president Tim Geithner indicated that both companies had excess capital above their regulatory capital requirements. Geithner announced that because Fannie and Freddie's operations were improving, he was reducing their capital requirements so that they could loan even more to the rapidly falling mortgage market. He made similar announcements through August 2008, with, it appeared, at least the tacit approval of Treasury Secretary Paulson.

Then, on September 6, 2008, both companies were put into receivership by the U.S. Treasury; they now trade for only pennies. In a subsequent announcement it became clear that both Fannie and Freddie had buckled under the intense pressure they were facing and had put substantially more money into "NINJA" (no income, no job or assets) mortgages, often with virtually no down payment. Naturally, all the senior Fed, administration, and congressional officials walked away, blaming Fannie for its poor lending practices. The carnage continued, and the S&P 500 Financial Select Sector SPDR (the market weight of all financial stocks in the S&P 500) dropped 83 percent from 2007 to early March 2009, the largest decline since the 1929–1932 crash and in a shorter period.

What went wrong with our analysis and those of most value manag-

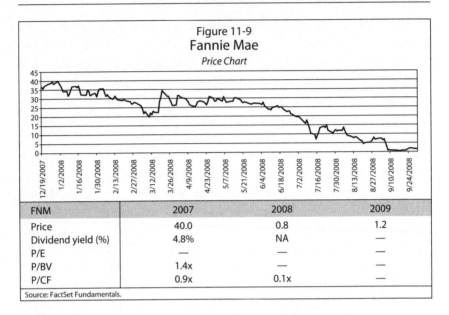

Figure 11-9
Fannie Mae
Price Chart

FNM	2007	2008	2009
Price	40.0	0.8	1.2
Dividend yield (%)	4.8%	NA	—
P/E	—	—	—
P/BV	1.4x	—	—
P/CF	0.9x	0.1x	—

Source: FactSet Fundamentals.

ers of Freddie and Fannie, the banks, and the investment banks? Here are a couple of important lessons which I have extracted from this painful experience:

1. Never buy a company that is losing money. Losses are an early-warning system that all is not well. Most good companies do turn around, but when they don't you get stung. The contrarian studies that we looked at always excluded companies that had an earnings loss in any quarter, and the results over time were just fine.

2. This one is hardly worth writing about but inevitably takes a major toll. Never, never believe senior officials up to the cabinet level when they say all is well in trying times for a company or an industry. In most cases that's the time to let the stock or industry go. (See Figure 11-9.)

Using the Low-Price-to-Book Value Strategy

JPMorgan Chase

Price to book value, even more than price to cash flow, is an excellent contrarian indicator when a company stumbles and earnings crater. A good example was the bank stocks in the financial crisis of 2007–2008. As the subprime crisis intensified, financials, as we saw, plummeted. JPMorgan Chase, under Jamie Dimon, its savvy CEO, was one of the first of the major banks to recognize the gravity of the subprime situation, and in 2007–2008 it began to both lessen its activities in those markets and reduce its sizable portfolio of those and other lower-rated mortgage holdings. Its price to book value was substantially lower than the market's, as were those of most financial stocks.

But there was one major difference: JPMorgan Chase's book value was by and large real. Because of its greater liquidity as a result of its pulling back on the purchase of illiquid mortgages, the Federal Reserve and the Treasury struck an advantageous deal with it that allowed it to buy Bear Stearns, one of the largest Wall Street investment banks, on Sunday, March 16, 2008. The price was $2 a share,* a 93 percent discount from where Bear had closed the previous Friday. Although there were other bidders, JPMorgan Chase was the only credible contender and got a sweetheart deal from the Fed, paying only $1.5 billion for the firm, whose assets included its headquarters building, worth an estimated $1.2 billion. The Fed also agreed to fund up to $30 billion of Bear Stearns' troubled assets as well as provide it with special financing for the transaction.[13] The purchase gave JP Morgan Chase a major foothold in the investment banking business, where it had lagged behind other major competitors.

If lightning is not supposed to strike twice in one spot, there is no such idiom about "white magic." In late September 2008, the FDIC, after a bank run on Washington Mutual (WaMu), sold the nation's largest thrift to JPMorgan Chase for approximately $1.9 billion. Included in the sale were $307 billion in assets, $188 billion in deposits, and 2,200 branches in fifteen states.[14] To put the size of the WaMu sale into context, the company's assets were equal to about two-thirds of the combined book values of all the 747 thrifts that had been sold off by the Resolution Trust Corporation, the government body that had handled the savings and loan crisis from 1989 through 1995.[15] The deal vaulted JPMorgan Chase into first place nationwide in deposits.

The company's strong price-to-book-value ratio and the high quality of its financial assets allowed it to build a financial empire. True, it was

---

* The offer was raised to $10 to complete the transaction quickly and avoid threatened suits by Bear Stearns stockholders.

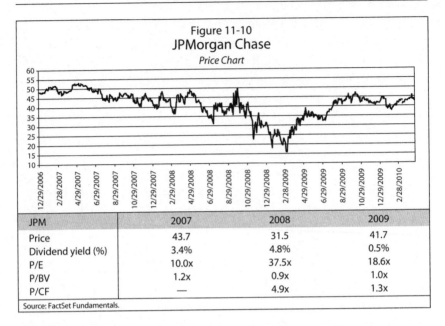

Figure 11-10
JPMorgan Chase
Price Chart

JPM	2007	2008	2009
Price	43.7	31.5	41.7
Dividend yield (%)	3.4%	4.8%	0.5%
P/E	10.0x	37.5x	18.6x
P/BV	1.2x	0.9x	1.0x
P/CF	—	4.9x	1.3x

Source: FactSet Fundamentals.

tough sledding for a while. In March 2009, it traded at just over 40 percent of book value, at $16. But by April 2010, it was once more above $45.

The enormous advantages of expanding profitability: it added the largest branch banking systems in the country; and a fully integrated investment banking department, given to it by the regulators for pennies on the dollar, was achievable only because of its financial strength. These acquisitions will be likely to lead to major payoffs over time. (See Figure 11-10.)

Using the High-Yield Strategy

Southern Company

The high-yield strategy, as we have seen, also provides above-average returns. At its most effective, it can be used with other contrarian methods to ferret out undervalued stocks, providing a combination of above-average income and reasonable appreciation. As noted, a high yield, even if earnings are temporarily depressed, indicates management's confidence in the future. How management and the board of directors react to a serious problem is usually worth noting.

At times the utility stocks are an example of a group where a combi-

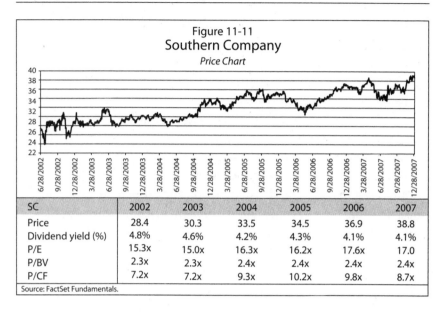

Figure 11-11
Southern Company
Price Chart

SC	2002	2003	2004	2005	2006	2007
Price	28.4	30.3	33.5	34.5	36.9	38.8
Dividend yield (%)	4.8%	4.6%	4.2%	4.3%	4.1%	4.1%
P/E	15.3x	15.0x	16.3x	16.2x	17.6x	17.0
P/BV	2.3x	2.3x	2.4x	2.4x	2.4x	2.4x
P/CF	7.2x	7.2x	9.3x	10.2x	9.8x	8.7x

Source: FactSet Fundamentals.

nation of high yield and low P/E allows investors to score well. High yield also works well in tandem with low price to book value.

This brings us to Southern Company, a utility company that operates four utilities with 4.4 million customers in Georgia, Alabama, Florida, and Mississippi. The company has shown slow but reasonably consistent growth for years. Every once in a while, as with most utilities, its stock price dips because of minor concerns that dissipate shortly thereafter. One such case came in mid-2002, when Southern's stock fell to $24, where it traded at a P/E of 13× and yielded 5.6 percent. The stock's earnings and dividends continued to grow over the next 5½ years, together returning 109 percent through 2007, when it yielded 7 percent on its original purchase price. Investor overreaction, as this example shows, is not confined solely to high-volatility stocks; utility and consumer nondurable buyers also get their chance on occasion. (See Figure 11-11.)

Contrarian Strategy Performance Summary

All five of the successful examples—Altria Group, BHP Billiton, Apache Corporation, JPMorgan Chase, and Southern Company—demonstrate a beneficial side effect of these strategies. Often contrarian stocks can move substantially higher in price and still be good holdings. The reason: earnings are moving up rapidly enough that the P/E, price-to-book-value, and price-to-cash-flow ratios remain low.

The contrarian approach I present has worked well both for my clients and for myself over time. Though I would be the last to argue that the record is definitive, the strategy has succeeded through both bull and bear quarters.[16] Although the degree of success will certainly vary among individuals—and for the same individual over differing time periods—this approach seems to be an extremely workable investment strategy, eliminating most complex judgments.

Indicators 1, 2, 4, and 5 are reasonably straightforward calculations, avoiding the major portion of Affect, configural, and information-processing problems previously discussed. And Indicator 3, which projects only the general direction of earnings, is much simpler and safer to use, and consequently should have a better chance of success, than the precise estimates ordinarily made by security analysts. Obviously, this is one of the methods I favor most.

As an investor, you may choose to follow this strategy as I have laid it down or look at other variations in the next chapter that should also allow you to outperform the market. But before you do this, let's visit the contrarian casino. You should really like this one because the odds in the casino favor the players. In fact, the question is: who really owns the casino?

▣ Section IV. What Are the Probabilities of Success Using IOH?

FINDINGS

At this point I think I hear a few murmurs out there—and rightly so. There are zillions of how-to investment books touting this method or that. Are there any real odds that contrarian strategies will beat the market over time? Indeed there are.

Calculating the returns of our forty-one-year study of the 1,500 largest stocks on the Compustat database, we find that the odds of contrarian strategies' outperforming the market are about sixty–forty in any single quarter. The casinos in Las Vegas and Atlantic City make a bundle with odds 5 to 10 percent in their favor. The probabilities of beating the averages using contrarian strategies, then, are even higher than the casinos'.

Let's look at these probabilities in detail. The results, I think, will surprise you.

First, in investing, unlike in Las Vegas, even if you do only as well as the market, you will walk away with your pockets bulging. You don't just get your cash back; you get it compounded. Ten thousand dollars invested in the market, as Figure 10-3 showed, results in a portfolio value of $913,000 forty-one years later. In the market casino, just breaking even would give you ninety times your money in forty-one years.

However, Figure 10-3 also demonstrated how well you would have done in contrarian strategies over time. Using the low-price-to-cash-flow strategy, you would have more than doubled the performance of the market, increasing your $10,000 of initial capital 216-fold. With price to book value, you would have outperformed price to cash flow somewhat, increasing your capital a modest 242 times. Investing in stocks produces enormous returns, even if you do only as well as the market. If you adopt a contrarian strategy, the results are spectacular.

You may have some questions at this point. First, is forty years a realistic time frame? How many people invest for anything near this time? If you are in your twenties or thirties, twenty-five or thirty years is not unreasonable, particularly if you are building your nest egg in an IRA or another retirement plan.

But as Table 11-2 demonstrates, you also get mouthwatering gains for shorter periods. The table indicates the amount that $10,000 would become in periods of five to twenty-five years relative to the market using the four contrarian strategies we have examined.[17] As you can see, all four strategies whip the market in every period. And the percentage they do it by goes up dramatically with time. Low P/E had the best returns overall. In five years, using the low-price-to-earnings strategy, you outdistance the market by 18 percent. This rises to 69 percent in fifteen years and 101 percent in twenty. And look at the difference compounding makes. At the end of five years, again with the price-to-earnings measure, the return is $3,203 over the market's; by ten years it increases to $12,419; and by the end of twenty-five years to $209,687. Remember, this is an initial onetime investment of only $10,000.

"There's no question that contrarian strategies look impressive, if not overwhelming, in studies," some readers would say, "but what are my chances of beating the market in practice?" Then there are other prob-

		Table 11-2			
		The Payoff Using Contrarian Strategies			
		Return on $10,000 Initial Investment, 1970–2010, with Annual Rebalancing			
	5 Years	10 Years	15 Years	20 Years	25 Years
Low P/E	$20,535	$42,165	$86,167	$176,964	$361,103
Low P/CF	$20,567	$41,980	$86,160	$174,939	$356,489
Low P/BV	$19,974	$39,972	$79,894	$158,468	$316,463
Low P/D	$18,757	$35,027	$65,363	$121,326	$226,288
Market	$17,332	$29,746	$51,035	$88,087	$151,416

Median compounded return in a Monte Carlo simulation of 10,000 trials.

Source: © David Dreman, 2011. Data Sources: Compustat North American data and Thomson First Call.

lems to deal with, such as the 2007–2008 crash, which cut out a large chunk of most people's retirement and savings plans.

Again, let's look at our chances of outdistancing the market over time in terms of the odds at a casino. Using our forty-one-year study,[18] we know that the odds are sixty–forty in our favor in any single play. But what are they over a large number of hands? In market terms, that would mean playing these strategies over some years.

To determine the answer, we use a statistical calculation, not by coincidence called the Monte Carlo simulation. We treat each quarter as a single card. Since we have a forty-one-year study, we have 164 quarters. Using low P/E as our strategy, we randomly pick a quarter from the 164 quarters in the forty-one years and calculate the return against the market, whether it is positive or negative. The card is then put back into the 164-quarter deck. We then randomly select another card in the same manner, calculate the return, and again put it back into the deck. This allows any quarter to be drawn more than once and other quarters to be missed entirely.

In effect, we are taking any possible combination of market returns over the 164 quarters of the study to determine just what the probabilities of beating the market are. A game would consist of 100 draws for each hand, which would total twenty-five years.[19] This gives us an almost unimaginably large number of combinations, which provides very accurate odds of how well a strategy will work over time. The Monte Carlo simulation allows us to get billions of possible combinations (actually 164^{100}, or more than the number of inches from here to the Andromeda galaxy, which is two million light-years away).

But most investors don't make a onetime investment in the market; they put away a few thousand dollars or more each year. Not wanting to bore the computer, we asked it to calculate the odds of beating the market for 10,000 plays of each strategy, investing sums from $1,000 to $20,000 dollars annually. The computer did this for the four value strategies, with only a minor whine at the monotony.

Table 11-3 shows the result of investing these amounts using the low-P/E strategy against the market over time. As you can see, the dollars you accumulate using a contrarian strategy are almost mind-boggling. An investment of only $1,000 a year over twenty-five years in a tax-free account would become $262,709. An investment of $20,000 a year would, by the same method, become $5,254,173.

If you used the low-P/E strategy and repositioned your portfolio quarterly into the lowest-P/E group, what would be your odds of beating the market over twenty-five years? High enough to make the owner of the plushest casino drool. If you play a 100-card series 10,000 times, your probabilities of winning are 9,978 out of 10,000! That's right, chances are you would underperform the market only twenty-two times in 10,000, or about two tenths of 1 percent on each hundred-card play.[20] And remember, this casino is different; even underperforming the market sends you

		5 Years	10 Years	15 Years	20 Years	25 Years
$1,000	**Low P/E**	**$7,860**	**$23,999**	**$56,948**	**$124,763**	**$262,709**
	Market	_$7,039_	_$19,119_	_$39,853_	_$75,755_	_$137,299_
$5,000	**Low P/E**	**$39,300**	**$119,995**	**$284,738**	**$623,816**	**$1,313,543**
	Market	_$35,196_	_$95,595_	_$199,264_	_$378,775_	_$686,494_
$10,000	**Low P/E**	**$78,600**	**$239,989**	**$569,477**	**$1,247,632**	**$2,627,086**
	Market	_$70,392_	_$191,189_	_$398,529_	_$757,549_	_$1,372,988_
$20,000	**Low P/E**	**$157,200**	**$479,978**	**$1,138,953**	**$2,495,263**	**$5,254,173**
	Market	_$140,784_	_$382,378_	_$797,058_	_$1,515,099_	_$2,745,976_

Table 11-3
Building a Nest Egg the Easy Way
Adding to the Investment Each Year, 1970–2010

Median compounded return in a Monte Carlo simulation of 10,000 trials.

Source: © David Dreman, 2011. Data Sources: Compustat North American data and Thomson First Call.

away not with empty pockets but with a large stack of chips if you get even a reasonable percentage of the market's return.

But say that twenty-five years is much too long for you to invest—what would happen if you move to a ten-year span? Using this strategy for ten years would reduce your chances of beating the market, but not by much. You would still come out a winner 9,637 times out of every 10,000 hands you played, not bad in casinos or markets. If you invested for five years in this manner, your odds of beating the market would still be 90 out of every 100 hands. The probabilities of winning with this strategy are a gambler's or an investor's fantasy.

But let's stop for a moment. Maybe you don't like to turn a part of your portfolio each and every quarter. Such a strategy might be too anxiety-producing; it might drive you, along with the rest of the players, to Prozac. How do we do if we opt for a longer holding period, say a year, without changing any part of the portfolio? Once again, this casino pays off like a dream. If you play this strategy for one-year periods for the full length of the study, making modest changes to the portfolio annually, your odds go up. But I'm sure you'll take them—try winning 9,998 of 10,000 hands. If you want to go for shorter periods, your odds of beating the market decrease somewhat but are still high—99 percent for ten years and 94 percent for five years.

The probabilities are nearly identical for price to cash flow and price to book value. A casino owner would die for these odds rather than the roughly fifty-five–forty-five the house gets. In fact some casino owners, including "Bugsy" Siegel, pushed daisies for far lesser odds.

These odds are by far the highest consistently available of any investment strategy I am aware of. There is nothing closer to a sure thing for millions of investors, yet, strangely enough, few play this game.

The contrarian wing has always been sparsely populated, and, despite all the statistics, it's likely to remain so.

Walking Away from the Chips

It's important to realize that investing using contrarian strategies is a long-term game. One roll of the dice or a single hand at blackjack is meaningless to a casino owner. He knows there will be hot streaks that will cost him a night's, a week's, or sometimes even a month's revenues. He may grumble when he loses, but he doesn't shut down the casino. He knows he'll get the money back.

As an investor, you should follow the same principle. You won't win every hand. You'll have periods of spectacular returns and others you might diplomatically describe as lousy. But it's important to remember that contrarian strategies, like a casino's odds, put you in the catbird seat. Professional investors, along with everyday folks, often forget this important principle and demand superior returns from every hand.

Even though a strategy works most of the time and generates excellent returns, *no strategy works consistently.* The fast-track, aggressive growth stocks will, on occasion, knock the stuffing out of low-P/E or other contrarian methods for several years at a clip—sometimes for much longer, as they did between 1996 and early 2000. But over time, it's simply no contest. Low P/E came back strongly in 2000 and 2001, sharply outperforming growth for the preceding ten years. Still, human nature being what it is, our expectations are almost always too high.

Is it possible for everyone to handle contrarian strategies? I'm confident that the underlying psychology we've looked into in some detail will remain valid, and I think most of us would take the bet that human behavior is remarkably invariant. But attitudes do change, and strong market movements, particularly by groups of exciting stocks, invariably bring about changes in the way people think. It is very hard for many, no matter how much they know, to take the odd cold shower while everyone else seems to be having a great time in the Jacuzzi.

It's almost impossible to underestimate the power of Affect, neuropsychology, and other psychological influences on our decisions. As a trained professional investor well versed in the new psychology, I'm certainly not immune, nor is anyone else. Enthusiasm, despondency, and fear tug at me just as hard as at most people, but knowledge gives you a better hand far more often than not. Still, it's no whitewash.

Even when we look at the record of these superb returns, which encompass both bull and bear markets over decades, we are still disappointed that a contrarian strategy doesn't win each and every year. The probability is very low that any investment strategy will, just as it is that you'll win a hundred straight hands at blackjack. That's obvious—if we were totally rational data processors. But we are not. We demand the impossible and repeatedly make poor decisions in pursuit of the unattainable.

Take the following example of how easily a winning strategy can be abandoned. In 1998 and 1999, growth investing sharply outperformed the value approach. Many value managers trailed the S&P 500 by 14 or 15 percent when the market was up 56 percent in the 1998–1999 period. These strategies continued to underperform for several years. The chant went up from some consultants and sophisticated clients that value was dead. "Contrarian strategies might have worked well in the past," many said, "but now, with almost everyone using them, they aren't effective anymore."

Then contrarian strategies did the unthinkable—they underperformed by even more in the first two months of 2000. How could this happen? Fidelity Investments replaced its leading contrarian manager, George Vanderheiden, in early 2000 with a growth team. Vanderheiden had managed the $7.2 billion Fidelity Destiny I fund as well as two other funds for almost twenty years.

The over $4 billion contrarian fund I was managing saw its assets drop by almost 50 percent as shareholders fled to hot Internet and fast-growing dot-com funds. The underperformance by contrarian stocks was worse than I had ever experienced. I wondered how many years it would take for me to catch up with the high-flying NASDAQ market, where the large majority of those hot stocks traded.

The answer was not years but months. By mid-March, the Internet bubble began to disintegrate and dot-com and high-tech stocks plummeted. Concurrently, Dreman Value Management's contrarian portfolios and mutual funds skyrocketed. By the end of 2000, our portfolios were up 40 percent, while the S&P 500 dropped 9 percent. We had made up not only all the underperformance we had lost between 1997 and 2000 in a little under ten months but a good deal more. As for George Vanderheiden, a *Wall Street Journal* article written several years later calculated that had his original portfolio been left intact, the fund he had managed so successfully over time would have been 40 percent above where it was under the new managers.

Again, it was simply the laws of probability. Contrarian stocks have an excellent record of doing better in bear markets, but that doesn't mean they will do so every time (they don't have to in order to get the well-above-average returns we saw in bear markets in Figure 10-5a). Still, when they don't do better, consultants and professionals, as well as individual investors, believe the strategies have lost their edge. Large numbers of investors, from giant institutions to individuals, abandoned them at that point, which happened to be right at the bottom of their performance cycle. From then on, those strategies outpaced the market handily for years.

Experience Is a Good Teacher

My own experience, as well as that of many other contrarian money managers, is similar. Over the past thirty-five years, I've seen this same syndrome occur virtually every time contrarian stocks underperformed the market for any length of time. If you can live with the few bad periods and the odd terrible period, you should do very well. However, following through is much more difficult than it may appear. One last but very important Psychological Guideline:

PSYCHOLOGICAL GUIDELINE 25: The investor psychology we've examined is both your biggest ally and your worst enemy. In order to win you have to stay with the game, but for many people that is difficult to impossible.

Though the strategies are simple and easy to use, the influence of immediate events is very powerful. We looked at why most people can't shake off these influences and at some of the principles that can help you to do so in Part I. Next let's look at the new, sometimes alien, world we face as investors and the strategies we can use to get through it.

Chapter 12

Contrarian Strategies Within Industries

WE'VE SEEN THAT the four contrarian strategies discussed in the previous chapter held up better than the market through both the Internet bubble and crash and the 2007–2008 market debacle.

Next we'll examine a new strategy that works on exactly the same behavioral principles as contrarian stocks but in a very different way. This method will allow you to participate in virtually every major industry in a manner similar to an index fund. Unlike an index fund, however, it should provide well-above-market returns. As we've already documented, investors are entirely too confident of their ability to forecast which stocks will win and which will lose, and fashions in the marketplace play a powerful role in drawing people to popular stocks. Does that extend beyond absolute "best" and "worst" stocks, as measured by absolute contrarian indicators in the previous chapter? It should.

▨ A New Contrarian Strategy

If trends and fashions exist in the marketplace as a whole, it is reasonable from a psychological perspective to expect that they exist within specific industries.[1] Analysts' research, expert opinion, current prospects, and a host of other variables should work on investors' expectations almost the same within industries as in the overall market. The result again should be expectations set too high for favored stocks within an industry and too low for out-of-favor stocks. Thus, Apple might be a favorite in the computer and peripheral industry, while Dell might be thought of as a laggard. Similarly, Chubb might be a favorite in the insurance industry, while Hartford is unloved and unwanted. Overpricing and underpricing of favored and unfavored stocks within value and growth industries would thus appear to be a natural extension of contrarian strategies. Sounds great in theory, but, unlike our academic friends, we're going to ask a rude question: does it work?

First we should ask how well the contrarian industry strategy does in the difficult environment we have recently experienced. The harsher the environment, the more accurate your judgment must be. Contrarian industry or relative strategies, like the absolute contrarian strategies we looked at in the preceding chapter, should also reduce the number of judgment errors significantly by not allowing us to overpay for stocks and not using disproved beta or other volatility measures, as well as by providing other safety checks.

To get the answer, first in collaboration with Eric Lufkin from 1970 to 1996[2] and then in a follow-up study with Vladimira Ilieva from January 1, 1995, through December 31, 2010, I examined the 1,500 largest companies on the Compustat database by market size. In the later study we divided the 1,500 stocks into the sixty-eight industries as classified by Standard & Poor's Global Industry Classification Standard (GICS) for the period measured.[3] The most favored stocks consisted of the 20 percent of companies in each industry with the highest P/E ratios, price-to-cash-flow ratios, and price-to-book-value ratios or lowest yields. The most unpopular were the 20 percent of stocks in each industry that had the lowest ratios by the first three measurements and the highest yield by the fourth. Returns were calculated in the same way for the remaining 60 percent of stocks in the middle quintiles.

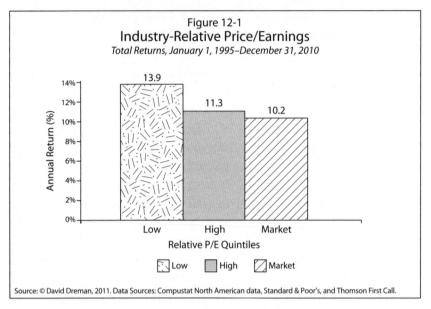

Figure 12-1
Industry-Relative Price/Earnings
Total Returns, January 1, 1995–December 31, 2010

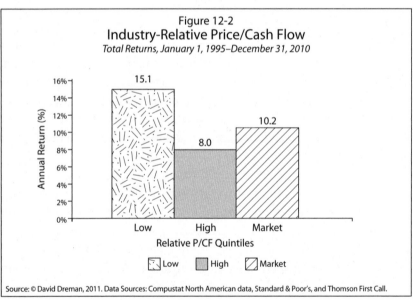

Figure 12-2
Industry-Relative Price/Cash Flow
Total Returns, January 1, 1995–December 31, 2010

If we used the industry strategy and took low P/E as our example, the lowest multiple in one industry, such as commercial banking, might be 10; in another industry, such as biotechnology, it might be 40. Yet, if we were right, the lowest-P/E stocks in both industries should provide well-above-market returns. Remember, in this strategy, we speak of relative P/E or the lowest 20 percent of P/Es (or price to cash flow or price to book value, or highest yield) within an industry, versus using the absolute lowest P/E measurement for the entire market, as we do for the four other contrarian strategies.

Figures 12-1 and 12-2 give the results of our most recent study for low price to earnings and low price to cash flow. Looking at Figure 12-1, for example, we see that the lowest 20 percent of stocks in each industry as measured by P/E, the first bar, returned 13.9 percent, the highest (second bar) returned 11.3 percent, and the market returned 10.2 percent. The lowest-price-earnings group outperformed the highest by 2.6 percent annually over the life of the study. Most important, the low-P/E stocks in each industry outperformed the market by 3.7 percent annually.

Figure 12-2 shows that the total annual return with the price-to-cash-flow strategy is 15.1 percent, which is higher than the low-P/E return. The lowest-price-to-cash-flow stocks in each industry group outperformed both the highest-price-to-cash-flow stocks and the market by more than the low-P/E group did in Figure 12-1.

Table 12-1 shows the returns of buying low-P/E stocks by this method and holding them for periods of two, three, five, and eight years. Again, the results of investing in the most out-of-favor stocks within industries are similar to those of buying the most unpopular stocks overall; however, the industry returns are somewhat lower. As Table 12-1 indicates, the returns of the laggards continue to outperform the market but fall off more rapidly against it over longer periods of time than do absolute contrarian strategies. It is best to rebalance portfolios annually when this strategy is used. The returns of price to cash flow and price to book value (not shown) are also similar.

Table 12-1
Industrial-Relative Price/Earnings
Buy-and-Hold Returns
January 1, 1995–December 31, 2010

P/E Quintiles	2 Years	3 Years	5 Years	8 Years
Low P/E	**11.9%**	**10.1%**	**9.9%**	**9.2%**
High P/E	**9.1%**	**7.9%**	**8.0%**	**7.2%**
Market	9.8%	9.0%	9.1%	8.0%

Source: © David Dreman, 2011. Data Sources: Compustat North American Data, Standard & Poor's, and Thomson First Call.

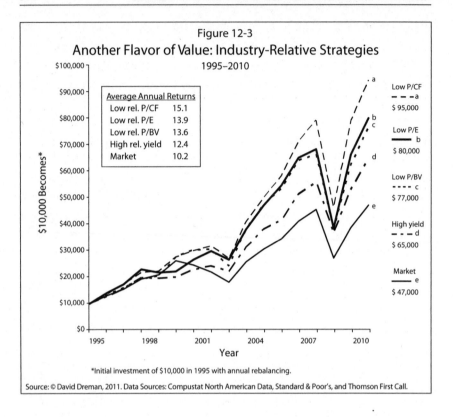

Figure 12-3
Another Flavor of Value: Industry-Relative Strategies
1995–2010

*Initial investment of $10,000 in 1995 with annual rebalancing.

Source: © David Dreman, 2011. Data Sources: Compustat North American Data, Standard & Poor's, and Thomson First Call.

Figure 12-3 demonstrates how soundly the relative (or industry) contrarian strategies beat the averages over the full sixteen years of the study. Low price-to-cash flow does the best. Ten thousand dollars invested by this method at the beginning of the period becomes $95,000 sixteen years later, outperforming the market by 102 percent.* Low relative price-to-book value and low P/E also work, while high yield also outperforms the market but lags behind the three other strategies.

Figure 12-4 once again shows that the market outperforms the highest industry-relative strategies, with the exception of high P/E, in a manner similar to how absolute contrarian strategies outgunned "best"-stock metrics. The resemblance in performance between the absolute strategies we looked at in previous chapters and the relative strategies we are looking at now is extraordinary. All of the "worst" industry-relative strategies in Figure 12-3 outperform the market.

_____

* Dividends are reinvested.

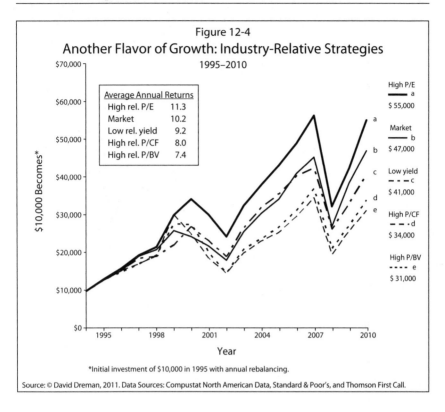

Figure 12-4
Another Flavor of Growth: Industry-Relative Strategies
1995–2010

Average Annual Returns	
High rel. P/E	11.3
Market	10.2
Low rel. yield	9.2
High rel. P/CF	8.0
High rel. P/BV	7.4

High P/E
— a
$ 55,000

Market
— b
$ 47,000

Low yield
– – c
$ 41,000

High P/CF
– – · d
$ 34,000

High P/BV
- - - e
$ 31,000

*Initial investment of $10,000 in 1995 with annual rebalancing.

Source: © David Dreman, 2011. Data Sources: Compustat North American Data, Standard & Poor's, and Thomson First Call.

Are these returns simply due to the superior performance of industries loaded with unloved stocks? No. The most out-of-favor stocks in an industry, regardless of whether they were dirt cheap or highly priced, outperformed the most popular stocks in each group and the market average. Low P/E beats high P/E, for example, by almost 50 percent. The evidence suggests that the relative value has a potent effect in all industries.[4]

So a new strategy is born. Let's make that a Psychological Guideline to summarize the concept:

PSYCHOLOGICAL GUIDELINE 26: Buy the least expensive stocks within an industry, as determined by the four contrarian strategies, regardless of how high or low the general price of the industry group is.

This strategy will beat the market handily most of the time. The psychological reasons are identical to those behind the contrarian strategies we looked at previously. It appears that the driving force behind these

Table 12-2
Contrarian Industry Ratios, 1995–2010

The price-to-value ratio of the cheapest stocks in the lowest 20% of industries is much lower than the price-to-value ratios of the cheapest stocks in the highest 20% of industries, while the overall returns of the stocks in the lowest 20% of industries are somewhat better.

Lowest 20% of Industries			Highest 20% of Industries		
	Ratio	Return		Ratio	Return
Low P/E	8.9	14.1%	Low P/E	17.4	13.2%
Low P/CF	4.1	15.7%	Low P/CF	10.7	14.8%
Low P/B	0.9	13.4%	Low P/B	2.2	14.1%

Source: © David Dreman, 2011. Data Sources: Compustat North American Data, Standard & Poor's, and Thomson First Call.

surprising results is Affect, as it is with absolute contrarian strategies. Regardless of how high or low the stock is valued absolutely, it has a nearly identical influence on investors in choosing the most popular and least popular stocks in an industry, as it does on the most popular and least popular stocks in the market itself. *The industry-relative price-to-value strategies appear to rely more on Affect than on fundamentals in the two periods ranging over the thirty-seven years the studies covered.*

Table 12-2 shows just how different the various contrarian value measurements are for the cheapest and most expensive industries. Price is only 90 percent of book value (0.9), for example, for the lowest-price-to-book-value group (PBV) in the cheapest 20 percent of industries, and this group returned 13.4 percent annually over the length of the study (above the market's 10.2 percent). By contrast, the lowest-PBV stocks in the highest 20 percent of industries are 2.2 times PBV by this measure. This is more than 2.4 times the price-to-book-value ratio of the cheapest 20 percent. Still, the lowest PBVs in the highest-value group provide an above-market 14.1 percent return. A glance at Table 12-2 also shows that the returns of the lowest relative strategies outperform those of the highest, with the exception of PBV. So we now have two separate and distinct effects that allow you to beat the market, both of them strongly backed by statistical evidence.

▧ Why Buy the Cheapest Stocks in an Industry?

Perhaps you're wondering, "What is the advantage of buying the cheapest stocks within an industry rather than the cheapest stocks overall?" There are several reasons why it can make good sense. As we just saw, millions of investors, tired of being battered by bad advice, have moved into index funds, as have large numbers of their institutional counterparts. Index funds, including exchange-traded funds (ETFs), now account for over $1 trillion of investment.

The new research about buying the cheapest stocks in a group of major industries leads to excellent long-term returns, while allowing you the chance to participate in stocks across the board—any investor can use this formula. Our study indicates that the returns are well ahead of those of an index fund. Though it's not a strategy for everybody, it will work for investors who can afford to own a broadly diversified portfolio of stocks: two in each industry across sixty-eight industries.

This is not an index fund as such, because it does not own hundreds of stocks, but it does own the most unfavored stocks in each of the sixty-eight major industries. As we saw, the returns have been well ahead of the S&P 500 over time. It can be used in lieu of an index-plus fund, a fund that attempts to outperform the S&P 500 with a somewhat similar portfolio. Unlike an index-plus fund, industry-relative portfolios have long records of outperforming this way.

Our research also shows that once a portfolio is in place, as Table 12-2 demonstrates for contrarian stocks, it needs some fine-tuning. Buying a portfolio of the lowest-valued stocks in an industry and holding it without any changes—regardless of the contrarian strategy you prefer—unlike buying absolute contrarian strategies, results in some "decay" in results in statisticians' terms, but they are still well ahead of the market. *You are better off rebalancing the portfolio every year or two.*

Though we continue to research the industry strategy work, we believe, as previously stated, it is caused by Affect and other psychological influences.

It also appears in relative industry strategies, as in absolute ones, that company fortunes change over time, as Graham and Dodd noted in *Security Analysis.*[5] Industry laggards often tighten their belts, improve their management, and find ways of increasing their market share or developing new products, resulting in their outperformance of the market for fairly long periods.

However, such changes could certainly be Affect-related. Analysts and investors slowly change their opinions of these laggards. Now, when companies' performance surprises pleasantly, the market applauds and awards them higher stock prices. For favored-industry stocks, the process is exactly the opposite: expectations are too optimistic—so high that even a brilliant management cannot meet them. Something has to go wrong and usually does.

Moving back from the "why" to the "how," let's look at another reason this approach can help you. Buying the lowest-valued stocks in each major industry opens a much larger investment universe than is available with an "absolute" contrarian strategy. Investing in the absolutely cheapest stocks, no matter which of the previous methods you pick, gives the investor only the bottom 20 percent of stocks in the marketplace from which to select. With an industry-relative strategy, you can get a crack at every industry in the entire market.[6]

The advantage of the contrarian industry strategy is that you have far more diversification by industry than you do in the original contrarian strategies. This diversification should protect you from the underperformance that occurs when the most out-of-favor stocks and industries in the market are taboo. Thus, if industries such as communications equipment or biotechnology are headed for the stars, you will not feel left out. You will also not be positioned only in the most disliked groups, which may underperform for months or sometimes years.

Although the returns of the industry-relative strategies are below those of the absolute strategies, they still significantly outperform the market. As we've learned, it is difficult for individual investors, and even more for professionals, to take unpopular positions for long periods, even if they are right in the end.

With the inane focus on quarterly performance by too many consultants and clients continuing to increase, a manager who lags behind for too long can easily get the ax. True, he or she may prove right, but all too frequently it is "dead right." For individuals, the psychological pressure to run for the hills is difficult or impossible to resist. After all, it is psychological pressures that keep people from following contrarian strategies in the first place.

■ The Defensive Team

"Do I still get to eat my cake and have it too?" many investors might ask ᴜ the industry-relative strategies. "We see that they provide impressive returns over time, but how good are they in down markets?" Pretty good, as Figure 12-5a demonstrates. As with the absolute contrarian strategies in Figure 10-5a, we measured the bear market returns for all the down market periods. Relative value, like the other four absolute contrarian strategies, outperformed the market in the twenty down quarters in this study. The high-yield method again shines, declining only 5.1 percent quarterly on average in down quarters (the best of the litter) against –8.1 percent for the overall market. Similarly, Figure 12-5b shows that all industry-relative strategies outperformed the market in the forty-four quarters of our study when stocks were heading up.

The results are both robust and remarkably similar to those that Eric Lufkin and I obtained in *Contrarian Investment Strategies: The Next Generation* in 1998 (for 1970–1996), although the databases and time periods are very different. The main point is that these strategies are time-tested and work.

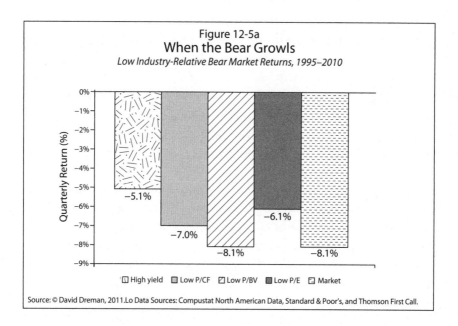

Figure 12-5a
When the Bear Growls
Low Industry-Relative Bear Market Returns, 1995–2010

Source: © David Dreman, 2011.Lo Data Sources: Compustat North American Data, Standard & Poor's, and Thomson First Call.

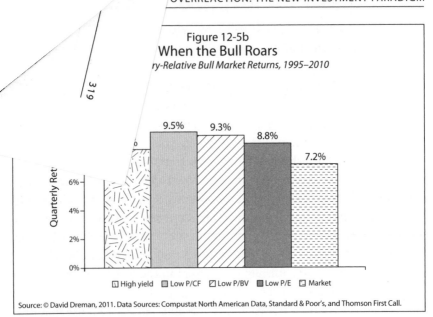

Figure 12-5b
When the Bull Roars
ry-Relative Bull Market Returns, 1995–2010

Source: © David Dreman, 2011. Data Sources: Compustat North American Data, Standard & Poor's, and Thomson First Call.

▨ Additional Portfolio Considerations

WHERE DO I GET MY STATISTICS?

You might ask how one determines quintiles. Brokerage firms, advisory services, and financial publications often advertise long lists of contrarian stocks (the Value Line Survey, for example, presents weekly tables of the hundred lowest P/E ratios, price-to-cash-flow ratios, price-to-book-value ratios, and highest-yielding stocks of the 1,700 companies in its universe). Two other statistical database providers, the American Association of Individual Investors (800-428-2244) and Investors Alliance (866-627-9090), also offer discs of company information that allow screening for a minimal fee.

To select contrarian stocks on your own, some simple rules should suffice. First, take a broad market index, like the S&P 500, for which the current P/E, price-to-cash-flow, and price-to-book-value ratios and dividend yield can easily be found in a variety of sources. The current P/E ratio of the S&P 500, in September 2011, was about 12×, its price-to-cash-flow ratio 7×, its price-to-book-value ratio 1.9×, and its yield 2.3 percent.

Pick well-established companies. A rule of thumb might be to use a 20 percent discount or more from the S&P 500 for any of the first three measures and a yield of at least 1 percent above the market for the fourth. The deeper the discount from the S&P 500, the further into contrarian land you go.

There is nothing magical about picking the bottom 20 percent by any of the first three measures. It's simply a good cutoff point for a computer. As we found in virtually all of the contrarian studies, this group consistently outperformed the market.

A simple method should work fairly effectively if you do not have the quintiles for these strategies. How can you find the ratios? Your broker should be able to procure all the ratios for you very easily. The Value Line Investment Survey, among others, normally runs a list of these metrics weekly, as well as one of high-yielding stocks. Yields are also published daily in the financial section of any large newspaper. Once again, you can compare them with the average yield of the S&P 500, which is readily available from a number of sources. As indicated, the price-to-cash-flow and price-to-book-value ratios can be obtained at low cost from the Morningstar or Value Line Web sites or a variety of other services.

Though I don't believe contrarian investing need necessarily be the final answer to stock selection for everyone, it has consistently performed better in both good and bad markets. It is also the only strategy that I know of that effectively and systematically checks investor overreaction— by far the largest and most important source of investor error.

WHAT CONTRARIAN STRATEGIES WON'T DO FOR YOU

Whether you opt for the eclectic contrarian strategy or take the contrarian bit between your teeth and attack the market without any form of security analysis, keep in mind that the strategies are relative rather than absolute. This means that they won't help you decide when to get into or out of particular stocks. But no strategy that I am aware of does so successfully. We saw in chapter 4 that the technical analysis that claimed to be able to do so crashed and burned. Whether the market is high or low, you will receive no warning signals to sell in the first place or buy in the second.

What contrarian strategies should do is give you the best relative opportunities for your capital, particularly in the present difficult environment. This means that in a falling market, your stocks ought to decline less than the averages, and in a rising market, they should perform somewhat better. But remember that averages are deceptive. Even if contrarian stocks provide better returns in most bear markets, they don't do so for all bear markets. Similarly, though contrarian strategies provide far-above-average returns over time, they don't do so every time. Think of yourself as the owner of a casino. The odds in your favor are extremely high, but in this financial casino, unlike a regular casino, you will have a few years of poor results, as was the case from 1997 to 2000 or 2007 to 2008, eventually followed by some years of staggering returns. Your greatest enemy is the psychology highlighted in the first section of the book. If you can control the strong urge to play the winners, your chances of success even in an alien environment are high.

As we have seen, the long-term returns of holding contrarian stocks through bull and bear markets are breathtaking; the longer the period, the more impressive the results. We will shortly provide some impressive evidence that owning stocks has been one of the two best ways to go, not only for the past decade but for the past two hundred years.

Chapter 13

Investing in a New, Alien World

TODAY'S INVESTMENT WORLD seems as foreign to many as being encased in a spacesuit on a meteoroid. Through the suit you can hear the hissing of fissures and somewhere farther away the explosion of meteorites crashing into rocks. Craters whose depth is impossible to gauge in the semidarkness seem dangerously close. The only light is from Earth, which seems very large but impossibly far away. If you walk too vigorously, you may catapult into a crater or onto a jagged peak because there is almost no gravity. In short, welcome: this is the investment world many people feel they are in today.

The investment arena is a disjointed, difficult world far different from the one we approached so enthusiastically only a little over a decade ago. Here we'll look at a set of particularly important new threats and how you can cope with them as well as the new opportunities available now.

Most of the rules of investing that we were taught, and thought we had mastered, at times seem altered and unfamiliar. Now we face high volatility, flash crashes, an economy only just crawling back after the Great Recession, derivatives so complex that even major institutions such as AIG have imploded using them, and stock and bond markets that often seem dysfunctional. We'll have to be at our intrepid best to adjust to the conditions of investing in this altered and unfamiliar investment environment.

The Flash Crash and the August 2011 Panic

E-world technologies make possible market strategies that were never practicable before, but some of the results can have all the characteristics of a major crash—only it all happens so much faster. On May 6, 2010, out of nowhere, the Dow Jones Industrial Average dropped 9.2 percent. This was its biggest tumble since the 1987 crash: $862 billion in U.S. stocks were erased in less than ten minutes. Although the worst trades were canceled and the markets pared back the decline to 3.2 percent at the close, investors still took major losses that day. Worse, their confidence, already badly battered by the crash of 2007–2008, was further rattled by what was soon dubbed the "flash crash." The report the SEC and the Commodity Futures Trading Commission (SEC-CFTC) released on the crash on September 30, 2010, appears to have only scratched the surface of the problem. To date, the SEC has continued to move in a slow but methodical manner. Many professionals knowledgeable about the flash crash worry that the SEC's reaction was far too slow, as it was in 1987, opening up the possibility that a far more severe crash could be in the wings.

What has not been analyzed to date is the effect of a giant new force in the stock market called high-frequency trading (HFT). The best of the traders who use these methods have built trading systems that move almost in milliseconds (thousandths of a second) to almost instantaneously get a slight advantage in any trading patterns their computers spot. The profit is only a fraction of a penny per share in most cases, but the volume of trades is enormous. Although precise figures are elusive, some trade sources estimated that by mid-2009, high-frequency trading accounted for almost 75 percent of the volume on all U.S. markets, up from 33 percent in 2006 and only about 10 percent in the early years of the last decade. Despite their huge trading volume, HFT firms represent only 2 percent of the approximately 20,000 brokerage firms operating in the United States today.[1]

High-frequency trading firms are made up primarily of scientists, software developers, math whizzes, and information technology developers whose mission is to squeeze out a fraction of a penny in profits per share on each of these trades. At RGM Advisors, a major high-frequency trader in Austin, stone urns in the lobby are stuffed with pennies as a reminder that the firm trades hundred of millions of shares a day, for well under a penny profit apiece, and makes money doing it. High-frequency firms such as RGM are a driving new force in the U.S. securities markets. Speed is king; even millionths of a second can make a big difference.

High-frequency traders have set up headquarters from Chicago and Austin to Red Bank, New Jersey. Algorithms, enormously fast computers, and direct cables that transfer data almost at the speed of light give them a precious few milliseconds of advantage. Using their enormous speed, they scour public and private markets for deviations from historical price relationships between stocks and jump on discrepancies, rather than playing the stocks themselves. They also use puts, calls, or futures when they work.

The burgeoning HFT industry has spawned legions of jeans-wearing techies who arm their machines to outwit rivals. Programmers write formulas to sniff out the buy and sell intentions of mutual funds and jump in ahead of them in a practice called "gaming." HFT firms also employ strategies such as iceberging, breaking a single large order into chunks and leaving just a small order, or the tip, visible. The gamers, also called sharks, place small buy and sell orders to uncover the hidden larger ones, which they then front-run.

High-frequency trading played a large role in the ten-minute U.S. market crash on May 6. The automatic execution of the sale of futures contracts valued at about $4.1 billion on the Chicago Mercantile Exchange played a major part in triggering the plunge, according to the joint SEC-CFTC report. The initial sales of the contracts led to a burst of trading among HFT firms, the report added.[2]

The SEC-CFTC report indicated that the market was already down 3 percent that day, when Waddell & Reed, a major Kansas mutual fund complex, put in an order to execute 75,000 mini E contracts* of the S&P 500 as a "routine hedge" transaction. Despite Waddell & Reed's protest, the transaction was anything but routine. It was carried out for its most aggressive, free-swinging mutual fund, which accounted for more than 15 percent of its assets. Although the order was supposedly put out

---

*Futures contracts on the S&P 500 that are one-fifth as large as the normal S&P futures contract.

carefully, high-frequency traders and a few brokerage firms played a major role in driving prices down. Critical to the debacle was that they stopped buying and started selling futures as S&P minifutures plummeted, putting more pressure on the downward-spiraling prices. Brokers, through various sophisticated techniques, reduced their executions of clients' sell orders, which they normally took the other side of, but continued to execute buy orders. This in effect allowed the brokers and market makers to sell their own inventory to their customers and get shorter.

The lack of liquidity was major. The next day, the regulators and the exchanges reversed some of the trades, but the reversals were only for trades that had taken place at 60 percent or lower than pre–flash crash price levels.

The damage to investors was serious. Twenty thousand trades, totaling 5.5 million shares, executed 60 percent or more below the pre–flash crash price, were canceled. At least half of those were retail orders. And that does not include the far larger number of trades that were executed at a steep discount to the precrash level that were not canceled.[3] What caused the regulators' overly timid actions?

For investors to lose 60 percent of their stocks' value in minutes is unheard of. Since this crash, circuit breakers* have been posted for various categories of trades. If the market rises or drops by a predetermined amount, the circuit breakers kick in, allowing various stocks to move from 3 to 15 percent for the NASDAQ 100, depending on the stock price, 10 percent for most large listed stocks, and additional limits for the Dow Jones Industrial Average and other indices. The circuit breakers at this time are extremely complex and vary widely for different stocks and markets.

Why did the regulators, only months before, let individual investors take losses as high as nearly 60 percent—up to as high as twenty times the amount of the new limits? That question has never been answered. Surprisingly—or perhaps not—the only ones who could make money from the original flash crash were the high-frequency traders and a handful of brokers.

Unfortunately once again, we see our exchanges and regulatory agencies at work. Who benefits from crashes: small investors and mutual funds or the flash traders and hedge funds that feed on them? The

---

* Circuit breakers determine how much a stock can rise or fall before trading is temporarily stopped. They are also used for S&P 500 and other stock options.

question is rhetorical. The institutions and small investors were taken out by the bottom-feeders as the regulators looked the other way. Does this remind you of another crash not much earlier?

This crash may be only the tip of the iceberg. The question is asked more frequently whether rather than providing liquidity at the most critical times, as the HFT crowd strongly claims it does, HFT actually drains liquidity. The initial SEC-CFTC report written after the flash crash on May 18, 2010, contradicts the high-frequency traders' assertions, stating that "preliminary analysis shows that between 2:30 p.m. and 3:00 p.m., trading volume spiked, bid/offer spreads widened, and depth declined. The latter two observations are consistent with a significant decline in liquidity with the bulk of that decline occurring between 2:42 p.m. and 2:45 p.m."[4] The SEC-CFTC report further comments, "During the 30-minute period from 2:30 p.m. to 3:00 p.m., trading volume was about 10 times the average daily trading volume for the same intraday time period calculated over the prior 30 days."[5] The report states that the heaviest trading occurred after liquidity dried up in the critical 2:42 to 2:45 P.M. time period.

The S&P 500 futures did not provide additional liquidity, as virtually all the high-frequency traders claim; they actually decreased liquidity in much the same manner as in the 1987 crash. Heavy short selling slammed prices downward. When panic is created, the standard operating procedure of the short sellers is to stand aside as prices plummet, reappearing only when buyers begin to come back. This creates big-time profits for the high-frequency traders. And it was all made in the U.S.A.

Insiders knowledgeable about HFT suggest that there are many similarities between these events and the price drops prior to the 1987 crash. On this basis alone, HFT is not a boon to liquidity but a serious danger to the destabilization of the market, with the risk of possibly triggering another 1987-type crash.

Other Potential HFT Problems

Unfortunately, the danger does not end there. According to a report in Bloomberg News, Nanex, a data firm located in Winnetka, Illinois, says that some activities are definitely underhanded. Its researchers have found instances in which thousands of quotes a second in a particular stock are fired and canceled almost instantaneously, overwhelming trading systems.[6] This process has added the term "quote stuffing" to the lexicon. "High-frequency traders are not interested in the fundamental worth of a company," says George Feiger, the CEO of Contango Capital Advisors, a San Francisco money management firm with $2 billion in assets. "They are only interested in making a quick killing and moving on."

Regulators are struggling to find solutions for reining in the HFT crowd and its computers. The SEC is looking into establishing and then enforcing a minimum time period, such as fifty milliseconds, in which a quote to buy or sell a stock would remain valid, according to firms that have met with the agency. The SEC is also considering whether to require high-frequency firms to remain in a market, rather than pulling out when times get tough, to maintain liquidity, which is after all their primary function.

Ted Kaufman, at the time a senator from Delaware, proposed a number of protective measures that would limit the damage of plummeting S&P futures. He wanted the SEC to limit the number of quote cancellations. The agency has proposed rules to monitor firms that trade more than two million shares a day.

However, such changes assume that enforcers are as agile as the high-frequency firms. "'Technological advances have outstripped our ability to regulate them,' says Andrew Lo, director of Massachusetts Institute of Technology's Laboratory for Financial Engineering and chief scientific officer of quantitative-analysis hedge fund AlphaSimplex Group. 'It's like the Wild Wild West.'"[7]

▓ HFT 2: The Guns of August

Through the end of 2010 and continuing in 2011, as we saw, the SEC and the Exchanges put in circuit breakers and limits that determined how much a futures index or stock could fall or rise in a given period of time. The SEC also continued its investigation of the flash crash and subpoenaed firms that do high-frequency trading.

Although there appeared to be widespread skepticism that high-frequency trading was under control, the regulators allowed it to continue with the curbs that had been put on it, as the investigation continued. Volatility stayed very low and stock prices were rising. The SEC and other regulatory bodies' investigations dragged on at a snail's pace.

Then things began to change. On July 27, 2011, the S&P 500 dropped 27 points, or 2 percent. For that month as a whole, though, the S&P was down only slightly (2.1 percent), volatility was still very low and the correction was minor relative to the market's major rise for 2009–2011. But moving into August, the roof began to fall in. After declining moderately on August 1 the S&P plummeted 33 points, or 2.6 percent, on August 2, and suffered an enormous 60-point drop, or 4.8 percent, on August 4, followed by a drop of 80 points, or 6.7 percent, on the eighth. The Dow Jones, meanwhile, plummeted 635 points on the eighth. From July 8 through August 8 the S&P had fallen 17.3 percent—13.4 percent in the first six trading days of August alone—and was on the doorstep of a new bear market (considered a drop of 20 percent or more).

Volatility skyrocketed. The VIX volatility index traded on the Chicago Board Options Exchange (CBOE), also known as the "fear index," measures the implied volatility for the S&P 500 Index options. The lower the VIX, the more confidence people have that markets will not move up or down rapidly. For the previous eighteen months through July the VIX normally traded around 20, which is considered a low-volatility level. Then a tidal wave of fear swept through markets.

The S&P 500 cratered as the VIX soared. In a matter of days the VIX index doubled. From 16 in early July it began to move up and by early August it took off. From 32 on August 4 it rose to 48 on August 8, a rise in volatility almost never seen this quickly, even in a free-falling market. Panic was everywhere spurred on by the enormous volatility. Global markets, taking their cue from the United States, dropped as much and in many cases more than the domestic ones.

Over three trillion dollars had been lost by investors and institutions domestically, the great bulk in less than three weeks. The rush out of stocks was like a panic at the exit in a theater fire. In the four months ending in mid-September investors had pulled $75 billion out of U.S. stock funds, more than in the five months after the collapse of Lehman Brothers.[8] Meanwhile, gold and almost-zero yielding treasuries rocketed upwards. Investors globally yanked $92 billion from stock funds in the three months through the end of August, which was more than the total moved into stock funds from the spring of 2009, when the market rally began.

Fear turned into contagion among investors. Many sold at any price, thinking that after the twenty-seven-month rally following the 2007–

2008 crash, stocks were heading down to major new lows. The falling prices and volatility continued to the time of this writing in early October.

Inflows to some banks were so high that a number of them, including Bank of New York, announced they would post fees to take in new deposits for large accounts, something almost never done before. How did this all come about?

While the thick smoke from this battlefield has not cleared and likely won't for many months, the regulators and experts are increasingly focusing on high-frequency trading as one of the chief culprits. HFT trading tripled during this period and was the dominant force in U.S. markets. According to a report in *The Wall Street Journal,* the market research firm Tabb Group estimated that the increase in the volume of HFT trades in August brought their share of total U.S. stock trading volume to 65 percent from 53 percent in the prior months.

Volume including HFT was up 80 percent, indicating that these firms were on a highly profitable trading tear during this period, while most other investors suffered substantial losses. The overall volume of equity trades between August 4 and August 10 averaged 16.0 billion shares daily, the busiest five days of trading on record. The report further states that the volume of trading was especially high on August 8, with the Dow dropping 635 points—making it the fourth busiest trading day on record—and Tabb estimated that HFT traders made approximately $60 million in trades in U.S. stocks and futures that day. Profits ranged from $40 million to $56 million on other days of that same week.

The article cites a number of firms that made large gains, pointing out that August 8 and 9 were both big winning days for Tradeworx Inc. of Red Bank, New Jersey. Getco LLC, based in Chicago, was also a big winner. And hedge fund Renaissance Technologies LLC of East Setauket, New York, was said to have earned total gains of $200 million in the first two weeks of August in two funds it manages.

To provide a comparison, the article states that Tabb estimates that the profits from HFT in stocks for all of 2009 were $7.2 billion. HFT traders are also active in stock futures and in major commodities such as oil and gold, among other markets. The large high-frequency profits came as other stock buyers including some major hedge funds, mutual funds, and individual investors were badly bruised. Adam Sussman, director of research at Tabb, said in the article that "Retail investors are just going nuts, and high-frequency traders are feeding off the volume."[9]

Further illuminating the problem, in an interview with Bloomberg News, Gary Wedbush, executive vice president of Wedbush Securities, whose company is one of the biggest execution and clearing firms catering to HFT, said, "Some of their algorithms and automated systems are trading two, three or five times as many shares as they would have in a more normalized volatility environment." Wedbush added, "We're seeing a tremendous amount of high-frequency trading. Their business is a trading business, and volatility creates far more opportunities." Putting a fine point on the matter, he further stated, "*You can look at a VIX chart [the most widely used volatility measure] and that's almost perfectly correlated to high-frequency trading volumes* [italics mine]." [10] What Wedbush is saying in non-Street parlance is in effect that high-frequency trading is a primary cause of the panic because it was the prime reason for the enormously increased volatility of stock and index futures prices. Remember in the flash crash stocks fell as much as 60 percent or more because of similar volatility in minutes.

The skyrocketing volatility, while highly profitable to HFT traders, terrified almost all institutional and individual investors because of the rapidity of the moves both up and down. Such volatility in a very short time period was almost unheard of. This is a proven way to create market panic.

Along with many others, I find it difficult to say the HFT group are legitimate market makers; to many, including myself, they can be far more accurately thought of as major destroyers of wealth.

Some traders believe that the market volatility during this period was due to market manipulation. A number of knowledgeable traders interviewed on CNBC strongly agreed. Jon Najarian said that everything that happened since August 3 deserves to be the subject of this debate. He particularly cites the 33 percent increase in the capacity to report trades in the Consolidated Quote System to 1 million quotes per second on July 5, 2011. "In a turbulent market," he continued "[investors] can't even see what's going on." Other traders agree. Tim Seymour says, "It reeks of manipulation." Trader Joe Terranova said any way you add it up, it equals trouble. "Because of machines, things are happening much more quickly and much more deeply." Jon Najarian added, "We need the SEC and the CFTC to step in and say 'no more.'" [11]

Some high-frequency tactics have in fact attracted the attention of regulators. They are probing into whether laser-like orders placed in large batches and withdrawn in milliseconds have distorted security prices, particularly if they were placed almost at the same time by a dozen or more firms using similar algorithms to trigger them. If the market is moving down sharply and a tidal wave of potential sell orders suddenly appears to be coming in, the natural tendency is to get outta Dodge fast.

The SEC in these weeks subpoenaed a number of HFT firms' records to analyze their role in major swings, including the flash crash, as well as to probe into other activities not related to it. SEC chairman Mary Schapiro said in a speech earlier in the year, "We need to assess the entire regulatory structure surrounding high frequency trading firms and their algorithms."[12] An issue she highlighted was whether these algorithms work properly in stressed markets. According to CFTC commissioner Scott O'Malia, three other such crashes that have occurred since the May 2010 flash crash have also been related to algorithmic trading.[13] The Justice Department and SEC are now investigating whether HFT practices may be manipulative.[14]

Actions on HFT spread to Europe months ago. Similar reactions in these markets resulted in Europe's top securities regulator, The European Securities and Markets Authority (ESMA), outlining a series of tough new rules to clamp down on HFT. The rules will be fast-tracked to passage by including them with two existing pieces of security legislation, and should be adapted in 2011. The rules are being introduced after NYSE Euronext suffered three trading halts due to excess volatility in six trading days earlier this year while alternative platform CHI-X suffered three stoppages in May and June. Andrew Haldane, executive director for Financial Stability at the Bank of England, said in early July that the rapid growth of high frequency trading caused price "abnormalities" and was raising contagion concerns.[15] More new evidence questioning high frequency practices seems to come in almost daily.

What seems clear to me, if anything can be clear in the murky HFT environment, is that high-frequency trading may be used for many dozens of trading strategies. But in my opinion from what we've seen, in these two recent periods of market crisis, one strategy stands out. The HFT traders use their enormous speed, measured in thousands of a second, to accentuate market moves up or down. If markets are down a few hundred points, as in the flash crash, and selling begins to pick up, HFT firms short S&P futures or other stock vehicles heavily. All of this is computer driven because of the enormous speed required. HFT firms can also be very active on openings and closings, when the market is down or up fairly sharply, accentuating the moves in either direction significantly.

It would seem the algorithms of most HFT firms are programmed similarly for this type of scenario, so if one flash trader begins to short the computerized algorithms of many others, HFT firms fire off short sell orders almost instantaneously. We have already seen how this tactic worked in the flash crash to drop the Dow 600 points in eight to ten minutes and can lead to widespread contagion in the marketplace. The panic moves through the S&P stock futures pits into the stock market itself and results in the selling of individual stocks. As we saw in the flash crash, the carnage was very heavy, with many stocks dropping as much as 40 to 60 percent.

We also know that the HFT firms fire off enormous numbers of bids or offers for futures and stocks in milliseconds and cancel them a few milliseconds later. Some of the reasons given seem valid, such as trying to uncover a buyer's position. But this is very different from placing enormous orders that they don't intend to follow through on. The latter practice in a sharply falling market is dubious at best. One reason in a panicky market might be to drive prices even lower. If a flotilla of HFT firms are attempting to drive prices down and a large tidal wave of flash sell orders show up on the screen, canceled in milliseconds, other investors can easily be fooled into thinking that heavy potential waves of selling will hit the floor in seconds, resulting in investors and traders selling immediately to escape the deluge.

The same strategy may apply in a market which is rising substantially, only in this case the tactics would be used to keep the market rising, and if possible on an accelerated basis. HFT firms thus win on both the upside and the downside. All they require is enormous volatility in either case, which from the evidence available they help to create. The net result is that volatility is far higher than it should be and all too many people abandon markets because of their casino-like behavior.

Markets thrive on low volatility and a stable environment in which to make investment decisions. Flash traders thrive on instability and rapidly rising or falling markets. The very instability they require to make major profits is what drives tens of thousands of investors out of the marketplace as we have seen. It is interesting to know how attuned flash traders are to the art of creating panic by aiming to increase the market's volatility. Their profits in the August 2011 crash were huge while most investors, including most professionals, lost money. For HFT firms to make instant profits by these activities is certainly against the best interest of the overwhelming majority of market participants.

The HFT firms' actions are not unlike the allegoric snowball that rolls down the mountain gathering mass and creating an avalanche. Remember we've heard a number of times from HFT participants that the more volatility, the better. HFT firms like it because it does create great volatility and what they don't say—major panic.

We don't know yet whether there has been manipulation by some of the major HFT firms. But if my portrayal is correct, this is not only a challenge for the SEC, it is a serious challenge for investment professionals and individual investors, in their efforts to keep markets sound. This band of traders who haven't the least interest in owning stocks or indexes themselves or participating in markets for more than a few milliseconds are a real danger to markets as we know them. Though destroying our markets, which high-volatility trading does, is certainly not intentional. The last thing the HFT firms want to do is kill the goose that lays their golden eggs. But it would seem that in their rush for profits that's exactly what their actions threaten to do.

How can we stop this major threat to markets? It won't be easy. As we saw, we faced a similar situation during the 1987 crash because of the interaction of index arbitrage and portfolio insurance. However, in 1987, the explosion was accidental, while here it seems to be intentional. HFT seems to be a far more effective weapon to keep volatility high over prolonged periods of time, if not dealt with quickly.

One solution might be to raise the margin requirements up to 25 or even 50 percent for these firms on the stock futures they trade. Another would be to place limits on the size of positions they can buy or sell very quickly in S&P 500 and other futures, which do disrupt markets. A third is the SEC's proposal in late September to set tighter limits on circuit breakers, reducing them down to 7 percent from 10 percent, and using the much broader S&P 500 instead of the Dow Jones Industrial Average.[16] A fourth is to increase the transaction costs per share slightly on trades. Since most HFT firms trade for profits of only a fraction of a penny a share, marginally higher transaction costs will sharply reduce their trading. I'm sure sophisticated thinkers on the matter can come up with many more. Hopefully soon, because our markets do seem to be seriously threatened.

A Fast Track to Disaster?

The SEC's and CFTC's mission is to protect the public, not a group of brilliant computer jocks in T-shirts and jeans whose sole reason for being is to rip off investors by getting an edge on their trading. If the traders provided a consistent legitimate service and did not increase the danger to the average investor or mutual fund, it would be hard to find fault with their activities. But from what we've seen from our brief overview of the flash crash and the far more devastating drop in late July and through September 2011, this does not seem to be the case. The SEC itself noted that in the flash crash, volatility increased as the stock market crumbled. Moreover, practices such as bid stuffing, where an HFT trader can fire and cancel thousands of shares a second, and other schemes we have viewed, are potentially very dangerous.

These strategies have been put together by some of the smartest people in the investment business after investing tens of millions of dollars in the high-speed systems and the professionals necessary to make them work. It doesn't quite seem that they are doing it for charity. Knowing what we know, we see that flash trading may be a danger to both the public and our major financial institutions. Although this writer and many others believe there is widespread manipulation caused by HFT, the SEC is still investigating the charge. Many of us are curious why HFT trading firms seem to be the only ones making large profits through these debacles. The end result is that the damage to investor savings and to their confidence in our markets has been enormous. There are certainly serious questions to ask about its many moving parts that require thorough analysis. The prudent move to protect the large majority of investors would be to severely restrict HFT operations until these questions can be answered.

What Should You Do?

If I am right, there are a number of ways you can get hurt by high-frequency trading. The worst, of course, is if HFT causes a serious crash. But this is not a reason you should get out of the market. First, the regulators are moving slowly in the direction of taking action on this issue. A worst case is that they wait too long and the wheels come off the market.

In this case, if the facts are widely known, I'd expect the market to come back fairly quickly in a manner similar to the recovery rally after the 1987 crash.

However, there is something you can do to avoid being bloodied in the interim. High-frequency traders can profit big-time from a panicky market that they've created, though most traders would swear on their mothers' lives that it isn't true. To avoid this, do not put in stop-loss or sell-at-the-market orders. Instead, always put in limit orders, which limit the price at which a broker can sell. If you do this, your stock, derivative, or futures contracts cannot be sold off many points down in a crash. Don't use stop-loss orders until the problem is cleared up, or you could lose big. Stop-loss orders worked in the past, but, given HFT, they could be as bad in these times as Russian roulette.

▓ Volatility Twisters

High-frequency trading, which instigates enormous volatility, is but one threat in the, at times, alien world we are in now. The possibility of greater volatility, aside from that generated by these crashes, is another. Volatility was at more than three-year lows in June but can change on a dime and can continue to fluctuate violently with any sharp move in prices or serious financial or economic events. In the fall of 2008, fear shot up like the flames of a roaring forest fire. Some investors tried to protect their blue-chip stocks by buying puts, which gave them the right to sell a stock at its then-current, highly depressed price if the market went lower. The cost to do so can be exorbitantly large with ultrahigh volatility, premiums sometimes rise to 20 to 25 percent of the entire principal for 90 to 100 days. For a year, if the put premiums remained relatively unchanged, the cost increased to 80 to 85 percent annually. For some of the smaller names, option prices rose as high as 130 percent annualized.

In effect, the insurance provided by buying a put would have almost wiped out any blue-chip portfolio in little more than a year. Insurance rates through buying puts, as a matter of comparison, were far higher than those Lloyd's of London sold on merchant ships and their cargoes coming back from the New World and the Far East in the eighteenth and early nineteenth centuries.

What I hope this example shows you is that in periods of crisis, using options clearly does not work. The person taking the other side of the trade is usually an experienced trader who has almost fully protected himself from the risk you are trying to shed and is probably charging you a pretty healthy premium above the going rate for the risk, because there are so few traders who even want to do the transaction.

There are other alternatives, such as shorting against the box, that are less costly, if you're bound on this course, but again the problem when we sell in a panic is that we are normally near the bottom. Even if you protect your downside, shorting against the box leaves you with no stock position if the market rallies. If, for example, I had forgotten my contrarian training and panicked in March 2009, when stocks were approaching their lows, this tactic would have resulted in my totally missing the market upside of over 100 percent for the S&P 500 to June 2011. The trouble is that this happens all the time.

About a decade ago, the head of customer service at our firm grew nervous about the market and took all of his funds out of stocks because he thought the market would go down another 5 percent. I advised him not to do it because market timing rarely worked. He followed his inclination and proved wrong. Before he bought back into the market, stocks had advanced another 10 percent. Fortunately, our firm does not market-time, nor do we do so for our clients.

Volatility, unfortunately, is something we just have to live through. Yes, every eight or ten decades or so, we'll be wrong to do this, but we or our families will have far larger portfolios in the end if we stay the course. Recall also that contrarian portfolios, on average, outperform the market on the downside.

Protective Actions

PROTECTIVE ACTION 1: PUTS AND CALLS

Should you buy puts and calls to protect your portfolio? We've just said that puts are not a good investment in a panic. Put and call options can protect the investor in a volatile market. An investor can stay out of the market and buy a call option if he thinks prices will rise. If he buys it at today's market price, he will pay a hefty premium and be able to call the stock at that price. Similarly, in a more normal market, if he thinks the market is going down, he could sell a put and for the premium be able to sell at the market price or close to it for a period of time; the longer the period, the higher the premium.

This may sound simple, but in a volatile market it is a devilishly tricky game. First, premium prices are high, and the greater the market volatility, the higher they become. In December 2008 and January and February 2009, premium prices rose as high as 20 percent, as noted, for some stocks on a quarterly basis and much higher annually. This means that if you buy a call option that gives you the right to buy a stock, you could pay a good part of the principal to hold it for, say, nine months. If it goes up 50 percent, you still might come out only breaking even. Great idea, but the cost is often much too high.

There is also a series of options issued on each stock that makes this exercise far more difficult to calculate. And then there are the sharks. The options traders want to get as much of an edge on you as they can. Hey, that's the game. What this translates into is that you pay the normal premium (calculated by the Black-Scholes model)* and something more, possibly a significant amount if the stock is illiquid, to the seller.

The bottom line here is not to buy puts or calls unless you are highly experienced with them. Even then, the odds are against most people. On the other side, never, never sell these options unless you are very well trained in all the risks they entail.

What about the VIX that we just discussed in some detail; does it help investors to protect themselves in markets such as these? When volatility moves up sharply, buyers of VIX products will make money, and when volatility moves down sharply, they will lose money. This is one of the ultimate new market casino games. The VIX is a statistic that the CBOE calculates and disseminates using real-time S&P 500 Index option bid/ask quotes. Though widely disseminated, this statistic is not available for purchase.

But never fear: the croupiers in the Chicago markets have devised many ways for you to bet on this fast-moving action. After all, the house has to be rewarded for its ingenuity. A number of VIX derivatives allow traders to take positions on the VIX without owning the underlying index; these positions include VIX options, standard VIX futures contracts, the recently added mini-VIX futures, and other more exotic variations.

---

* The risk premium is not correct, but that doesn't help you.

   Buyers make money if volatility goes up; sellers win if it goes down. This is an interesting instrument but is again more of a speculative tool run primarily by sharks on the trading floor. I think one example should be more than enough to show why. On January 30, 2009, a new exchange-traded fund, the VXX ETN, started and bought the VIX options. Since that time to now (June 2011) the fund has dropped 94.9 percent. The VIX index, with which it is calibrated, has fallen 63.2 percent. The calibration disappeared because of the cost of contract expirations, commissions, and the high markups on buying each new contract. The fund, as a result, lost an additional 31.7 percent. VIX options have no place in a conservative portfolio—or, come to think about it, in any sane account.

PROTECTIVE ACTION 2:
EXCHANGE-TRADED AND INDEX FUNDS

An exchange-traded fund (ETF) normally has smaller charges than the great majority of mutual funds. It usually has a fixed portfolio, so transaction costs are also normally lower. Unlike a mutual fund, it is not redeemed but sold on the open market. There are literally hundreds of ETFs that are set up to do everything from short-selling 30-year Treasury bonds* to buying and selling gold to investing in a particular industry. An ETF can help you accomplish your investment objectives if you carefully examine its portfolio, by providing you with diversification in a volatile industry that you believe has potential. Diversification is important in a volatile market, as there is more than enough danger in owning any one industry. Owning a single stock in that industry is often too risky. Not only are you taking the industry risk, which can be substantial, but if you put all your eggs into one basket, you increase that risk significantly.

   Two examples here: First, if you had bought financial stocks outright in 2008, you would have suffered major losses; if you owned the wrong stock, you were gone. However, had you bought an ETF, such as the XLF, a weighted average of all the financial stocks in the S&P 500, then, although you would have taken devastating losses—the XLF dropped

---

* You can also short double the amount of Treasuries if you want to lose your money more quickly, as some of the younger analysts in my office did several years back when they were convinced that bond prices would drop rapidly.

83 percent from its 2007 high to its early-2009 low, the worst drop since 1929–1932—your investment would have rebounded since then. It was up more than 158 percent from its March 2009 low to June 2011. This is an industry that I believe will recover strongly over time.

Another example is the SPDR S&P Oil & Gas Exploration & Production ETF (ticker symbol XOP), which consists of a fairly broad portfolio of oil and gas exploration and development companies. After hitting an all-time high of $71.38 in late June 2008, the index free-fell, reaching a low of $23.01 on November 20, down almost 70 percent in less than five months. Since then it has recovered smartly, along with oil, up 161 percent to June 2011. These two ETFs are good examples of what's out there that can give you more diversification in an industry you like. Just be aware that these ETFs will have wider fluctuations in the volatile markets we just experienced and may experience again, hopefully without the ferocity of 2008 to early 2009 or of August/September 2011.

Another word of caution: many ETFs are small and thinly traded and are best left alone. Make sure the daily trading volume is sufficient to make your order inconsequential to it. Also, check the asset value, which you can determine each day, and be careful to check that the market price is within pennies of it.

PROTECTIVE ACTION 3: SECTOR FUNDS

Industry-sector funds are different from ETFs in that they have a money manager select the stocks. Here you are faced with higher fees in almost all cases and are dependent on the performance of the manager. Still, there may be good opportunity in some. I would recommend you first look at the manager's performance over at least a ten-year period. If he outperforms his industry, he is certainly worth looking at. It's also a good idea to check the fund's fees. High fees are a major cause of underperformance over time.

PROTECTIVE ACTION 4: MUTUAL FUNDS THAT BEAT THE MARKET

As we have seen, only 10 percent of managers have beaten the market in any ten-year period since performance measurements began to be used. Those are not great odds. Mutual funds do give you the diversification

Table 13-1
Best-Performing Large-Cap Value Funds: 10-Year Ranking
as of 6/30/2011

Company	Asset Size ($Millions)	10-Year Return
Wasatch Large Cap Value Fund	1,812.8	7.2%
ING Corp Leaders Trust Series Fund; B	580.9	7.1%
American Independence Stock Fund	158.5	6.4%
Pioneer Cullen Value Fund; A	5,354.5	6.4%
Valley Forge Fund	27.1	6.0%
Federated Clover Value Fund; A	945.5	5.9%
Forester Value Fund; N	12.2	5.6%

Source: © David Dreman, 2011. Source of Data: Lipper Inc. and Factset Research Systems Inc.

you need if you don't want to invest on your own, but we all want performance, too. Fortunately, there are a couple of good answers. The first is to buy a mutual fund with a long record of outperforming the market after fees and costs; I would suggest a record of at least ten years. Make sure the fund is still run by the same manager who created the record. Many times it isn't.

With limited funds, the best approach would be to purchase a mutual fund with a broad portfolio. There are a large number of sources to help you in the selection process, including Lipper, Morningstar, Value Line Mutual Fund Service, *Forbes,* and *Barron's.** These will provide you with quarterly information on the fund's performance and its record over the number of years it has been in public hands. Select a fund that has a strategy you are in tune with and that has outperformed the market for a significant period. This will narrow the bewildering number of funds down to a handful. Table 13-1 gives you the returns of some of the better-value large-cap mutual funds through bull and bear markets in the last ten years. The results are taken from Lipper.

PROTECTIVE ACTION 5: INDEX FUNDS

Unless the mutual fund you chose has a solid record of outperforming the market over time, I would suggest you buy an index fund that replicates the S&P 500 and has very low fees. The Vanguard 500 Index Fund

---

* *Forbes* ranks funds through at least two bear markets to get its bear market rankings. The best funds are the top 5 percent relative to all stock funds, the F's the bottom 5 percent.

Investor Shares* ($112.6 billion in assets) is such a fund with costs and fees of just 0.17 percent annually. It is a low-cost index mutual fund that replicates the S&P 500. Another choice is an S&P 500 ETF. The largest is the SPDR S&P 500 ETF, with $94.2 billion in assets and an expense ratio of 0.15 percent.† If you prefer a large-cap value index, one of the largest is the iShares Russell 1000 Index Fund, $12.0 billion in assets, expense ratio 0.15 percent. The Russell 1000‡ is the most widely followed domestic value index today.

Some of you may prefer a smaller-cap index. Here are two to look at: the iShares Russell 2000 Index Fund, with $15.6 billion in assets and 0.20 percent expense ratio; and the Vanguard Small-Cap Index Fund, with $22.6 billion in assets and 0.26 percent expense ratio. Both are small-cap index funds holding both value and growth stocks.

There is one other intriguing strategy for the investor, another, newer variation of contrarian strategies, which we will look at next.

Buy-and-Weed Strategies

We've looked at the success of buy-and-hold strategies. A twist to this approach is to buy a portfolio of contrarian stocks and weed it periodically of stocks if they move up to or above the market ratios or if they fail to perform as well as the market after a certain time, at the same time replacing the stocks sold with new contrarian stocks. If, for example, you owned a low-P/E portfolio of forty stocks with roughly 2½ percent in each holding and sold 10 percent of it, you would replace the 10 percent with four low-P/E stocks each with about a 2½ percent portfolio weighting. An overview of the studies indicates that returns normally diminish with long holding periods (five to six years or more). Some methods, such as this, should raise overall return above that of the simple buy-and-hold strategy.

The pruning process should also allow you to maintain a portfolio of contrarian stocks with above-average yields. In any case, whichever

---

*For information, contact the Vanguard Group at 1-800-860-8394 or go to www .vanguard.com.

† For information, contact State Street Global Advisors at 1-866-787-2257 or go to www .spdrs.com.

‡ For information, contact iShares at 1-800-474-2737 or go to www.ishares.com.

strategy you choose, you should have a good chance of outdoing the market while taking below-average risk and spending minimal time making selections.

Other Alternatives to Contrarian Strategies

FOREIGN AND COUNTRY FUNDS

Until recently, with the stumbling domestic economy, foreign markets were all the rage. Billions of dollars were flowing into China, the Pacific Rim, Latin America, Brazil, and Argentina, while more conservative investors bet on the European and Japanese markets. Should you get into the act? Yes, but be careful.

First, foreign markets have already had enormous moves. Second, pessimism, though improved from 2008–2009, when it was at the highest level since the Great Depression, is still widespread. There's no question that people are very frightened, though the U.S. economy should pull out of this morass within a few years. If this is correct, we have a very powerful domestic bull market ahead, particularly if inflation begins to move up rapidly several years out; as we'll see, this is a distinct possibility.

Still, foreign markets do present more potential than at any time in the past because of their growth, financial strength, and increasingly more responsible investment regulation. Remember, the same investment guidelines apply abroad as they do domestically. First, don't jump in just because the concept is exciting. Speculative activity in China, Hong Kong, Russia, and Mexico has cost investors billions of dollars in the not-so-distant past. Lesson one, then, is that foreign investing is not a panacea. You have to apply the same contrarian principles you apply in U.S. markets. The 1997 debacle in the Pacific Rim markets is a classic example of investors' not doing so. Be extra careful to avoid the waves of speculation that often dominate in these areas.

Another important consideration is that when you buy foreign companies, you are taking an exchange-rate risk that can greatly add to or detract from your total return. In the years that foreign markets outpaced those in the United States, the gains were often more a consequence of a weak dollar than of strong markets overseas. Thus, when the dollar dropped in recent years, a good part of the fabulous returns on foreign

Table 13-2
Total Returns of MSCI EAFE Versus the S&P 500
December 31, 2010

	3 Yrs	5 Yrs	10 Yrs	15 Yrs	20 Yrs	25 Yrs	Average P/E	Average Market Capitalization*
MSCI EAFE	−6.5%	2.9%	3.9%	5.1%	6.2%	8.5%	14	50.2
Standard & Poor's 500	−2.9%	2.3%	1.4%	6.8%	9.1%	9.9%	15	88.2

*In billions of dollars.

Source: © David Dreman, 2011. Data Sources: FactSet Research Systems and Bloomberg LP.

portfolios—trumpeted in many funds' advertising—was not from the markets themselves but from the fact that stocks were simply worth more because of the cheaper U.S. dollar, as may be the case again today. If the dollar gets stronger, the situation is likely to reverse.

Table 13-2 gives you the returns of domestic and foreign stocks taken from the S&P 500 and the MSCI EAFE index data. The MSCI EAFE (acronym for Europe, Australasia, and Far East) index is designed to measure the equity market performance of developed markets outside the United States and Canada.

Look at the six performance columns. The performance of foreign stocks, as measured by MSCI EAFE against the S&P 500, is mixed. The two indices changed lead in four out of the six periods measured. What is clear is that these two indices are in a real horse race. Which will do better over time may involve a photo finish.

But let's make the choice even more difficult. Stocks, as we know, are exceptionally ornery critters, and their behavior in different time periods is unpredictable. There are other factors that you as an investor should consider. Owning domestic stocks allows you to avoid the worries of currency fluctuations and also stay clear of thinly traded speculative markets and geopolitical considerations.

The results are a standoff. There's no question that foreign markets, with the exception of the European Union, are healthier today, but should we bank on this indefinitely? As the chart shows, they are pricey by P/E but have smaller market caps.

Remember, too, that not all foreign countries are equally safe. I feel more comfortable investing in Western Europe and Canada or, if the P/Es come down, in Japan. I would invest much more sparingly in China, the

Pacific Rim, South America, or Russia. Banks and foreign investors have taken a whipping in Brazil, Argentina, and Russia because of their record of defaults and restructurings; these investors often lost 50 cents or more on the dollar. The underwriters of foreign securities assure us that things are different now. Maybe, but who can say that a government that has defaulted on its debt once won't do so again?

Having talked about the dangers involved in investing abroad, I should note that there are opportunities in foreign stocks. One of the best strategies for individual investors is to buy foreign securities traded on the U.S. markets that fit in with a contrarian strategy. The latter is something I have often done with the portfolios I manage, with good success.*

This avoids the higher costs of overseas brokerage and safekeeping charges and converting small amounts of foreign exchange at high spreads. American Depository Receipts (ADRs) represent a stated number of shares of a foreign stock traded in the United States. Many of the larger ADRs, such as Royal Dutch/Shell, Sony, and Koninklijke Philips Electronics, are listed on the New York Stock Exchange, and most have detailed financial information available—in English.

The mechanics are simple, since a large number of foreign stocks, funds, and other financial instruments are actively traded here. Foreign stocks can make good sense because they sometimes trade at lower values, using contrarian indicators, than do domestic companies in the same industry. For example, Unilever, the giant Dutch-based consumer products company, is about half the size of Procter & Gamble; nevertheless, with a market value of $90 billion, it is huge. The company has a lower P/E ratio and a higher yield than the U.S. consumer products companies, with similar growth rates expected by analysts over the next several years. Other foreign companies that present better value than their U.S. counterparts can be found by looking through the Value Line Investment Survey and the Morningstar Web site, while professionals can use Bloomberg, FactSet, or other systems.

You might use these stocks, as I do, to find better values in a particular industry than are available domestically, or else to produce a diversified portfolio both by country and by industry. Using ADRs, you

---

* Our firm has a low-P/E ADR international fund that invests precisely in this manner. It has been ranked by Lipper in the 13th percentile since its inception.

can structure a well-diversified foreign portfolio. By coincidence, many of these large, well-established ADRs pass the contrarian criteria easily. But remember, the currency risk doesn't disappear. If the dollar spikes up against the currency the stock was issued in, the price will drop; and if the dollar drops, the price will rise.

There are a number of conservative ways, then, to approach markets abroad. The first is to buy an index fund, or a close substitute, that represents the weighted value of stocks outside the United States. If I were to buy a foreign fund, my preference would be an index or a contrarian fund with an acceptable record in foreign markets.[17]

A second alternative that sometimes proves quite lucrative is to buy closed-end funds that invest in major countries with good outlooks and political stability when these funds are unpopular.

The first rule of investing abroad is identical to the first rule of investing at home: buy 'em when they're cheap, not when everybody is already on the bandwagon and the media hype is in full swing. Just as with hot IPOs and concept stocks at home, we know that after a euphoric price run-up there is an inevitable hangover.

Finally, we'll turn to one of the toughest questions that must be addressed using contrarian strategies—or for that matter any other strategy: when should you sell?

When Should You Sell?

Regardless of the strategy you use, one of your most difficult decisions is when to sell. There are almost as many answers to the problem as there are investors, but even among professionals, few religiously follow their own sell rules. Psychological forces misdirect most sell decisions, often disastrously. I have seen many a money manager set stringent sell targets and did so myself in my earlier years. But as the stock moved rapidly toward the preset price, more and more good news usually accompanied its rise.

If the stock was originally purchased at $20 with the sell target at $40, and it shot through $40, a manager would often bump the sell price higher. Forty would become $50; $50 would be stretched to $60. This frequently resulted in the manager's taking the "round trip": riding a stock all the way up, only to ride it all the way down again.

Given what we know, it seems that the safest approach, once again, is to rely on mechanical guidelines, which filter out much of the emotional content of the decision. The general rule I use is this, which I'll call a Psychological Guideline.

PSYCHOLOGICAL GUIDELINE 27: Sell a stock when its P/E ratio (or other contrarian indicator) approaches that of the overall market, regardless of how favorable its prospects may appear. Replace it with another contrarian stock.

For example, assume we are using the low-P/E strategy and the market P/E is 16×. If one of our stocks (say, Chevron), bought at a P/E of 10×, went up to 16×, we would sell it and replace it with another low-P/E stock.*

The first guideline, then, is simple: pick a sell point when you buy a stock. If it reaches that point, grit your teeth, brace yourself, and get rid of it. You will probably be unhappy because the issue will often go higher. But why be greedy? You've made a good gain, and that's what the game is all about. (The only exception is when you have an almost sure takeover situation.)

Picking a sell point, however, doesn't necessarily mean selling a stock just because it has gone up. If you are a low-price-to-book-value (P/BV) player, you may find that even after a stock has risen sharply it still sells at a below-market P/BV because its book value has continued to go up. Often, stocks remain at low P/BVs for years, despite doubling or even tripling in price, because their book value has also doubled or tripled, keeping the P/BV ratio low. The same is true for low-price-to-earnings and low-price-to-cash-flow ratios, and high dividend yields.

Another question is how long you should hold a stock that has not worked out. Investors all too often fall in love with their holdings. I have seen portfolios loaded with dozens of companies that look good on paper but have long been dogs in the market, resulting in poor returns.

Again, there are many partial answers to this problem, but I think two and a half to three years is an adequate waiting period. (For a cyclical stock with a drop in earnings, this might be stretched to three and a half

---

* Naturally, as prices change over time, the weightings of stocks in the portfolio will differ. When stocks are sold, the effort should be made to bring the weightings more into balance with one another.

years.) If after that time the stock still disappoints, sell it. The late John Templeton, one of the masters of value investing, used a six-year time span. You be the judge, but stick to your time frame and don't be stubborn.

Another important rule is to sell a stock immediately if its long-term fundamentals deteriorate significantly. No matter how painstaking the research, something can go wrong, worsening a company's or an industry's outlook dramatically. I'm talking not about a poor quarter or a temporary surprise that a stock will snap back from but about major changes that weaken a company's prospects, as the financial crisis did with scores of financial stocks. Under these conditions, I have found that taking your lumps immediately and moving on usually results in the smallest loss.

To summarize: don't be stubborn, don't be greedy, and don't be afraid to take small losses. Above all, when you buy a stock, make a mental decision as to the level at which you will sell it—and stick to that decision. You may lose a few points at the top, but in the long run you'll make a lot more than you'll lose.

A further question may arise with sell strategies using the eclectic approach. Suppose you have a portfolio of thirty to forty stocks and find a new one that ranks much higher by our indicators, while trading at a lower contrarian ratio than stocks you already own. A switch might then be made, but keep in mind the principle of a fixed number of stocks in the portfolio: each time one is purchased, another should be sold. Because you are bringing in more judgment in switching, and therefore more opportunity for error, changes of this sort should be relatively rare in order to avoid the dangers of overtrading. Or, as horse players like to say, "Stay away from the switches."

A supplementary rule, which I followed for years, was not to sell a stock that attained a high P/E multiple solely because of a decline in earnings, either through a large onetime charge or because of temporary business conditions. I've mulled this rule over since the 2007–2008 market meltdown and have revised my thinking. Unless you know for certain it is a onetime charge and will not recur, I think it is wiser to sell immediately. What the crash showed us was that a onetime charge could often be only the beginning of a series of crippling charges. "Onetime charges" felled the financial sector and hurt a lot of value managers' clients, including my own. It is better to take a onetime charge immediately and, if you still like the stock, buy it back when the company restores its earning power. Further reflection led me to remember, in choosing our low-P/E portfolios, that our computer simulation always dropped stocks that had no earnings in a given quarter; it adhered to the reevaluation I am making here.

Having examined this key set of new risks and opportunities, let's now turn to a topic that's been needing urgent attention for some time: a better theory of risk to replace the bankrupt theory so widely used today.

Chapter 14

Toward a Better Theory of Risk

RISK CAN BE a temptress or a savage god. It beckons us to casinos or markets and sometimes provides us with amazing rewards that defy all odds. When we win, we often don't pocket the money and walk away. Rather, we play on, too often giving back everything we've won and more.

History is replete with great generals who won repeatedly against staggering odds: think of Napoleon, Robert E. Lee, and Erwin Rommel. But the odds—that calculation that mixes the might of armies, the will of warriors, and the economic power of a nation's industries—always came back one time too many and too powerfully and in the end overwhelmed them all. In the civilian world, the investment media feature interviews with money managers, analysts, and investment managers who have had a superb run of three months, one year, maybe even three years. Every word they utter, no matter how nonsensical, is taken as the new gospel— until the law of probabilities sinks their records and, as in vaudeville, the long hook comes out from the wings to pull them off the stage. New stars with similar spectacular short-term records replace them as the audience roars its approval. But the Great Show of defying risk goes on.

Most of us are more than a little ambivalent about risk. We love to see the underdogs triumph and repeatedly root for them, delighted when they upset the favorites, more so if an underdog is a team we like or bet on to win. But in markets we want none of that. We want to stay with the odds, the higher the better. The only objective, naturally, is to win. The trouble today is that with complex situations we often have difficulty determining what the odds really are.

It all seemed so simple under efficient markets. Mr. Risk, aka Mr. Volatility, was a real mensch. He told you exactly who he was and what he did, and for decades we loved him for telling us expressly how much risk we could take to fine-tune our portfolios as precisely as a violin virtuoso tunes his strings. We thought we had finally caged the risk devil that had run amok since the beginning of history.

But then things began to change. We are increasingly finding out in this new, more difficult investment world that Mr. Volatility is not the mensch he claimed to be. In fact, he began to seem more like a heavy, a wise guy who ordered investors around, threatening them when they asked why their returns weren't what was promised if they followed his recommendations.

Let's translate that into slightly more technical terms. As we've discussed, beta and other volatility measures were introduced as objective gauges of risk, promising no more messy, inaccurate human guesses, and beta in particular became the touchstone calculation of risk in efficient-market theory. That was all to the good, except for one small problem that became apparent from the long-term performance data of the stock market: greater (or lesser) volatility did not correlate with the actual returns. Mr. Volatility's numbers just didn't work. Oh, he was more than articulate, and he proposed an elegant theory that was so easy to understand that most investors happily anchored their portfolio strategies on it. But he encountered the same argument made by Thomas Huxley, who defended Charles Darwin's theory of evolution against avid creationists more than 150 years ago. Huxley said back then of creationist thinking, "The great tragedy of Science [is]—the slaying of a beautiful hypothesis by an ugly fact."

As if the data were not enough, we saw in chapter 2 that the untested economic theory of risk collides head-on with Affect research findings about risk behavior. Over a number of experiments, Affect research has found that risk and benefits are negatively correlated. Taking on higher risk results in lower, not higher, perceived benefits, and conversely, taking on less risk results in higher perceived rewards. These findings are the direct opposite of core EMH risk beliefs.

Finally, the headlong charge into aggressive stocks in mania after mania, stocks that were characterized as low risk but were actually highly volatile, certainly at least partially documents the validity of the recent findings in Affect research. From the beginning, then, this hypothesis of risk seemed unrealistic. And with time its problems only became larger. Once again, and from a surprising source, modern risk theory is being questioned.

Nonetheless, as we discussed, when the assertion that volatility is the best measure of risk couldn't be proved, rather than giving up on the concept, its advocates started altering their calculations of volatility in the hope of finding a new correlation between the two. They continued to put forward new risk models, but, as we saw, none of them worked reliably, and at best the scientific methodology used was questionable. In the meantime we're left with one of the most glaring problems of today's investment world: that the risk analysis most investors rely on is . . . specious.

Toppling Stalin's Statue

Most of us recall dozens of scenes of statues of Joseph Stalin being toppled throughout Eastern Europe after the Soviet Union collapsed in 1989. The smaller ones were knocked down by workingmen using ropes and chains, the larger ones with tractors or other heavy construction equipment. Russia's future was unclear, but there was no turning back. As with the fall of communism, we must ask: if volatility is toppled, what will take its place? The essence of this chapter is to provide you with risk measures that will hold up under many differing circumstances.

Let's start with some of the key elements that were ignored in the old risk paradigm. We'll see the damage each of these has inflicted for hundreds of years, if not longer. More important, we'll also see that much of the damage can be halted for both investors and the economy.

Yes, there is life after beta, and we can begin to put together some far better principles for today's investor. Let's start by looking at risk factors that, as we saw, caused significant damage to our portfolios in recent decades but have on the whole been ignored by investors to the present time.

Liquidity: The First Horseman of the Financial Apocalypse

To begin, we'll look at one of the most serious risks contemporary investors face: the improper understanding and treatment of liquidity. In chapter 5, we examined in some detail the major role the almost absolute lack of liquidity played in three major crashes, driving illiquid stocks and futures down sharply lower and resulting in market panics.

The lack of liquidity is anything but a new risk; it's probably been around since the birth of markets. Just the whisper of a lack of liquidity in the nineteenth century in England and other countries was enough to make depositors rush to withdraw their funds from banks, often sending the banks into insolvency. And of course we've all read about the bank holiday of 1933, with the long lines of depositors, waiting to withdraw whatever money they still could.

The damage that lack of liquidity can cause, of course, extends well beyond banks. A recent example is loans to housing and real estate companies in the past few years. Because a good part of the credit received by home builders and other real estate companies is originated by banks or other commercial lenders, if loan levels are cut sharply or not renewed, the borrower is often in an impossible situation. He can either try to dispose of his inventory, at fire-sale prices, or, if prices have dropped dramatically, go into Chapter 11 bankruptcy or make a deal with a bank that is not much better. The same situation has also occurred in the past year with some commercial property loans.

Throughout 2007–2009, U.S. companies, particularly those with less than a hundred employees, where most jobs are created, were plagued by the problem both of not being able to hire because bank capital was unavailable for expansion and of being forced to cut back operations because they could not get the credit they had always relied on. Lack of liquidity, then, is far more than a subprime problem, although the subprime crisis magnified its effects immensely; it is an ongoing problem even for safer and healthier companies.

The damage we are primarily concerned with in this section occurs in periods of abundant monetary availability. In such periods banks and other financial institutions ease their lending standards signifi-cantly. The lending standards on subprime mortgages, as we now know, were wretched. Hedge funds and other lenders were supplied with large amounts of leverage on loans of very poor quality, and the lenders, at best, made cursory examinations of the toxic mortgages they were lend-ing against.

We've seen this also with commercial real estate in periods of boom-ing prices, such as the late 1980s and early 1990s, when bankers failed to adequately scrutinize the economics of major projects. Builders were given up to 105 percent of the cost of a project because of the intense competition by banks to issue these loans. Such real estate bubbles have occurred almost once a decade since the 1960s.

Their endings have all been remarkably similar: At some point the banks and other financial institutions woke up to the fact that projects would not be nearly as profitable as originally projected. Worse, they were highly illiquid, as nobody wanted to touch them except at a huge dis-count, and the borrower was often completely illiquid, as in the case of Donald Trump circa 1992. Financial institutions were stuck big-time as in the bank crisis of the late 1980s to early 1990s; President George H. W. Bush organized the Resolution Trust Corp. to take over insolvent banks and thrifts and raised capital for some struggling institutions. Bank stocks tumbled as much as 50 to 60 percent on the dollar, and the real estate market crashed.

With the repeal of the Glass-Steagall Act in November 1999, which resulted in far more liberal bank lending, the illiquidity problems began to become significantly worse. Yet most banks and many other classes of professional investors completely dismiss this serious threat from their risk screens.

Liquidity Does Not Beget Liquidity

As we've discussed, liquidity played the crowning role in the 1987 crash. A serious but little realized problem is that liquidity can vary sharply with changing market conditions. The efficient-market hypothesis assumes that "liquidity begets liquidity," meaning that as prices fall, swarms of buyers will appear. However, there is no proof that this has ever been ac-curate, but a good deal of evidence that in periods of severe strain, liquidity dries up, in the face of sharp drops in price. Recall that this occurred with S&P 500 futures markets during the 1987 crash. Still, this untested EMH assumption is held as a cardinal principle of markets, even after the crashes we have discussed. Other crashes, as well as the flash crash of 2010 and the July–August/September 2011 panic, also clearly showed that liquidity does not beget liquidity. Quite the opposite: as a result of rapid downward movements in stock or index futures, liquidity can decrease sharply and, in worst-case situations, dry up almost completely, significantly increasing the magnitude of the downturn, as the above examples demonstrated. A new Psychological Guideline should prove helpful here.

PSYCHOLOGICAL GUIDELINE 28(a): Liquidity does not increase as stocks fall sharply; quite the opposite. In rapidly falling markets, liquidity can decrease significantly; the less liquid a stock or other financial instrument, the greater the negative effect this will have on its price.

PSYCHOLOGICAL GUIDELINE 28(b): Increasing liquidity normally occurs in rapidly rising stocks or other financial vehicles in a sharply rising market.

Leverage: The Second Horseman of the Financial Apocalypse

Leverage is on a par with liquidity for the damage it can render. High margin by itself has been a major cause of crashes. Like liquidity, leverage is difficult to handle because of the similarity of interactions with Affect and other psychological forces. As we have seen, when the two work in tandem, as was the case in the 1987 crash, in that of 2007–2008, and with Long-Term Capital Management, the results are disastrous. As Psychological Guideline 29 warns, leverage is a risk that the conservative investor should avoid.

A point worth repeating on leverage: buying the S&P 500 and other financial futures requires significantly less margin than buying the stocks themselves (7 percent initial margin on hedging S&P 500 futures positions versus 50 percent margin on S&P stocks). This is less than the 10 percent margin allowed in 1929, cited by Congress as a major factor in that crash. In fact, in 1934 Congress allowed the Federal Reserve to set margins on stocks. Since that time, margin requirements have been set by the Fed, from 50 percent to as high as 100 percent of stock purchases. Allowing the Chicago Mercantile Exchanges and other exchanges to set futures margins as low as 7 percent—5 percent prior to the 1987 crash— has encouraged both greater speculation and more volatility in markets, as shown by both the 1987 crash and the flash crash.

Liquidity and Leverage: A Deadly Combination

We are not likely to soon forget the financial panic of 2007–2008, in which liquidity and leverage played a major role in almost annihilating financial markets in the worst credit crisis in modern history. The combination of high leverage and enormous illiquidity almost wiped out the financial system. Leverage also played a major hand, working in tandem with the lack of liquidity, in crashes from 1929 through 1987.

HOW CAN YOU PROTECT YOURSELF AGAINST ILLIQUIDITY PROBLEMS?

Because of the numerous forms of illiquidity, there is, unfortunately, no catchall answer. In a crash, there's not much you can do but ride it out. Normally stocks come back fairly quickly, when it is realized that the crash was liquidity-driven. This happened with the 1987 crash, when stocks regained virtually all of their liquidity-driven losses in a little over one year, and in the flash crash last year, when stocks gained back most of the losses the same day and the entire amount in a matter of months. *In a liquidity-driven market crash, do not sell your stocks.*

HOW CAN YOU DEAL WITH LIQUIDITY AND LEVERAGE?

Unfortunately, both liquidity and leverage are very tempting in rising markets and hard to resist, particularly if credit is easy. The more we like an illiquid stock or bond or a group of them and the better the returns, the greater the temptation to buy additional amounts, using more leverage to enhance the upside. Both using too much leverage and having too little liquidity seem to be by-products of strong positive Affect. It is almost like a psychological addiction for many thousands of investors, including hedge funds, banks, and investment banks.

The only way to defend against the liquidity and leverage problem is to strictly limit your leverage and your ownership of securities that are not liquid, particularly if the latter are in the same sector of the market. For most people it is a good idea to go cold turkey. A Psychological Guideline as good now as it was in the 1920s is:

PSYCHOLOGICAL GUIDELINE 29: The prudent investor should stay away from leverage or margin and hold only a small part of his or her portfolio in illiquid securities.

Following are some booby traps to avoid.

1. If you do decide to use futures, make sure you don't get in over your head. First decide how much stock you want to buy or sell. If, say, it is $20,000, and the smallest contract available is $200,000, run for the exit or you will have to buy ten times the amount you actually want. You'll be surprised at how many people sink themselves by not following this simple rule.

2. Be careful of packaged concept products, complex mortgages, and other intricate offerings by hedge funds, investment banks, or banks. They normally get big markups on these structured deals, which are often partnerships. Liquidity is notably poor in most cases. And their record is usually not good. Ask the banker or broker how much his firm intends to keep invested in each over time. Don't be surprised if the answer is a touch evasive.

    These products have a common denominator. They are almost all intriguing concepts that, you will be told, should earn higher returns. I never buy them because the fees are much higher than stock commissions, sometimes going up to 20 percent of profits with ample annual charges on top. More important, I don't have a warm, fuzzy feeling that these deals will work out well. I'd advise you to stay well away unless you like financial products with no record, no liquidity, and high fees. Strangely enough, a lot of investors with a pretty high net worth latch onto these products. Hopefully you will not.

3. Tread cautiously when you buy little-traded issues either on your own or in a secondary offering. You can again run into liquidity problems that often cost. Make sure that when you buy there are at least a

few market makers, and don't take positions above a few percentage points of the daily trading volume.

4. Stay away from exotic derivatives such as European puts and calls written on U.S. stocks, often by a U.S. broker. These are normally both more expensive than trading derivatives on a U.S. exchange and far less liquid to sell if you decide to.

5. If you don't understand a bond or a hedge fund, or any other security—don't buy it. Forget the yield, no matter how alluring, and protect your principal; better opportunities will come that you will understand, and probably sooner than you think. Remember, the buyers of the subprime AAA and AA bonds lost as much as 70 cents on the dollar. That's a heck of a lot to lose only to collect maybe an extra 2 to 3 percent a year in yield when the going is good.

Other Risk Factors

When the efficient-market risk theory put its focus exclusively on volatility, doing so wiped out important guidelines that had been followed for risk analysis for centuries. Prudent security analysis on risk, much of it codified by Graham and Dodd and other leading financial theorists, was cast aside or else not looked at carefully, because it wasn't all that important, according to EMH believers. Why bother? they thought. It was all factored into volatility anyway.

We must now resuscitate those established principles of risk assessment, which are far more useful in determining many types of risk that volatility completely bypasses, including:

1. Lack of liquidity
2. Excessive leverage
3. Bond risk-control techniques
4. Stock risk-control techniques

It's beyond the scope of this book to go through the lengthy list of stock and bond risk control measures. Many are presented in Graham and Dodd's *Security Analysis* (6th edition, 2008) and other good books on the subject that can provide you with the fundamentals you need. The principles are very important and haven't changed significantly over recent decades.

Next we'll look at a new set of new risk factors that we should pay special attention to in the years ahead.

▦ The Third Horseman of the Financial Apocalypse: Inflation

Let's start this section with a quick review of the history of some of the risks out there and how they can destroy the unwary. Frank H. Knight, one of the cofounders of the Chicago School of Economics, in his seminal work *Risk, Uncertainty, and Profit* (1921),[1] stated that there is a major difference between risk and uncertainty. Risk, according to him, was "a quantity susceptible of measurement," while uncertainty is not capable of being measured.

By his definition risk applies to many types of gambling games, horse racing, betting on baseball and football, and many other activities— anything where the risks can be calculated. Uncertainty applies to situations where the gains or losses are indeterminate either on the upside or on the downside, such as the value of stocks in a revolutionary period, shorting futures or derivatives positions and leverage on real estate, or scores of similar situations.

By far the most dangerous new risk over the past sixty years has been inflation, which can attack our savings in many ways. In the past we did not focus on inflation, as rising prices have been pretty much a nonevent for centuries, with only a few flare-ups such as those during the Revolutionary War and the Civil War in this country and similar periods abroad. Inflation was a minuscule one-tenth of 1 percent from 1802 to 1870 and six-tenths of 1 percent from 1871 to 1925.[2]

When all major nations were on the gold standard, most government and many corporate bonds could be redeemed in either the national currency or gold at maturity at the holder's option. Given that inflation was almost nil, the "prudent-man" rule was introduced by Justice Samuel Putnam of the Massachusetts Supreme Court in 1830 and has served as an important guideline for money management for 150 years. A prudent man did not speculate, according to Putnam, who directed trustees "to observe how men of prudence, discretion and intelligence manage their own affairs" and act accordingly. So it made the best sense to stay in bonds with a number of preferred shares and a sprinkling of blue-chip stocks.[3]

But risk is a cunning beast, and inflation is a major weapon it unleashes against our capital, stealthily sneaking through our defenses time and again. Inflation caught investors following Justice Putnam's prudent-man edict flatfooted after World War II. Anyone who had put $100,000 into bonds at the end of that war would have $280,000 in 1946 purchasing power left today.[4] However, that's before income taxes, which averaged 60 percent between 1946 and 2010. After those two horsemen of the Financial Apocalypse—inflation and taxes—trampled over the bonds, investors or their estates who paid income tax in the top bracket would have had only 27 percent of their original 1946 purchasing power remaining in 2010.

The law is often decades behind economic and financial changes, and many investors and their managers still continue to believe in and follow Putnam's seriously outdated principle, which was appropriate in his time. The truth is that following the prudent-man rule, which had worked so well for so long, devastated the savings of many millions of Americans after World War II. Risk, this time in the form of rapidly rising prices, leaped from the heart of Justice Putnam's well-designed law to protect people's capital and is now one of the greatest dangers investors have faced and will continue to face in the twenty-first century.

Let's next turn to how we can best handle risk in the stock and bond markets.

▥ Beyond the Prudent-Man Rule

Inflation permanently entered the investment environment for the first time after World War II. Nothing is safe from this virulent virus, although its major victims are the supposedly safest investments we own: savings accounts, T-bills, Treasuries, corporate bonds, and other types of fixed-income securities. Whereas a relatively small number of companies may flounder financially or go under in any normal period* and far more in a financial crisis such as we are currently moving through, *the risk of inflation for most investors has proved more costly over time than credit risk.* Rising prices after World War II have radically and completely altered the return distributions of stocks, bonds, and T-bills.

---

* With the exception of some calamitous event such as the current financial crisis or the Great Depression.

▓ Are Stocks Riskier?

The wisdom of the ages, as we have seen from Justice Putnam's prudent-man rule, has always been that bonds are less risky than stocks over time. A company's bondholders, after all, had far less financial risk than the shareholders. If a company ran into financial problems, it could cut its dividend to shareholders, but it had to maintain interest payments and repay the bond principal when it was due. Otherwise, the company would go into default and the creditors would take everything the company owned before the shareholders got a penny. In the pre–World War II period, the major risk investors had to face was financial: the risk that a bond or a company would go under. The risk of inflation was an insignificant concern at that time.

The rapid inflation of the postwar period has turned all risk calculations topsy-turvy. While stocks have always had higher returns than Treasury bills or bonds over time, the disparities among the three classes of financial investment widened enormously after 1945. If an investor put $100,000 into T-bills in 1946, after inflation it would have increased to only $133,000 by 2010, a gain of only four-tenths of 1 percent annually. At that rate it would have taken about 160 years to double his capital. Bonds did only slightly better; $100,000 in 1946 became $280,000 by the end of 2010, for a return of 1.6 percent annually.* By comparison, investing $100,000 in stocks in 1946 hit the jackpot. It became $6,025,000, forty-five times as much as T-bills and twenty-one times as much as bonds (before-tax figures). After taxes the relative return for stocks over bonds and T-bills widens considerably, as both of the latter two categories have significant negative yields over time.

We see, then, that since World War II, inflation and taxes have taken an enormous toll on T-bills, Treasury bonds, savings accounts, and corporate debt. Yet few investors put the major outperformance of stocks over debt securities into their risk calculations even in normal times. In spite of the far superior returns over the past sixty-five years, capital to the time of this writing (September 2011) is still flowing out of stocks and mutual funds into Treasuries, yielding only one-twentieth of 1 percent on the very short end to 1.9 percent on ten-year Treasury bonds and 2.9 per-

---

* Both are before taxes, as noted earlier.

cent on thirty-year Treasury bonds. In the final chapter we will look at why these flows into bonds and T-bills may prove disastrous.

▇ Transforming Risk into Odds You'll Like

Table 14-1 shows the inflation-adjusted returns of stocks, bonds, and T-bills for periods of one to thirty years since 1946. As the table demonstrates, the longer the holding period, the greater the difference in the returns of stocks, on the one hand, and bonds and T-bills, on the other. The first row in column 1 shows that stocks provided a 6.5 percent annual return after inflation, on average, over the entire 1946–2010 period. At the end of five years, capital invested in stocks increased an average of 37.1 percent, after ten years an average of 87.9 percent, and after thirty more than sixfold. With Treasuries and T-bills, the rate of increase moved up at almost a snail's pace. After ten years, bonds (column 2), after inflation, expand initial capital by 17.2 percent, after thirty years by only 61 percent. The rate of increase for T-bills is lower yet (column 3). After a decade, capital, adjusted for inflation, would have increased by 4.5 percent, after two decades by 9.2 percent.

"That's well and good," you might say, "but stocks fluctuate. What are the odds that stocks will outperform bonds or T-bills over various periods of time?" Good question. It is one thing to see that stocks outperform

Holding Portfolio for...	Returns			Percent of Times Stocks Beat	
	Stocks	Bonds	T-Bills	Bonds	T-Bills
1 year	**6.5%**	1.6%	0.4%	63%	68%
2 years	**13.4%**	3.2%	0.9%	67%	73%
3 years	**20.8%**	4.9%	1.3%	71%	79%
4 years	**28.7%**	6.6%	1.8%	73%	77%
5 years	**37.1%**	8.3%	2.2%	74%	75%
10 years	**87.9%**	17.2%	4.5%	84%	82%
15 years	**157.5%**	26.9%	6.8%	94%	88%
20 years	**252.9%**	37.3%	9.2%	98%	100%
25 years	**383.7%**	48.7%	11.6%	98%	100%
30 years	**563.0%**	61.0%	14.1%	100%	100%

Table 14-1
Compounded Returns After Inflation
1946–2010

Source: © David Dreman, 2011. Data Source: Ibbotson® SBBI® Classic Yearbook 2011.

over time, but, as John Maynard Keynes once remarked, "In the long term, we're all dead." How, then, do they perform for somewhat shorter periods, while we can still enjoy spending the gains?

Column 5 shows the percentages by which stocks beat bonds for periods varying from one to thirty years, and column 6 provides the same information for T-bills. As you can see, it's a slam dunk for stocks after four years on average. Holding stocks, you have a 73 percent chance of doing better than bonds after inflation on average and a 77 percent shot at outperforming T-bills after forty-eight months, moving up progressively to a 94 percent chance at outperforming bonds and an 88 percent chance of beating T-bills in fifteen years. Beyond fifteen years, the odds favoring stocks surge to almost 100 percent against both bonds and T-bills. For longer periods, stocks are clearly the least risky of these three categories of investments.

Let's look at how stocks and bonds have performed over other periods in the past. Table 14-2 shows the probabilities of stocks outperforming

Table 14-2
Frequency of Stocks Outperforming Bonds and T-Bills, Bonds Outperforming T-Bills, Inflation-Adjusted, 1802–2010

Holding Portfolio for...		Stocks Beat Bonds	Stocks Beat T-Bills	Bonds Beat T-Bills
1 year	1802–1870	63.8%	59.4%	44.9%
	1871–1945	57.3%	61.3%	58.7%
	1946–2010	63.1%	67.7%	49.2%
2 years	1802–1870	63.8%	59.4%	42.0%
	1871–1945	60.0%	62.7%	65.3%
	1946–2010	67.2%	73.4%	57.8%
5 years	1802–1870	65.2%	69.6%	40.6%
	1871–1945	65.3%	69.3%	69.3%
	1946–2010	73.8%	75.4%	60.7%
10 years	1802–1870	78.3%	75.4%	40.6%
	1871–1945	80.0%	85.3%	76.0%
	1946–2010	83.9%	82.1%	48.2%
20 years	1802–1870	87.0%	87.0%	30.4%
	1871–1945	92.0%	98.7%	74.7%
	1946–2010	97.8%	100.0%	50.0%
30 years	1802–1870	98.6%	92.8%	17.4%
	1871–1945	97.3%	100.0%	76.0%
	1946–2010	100.0%	100.0%	50.0%

Source: © David Dreman, 2011. Data Sources: Jeremy Siegel and Ibbotson® SBBI® Classic Yearbook 2011.

bonds and Treasury bills after inflation over different intervals between 1802 and 2010. Three periods are analyzed, 1802–1870, 1871–1945, and 1946–2010. In each period the probability of stocks outperforming bonds, stocks beating T-bills, and bonds beating T-bills is measured from one to thirty years. The table shows that the probabilities of stocks outperforming bonds or T-bills increase with time. More important, *the odds were higher for the outperformance of stocks over Treasuries and T-bills for any period from one to twenty years in the post–World War II period than in the previous 145 years.*

For five years the probability of stocks beating Treasury bonds rose from 65 percent in the two earlier periods to 74 percent after World War II. In the 1946–2010 period, stocks had a 100 percent chance of outperforming T-bills for all twenty-year periods. Stocks had an 87 percent chance of beating T-bills after twenty years over the 1802–1870 period; the chance increased to 99 percent for the 1871–1945 time span.

But wait—there is more.

▓ Taxes: The Fourth Horseman of the Financial Apocalypse

Enter the fourth horseman of the Financial Apocalypse—taxes, riding down the owners of bonds and T-bills, and other fixed-income issues. Table 14-3 is identical in format to Table 14-1 but shows the returns after both inflation and taxes for stocks, bonds, and T-bills for periods of one to thirty years through the postwar period using the average top federal income tax rate of 60 percent between 1946 and 2010 over the entire period.* Stocks compound at 4.4 percent annually, adjusted for inflation and taxes. In ten years investors would have increased their capital by more than 53 percent, in twenty years by 135 percent. As Table 14-3 also shows, the returns on fixed-income securities after taxes drop even more dramatically. For all their allure, buying long-term government bonds is about as safe and profitable as having been heavily margined in stocks just before October 24, 1929. If an investor in a 60 percent tax bracket had put $100,000 into long Treasury bonds after World War II, he would have had

---

* The average top tax bracket was 62 percent between 1946 and 2010. I used 60 percent to be conservative. I also did not include state and municipal income tax, to bring the top tax bracket down further. Please see note 5 for a more complete breakdown of the tax rate through the entire period.

Table 14-3 Compounded Returns After Inflation and Taxes 1946–2010					
Holding Portfolio for...	**Returns**			**Percent of Times Stocks Beat**	
	Stocks	Bonds	T-Bills	Bonds	T-Bills
1 year	**4.4%**	−2.0%	−2.2%	65%	71%
2 years	**8.9%**	−4.0%	−4.4%	77%	77%
3 years	**13.7%**	−5.9%	−6.5%	78%	81%
4 years	**18.7%**	−7.8%	−8.6%	81%	82%
5 years	**23.8%**	−9.7%	−10.6%	80%	79%
10 years	**53.4%**	−18.5%	−20.2%	91%	88%
15 years	**90.0%**	−26.4%	−28.6%	100%	98%
20 years	**135.3%**	−33.5%	−36.2%	100%	100%
25 years	**191.4%**	−40.0%	−43.0%	100%	100%
30 years	**260.9%**	−45.8%	−49.1%	100%	100%

Source: © David Dreman, 2011. Data Source: Ibbotson® SBBI® Classic Yearbook 2011.

only $27,000 of his original purchasing power left in 2010. That's right, inflation and taxes would have eaten up 73 percent of the investment.[5]

The results are equally bad for T-bills, and being in a lower tax bracket doesn't help the T-bill or Treasury bond buyer much. Finally, had the investor put $100,000 into blue-chip stocks, the supposedly "riskiest" investment, with the same 60 percent tax rate after inflation, the portfolio would have appreciated to $1.6 million over the sixty-five-year period. The capital invested in equities would be worth fifty-seven times as much as if placed in bonds.

With bonds or T-bills, it's a dirge. The longer you hold them, the louder the organ plays. After ten years, both will cost you about 20 percent of your capital after inflation and taxes; after twenty years, about 35 percent; and so it goes. The last two columns again demonstrate the probabilities of stocks outperforming bonds and T-bills for periods of one to thirty years. After four years, there is better than an 80 percent chance that stocks will outperform bonds and T-bills, and the chance builds up significantly with time. By fifteen years, the chance is nearly 100 percent that you'll do better in stocks than in government bonds and 98 percent that you'll do better than T-bills. Investing in government securities, then, considered by most people to be almost "riskless," is a loser's game.

Common stocks, as Tables 14-1 and 14-3 indicate, though a more volatile asset in any short period of time, provide much higher returns than T-bills and bonds over longer periods.

▨ Is There Something Wrong with This Picture?

As we've seen, the starting point of modern portfolio theory is the return an investor receives on a "riskless" asset, normally a Treasury bill. The investor then merrily selects a portfolio made up of risk-free and riskier assets, measured by their volatility, to get the optimum mix. *The trouble is that the "risk-free asset" of the academic theory, the T-bill, is one of the riskiest assets over time.*

It's apparent that this assumption of academic investment theory is far removed from reality. Rational investors should be concerned with the probability of maintaining and enhancing their savings, adjusted for inflation and taxes, for retirement or other future needs. This is one of the greatest risks they face. The time horizon of the large majority of investors is not months, quarters, or a year or two away. It is many years away, because the need for funds to meet costs such as retirement, college tuition, and similar requirements usually far off in the future. After all, that is why the government set up tax-deferred pension funds, IRAs, and similar programs, which tens of millions of investors participate in. The investment objective for most people is to maximize savings as safely as possible for the time when they will need to draw on them.

The major risk is not the short-term stock-price volatility measurements, which have been shown to be specious. Rather, it is the possibility of not reaching your long-term investment goal through the growth of your funds in real terms. *It is counterproductive for investors with investing time horizons of thirty, twenty, ten, or even five years to focus on short-term fluctuations.* Shorter-term volatility measurements provide an illusion of safety while derailing the higher returns that are provided by holding equity or equity-equivalent products (real estate, housing, better-grade private-equity investments, and so on) over time. This leads to another important Psychological Guideline.

PSYCHOLOGICAL GUIDELINE 30 (a): To invest successfully over time, risk measurements should be established using longer-term rates of return for stocks, bonds, T-bills, and other investments. The performance benchmark should be appropriate for the time period the investments are anticipated to be held.

PSYCHOLOGICAL GUIDELINE 30 (b): Using short-term risk measurements as benchmarks for longer-term capital performance is likely to result in a significant shortfall in an investor's returns. It is one of the most serious risks investors can take today.

The Treacherous T-Bill

Stocks may blow away T-bills and bonds over time, but, as we have seen, the focus of most investors, fiduciaries, and courts is still on shorter-term financial risk. The far more potent and universal risk of inflation and taxes is a secondary consideration at best. Academic risk theory also accepts the conventional wisdom by making the T-bill the risk-free investment. But financial academics, like most market participants, have not incorporated into their equations the fact that *the largest risk factor today is the decrease in purchasing power of your investment through inflation.*

When we adjust for inflation, supposedly risky assets such as stocks become far safer. The probability that investors holding stocks will double their capital every ten years after inflation and quadruple it every twenty, combined with the 100 percent chance that they will outperform T-bills and the 98 percent chance that they will outperform government bonds in twenty years, can hardly be called risky.* Conversely, the supposedly "risk-free" assets actually display a large and increasing element of risk over time. For that reason we must incorporate into a new definition of risk the effects of higher inflation on investors in recent decades, including contemporary markets, along with the other types of risk inherent in these investments.

A Better Way of Measuring Risk

What, then, is a better way of measuring your investment risk? While there can be many definitions, even in the business and investment worlds, a good starting point is the preservation and enhancement of your purchasing power in real terms. The goal of investing is to protect and increase your portfolio on an inflation-adjusted basis and (where appropriate) tax-adjusted dollars over time.

---

* Through the post–World War II period.

A realistic definition of risk recognizes the potential loss of capital through inflation and taxes and includes at least the following two factors:

1. The probability that the investments you choose will preserve your capital over the time you intend to invest your funds.
2. The probability that the investments you select will outperform alternative investments for the period.

Unlike the academic volatility measures, these risk measures look to the appropriate time period in the future—five, ten, fifteen, twenty, or thirty years—when the funds will be required. Market risk may be severe over a period of months or even a few years, but, as we have seen, it diminishes rapidly over longer periods.

Tables 14-1, 14-2, and 14-3 tell us how stocks stack up against bonds and T-bills after inflation and taxes and the probability that stocks will outperform them in any period of time. The careful reader might ask another question here: "Okay, I know the odds of stocks beating bonds and T-bills are increasingly high over time, but stocks have very good periods followed by years of lackluster results. What are my chances of capturing returns above those provided by bonds or T-bills?"

The answer is provided in Tables 14-4 and 14-5. Table 14-4 shows the probability of receiving stock returns as low as 50 percent of the average return for stocks in the postwar period (column 2) to as high as 150 percent of the average return (column 6) after inflation. The probability of returns above these levels is shown for periods of one to thirty years.

Table 14-4, column 1, shows the total portfolio value, or *wealth relative,* in academic jargon, for every period from one to thirty years, if you earned only 50 percent of the average return for stocks for each period through the 1946–2010 study, after inflation. This is a very severe worst-case situation, as will be explained shortly. Column 2 indicates what your probabilities are of earning more than 50 percent of the average return for any period between 1946 and 2010. The probabilities, with minor exceptions, of earning more than half the market return increase with time. Thus, holding a portfolio with a starting value of 100 in the first year, you have a 62 percent probability or better of returning above 3 percent (103, column 1) at the end of one year. After ten years, the portfolio has a 73 percent probability (column 2) of increasing more than 38 percent (138 in column 1); after twenty-five years, it has a 93 percent probability

	50% of Market Return		100% of Market Return		150% of Market Return			
	(1)	(2)	(3)	(4)	(5)	(6)	(7)	(8)
Holding Portfolio for...	Average Stock Portfolio Value	Probability*	Average Stock Portfolio Value	Probability*	Average Stock Portfolio Value	Probability*	Average Bond Portfolio Value	Average T-Bill Portfolio Value
1 year	103	(62%)	107	(55%)	110	(52%)	102	100
5 years	117	(70%)	137	(59%)	159	(43%)	108	102
10 years	138	(73%)	188	(63%)	254	(43%)	117	104
15 years	162	(75%)	257	(59%)	404	(37%)	127	107
20 years	190	(74%)	353	(52%)	644	(26%)	137	109
25 years	223	(93%)	484	(51%)	1026	(12%)	149	112
30 years	261	(100%)	663	(42%)	1635	(0%)	161	114

Table 14-4
Probability of Stocks Meeting Various Levels of Return
1.0 = Starting Investment, Inflation-Adjusted
1946–2010

100 = starting investment
* Probability that a portfolio will be above the value shown.

Source: © David Dreman, 2011. Data Source: Ibbotson® SBBI® Classic Yearbook 2011.

of returning 123 percent above your investment (223 in column 1). So cutting the market return by half, which has happened only several times in our market history during the Great Depression, still provides significant stock returns over time.

Next look at columns 7 and 8, which show the cumulative returns of bonds and T-bills. *You can see that even if you receive only 50 percent of the stock market's average return, you still do much better in stocks than in either bonds or T-bills for any given period.* Again, this is a doomsday scenario, as the chance of making only 50 percent of the normal market return is near zero when you invest for as long as twenty-five years. You have a 93 percent (column 2) chance of doing better. But worst case or no, you still do better in equities than in T-bills or bonds.

As you increase the number of years you hold stocks versus debt securities, the comparisons only get better. If you receive the market return over time, as we saw before, you score big; after fifteen years your portfolio would appreciate 157 percent, or six times as much as in bonds and over twenty-two times as much as in T-bills. After twenty-five years, your net worth would be three times what it would be in bonds and over four times that of T-bills, and so on. Not that you need to strike it rich with the types of returns we have just seen, but there is also a reasonable probability that your return can be above-market averages. If you return 150 percent of the market, as column 5 indicates, the returns bury those for bonds and T-bills. In this happy situation the investor receives almost eleven times the return he would on bonds in fifteen years and about fifteen times in twenty years.

There you have it. Once again, stocks provide higher rewards over time than bonds or T-bills even under poor circumstances and shoot out the lights under better conditions. The decision of where to place your money should not be difficult.

Introducing taxes in Table 14-5 (which is set up in an identical manner to Table 14-4) of course reduces the absolute returns for stocks but will reduce them significantly more for bonds and T-bills. Again, as the time periods increase, stocks substantially outperform bonds and T-bills under all the scenarios.[6]

Looking first at the average market return (column 3), we see that

Table 14-5

Probability of Stocks Meeting Various Levels of Return

1.0 = Starting Investment, Inflation-Adjusted and Tax-Adjusted

1946–2010

	50% of Market Return		100% of Market Return		150% of Market Return			
	(1)	(2)	(3)	(4)	(5)	(6)	(7)	(8)
Holding Portfolio for...	Average Stock Portfolio Value	Probability*	Average Stock Portfolio Value	Probability*	Average Stock Portfolio Value	Probability*	Average Bond Portfolio Value	Average T-Bill Portfolio Value
1 year	102	(58%)	104	(57%)	107	(54%)	98	98
5 years	111	(64%)	124	(59%)	137	(52%)	90	89
10 years	124	(73%)	153	(64%)	189	(50%)	82	80
15 years	138	(71%)	190	(61%)	259	(51%)	74	71
20 years	154	(63%)	235	(52%)	356	(48%)	66	64
25 years	172	(66%)	291	(44%)	489	(29%)	60	57
30 years	191	(89%)	361	(42%)	672	(6%)	54	51

100 = starting investment
* Probability that a portfolio will be above the value shown.

Source: © David Dreman, 2011. Data Source: Ibbotson® SBBI® Classic Yearbook 2011.

stocks outperform bonds (column 7) for ten years by 71 percent, with a 64 percent probability that stock returns will be higher. After inflation and taxes, bonds actually lose purchasing power.

T-bills do even worse over the same period. Over time, the increase in capital invested on $100,000 in stocks rather than bonds increases dramatically. In ten years, your investment is almost 90 percent ahead; in twenty-five years it is almost four times as much. In the interim, both bonds and T-bills have lost over 40 percent of their original purchasing power.

Last, let's take a brief peak at what could happen to stocks if they outperform their long-term rates of return for a decade. Most investors believe this is very unlikely today, but a few, including myself, for reasons presented in the final chapter, believe it is a distinct possibility. If this impossible dream were to come true, your capital would increase by 89 percent in a decade, 159 percent in fifteen years.

▮ Toward a Better Analysis of Risk

The evidence indicates that in the post–World War II inflationary environment, bonds and T-bills are no match for equity-type investments over time. I have tried to answer the question of how much risk there is in holding stocks instead of bonds and T-bills in two ways. First, I asked how often stocks would outperform T-bills or government bonds after inflation for periods varying from one to thirty years in the postwar period in Table 14-1 and after inflation and taxes in Table 14-3. We saw that stocks won in a breeze in both cases; the longer the time period, the more they outperformed. The probability that T-bills or bonds would provide inferior returns relative to stocks is large and increases after three to five years.

Second, I examined the risk of owning stocks if their returns dropped off sharply from their long-term norms in Tables 14-4 and 14-5. Once again, even if this happened (if, for example, stocks provided only 50 percent of their normal return over time), they still outperformed debt instruments by a significant amount after five years and by a more moderate amount up to five years.

Let's now go back to the two measures we said should be incorporated into a good definition of risk:

1. The probability that the investment you choose will preserve your capital over the time you intend to invest your funds
2. The probability that the investments you select will outperform alternative investments for this period

The conclusion is obvious: stocks meet both these criteria. If we apply this standard of risk in the postwar period, stocks are the least risky investments over time. If you are in your thirties, for example, and have a goal of retiring at sixty-five, you should buy blue-chip stocks because you have a 100 percent chance of both enhancing your capital and outperforming bonds and T-bills. The probabilities are also high that you will outperform debt securities many times over. Though not as high, the odds are still very high for fifteen years and reasonably good at four or five years. From a risk perspective, bonds and T-bills give you increasingly short odds after only a few years. They are not the investments you want to build your future upon and have not been for almost sixty-five years.

What we see, then, is the development of a new approach to risk analysis that tries, before funds are invested, to more realistically appraise the risk of holding various types of investments over the time the investor might need. The analysis allows you to determine not only the odds that your returns will outperform or underperform other types of investments but also the probability of by how much. This risk measurement framework could also be adapted to valuing real estate, precious metals, or other investments, if you have the records of their performance over longer periods. If you choose to measure how you might do in Impressionist art, other art, or collectibles relative to equities, as an example, there is an index dating back to the 1960s from Sotheby's, which *Barron's* reports each week.

While this approach to risk can certainly be fine-tuned, it allows you to more accurately assess your exposures in the postwar investment world, one very different from any investment environment in the past.

What we've clearly seen from the tables is that since 1945 we have entered a new world of investing. Inflation and higher taxes have an immediate and lasting effect on holders of fixed-income securities.* This sit-

---

* Fixed-income denotes all interest-bearing securities, including Treasuries, corporate bonds, debentures, and savings accounts.

uation did not reduce stock returns in the early postwar years but actually saw them increase because of rapidly rising stock prices and dividends. From the middle of 1949 to the end of 1961, the Dow rose 355 percent.

In summary, then, there is a very important lesson about risk to learn from these events, which we'll make an investment Psychological Guideline.

PSYCHOLOGICAL GUIDELINE 31: There has been a permanent shift in the structure of risk because of higher inflation and taxes that strongly favors equity investments, real estate and housing, and other investments that benefit from it, and puts bond and other fixed income at a major disadvantage over time.

This change, as noted, has been going on for well over sixty years, but because psychologically we focus on much shorter time periods, it is hard to react to the current dynamics of risk.

Second, because stock performance is volatile, we don't pick up the full scope of this sea change in risk psychologically, even though many of us know that inflation affects stock prices positively over time. As a result, many people don't see the conclusions clearly. Let's also make this a Psychological Guideline:

PSYCHOLOGICAL GUIDELINE 32: The changed economic environment unambiguously indicates that the longer we hold equities or other investments that outperform inflation, the better off we will be financially over time.

The findings almost jump out of the tables in this chapter.
A further Psychological Guideline is in order here.

PSYCHOLOGICAL GUIDELINE 33(a): Try to ignore near-term market fluctuations; if you intend to be invested for a five-year or longer period, the true risk is in not owning stocks or similar investments that appreciate faster than the rate of inflation over time.

PSYCHOLOGICAL GUIDELINE 33(b): Unless yields are very high, don't consider bonds, savings accounts, or other low-interest fixed-income securities as longer-term investments. They are high-risk vehicles with the odds heavily against them; the longer they're held, the greater the risk. Consider them only as a repository of cash for short- to intermediate-term needs.

Although the tables make this crystal clear, conventional wisdom changes all too slowly.

Professor Knight's distinction between risk and uncertainty holds a very important lesson for us here. The performance of the stock and bond markets is uncertain for any short period of time. But over time the uncertainty turns into risk. Risk is our friend if the odds are heavily in our favor, as they are with stocks. What we must remember is that for stocks and similar investments, risk turns into an increasingly high probability of winning over time.*

Focusing on short-term periods, rather than the period the capital is intended to be held, will result in subpar returns. The investor should focus optimally on the time for which the stock portfolio is likely to be held, rather than on its short-term volatility.

The following Psychological Guideline encapsulates these findings.

PSYCHOLOGICAL GUIDELINE 34(a): Inflation and taxes sharply reduce your risk in owning stocks over longer periods of time.

PSYCHOLOGICAL GUIDELINE 34(b): Inflation and taxes sharply increase your risk in owning Treasuries, other bonds, and savings accounts over longer periods of time.

Richard Thaler of the University of Chicago, one of the pioneers of behavioral finance, once told me he wished that stock quotes were not published every day. His reason was that overexposure, particularly in bad times, precipitates hasty and often foolish decisions. If people treated stocks like real estate, where they can't get a quote every day, they'd be far better off. Thaler was right. If we could clearly focus on the long-term probabilities and not be thrown off course, sometimes badly,

---

* In the past sixty-five years there has been only one period when stock prices did not go up for fifteen years, 1969–1982. Still, even in that disappointing time, total return was 5 percent a year because of dividends. Stocks prices rose more than twelvefold to 2000. The performance of bonds, as we have seen, was pitiful by comparison.

by month-to-month or year-to-year events, we would all very likely be much better off.

These results are something to ponder carefully, especially as our final section will try to do a little crystal-ball gazing and reasonably project what is likely to lie ahead for investors. Notice that I've said "reasonably." This is still a world of surprises, and the last thing I ever want any investor to do is to think that the future is a settled bet.

Part V

The Challenges and Opportunities Ahead

Chapter 15

They're Gambling
with Your Money

WELCOME TO THE internationally acclaimed House of Goldman Sachs. We are proud to be your host at one of the most spectacular casinos in the world. Our well-dressed, highly courteous staff members are some of the most talented and intelligent employees in the business today, as almost all of them have advanced degrees, including some doctorates. They are well trained to help you in every aspect of what you might call gambling. Further, they will make their expertise available to you on any of the hundreds of games we are proud to feature at our exquisite investment casino. Some of the most unusual player opportunities, ranging from exciting "synthetics" to the all-new "exotics," can be found only here. You can be sure you will always maximize your odds of winning, as our outstanding staff is ready and eager to let you know the probabilities of any game you select.

I see that you are walking to the beautifully appointed gaming room. From the foyer you can see that there are many enticing games in the casino, including some that you've never seen before. The players are excited, and the chips on the tables are piled high. You wisely decide to play a game you know and walk over to a beautiful mahogany roulette table. You put a few chips down, and the handsome and expensively dressed croupier drops the tiny silver ball. After he spins the wheel around, it lands in a green slot. Knowing that green is normally a 1-in-37 chance, you decide to play red, which should give you almost fifty-fifty odds of doubling your money. The dealer drops the ball, which, after circling the wheel again, lands on green. You know the probabilities of that are exceptionally small. So you continue to play red. But to your amazement green comes up on eight of the first ten spins.

Astounded at this enormous run of luck that defies all probabilities, you put your entire stake on green. The croupier removes it and puts the chips back in front of you. You look up and ask why. He politely says, "I'm sorry, sir, green is not allowed to be played against the house."

An old-timer standing behind you watching the action says, "That's a heck of a wheel, son. The casino spent years making alterations to it." He goes on to tell you that it took masterful financial engineers to get it just so. The first attempts resulted in the ball's landing on green only a few times in every ten times it was spun. But with intense work by outstanding financial engineers, the number of times the ball landed on green kept going up. Now it's eight of every ten times the ball is dropped, which is exactly what the house targeted.

"Since it pays thirty-five to one, it makes a bundle for the casino. There are dozens of other games that pay off for the house just as well. If you walk down the Strip, you'll see the casinos of Morgan Stanley, Credit Suisse, Citigroup, and a dozen others just as nice. Lehman and Bear Stearns also had great places; it's too bad they burned down," he finishes.

You wisely decide to leave but wonder how it is that a casino is allowed to have such odds in its favor. In Las Vegas, it would be shut down in less than an hour. In the Old West, the proprietors would immediately have been strung up for high-handed cheating. But on Wall Street it wins rave reviews. And you can't go to the government regulators because you know they work with the casinos.

This story is, of course, total fiction. We all know investment banks and banks don't own casinos—at least not directly. The details, too, are not literally true. So, as you read on, any similarities you may deduce are simply a matter of coincidence.

Or, then again, are they?

Singing the Bailout Blues

"How could the U.S., the strongest country on earth, put itself into this horrific situation?" I wrote in *Forbes* shortly after the $700 billion Troubled Asset Relief Program (TARP) was passed by Congress in late 2008. "I wince at the $700 billion bailout," I continued. "It was a necessary evil, but it doesn't make me feel good as an investor." The article went on to describe what we knew back then had caused the worst financial crisis in history.[1]

The public is still very perturbed about the financial bailout, as well as the high levels of unemployment the financial crisis has caused. Further resentment has been stoked because millions of people have been forced out of their homes. Many Americans are furious that virtually all of the perpetrators of these financial acts are walking off not with prison sentences but with severance payments up to a hundred million dollars. The final and possibly bitterest blow is that the financial executives who almost brought down our economy received seven- and eight-figure bonuses for what they did. The rise of the Tea Party and the sweep of the House of Representatives by Republicans in November 2010 showed quite clearly that voters are unhappy with the slow progress of both constructive change and job creation. Is popular opinion close to the truth on what actually happened, or is it out of whack with the facts?

Three congressional committees (which were surprisingly bipartisan) subpoenaed hundreds of thousands of e-mails and took voluminous testimony. Prior to the hearings, few explanations were forthcoming from the Fed and the Treasury about the banks and investment bankers who received the bailouts. But thanks to the congressional committees' thorough work, we know much more today.

What we have learned is at times shocking. Bankers were enormously deceitful to the public, and their greed was on a par with almost any in our history. Yes, Congress has taken actions to prevent a recurrence of some of the folly, but all too many questions remain. In order to highlight possible causes of future crises, let's take a quick look at what we've learned.

First we'll look at the roles played by the Federal Reserve under its current and previous chairman, as well as by senior administration officials through the previous two administrations and the present one. We'll then move on to the banks, investment banking firms, and other key players. No one group can be singled out for causing the financial crisis or the Great Recession. As most of us know, they were caused by a powerful confluence of factors, almost a perfect storm. What many people don't know was the degree of incompetence and misguided ideology, as well as the powerful role played by little-known special-interest groups and the intensity of greed displayed by so many, all of which were critical elements.

The solutions to these serious problems are certainly beyond the scope of this book, but an understanding of the insidious effects they inflict should prove helpful to us as investors in understanding the problems we must continue to cope with for some time.

Mr. Chairman

May I introduce you to one of the major economic powers in U.S. history? No, he wasn't a political figure such as FDR or Ronald Reagan, but he was reverently called "the Oracle" by many thousands for the brilliant economic moves people thought he had made, which they believed had saved not only the U.S. economy but businesses globally. I'm referring, of course, to Dr. Alan Greenspan. He holds a Ph.D. in economics and served as chairman of the Federal Reserve of the United States from 1987 to 2006. For Wall Street, he was the closest thing to a Delphic oracle that investors had ever seen.

During his tenure as Fed chairman, he appears to have been strongly driven by ideology. As many know, Greenspan is a disciple of Ayn Rand, the author of *Atlas Shrugged* and one of the prime intellectuals from whom libertarianism took its ideas. In his late twenties, Greenspan fell into the Objectivist movement, dominated by Rand, which favored free markets and opposed strong government, and he contributed several essays to her book *Capitalism: The Unknown Ideal.* He was even a strong advocate of the gold standard and in his earlier years would have denied the power of the Fed to increase or reduce the money supply. Through the years he remained close to Ayn Rand and was a strong believer in deregulation. She and his mother were present as the witnesses when President Reagan swore him in as the chairman of the Federal Reserve in the summer of 1987.

In his prepolitical years, his philosophy was relatively simple: regulation bad, free enterprise good. He went so far as to state on *Meet the Press* that antitrust laws should be abolished. Not only did he want to cast out the New Deal in its entirety; he even wanted to undo the Republican president Theodore Roosevelt's trust-busting work in the early twentieth century. His perspective is encapsulated well in this quote from a speech he gave to the American Bankers Association in 1996: "If banks were unregulated, they would take on any amount of risk they wished, and the market would rate their liabilities and price them accordingly."[2] Simple, yes; naive, yes; and to a large degree successful. So successful, in fact, that the deregulation of the banks played a major role in their blowing up both themselves and the economy a little over a decade later. The complexity, scale, and interdependence of modern banks were never considered by the man who led the Fed for twenty years.

Greenspan appears to be an advocate of the much earlier form of free enterprise, the laissez-faire of the 1830s and 1840s. Back then, all the fundamentals he would like to see in the current world were functioning. What his almost zealous idealism seems to overlook was that it was anything but a perfect time. Most people lived in enormous poverty. Fifty to 60 percent of the English population suffered from malnutrition. Child labor was widespread, and most people worked a seven-day week. "Don't come in Sunday, don't come in Monday" was a sign industrialists often posted on British factory doors. Debtors' prisons dotted the country. Several major riots took place in manufacturing cities and London, protesting the terrible conditions, while Wellington, "the Iron Duke," who won the Battle of Waterloo, was prime minister. Ironically, had Greenspan lived in those halcyon times, his chances of achieving the success he did would have been almost nil, because major positions went to the upper class. At heart he is a man of the early nineteenth century.

Fortunately for him, he was born much later and achieved enormous success. Greenspan at his pinnacle was widely considered to be the most able central banker who ever walked the face of the earth. He was a financial savior, affectionately called "the Prophet" or "the Oracle," whose understanding of evolving financial and economic problems and his adept handling of them as they arose led, most believed, to a world of peace and prosperity.

Every statement or speech he gave was a news event and was immediately flashed to financial markets globally. No economic forum was considered important if he did not speak or attend. His portrait sold for as much as $150,400,[3] and a dinner with him went for $250,000.[4] More important, he had the ear of every president of the United States from Ronald Reagan to George W. Bush, as well as most congressmen and senators, whether Democrats or Republicans, almost since his appointment as chairman of the Fed.

Wall Street speculated on what he would say prior to his every major appearance before Congress. His speeches were often televised live, and their content was distributed to the media before the actual delivery of the talk. Greenspan's speeches and statements were convoluted and difficult to decipher, although every word was studied by tens of thousands.

To me his statements not only were difficult to decode but often seemed to contradict previous ones he had made. When I mentioned this to other money managers I knew or when I wrote about his lack of clarity in my *Forbes* column, I was told that this was the way a major chairman of the Fed should present himself. Others said that this was the way an oracle should speak. Greenspan told Bob Woodward, the noted journalist and political author, that he wanted to keep the financial community off balance by doing this so it never fully understood his course of action. He called it "constructive ambiguity."[5]

If his speeches were opaque, his actions as Fed chairman for almost twenty years certainly were not. And it was those actions that played an important role in the worst financial crisis in history. What is striking was that although his decisions on key matters were consistent, predictable, and repeated numerous times, few Fed watchers caught on to the pattern.

Greenspan did not want outside regulation by governmental agencies at any level, and he did not want the Fed to carry out many of its assigned responsibilities to regulate banks and other financial institutions or to provide the consumer protection it was mandated to give. He had an unshakable belief that companies, regardless of their size, industry, or circumstances, would, in their own self-interest, regulate themselves well. His belief in self-regulation colored most of his major actions over the almost twenty years he was chairman.

Greenspan was instrumental, along with Treasury Secretary Robert Rubin and Lawrence Summers, a powerful, politically connected Harvard economist, who would later become secretary of the Treasury, in repealing the Glass-Steagall Act under the Bill Clinton administration. The act, which restricted the power of commercial banks to compete with investment banks and significantly curtailed the amount of risk they could take, had by and large worked successfully to that time. The roots of the repeal came out of Greenspan's Federal Reserve, which in the late 1980s began reinterpreting Glass-Steagall in a series of actions that slowly increased the banks' abilities to expand into other activities.[6]

Enormous decisions that affected the welfare and livelihoods of most Americans were made by the ranking Fed and Treasury policy makers and were based on their personal ideologies, which were often far removed from those of the electorate.

Were It That Simple

Greenspan was also the "leading proponent of the deregulation of derivatives."[7] There were an ample number of knowledgeable people who were concerned that this deregulation would cause a serious drop in the safeguards on their use in the last year of the Clinton administration. Among the opponents was the former head of the Commodity Futures Trading Commission (CFTC), Brooksley Born. She attempted to have derivatives regulated, including the extremely complex and lethal credit default swaps, which sank AIG and came close to sinking dozens of other financial institutions and hedge funds. Born was met by enormous opposition from Secretary of the Treasury Robert Rubin, Lawrence Summers, and, oh yes, Alan Greenspan, all of whom, on April 21, 1998, took turns trying to talk her out of her position.[8] One account indicates that Summers's discussion was—to be charitable—very assertive. Born's stand resulted in her being forced out of the Clinton administration.[9]

Rubin and Summers, with the strong support of Greenspan, pushed through the Commodity Futures Modernization Act of 2000, which Clinton signed into law in his last month in office. The impact on markets resulting from the nonregulation of these toxic derivatives was enormous. President Clinton told *ABC News* in April 2009, when asked about the advice he had received from Secretary Rubin and his handpicked successor, Summers, "On derivatives, yeah, I think they were wrong and I think I was wrong to take it."[10]

Numerous warnings by highly knowledgeable financial types were given about the destructive power of derivatives years before the meltdown. George Soros, the hedge fund manager who "broke the Bank of

England" with his shrewd currency trades, avoids using such contracts, "because we don't really understand how they work."[11] Felix Rohatyn, who saved New York City from going bankrupt in the 1970s, described derivatives as potential "hydrogen bombs." Warren Buffett presciently observed, five years before the 2007–2008 crash, that derivatives were "financial weapons of mass destruction, carrying dangers that, while now latent, are potentially lethal."[12] Those warnings, like so many others, were ignored.

From 1990 and for the next four years, the Fed cut rates sharply. Easier access to credit and rapid advances in financial technology led to explosive growth in the over-the-counter derivatives markets, which reached $25 trillion in notional value by 1995 and increased tenfold to 2005.

Alan Greenspan took an active role in lessening the regulation of derivatives and did not see any cause for alarm, consistent with his unwavering philosophy that the derivatives markets were unregulated and therefore must be good. Even after derivative scandals sent shock waves through the market in the mid-1990s and derivative counterparties lost billions of dollars, Greenspan continued to press for greater deregulation of them. His policy never changed. In 2003, he testified to the Senate Banking Committee, "We think it would be a mistake" to more deeply regulate the contracts.[13] During the 2008 crash, in a speech at Georgetown University, Greenspan said that the problem was not the derivatives but the people using them—who got "greedy."[25] He was contradicted by Frank Partnoy, a law professor at the University of San Diego and an expert on derivatives and financial regulation, who said, "Clearly, derivatives are a centerpiece of the crisis."[14]

The consistency and obstinacy of Greenspan's push to deregulation in the face of failure after failure of his policies are remarkable. So, as we run quickly through a number of other major policy decisions that contributed to the magnitude of the financial crisis, an important question we should ask is whether the Fed's powers ought to be curtailed after the damage it has caused the economy.

As obstinate as Chairman Greenspan was about derivatives, he was even more so about not taking any action to curb the excesses of the housing bubble.

The subprime problems did not begin in 2004–2005. Rather, they go back almost a decade to the passage of the Tax Reform Act of 1986, which allowed the deduction of interest on a primary residence and one other home.[15] This made the cost of subprime mortgages cheaper than consumer loans, on which interest could not be deducted. A major new market was opened for people who could not get conventional mortgages because of low credit scores. Credit was now available, but at higher interest rates, and numerous financial companies, aka loan sharks, flocked into what looked like a very profitable new business.

By 1997, questionable accounting, higher-than-projected arrears, and defaults made it apparent that the industry had underpriced its loans and was floundering. Of the top ten originators of new mortgages in 1996, only one remained in 2000. Did the credit-rating agencies, the Federal Reserve, the regulators, and the banks remember this dismal performance? They did not, as we all painfully know. Only a year later, subprime demand roared ahead again and housing prices had turned up sharply. The housing bubble had started.

The Subprime Ball

After the 1996–2000 high-tech bubble collapsed, the Federal Reserve, under Chairman Greenspan, lowered interest rates significantly and a very easy monetary policy was established to cushion the enormous market losses, estimated at over $7 trillion, that investors had taken after the 2000–2002 crash. The Fed feared those losses might severely curtail consumer and to a lesser extent business spending, pushing the nation into a recession. To prevent this outcome, the Fed funds rate was dropped from 6½ percent in mid-2000 to 1 percent in mid-2003 in thirteen consecutive steps as the high-tech bubble disintegrated. Long-term Treasury rates fell from 7 percent to 4½ percent.[16]

After the 2000–2002 high-tech bubble collapsed, people realized that although many had lost heavily in the market, housing, usually accounting for by far the greatest portion of their net worth, was not only intact but moving steadily higher. Beginning in 2002, an enormous housing boom was triggered whose excesses, as we'll see, were the prime cause of both the near-destruction of the global financial system and the worst economic climate since the 1930s.

Twelve and a half trillion dollars' worth of new-home originations was completed between 2002 and 2007. Risky subprime originations shot up far more than conventional mortgages, increasing from 6.6 percent of total mortgages in 2002 to a whopping 21.7 percent in 2006.[17] The subprime industry had hit a grand slam!

However, as is so often the case in the financial sector, the truth is not found in the glossy pages of a self-congratulatory annual or quarterly report but squirreled away in the footnotes buried deep in the back pages, where, it is hoped, they will never be found.

▮ The Casino Has a Grand New Game

Mortgages were now available for buyers with only the most limited incomes and financial resources, housing prices soared, and buyers were lining up to get a part of the action. The mortgage companies and real estate investment trusts (REITs), along with banks and investment bankers, the major originators of subprime mortgages, were aware that they now had an opportunity that comes maybe once in a generation, and they were quick to exploit it.

Enormous incentives were paid to subprime marketers to encourage sales. Many mortgage bankers (a glorified name for a primarily unscrupulous bunch of mortgage sellers whose ethics make most used-car salesmen appear highly principled) made a million dollars or more a year as well as lavish perks. The merchandise they sold smelled worse than fish left unrefrigerated for days.

The object for the mortgage lenders was to make it easy for borrowers with little or no income or even without jobs to buy homes, by loosening the underwriting standards in the subprimes and Alt A's* enough so that anyone could buy. Quality was of little concern. Everything they bought was immediately packaged with pools of other similar mortgages and sold to hungry clients.

Oh yes, bankers from Citibank, Bank of America, and Wachovia to Goldman Sachs, Morgan Stanley, Lehman Brothers, and Bear Stearns were all major players in the game. They not only bought mortgages from

---

* Alt A's are mortgages with only partial documentation about the buyer, as well as other very flexible requirements.

mortgage bankers but aggressively acquired the mortgage banks them-selves; vertical integration meant even greater profits.*

The bonds were then rated by a credit-rating agency such as Moody's, Standard & Poor's, or Fitch. Normally they were given a credit rating that was, as we'll see, far too high for the quality of the mortgage pool rated. The higher the ratings the banks could get from the rating agencies, the more salable the mortgages were. Nobody cared to look under the hood to see what the collateral really was. It was just merchandise that had to go quickly. And it did, by the hundreds of billions of dollars.

If you've got the stomach, we'll quickly look under the hood. What we see is a variety of products, almost all guaranteed to be major losers for buyers. Let's take a quick peek into a mortgage broker's or originator's office. He has all kinds of goodies to offer the mortgagees to get their business.

"Over here we have the Ninjas, and they're going fast," he might say. "What is a Ninja?" somebody asks. "Well, actually, it's an acronym the sales folk use for this class of mortgage. It stands for mortgages where the buyer has no income, no job, and no assets. But don't worry, the housing market is sizzling and prices will go higher, so you are well protected," the mortgage broker might answer.

"Over there," another salesman might continue, "we're having a spe-cial on negative amortization mortgages. Ninja buyers really like this product." What's that in English? Again, simple! The buyer doesn't have to pay any interest on the mortgages for two or three years and gets to move into the home of his choice immediately. At the end of three years he owes about 140 percent of the original price because of the high interest charged, but no banks or mortgage bankers care. They unload the mort-gages like hot potatoes to their institutional buyers. It all goes down as profit to them and means big commissions today for some, multimillion-dollar bonuses at year-end for others.

Who's going to lend $200,000 to a Ninja buyer who will have to repay about $280,000 in three years and doesn't have a dime? In retrospect, the answer is once again simple—we did, as taxpayers paying off the bank bailout.

---

* Most of the mortgages, secured by the mortgages themselves, were quickly turned into securities and sold as bonds to institutional clients, hedge funds, and scores of other buy-ers. The process is known as securitization.

Next we come to the largest section of the subprime salesroom, featuring the adjustable-rate mortgage, or ARM. Normally customers were lured in with a low teaser rate as bait. Two very popular adjustable-rate mortgages were the 2-28 and the 3-27. The 2-28 gave the mortgagee a low fixed rate of 2 percent for two years and an 11 or 12 percent rate for the next twenty-eight. The 3-27 gave the buyer a 3 percent rate for three years and a 10 to 12 percent rate for the next twenty-seven. Adjustable-rate mortgages were very popular, accounting for 80 percent of all subprime originations in 2005, or more than 1.7 million mortgages, and 70 percent of originations through the entire 2000–2007 boom.[18]

Chairman Greenspan gave subprimes the Fed seal of approval, stating that they were often cheaper than fixed-rate mortgages. Because a conventional fixed-rate mortgage has much lower indirect and hidden charges than a subprime mortgage and the cost to maturity might be 6 percent rather than 10 percent or higher for a subprime mortgage, I don't quite catch his math.

Again, we are just skimming the surface of the subprime and Alt-A universe, but I hope you now have an idea now of what was under the hood. Many of the buyers of subprime loans were decent people. They were taken in by glib salesmen who often specialized in minorities, elderly people, and those who simply could not understand the lengthy and complex mortgage documents they signed. The FBI and local authorities, as well as the courts, have processed thousands of cases from such victims. Angelo Mozilo, the well-coiffed, Brioni-suited, perpetually tanned former CEO of Countrywide Financial and the largest subprime lender, settled with the SEC for $67.5 million for fraud in October 2010.[19]

Sure, there were speculators and hucksters among those taking out these mortgagees, but if someone has a chance to make big returns with little down in a rising market, doing so isn't much different from using cheap margin to buy stocks. And the sellers, if they so chose, had highly sophisticated methods to check buyers' credit and ability to meet payments of both interest and the principal when due—but that was rarely done. From the beginning the subprime industry was fatally flawed. Many people could not even afford the initial "teaser" rates of 2 percent or 3 percent, let alone the quadruple or quintuple rates after twenty-four or thirty-six months. The concept was doomed to fail, and it did.

Where Were the Fed and the Regulators?

It is disturbing that one individual can exert the influence that Alan Greenspan did during his twenty years at the helm.

The Oracle left us with a remarkable record during his tenure as chairman of the Fed. Two of the most serious financial crashes in U.S. history, in 1987 and 2000–2002, took place while he headed the Federal Reserve.* He was also at the helm and played a major role in the real estate bubble from 2002 to 2006, stepping down not long before the largest crash since 1929 and the worst financial crisis in Western history. No other chairman in Fed history has had more than one market debacle during his tenure. The great majority have had none.

Why didn't the Oracle or Ben Bernanke, his successor at the Fed, and other senior Fed officers see the mortgage problems that the national and local press wrote about repeatedly, starting in 2006? Why did they not realize there was a problem until months after the housing market had already turned down?

Nobel laureate Paul Krugman and Pulitzer Prize winner Gretchen Morgenson repeatedly detailed various aspects of the subprime problem dating back to 2006. Possibly Greenspan found *The New York Times* too liberal for him; after all, he is a professed libertarian. But the issues were also covered in *The Wall Street Journal,* and state governments around the country were taking steps to ban some of the worst practices of the mortgage originators. Greenspan admitted back in the fall of 2007 that he did not see the subprime crisis coming, more than ten months after it began.[20] Skimpy regulation practices appear to have been encouraged by the Federal Reserve. And even when Greenspan finally saw the crisis was about to hit, the Fed took no measures to halt some of the most blatant lending practices. In fact, around that time, it took steps to block North Carolina and other states from taking action against federally chartered banks using poor mortgage practices.

As far back as 2000, Greenspan rejected a proposal by Fed Governor Edward Gramlich to have the Fed examine the lending practices not

---

*To be fair, he had come into office only months before the 1987 crash. But he was a strong believer in efficient markets and was likely to have supported the policies that led to the 1987 crash. His statements after the crash support this line of thinking.

just of the banks but of subprime lenders. Gramlich frequently spoke out about the dangers of the latter's sales practices. An expert in the subprime area who realized the major danger that the subprime market would blow up, he pushed hard for greater regulation and spoke to Greenspan about the necessity for it. But mortals don't often defeat gods. Gramlich, one of the real heroes of the period, published a book entitled *Subprime Mortgages: America's Latest Boom and Bust* that strongly warned about those dangers shortly before he died of leukemia in 2007. In 2008, when asked about his failure to perceive the dangers, Greenspan merely said, "I turned out to be wrong, much to my surprise and chagrin."[21] That is scant recompense for the many millions of Americans who suffered from both the crisis and its aftermath.

Greenspan had the authority to control these lending practices under a law passed by Congress in 1994, the Home Ownership and Equity Protection Act (HOEPA), but his antiregulation beliefs were so strong that he was adamant in refusing to do so.

The Fed chairman in 2005 and then his successor, Ben Bernanke, in 2006 completely missed the opportunity to have the Fed take the strong measures necessary to puncture the bubble.[22] Worse, the Fed's refusal to act encouraged practices that led to the victimization of hundreds of thousands of subprime borrowers and a large number of institutional lenders. The Fed was reactive, not proactive, through almost the entire collapse.

By the time the Fed realized the enormity of the problem, it was far too late. In 2007, even after the bubble was already imploding, both Greenspan and Bernanke continued to issue reassuring statements that all was well. Bernanke said in late March 2007, "At this juncture . . . the impact on the broader economy and financial markets of the problems in the subprime market seems likely to be contained."[23] Three months before the collapse of Lehman Brothers, he stated, "The danger that the economy has fallen into a 'substantial downturn' appears to have waned."[24]

How did Greenspan and, to a somewhat lesser extent, Bernanke make blunders of this magnitude? According to Daniel Kahneman, one of the most revealing moments of the 2007–2008 economic meltdown came at a congressional hearing in 2009, when Greenspan admitted that his theory of the world was mistaken. He expected and believed that financial firms would protect their interests, because they are rational companies and the markets are rational, so they would not take risks that would threaten their very existence. Where he went wrong, according to Kahneman, was that there was a huge gulf in the goals between the firms and their managers' (their agents') interests. The firm takes the long view of profitability over time. The agents take a much shorter-term view, basing decisions on possible promotions, large salaries, and bonuses. As we saw, the executives did not commit suicide by taking such risks. They walked away unscathed. It was the corporations they managed that were crippled or committed suicide.

A close friend of Kahneman, Nassim Taleb, author of the financial bestseller *The Black Swan,* put it in these words: "People are simply unwilling to accept the fact that they are actually taking huge risks . . . Alan Greenspan, the former chairman of the Federal Reserve . . . was driving a bus full of children with his eyes closed while he was in office." [25]

Not only were the Fed's actions totally inappropriate to meet the crisis, but with the Fed's hand on the pulse of the economy and with the severe liquidity crisis having already cut deeply into the nation's financial arteries for almost eighteen months, it seemed totally unaware of the forthcoming collapse in September 2008.

Whether the Fed has too much power is a controversial topic. But it certainly appears that the power it has was not used in an appropriate manner during the liquidity crisis and the Great Recession. According to statements by knowledgeable central bankers, including Chairman Bernanke, the Fed also did not use it well during the Great Depression, but at a Fed meeting in Jackson Hole several years before the 2007–2008 meltdown, Bernanke implied that the Fed's methods were now too sophisticated ever to allow a devastating financial crisis to happen again.

Ironically, Congress and the Obama administration gave the Fed even greater supervisory authority in the Financial Reform Act of 2010.

Could such episodes happen again? It's possible. Bernanke did continue Greenspan's policies until it was far too late. Although he said in late 2010 that we needed more regulation, his statements were quite different in early 2007. I don't think Bernanke is another Greenspan, or that he will continue to pursue Greenspan's policies. But what will the next chameleon who becomes chairman do? There is little or nothing to restrain an ideologue who favors libertarianism at one extreme, or socialism at the other, from influencing monetary policy.

Next let's briefly look at another outcome of the Fed and the previous two administrations' support of the destructive non-exchange-traded derivatives, as well as the excess leniency in regulation of the banks in the post-Glass-Steagall environment, which allowed banks and investment bankers to take enormous advantage of the system before bringing themselves and the financial system to the brink of collapse.

Gaming the System

Earlier in the chapter, we glanced briefly at the credit-rating agencies (CRAs), Standard & Poor's, Moody's, and Fitch, and noted that their credit ratings on mortgage-backed securities were far too high. The CRAs had come through the 1929 crash and the Great Depression unscathed, and their ratings through those difficult times had been rock solid. They gained increasing respect over time. Investors relied on them to accurately assess the credit of the company securities they rated, and their decisions were almost universally accepted.

Why, then, did they blemish reputations built up over more than a hundred years? The answer is the same as the one the notorious bank robber Willy Sutton gave in the 1930s when a reporter asked him why he robbed banks: "That's where the money is, stupid." [26]

The three top credit-rating agencies became enormously prosperous, not unlike the mortgage lenders earlier in this chapter. From 2002 to 2007, their revenues more than doubled, from less than $3 billion to over $6 billion. Most of the rapidly increasing revenues came from rating complex financial instruments.

All of the securities sold by banks and investment bankers needed high ratings to sell. Moody's and S&P each issued thousands of AAA credit ratings on subprime mortgage products near the height of the subprime bubble. As Senator Phil Angelides, the chairman of the Financial Crisis Inquiry Commission investigating the credit-rating agencies, said, "Moody's did very well. The investors who relied on Moody's ratings did not fare so well. From 2000 through 2007, Moody's slapped its coveted Triple-A rating on 42,625 residential mortgage backed securities. Moody's was a Triple-A factory. In 2006 alone, Moody's gave 9,029 mortgage-backed securities a Triple-A rating." [27]

Standard & Poor's ran neck and neck. By comparison, only a handful of AAA ratings were given to the strongest U.S. corporations or foreign governments, whose creditworthiness was light-years above that of sub-prime.

The ratings were a very lucrative business for the credit-rating agencies, costing upward of $50,000 for plain-vanilla slices to $1 million or more for supercomplex, multilayered collateralized debt obligations (CDOs).*

The dollar signs were spinning. Moody's gross revenues from residential mortgage-backed securities (RMBS) and CDOs increased from $61 million in 2002 to more than $208 million in 2006. From 1998 to 2007, its revenues from rating complex financial instruments grew by a stunning 523 percent.[28] S&P's annual revenues from ratings more than doubled from $517 million in 2002 to $1.16 billion in 2007. During the 2002–2007 period, its structured finance revenues, a good part of which came from CDOs, more than tripled, increasing from $184 million in 2002 to $561 million in 2007.

Interestingly, after the collapse of thousands of AAA subprime rated issues that led to the worst financial crisis since the Great Depression, Standard & Poor's on August 30, 2011, gave a AAA rating to another subprime borrower. This after it downgraded U.S. Treasuries in the previous month.

Rating agency stock prices tripled or quadrupled, on average, in the 2000–2007 period, while Moody's stock was up more than sixfold. But there would be a terrible price to pay. Like Dr. Faustus, the rating agencies had sold their souls to the Devil.

The banks and investment bankers had a large and growing market for residential mortgage-backed securities, which if sliced and diced properly would give them major underwriting profits from a clientele that could not get enough of the right stuff, which consisted of high ratings from the credit-rating agencies as well as higher yields than they could obtain from non-mortgage-backed bonds or other paper. The bankers found the solution early in the decade: cut the quality of the AAA, AA, and A product, yet retain the same high investment-grade ratings. That was essential for buyers, many of whom could, by law, buy only investment-grade securities.

---

* A collateral debt obligation is a far more leveraged and complex mortgage security backed by a wide range of securitized assets from commercial mortgage-backed securities, credit card debt, non-mortgage bonds, and bank loans to complicated mortgage derivatives. The CDO is originated by a regulated and authorized financial institution.

This solution was not unlike that used by more questionable bars, which water down their Glenfiddich single malts or other good brands, serving them from the original bottles, or by drug dealers who cut their product. The pivotal point was the cooperation of the CRAs. Dozens of underwriters with some of the Street's largest investment bankers, including Merrill Lynch, Citigroup, UBS, Bank of America, Wachovia, Goldman Sachs, Credit Suisse, RBS, Lehman Brothers, and Bear Stearns, had years of experience working with the credit-rating agencies on RMBSs, more specifically subprime. They persuaded the CRAs to go along, using finesse and threats to take their business elsewhere. From that point on, it was a turkey shoot—or, more accurately, a client shoot.

Armed with the best credit ratings money could buy, the bankers sold the toxic mortgages to unsuspecting clients. The product gave the bankers the best of all possible worlds: both significantly higher yields, since a good part of the merchandise was junk, with very high credit ratings. Sales soared into the hundreds of billions of dollars, and the bankers' margins on the business were in the stratosphere.

But the antics only started there. Once the bankers had the high credit ratings in hand, they were able to sell all sorts of complex paper, such as CDOs and structured investment vehicles (SIVs) to their clients. From 2003 to 2006, the demand was almost insatiable; where else could an insurance company, bank or hedge fund, or CDO get a yield like this with a top credit rating? By selling notes and other credit instruments, CDOs, SIVs, and hedge funds leveraged themselves up thirty to thirty-five times the amount of their capital invested, as we saw in chapter 5. Their clients saw consistent returns of up to 15 percent annually or even higher.

The bankers, however, were not happy with the billions of dollars they were making. With a little ingenuity and a lot of inside knowledge of the toxic assets they were selling, they could do even better. More complex derivatives were devised, which the traders dubbed "exotics" and "synthetics," thanks to the work that Robert Rubin, Larry Summers, and Chairman Greenspan had done in pushing through the Commodity Futures Modernization Act of 2000.

Exotics were extremely complex derivatives normally written by a banker who wanted to short certain toxic assets, knowing that the odds were heavily on his side that they would go down in flames. Synthetics allowed a banker to short the worst toxic assets he could find, not once but many times the size of the poor-quality issue itself, by simply replicating these horrific mortgage portfolios. Replication was simple, since there were no rules to follow. All that was needed was the financial details and the composition of the pool of mortgages and the monthly return it provided. The odds for the short sellers of toxic junk were now almost as great as those for the house in our mythical casino. What's more, the payoffs were in the billions rather than in thousands of greenbacks from the players in the casino.

Although there were many players, Goldman Sachs was the superstar, according to the findings and e-mails that were released publicly by the various Senate and House committees investigating the crash and meltdown. Goldman's research in finding the worst groups of subprime or Alt-A mortgages in the marketplace was outstanding. It could then short them to its clients or other buyers, making a killing when they dropped. To get the maximum odds, it wanted to discover not only the poorest issuers of this junk—and there were dozens of them—but the absolutely worst issues each had put out.

To do this, its analysts scoured through every series of mortgages of each bad issuer with a high credit rating. Overall, their detailed research covered thousands of individual series of mortgages. Which of each poor issuer's mortgages, for example, had the worst "Ninja" series, combined with a high rate of negative amortization or other debilitating options, to give Goldman a strong possibility of higher default rates, regardless of how high a credit rating they had been assigned? Dozens of other tools were used by Goldman's highly sophisticated multimillion-dollar-plus research and trading teams. All were out to bag their regular clients or any other potential victim who showed enough life to sign a derivative contract. Goldman was not alone; many of the banks noted above played an identical game, but unquestionably this firm was the champ.

One of its biggest wins was AIG. Goldman and a syndicate of bankers bought credit default swaps, which effectively resulted in their shorting mainly AAA-rated but very poor quality subprime mortgages to AIG, the buyer. The giant insurance company's losses were so huge that it was on the brink of bankruptcy. The New York Fed, then under Timothy Geithner, stepped in and paid the syndicate of banks 100 cents on the dollar, or $62 billion in all.* The inspector general of TARP, Neil Barofsky,

---

* The New York Fed made a $27.1 billion payment and allowed $35 billion of collateral received prior to the transaction to be kept by the syndicate.

stated that the Fed, using taxpayers' money, had overpaid Goldman and the rest of the syndicate by tens of billions of dollars, but that is another story.*

Goldman was bearish on the subprime market and watched it begin to turn down in the fall of 2006. The company wanted to get out of its remaining inventory quickly. The market for subprime was becoming increasingly illiquid, and the sale of its inventory would be difficult and probably go at a sizable discount. What to do? Easy: sell to its own clients. As Table 15-1 shows, Goldman sold six issues totaling $6.5 billion, *all from its own inventory, to clients.* The six new issues of subprime mortgage pools were quickly brought to market in late 2006 and early 2007. Five had AAA ratings on 70 percent to 80 percent of the overall issue.

Goldman knew that the ratings would collapse because of the poor quality of the holdings, since it had been instrumental in getting high ratings on many of them from the rating agencies and had researched them all thoroughly. The largest issue was Hudson Mezzanine, which, although subprime, contained 72 percent of supposedly AAA mortgages. The issue dropped more than 50 percent in less than a year, and Goldman made major money on its sale, while its clients lost a big chunk of their own investment.

In early 2007, as the subprime market began to crumble, Goldman moved quickly to increase the sale of its toxic inventory to clients. Hudson Mezzanine was followed by two more deals, Anderson Mezzanine 2007-1 and Timberwolf 1. In total these two underwritings raised $1.3 billion. What did the clients buy in the "synthetic" packages? Naturally, more of the lethal inventory that Goldman wanted to bail out of. "Boy, that Timberwof [*sic*] was one shitty deal," wrote Thomas Montag, formerly the co-head of the global securities business at Goldman, according to the Levin subcommittee.[29] To sell it, the head of Goldman's Mortgage Department, Daniel Sparks, sent out a mass e-mail promising its sales force "ginormous credits" for disposing of these tainted securities.

The Hudson Mezzanine 2006-1 deal was rated AAA, the highest credit rating that Moody's gives, although it had a major slug of subprime instruments in it. The subprimes were quickly downgraded, and investors lost the majority of their capital, as Table 15-1 shows. Look at row 3,

---

* In a bankruptcy proceeding, the unsecured creditors were likely to receive only a small fraction of this amount years into the future.

which shows the highest credit rating for the issues in early April 2010, prior to their being sold to Goldman clients. Of the six issues, all of which contained sizable AAA portions, credit ratings had been entirely withdrawn by Moody's for two, Hudson Mezzanine and Timberwolf 1. Three others, Long Beach Mortgage Trust 2006-A, Anderson Mezzanine, and Abacus 2007-AC1, were lowered to low junk ratings; only GSAMP 2007-FMI, although downgraded significantly to Baa2 by Moody's, was just barely above junk status. Finally, the underwritings were downgraded very quickly by the credit agencies, the average time being remarkably short—six months.

Obviously, given Goldman's sterling record for integrity in the recent past, it would be hard for any of us not to accept the statements of Goldman's CEO, Lloyd Blankfein, made at the various congressional committee hearings, that Goldman had not been using its formidable research and marketing clout to its benefit against that of its clients. It would be even harder not to accept that a good part of the $11 billion in bonuses Goldman paid out for its 2008 year in early 2009 could not have come from its subprime businesses. Blankfein testified to the committees that the firm had lost money there.* Where it had come from was never quite answered.

Subsequently, in mid-2011, Blankfein and other officers hired criminal attorneys when the United States began a probe of matters raised by the Senate's Permanent Subcommittee on Investigations. The subcommittee report accused Goldman Sachs of misleading clients about complex mortgage-related investments. The subcommittee chairman, Senator Carl Levin, also alleged that Blankfein had misled Congress.[30] Other lawsuits have been filed on a number of highly rated issues Goldman sold or shorted to its clients from its inventory in this period. The odds played by Goldman short selling to its own clients seem above those of the hypothetical casino in the chapter's opening paragraph.

Goldman Sachs was not the only investment bank that was flagged by the House and Senate subcommittees in the 2010 hearings for this type of trading. Investigations are also being carried out at the time of this writing on Morgan Stanley and Citigroup. Goldman has also made a large

---

*Not quite correct. In another internal e-mail Blankfein wrote, "We lost money, then made more than we lost because of the shorts"—presumably a fair amount on the underwritings it sold to its clients described in this section.

	Long Beach Mortgage Loan Trust 2006-A	GSAMP 2007-FM1 (Freemont loans)	Hudson Mezzanine 2006-1	Anderson Mezzanine 2007-1	Timberwolf 1	Abacus 2007 AC1
Size	$495 million	$707 million	$2 billion	$307 million	$1 billion	$2 billion
Percent AAA*	71.0%	77.5%	72.0%	70.2%	80.8%	19.2%
Highest current rating	Ca	Baa2	Withdrawn	Caa3	Withdrawn	Ca

Table 15-1
The Goldman Sachs Conveyor Belt

*All ratings based on Moody's credit ratings.

Source: U.S. Senate Subcommittee on Investigations, April 2010.

settlement with the SEC entailing a payment of $300 million as a fine and $250 million as restitution to the institutional investors involved.

Not only did Goldman and probably many other banks not share the information about those investments with their clients, as was their fiduciary responsibility, but, as we have seen, they actually sold those securities to the clients. Though doing so may not be have been illegal, it certainly seems to have been a breach of ethics that is unforgivable to most. Just as bad, the firm and many others sold tens of billions of dollars' worth of low-quality mortgage-backed securities to their clients in new underwritings when they believed the subprime market was on the verge of collapse. An underwriter has the fiduciary obligation both to provide his clients with his views on the state of the market and to sell them securities he believes are very solid. Goldman and many other firms did neither.

Ironically, in the financial panic beginning in September 2008, there was a run by investors on their assets at Goldman Sachs and Morgan Stanley. The firms were saved only because the Fed transformed them into banks and extended major credit to them, as it was also forced to do with Citigroup. The bailout provided more capital to many of the major domestic banks involved as well. Most of the banks that had been instrumental in causing the crash came out whole, while all too many Americans suffered badly.

Are there lessons here for you as an investor? I think there are several. First, the banks resisted financial reform at every step, in spite of the bailout and the damage they caused. Financial reform will help, but, as noted, it's not perfect; nor has the SEC taken aggressive steps on the matter of conflict of interest—and this seems surprising when it is all over smaller investment firms for even minor technical infractions.

You should stay away from complex products offered by investment firms and banks. If you stick to contrarian strategies, you will be much better off over time. Also, with products not regulated by the SEC, take underwriting ethics with a grain of salt regardless of what you buy. The underwriters at banks and investment banks certainly do.

Chapter 16

The Not-So-Invisible Hand

ADAM SMITH, THE father of free-market economics, wrote about an "invisible hand" in his magnum opus *The Wealth of Nations,* published in 1776. The invisible hand, which guided resources and capital to where they would be most productive, is one of the best-known images in economic literature. In Smith's words, man "neither intends to promote the public interest, nor knows how much he is promoting it . . . He intends only his own gain . . . led by an invisible hand to promote an end which was no part of his intention. . . . By pursuing his own interest he frequently promotes that of the society more effectually than when he really intends to promote it." [1]

Smith was, of course, the major figure in the development of laissez-faire economics, the purest form of free enterprise. He was strongly opposed to monopolies and cartels and warned repeatedly of their "collusive nature," which would fix "the highest prices which can be squeezed out of buyers." [2] Smith also warned that a true laissez-faire economy would quickly become a collusion of business and industry against consumers, which would scheme to influence politics and legislation. So things seem to have turned out pretty much as Adam Smith foresaw.

The last few decades of the twentieth century and the first decade of the twenty-first were a time of economic experimentation for the United States—not at the command of big government or as the result of a clamor for change by the general public but as a result of the great American belief in the power of free markets. This faith was amplified by many leading economists and financial professionals and championed by both Republican and Democratic administrations from at least the time of Ronald Reagan.

Intrinsic to that faith in the market is trust in the operation of an "invisible hand" to guide buyers and sellers to the best possible outcomes. Whether it is housing, autos, construction equipment, goods at Wal-Mart, or products available from online retailers, the market mechanism adjusts supply and demand to reach fair prices, equitable distribution, and socially beneficial results. At any rate, that is the basic theory.

But is the invisible hand currently all that, well, invisible?

In short, some market participants are greatly tempted to "help" the invisible hand reach outcomes favorable to their own personal interests and wallets. This is the sort of anticompetitive behavior and market monopolizing that has been resisted with only partial success in the U.S. economy for generations.

Adam Smith clearly understood the dangers of monopolies and the necessity of their regulation—unlike our Mr. Greenspan, who as we saw in the preceding chapter, despite his reverence for the master, seems to have been more influenced by the school of absolute economic freedom espoused by Ayn Rand. Ironically, the founder of laissez-faire theory would be likely to side with the old trust-busting policies of Teddy Roosevelt in addressing these problems. We saw where Mr. Greenspan stands on this one.

Though the era of unfettered deregulation now seems over, one debate between the invisible hand and the helping hand, if you will, remains as fiercely fought as ever. That is the issue of "free trade." A cause célèbre of long standing, it's now an issue amplified by the concerns of a global economy, and how it plays out in the years ahead will have a formidable potential to enhance or disrupt every investor's holdings, whether domestic or foreign. When it comes to investing, there's no doubt that it's a global world, with an unprecedented level of interconnectedness among the major economies.

Given the world we must deal with, there are two subjects that should be of particular concern for all investors in trying to protect their investments in the global economy. These are the investment implications for the future of free trade (with the related conundrum of fair trade) and the ominous signs of future inflation, the monetary dragon that can never be permanently slain.

▮ The Case for Free Trade

Naturally, Adam Smith was a strong believer in free trade. He opposed the efforts of Alexander Hamilton, our first secretary of the Treasury, to put up barriers to protect the United States' infant industries in the early 1790s, as he was convinced that the country would benefit more by the open export of cheap agricultural commodities, where it had a strong comparative advantage.[3]

The law of comparative advantage has been the core of free-trade belief for almost two hundred years. It was first put forward by David Ricardo, an English economist, in 1817.[4] Ricardo used the example of England and Portugal to illustrate his thesis: Portugal can produce wine and cloth more cheaply than England. But in England wine is very costly to produce while cloth is only moderately more expensive. Even though it's less costly to produce cloth in Portugal than England, it is cheaper still for Portugal to produce more wine and trade that for English cloth. Portugal then has more of both. England also benefits from this trade because its cost of producing cloth is still the same but it can now get wine at a cheaper price, coming out better on the deal. Thus each country can gain by specializing in making the products in which it has a comparative advantage, and trading that good for the other.[5]

Free trade has been one of the most debated topics in economics for the last two hundred years, on economic, moral, and sociopolitical grounds. A recent survey in this country showed that as many as 65 percent of those surveyed were against it. Surprisingly, in high-income groups the percentage is even larger.[6]

In the last few decades, numerous new theories have come out that favor or disfavor free trade. The law of comparative advantage has been challenged, even by numerous new hypotheses that favor free trade. Paul Krugman writes: "Free trade is not passé, but it is an idea that has irretrievably lost its innocence. . . . There is still a case for free trade as a good policy and as a useful target in the practical world of politics, but it can never again be asserted as the policy that economic theory tells us is always right."[7]

Are We in a New Era of Free Trade?

There is one area where the invisible hand continues to face fewer restrictions in this country, even though it sometimes functions poorly. That is free trade. Ricardo's thought, which was true in his time, was that the masses in the Far East and other remote, underdeveloped regions would never be a part of the international labor force. In any case, even if they could be, the cost of shipping raw materials to them and finished goods back to Europe would make the final prices prohibitively high. In the last six decades, however, technology and skilled labor in those nations have turned what was true in the early nineteenth century upside down. Ease of transportation, highly skilled and educated workers, and easy movement of machinery to any country have dramatically lowered the costs of production in Asia and elsewhere.

The result is that higher-wage countries such as the United States are at an enormous disadvantage relative to their low-paying counterparts. In 2008, the average U.S. hourly pay was $18.00. When benefits of $3.60 an hour, including the Social Security tax of 6.2 percent, are added, the average U.S. working hour costs the employer about $22.90. Compare this figure with the average wage in China in 2008 of $2.00 an hour, in Indonesia of $.65 an hour, in India of $.41 an hour, and in Thailand of $1.67 an hour.[8]

The cost of one hour of labor of a Chinese employee is less than 9 percent of the cost of a U.S. employee. In fact, the Social Security tax on the average U.S. hour worked is almost two-thirds of the average Chinese worker's wage and more than three times the average Indian worker's wage. Taking this a step further, in a perfectly competitive world, if there are 150 million workers in the United States and two billion in China, India, Indonesia, and other low-wage Asian countries, the average wage for an American worker manufacturing the same product would have to drop very sharply to be competitive: from $22.90 an hour to a small fraction of this.

This is a worst case scenario, as many jobs obviously cannot be exported, but unfortunately, it contains far more than a grain of truth. It is the reason we are outsourcing millions of our best jobs abroad and will continue to do so in the future. Ricardo could not foresee the future, and most contemporary economists have not focused directly on this problem, which has a number of thorny aspects.

To begin with, American consumers, along with those in almost all countries, want lower-priced goods of equal or even higher quality. This demand fueled the rise of Wal-Mart from a start-up forty-five years ago to the largest chain in the country today. The Wal-Mart revolution has spread to thousands of other businesses in dozens of sectors, all of which must make or sell low-cost products.

Second, low-cost foreign labor allows many businesses to stay competitive with foreign firms. The U.S. auto parts manufacturers were at a competitive disadvantage for years because their foreign counterparts could supply parts at lower prices. The American Big Three had to force a good number of suppliers to open plants in Asia or be dropped. Building plants abroad was the way to survival for many hundreds of industrial companies.

Increasing cost pressures on other industries, plus the natural desire to increase profit margins, have also led U.S. business to use lower-cost services abroad. India, where English is the second language and often the first, is a natural provider of these services. Customer service is provided there for dozens of companies, from United Airlines' reservation, departure, and arrival information to American Express's credit card information to hundreds of other companies' customer service help lines. All displace American jobs at significantly lower wages. But the range of services can also be much broader and more sophisticated: U.S. firms needing software engineers can get the work done for about $10,000 a year in some cases, against the annual cost of $80,000 to $90,000 for a U.S. engineer. Brokerage firms can ship over the daily processing in some departments after the market closes and receive the completed results early the next morning. A good deal of routine accounting can also be e-mailed to India, with the completed work returned promptly at a much lower labor cost.

Although parts of the country are up in arms about illegal aliens crossing our border from Mexico and taking minimum-wage jobs away from Americans, government at the federal level somehow seems less concerned about our losing much higher-paying skilled jobs to Asian and other lower-paying countries.

Obviously, unrestricted free trade is good for consumers and business buyers because it keeps their costs down and should also dampen inflation in many manufactured products. But is it good for the country? Not necessarily, if in the end we lose millions of jobs because of the enormous disparity in wages. If the loss of jobs is significant enough, our purchasing power will go down as a nation and our standard of living will decline. We will be able to buy fewer goods regardless of the prices they are selling at.

The unemployment rate was 9.1 percent in September 2011. Unofficially, including people who are self-employed not by choice, part-time employees, and those who have dropped out of the labor force because of frustration at not finding a job, it was estimated in September 2011 to be 16.5 percent, not much lower than at times during the Great Depression.

For the United States, this could prove extremely damaging. By knowingly exporting high-paying jobs, we are confronting a situation never faced before on a scale of this magnitude. The cost of high unemployment, the social unrest that goes with it, and the continuing erosion of our industrial base could more than offset the benefit of lower-cost imports. Meanwhile, lower import costs here, while threatening our own standard of living, will certainly increase the standard of living of China, India, the Pacific Rim Tigers (Taiwan, Hong Kong, Singapore, and South Korea), and other low-wage countries.

We have the choice of intentionally lowering our standard of living, which we are now actually considering—witness an independent committee proposal to the president in late 2010 to reduce Social Security and other benefits and raise the retirement age over time, as well as the dismissal of teachers and policemen across the country because of lack of funds to pay them. Or we can take affirmative action to protect our standard of living.

The last but most important part of the picture is that almost no country—not even the United States—is really a free trader in the Ricardian sense of the term. Free trade is in reality an economic myth. Most nations are fair traders to a greater or lesser degree. Fair trade usually consists of trading partnerships or alliances based on negotiation, transparency, and dialogue, with the goal of greater equality in international trade. It attempts to offer better trading terms and conditions to cooperating nations as well as securing the rights—read protection—of marginalized producers and workers. Fair traders open their markets to some extent but make sure their workers are not seriously affected. Many countries, including our major trading partners in Asia, such as China, India, and the Pacific Rim Tigers, are certainly questionable even as fair traders.

China is a classic example of unfair trade practices today, just as Japan was twenty-five years back. Like Japan in the 1980s, China is pursuing an export-led growth strategy, limiting domestic consumption, encouraging saving, and guiding investments into strategic industries. It has a multitude of trade barriers and an undervalued currency. It also carefully protects its major markets, where it is at a large competitive disadvantage relative to U.S. competition, by means of a multitude of skillfully constructed trade barriers. A prime example is the financial industry, where the United States has a significant cost advantage. Restrictions on ownership of financial companies and a myriad of other barriers keep the United States from exploiting this. The same protection is used by many other countries to restrict U.S. access to their financial industries.

There are many industries where restrictions are placed on sectors in which the United States or another highly developed nation has a competitive advantage, particularly in service industries and technology. When this occurs repeatedly, we have a new board game called "Free Trade." The object is to parrot the words "free trade" continually while obtaining the largest trade advantage possible. It is like Monopoly in the sense that the winner takes all, but in this version, it is the nation that gains the largest continuing trade surplus by taking in the largest amount of foreign currency that wins.

Adam Smith would call the current trade situation neomercantilism, and from his writings and his letters to Alexander Hamilton, we know he would be strongly opposed to it. About a quarter of *The Wealth of Nations* was devoted to arguments against mercantilism, meaning a policy of protectionism that spurs exports while limiting imports. Free trade cannot exist unless all trading partners subscribe to it, and this is a virtual impossibility in today's world. Would Adam Smith expect any one nation to adopt free-trade policies in a world that does not? I would doubt it, as his was a multinational, not a single-nation, theory.

The United States is not unaware of the game or its tactics, but our major players change with every new administration, while our most wily competitors keep their All-Star trade negotiators playing for their countries for decades. The way the United States is playing the game must be of serious concern. In recent trade negotiations with South Korea, President

Barack Obama offered it the opportunity to build its own jet engines in its own plants in its own country, with U.S. help. If the offer was serious, we would be giving away an industry in which we still have a strong comparative advantage, as well as state-of-the-art technology. This action could allow South Korea to become a low-cost exporter, possibly increasing our trade deficit further and costing us even more skilled jobs.

In late January 2011, General Electric, one of the aviation industry's largest suppliers of airplane technology and jet engines, inked a deal for a joint venture in commercial aviation with a state-owned Chinese company that will share its most advanced airplane electronics, including technology used in Boeing's state-of-the-art 787 Dreamliner. China is seeking technological support in the world's most advanced industries to eventually challenge the best from Boeing and Airbus. Leading technological industries in highly developed countries are trading off their technological expertise for a share of what they hope will prove to be a gigantic Chinese market.[9] The larger the number of advanced companies that play this game, the faster China will probably leap ahead in the development of ultrasophisticated technological products that are likely to increase its exports and reduce the exports of countries with high standards of living. Moreover, the Pacific Rim Tigers, as well as other neomercantilist countries, are also adept at this new variation of "Free Trade," exacerbating the problem further.

China's commitments to strong protection of intellectual property rights are far more often breached than observed. To make matters worse, the Chinese outright piracy and replication of U.S. intellectual property, from computer software to CDs and DVDs of music and entertainment companies to video games to top-of-the-line fashion, runs into the tens of billion of dollars a year. A Bloomberg article estimated in 2010 that the dollar value of pirated software from 2005 to 2009 doubled to 7.58 billion dollars. According to Microsoft Chief Executive Officer Steve Ballmer, "China is a less interesting market to us than India, than Indonesia."[10] One source estimates that of the millions of copies of Microsoft's Windows used in China, only about 20 percent are purchased; the rest are illegally replicated there.[11]

With millions of Chinese entering the ranks of the middle class, knockoffs of such luxury brands as Prada, Louis Vuitton, Burberry, and Rolex are widespread and widely distributed. Movies and other intellectual property of media giants such as Time Warner are also continually pirated, along with those of the music and computer game industry.[12] The Chinese go one step further by not allowing distribution of more than several dozen U.S. movies, all censored, in Chinese movie theaters, whereas the United States allows them to distribute theirs here at much lower royalties.

Unfortunately, the problem does not end here. We are not only exporting jobs to China and other countries with very low-cost wages. Many thousands of other U.S. jobs are lost primarily to China through counterfeiting. Our patents are blatantly ignored, and Chinese workers manufacture American and other industrial countries' products by simply making the goods in China and ignoring patents and copyrights. The magnitude of the counterfeiting is significant. Estimates peg the Chinese counterfeiting at approximately $480 billion worth of goods annually, much of which comes from the United States. The amount is 75 percent larger than the entire U.S. trade deficit to China, which was $273 billion in 2010.[13] Although the sums are enormous, they have received little media exposure. Senator Carl Levin stated at the Congressional Executive China Commission hearing, "The Chinese government itself estimates that counterfeits constitute between 15% and 20% of all products made in China and are equivalent to about 8% of China's annual gross domestic product."[14] The statement was reiterated by Wayne Morrison, Specialist in Asian Trade and Finance, in a Congressional Research Service Report prepared for Congress, January 2011.[15]

China has thus also taken by illegal means many high-quality jobs out of our country and other industrial countries and given them to its own workers, presumably at a much lower cost, by ignoring patents and licenses. As a result, counterfeit goods are a not insignificant part of the Chinese economy, and have proved costly to both U.S. labor and U.S. industries.

Although the Clinton, Bush, and Obama administrations have attempted to stop these and other unfair trade practices, even going to the International Court of Justice, almost no progress has been made. Other factors, including political considerations such as Iran, North Korea, and global warming, mitigate the United States' desire to use stronger tactics.

We also continue to have other major disputes with China. For example, China has turned a deaf ear to our urgings to raise the value of the Chinese currency to a more appropriate level, which would increase our exports to them and decrease our imports. Similar negotiations are going on with several dozen other countries having large trade surpluses with the United States.

How should we deal with these problems—or can we? The most serious is our high rate of unemployment and the question of whether it will become chronic. In the past ten years no new net jobs have been created domestically, while U.S.-China trade alone has eliminated or displaced 2.8 million jobs, as well as others to the Asian Tigers and other low-wage countries, all of whom are not free traders. As noted, figures coming from the Obama administration state that 25 percent of the job losses since the 2007–2008 recession are expected to be permanent. Moreover, the accelerating trend of outsourcing U.S. jobs abroad is showing no sign of abating, which could mean that our unemployment rate will continue to stay high over time.

The shortfall of jobs in the United States is the most significant problem the country has faced in decades. In the four years since the recession began, the U.S. working population has grown by about 3 percent. Jobs in a healthy economy would have grown by the same amount. Today the country has 5 percent fewer jobs than before the last recession began.[16]

There are certainly ways to bring about change. The United States is still a country blessed with almost all the natural resources it needs, other than oil,* as well as the strongest manufacturing and technological base that has ever existed. We could play the trade game the way most countries, including those of the European Union, do by expanding and improving our negotiation capabilities and forcing countries with large trade surpluses to open their important but now restricted markets. There is very little that the Chinese or the Pacific Rim Tigers manufacture that we cannot.

Employing a stronger fair-trade policy, the United States could also erect temporary trade barriers against nations that refuse to open up important markets or that indulge in large-scale piracy: theft of our intellectual property or other products. The penalties would have to be rigorously enforced with major fines or other damages. If the penalties weren't paid, we could perhaps slap on tariffs until they were. This is, of course, only if we could put aside political considerations.

---

* Our gas reserves are enormous and with fracking have increased rapidly in recent years. If we converted our trucking fleets to natural gas, we would significantly reduce our imports of oil while creating thousands of new jobs.

Likewise, with China and other low-wage countries, if we demanded that they adhere to some minimal environmental, worker protection, and employee medical and benefit standards, these standards would raise their labor costs, helping to decrease their exports to us, perhaps significantly. This is dangerous ground and measures other than environmental standards are probably best not approached by the federal government. But we have flirted with such ideas before, with respect to restrictions on child labor and to the strong, effective embargo that was placed by companies, unions, and individuals on South Africa before blacks were given the right to vote in the 1980s.

Similarly, we could follow up with tax credits for companies that increase employment domestically. We could also decrease tax benefits to U.S. companies that continue to increase employment of workers abroad or raise the tax when such firms want to repatriate their earnings unless these funds go into creating jobs in the United States. To date, neither of the two previous administrations, nor any economic theorists, have really taken on or acknowledged the depth of the problem.

Government policy over a number of administrations has helped destroy our auto industry. For almost thirty years our cost per vehicle was $1,500 to $2,000 more than that of foreign competitors. Foreign companies that were not unionized used cheaper labor, while our domestic companies could not. They were also given tax incentives by various states that wanted them to locate in one of their areas. It was only after the bankruptcy of GM and Chrysler that the playing field was finally level, at least for the moment. Ironically, no other major manufacturing country that I can recall has given foreign companies a major competitive advantage in an important home market. Our policy for decades of maintaining unionization for domestic producers, while allowing foreign manufacturers in the United States not to be unionized, puts our domestic auto companies on the chopping block.

The United States cannot be the sole exponent of the very liberal fair-trade policies we practice without the serious consequences discussed. If we continue on our current fair-trade course, we will see an enormous transfer of wealth from the pockets of our citizens into those of China and other Third World countries and quite possibly suffer from chronic unemployment in the process. It's certainly not a problem we want to face, but not facing it is likely to make it progressively worse with time.

At this time, such actions seem nearly impossible, but times change.

If high unemployment remains a serious problem, and little on the horizon indicates that it will not, the fallout from this will affect and alarm increasing numbers of voters. We are seeing a glimpse of this in the demonstrations and crowds camping out near Wall Street and in a number of American cities, as well as in mounting numbers of cities in Europe. The internal political pressures for full employment will mount, and with them the demands for changes in trade policy. Neither political party will be likely to want to oppose this challenge. Whether in two years or five, it is likely that a U.S. administration will eventually start promoting more aggressive policies toward fairer trade.

Adam Smith and David Ricardo both wrote about the merits of free trade. Would they have considered the current problems this nation faces here simply a matter of disagreement among trading nations? I doubt it—particularly when the wealth of the nation, its labor force, is being systematically put out of work or forced to take lower wages. That's how we're managing to freely trade in our high standard of living for something less, especially for our children.

The Case for Future Inflation

Investors have come out of the Great Recession frightened, battered, and with their confidence shaken, if not shattered. How could it be otherwise? What we went through was not a recession but the second worst depression in the nation's history. Economists do not currently use the term "depression" and have not used it since 1945, no matter how bad the downturn has been. The D-word has not been used since the 1930s—not a bad application of Affect theory by economists, but hey, knowing the beating they would take if the D-word had to be used again, it's been any port in a storm.

But whatever the official name of what investors have been through, we are hopefully better armed, with our new psychological tools, than the average investor to deal with what lies ahead. We know the risks of forecasting, something almost nobody can do with precision. We also should remember from chapter 14 that stocks and real estate, along with other similar investments, do very well over time.

What most of us also know (and would not like to remember) is that our government is running some of the biggest budget deficits on record.

This is true not only on an absolute but on a percentage basis: $1.4 trillion in 2009 (fiscal year ending September 30), $1.3 trillion in fiscal 2010, and $1.3 trillion in fiscal 2011, plus more than $2 trillion in other Federal Reserve and Treasury bailout costs and monetary stimuli. The Treasury printed and continues to print enormous amounts of dollars. For a benchmark to measure it against, the entire TARP bailout of the banking system, which has been repaid, totaled $700 billion, or about 12 percent of the money the Treasury has already printed to meet the budget deficits, potential bailouts, and monetary stimuli.

Deficits will continue to push upward if the divided Congress does not cut spending or raise taxes to the tune of $700 billion plus a year. Now that the first waves of terror of the Great Recession are fading into the past, investors are beginning to look beyond sheer survival to what comes next.

What seems likely, even if employment continues to increase at a very modest pace, is that we will see inflation, perhaps modest for the first few years but then accelerating at a more rapid rate. It is not only the United States that has bailed out its economy but most of the world. Stimulus funds to China accounted for $2.1 trillion, the European Union for $500 billion, South Korea for $117 billion, Russia for $111 billion, Brazil for $80 billion, and Canada for $58 billion.[17] Money is being printed on a worldwide basis.

Notably, one of the precursors to actual inflation is the movement in the price of gold. From late October 2008 to the end of August 2011 the price of gold rose $1,117, or 156 percent. Oil and commodity prices have also surged ahead during this same period of time: oil by 42 percent, copper by 149 percent, wheat by 54 percent. The world is awash in currency, with the likelihood that the printing presses will continue 24/7 for months to come, if not longer.

What should the smart investor do? First, *not* what many frightened investors have been doing: selling their stocks and putting the proceeds into Treasuries or bank accounts. In fact, that's the last thing any knowledgeable investor should do today. We have seen how bonds and T-bills outpaced those investments in the period following 1945. With the lowest interest rates since the Great Depression, this is almost undoubtedly going to happen again and hurt large numbers of investors. After 2007–2008, it's like jumping from the frying pan into the fire. Moving heavily into Treasuries or other bonds will seriously compound the damage to portfolios.

During the Great Depression, the deflationary environment protected and increased bond prices until World War II. The situation today is very different. With the rekindling of inflation and a low to almost zero interest rate on Treasuries, the probability of sharp losses to Treasuries, T-bills, and other fixed-income securities—as chapter 14 demonstrated—is high; just how high, we'll see shortly.

I believe we are likely to have a period of very high inflation, possibly as bad as what the nation went through from 1978 through 1982, because of the enormous increase in our money supply since 2008. Printing money is also not likely to stimulate the economy because interest rates on the short end are already touching zero. This appears again to be the typical questionable decision making we've seen from the Federal Reserve in recent decades. Strong opposition exists to the Federal Reserve's buying back Treasuries and, in the process, borrowing more money, in the face of strong criticism from most of our major trading partners. These include not only the Chinese and Russians but also the European Union, particularly Germany and the United Kingdom. Brazil and other emerging economies also fear that by loosening credit the Fed could cause new destabilizing asset bubbles abroad.[18]

The international fear is that this is a blatant attempt by the Fed to weaken the dollar, thereby improving our exports and decreasing our imports. In the process it can cause higher U.S. inflation and, if other countries follow by printing even more money, higher inflation globally.[19] Given this situation, if we had only one trading partner, China, this might be a tool to lower our trade deficit with it, but with well over a hundred trading partners, it is a very dangerous tactic and one that is unlikely to succeed. The outcome would be only more virulent inflation.

In 1978–1982, prices rose at an almost unprecedented 9 percent annual rate. At their worst, long-term Treasuries yielded as much as 15 percent while short-term rates touched 17 percent. To take a worst case, let's assume that the 1978–1982 rate of inflation is repeated and bond yields duplicate those back then. Investors owning a thirty-year Treasury today would see the interest rate rise from 2.9 percent (the September 2011 level) to 15 percent. Treasuries would drop 63 percent, including interest received. But inflation would gobble up another 53 percent of the bonds' purchasing power, so that investors would have only about 17 percent of their original purchasing power left at the end of five years, and that is before taxes on the interest. As you can see again, long bonds are a disaster in this situation. Remember, the shorter the maturity, the less you lose if inflation becomes virulent.

If you agree with this analysis, stay with the recommendations of chapter 14. Stocks will do perfectly well, as they always have done. Studies show that they do well even in periods of hyperinflation. Some years back, Jeremy Siegel, the author of the excellent book *Stocks for the Long Run,* sent me a number of charts, at my request, of how stocks performed in periods of hyperinflation, from the Weimar Republic in Germany in the 1920s to inflation in post–World War II Brazil and Argentina. The purchasing power of those countries' currencies was as little as one-billionth of what it had been previously. Remarkably, in all three cases, after an initial decline for some months, the indices not only adjusted for inflation but also performed considerably better, in line with the Dow and other indices in major industrial countries.

In a depressed market, such as the one we're still in today, we don't have to hit a home run each time at bat. We will do very well by investing in a market index fund. If you believe that contrarian strategies do work over time, you will get significantly higher returns by buying a large, diversified portfolio of contrarian stocks, as chapters 11 and 12 showed, providing much higher returns than the market for decades. Real estate and art are also good hedges for the period I believe we are about to enter, but you have to know what you're doing. Gold will protect you against inflation but will not give you the significantly higher returns that stocks offer over time.

We've come a long way in sixteen chapters. Yes, it is a very different investment world out there today, and it is likely to continue to be difficult for some years to come. But it is not a world without major opportunities. Benjamin Graham used the following epigraph in his book *Security Analysis,* published in 1934, near the bottom of the Great Depression: "Many shall be restored that now are fallen, and many shall fall that are now in honor" (Horace, *Ars Poetica,* 18 B.C.).[20] And so it has always been and will be again.

We have come through a terrifying period, but our system, though banged up, is still intact. And it will recover. The financial damage has been great, but our institutions and our democracy are still very much in place.

Looking back at the Great Depression of the 1930s, now almost eighty years ago, we see a period when the social fabric of the country was severely torn. The U.S. system was sharply criticized by anarchists, Communists, and large numbers of average people, including many thousands of World War I soldiers, who, after having given their all, marched on Washington in 1932 because they believed the country had abandoned them in their destitution. Joseph Kennedy, fearing the dangerous mood at the time and fearing major change in our system, allegedly said he would give up half his wealth in order to be assured his family could enjoy the other half in peace and safety.[21] We are in difficult times today, but we have faced far worse throughout our history.

The tools that we have discussed in this book, almost all based on modern psychology, have worked and, unless human nature changes, should continue to work well in the years ahead. Remember, too, that this is a whole new set of tools that have not been tried by many, partly because of a lack of knowledge of their existence, partly because they have been frowned on by the prevailing academic theory, but mostly because they are psychological. It is hard to stay independent of the acknowledged best thinking of the day, even harder to avoid the strong tug of Affect, neuropsychology, overconfidence, and the plethora of other similar forces that will push at you to go the other way. These forces get to us all at one time or another. As much as I've studied them, they still creep up on me more than I'd like to think.

But if we can know them for what they are, we can not only escape the major damage they can inflict but also harness it. That's the implicit goal of the strategies in this book and the likely result based on all the evidence, research, analysis, investing experience, and sheer hours of sweating the day-to-day technicalities of this new path in markets. Solid contrarian investments, soundly selected and managed, could put us all well ahead.

Good luck to those of you who are willing to try the new psychological way. And good fortune.

ACKNOWLEDGMENTS

THIS BOOK HAS its origins in two camps that have been warring with each other for well over a century. Each has an enormous number of outstanding scholars and other experts on its side, has been rewarded numerous Nobel Prizes, and quite naturally believes that its theories, well defined and well documented scientifically, are the only ones that explain economic and financial behavior correctly. The first camp I am speaking of is that of the economists and financial experts who strongly believe we act with complete rationality in our economic and investment decisions. The second camp is that of the behavioralists, who state that while we can and do act rationally much of the time, we also deviate from this behavior fairly frequently. As luck would have it, from my earliest days on I had a foot in each camp.

My father was a commodities trader and investor who took me to visit the commodity pits starting when I was three. Although he was financially trained, he believed that psychology played a major role in our decisions and continually pointed out why. Naturally, I was influenced by this thinking and found merit in it from the time I was in college to the present.

Over the past several decades, I have been privileged to exchange ideas with many outstanding financial thinkers, including the late Jim Michaels at *Forbes* and Alan Abelson at *Barron's,* as well as large numbers of outstanding investors across the country. I have had the pleasure of many long discussions over time on both financial and behavioral finance with both Arnie Wood, the chairman of Martingale Investments, and Brian Bruce, the editor of *The Journal of Behavioral Finance* and the chairman of Hillcrest Asset Management. Both are avid behavioralists, as well as highly sophisticated investment thinkers.

On the behavioral side, I am privileged to be acquainted with many of the leading figures studying the psychology of markets. I have known and learned a good deal of behavioral psychology from Paul Slovic, whom I have exchanged ideas with for over thirty years, and was honored to coauthor a number of academic articles with, as well as the late Amos Tversky, one of the founders of the field.

In writing this book I have had the very good fortune in working with two people who were not only highly experienced in both investments and behavioral finance but were excellent researchers as well. I owe an enormous debt to Jason Altman, CFA and excellent senior money manager and analyst, who did an outstanding job researching important aspects of this work. I also am indebted to Dr. Vladimira Ilieva, a Ph.D. in behavioral finance, for her scrupulous statistical studies documenting many of the important findings in the text, as well as for her strong research knowledge of the behavioral finance field. Finally, both Mihal Spitzer and Sarah Joyce did a terrific job of making the charts readable. To all four I owe my heartfelt thanks.

My relationship with Simon and Schuster has been a pleasant one, and I'd like to thank my editor, Emily Loose, for the enormous contributions and time that she spent on editing this work.

Naturally, any errors in the work, or what surely some readers will undoubtedly consider misguided thinking, are solely the responsibility of the author.

—David Dreman
September 30, 2011

Notes

INTRODUCTION

1. Bradley Keoun and Phil Kuntz, "Wall Street Aristocracy Got $1.2 Trillion in Secret Loans," *Businessweek*, August 22, 2011.
2. J. C. Bogle, *The Little Book of Common Sense Investing: The Only Way to Guarantee Your Fair Share of Stock Market Returns* (Hoboken, N.J.: Wiley, 2007), p. 81.

CHAPTER 1: PLANET OF THE BUBBLES

1. Charles Mackay, *Extraordinary Popular Delusions and the Madness of Crowds* (New York: Noonday, 1974), p. 55. Originally published in London in 1841 by Richard Bentley.
2. Alan Greenspan, "Economic Volatility," remarks at a symposium sponsored by the Federal Reserve Bank of Kansas City, Jackson Hole, Wy., August 30, 2002.
3. Virginia Cowles, *The Great Swindle: The Story of the South Sea Bubble* (London: Crowley Feature, 1960).
4. Mackay, *Extraordinary Popular Delusions*, pp. 19–20.
5. Ibid.
6. Gustave Le Bon, *The Crowd* (New York: Macmillan, 1896), p. 2.
7. Ibid., pp. 23–57.

CHAPTER 2: THE PERILS OF AFFECT

1. M. L. Finucane, A. Alhakami, P. Slovic, and S. M. Johnson, "The Affect Heuristic in Judgements of Risks and Benefits," *Journal of Behavioral Decision Making* 13 (2000): 1–17.
2. Ibid.
3. Paul Slovic, Melissa L. Finucane, Ellen Peters, and Donald G. MacGregor, "Rational Actors or Rational Fools? Implications of the Affect Heuristic for Behavioral Economics," in *Behavioral Economics and Neoclassical Economics: Continuity or Discontinuity?* Sponsored by the American Institute for Economic Research, Great Barrington, Mass., July 19–21, 2002. This paper is a revised version of Paul Slovic, Melissa Finucane, Ellen Peters, and Donald G. MacGregor, "The Affect Heuristic," in *Heuristics and Biases: The Psychology of Intuitive Judgment,* ed. T. Gilovich, D. Griffin, and D. Kahneman (New York: Cambridge University Press, 2002), pp. 397–420. An earlier version of this paper was published in *Journal of Socio-Economics* 31, No. 5 (2002): 329–342.
4. S. Epstein, "Integration of the Cognitive and Psychodynamic Unconscious," *American Psychologist* 49 (1994): 710.
5. Slovic et al., "Rational Actors or Rational Fools?" p. 17.
6. Ibid., p. 13.
7. G. F. Loewenstein, E. U. Weber, C. K. Hsee, and E. S. Welch, "Risk as Feelings," *Psychological Bulletin* 127 (2001): 267–286.
8. Robert J. Shiller, "Initial Public Offerings: Investor Behavior and Underpricing," Yale University, September 24, 1989. Photocopied.
9. Y. Rottenstreich and C. K. Hsee, "Money, Kisses and Electric Shocks: On the Affective Psychology of Risk," *Psychological Science* 12 (2001): 185–190.
10. B. Fischhoff, P. Slovic, S. Lichtenstein, and B. Coombs, "How Safe Is Safe Enough? A Psychometric Study of Attitudes Towards Technological Risks and Benefits," *Policy Sciences* 9 (1978): 127–152.
11. P. Slovic, D. G. MacGregor, T. Malmfors, and I. F. H. Purchase, *Influence of Affective Processes on Toxicologists' Judgements of Risk.* Report No. 99-2 (Eugene, Ore.: Decision Research, 1999).
12. Slovic et al., "Rational Actors or Rational Fools?" p. 17.
13. A. S. Alhakami and P. Slovic, "A Psychological Study of the Inverse Relationship Between Perceived Risk and Perceived Benefit," *Risk Analysis* 14, No. 6 (1994): 1085–1096.
14. Y. Ganzach, "Judging Risk and Return of Financial Assets," *Organizational Behavior and Human Decision Processes* 83 (2001): 353–370.
15. D. T. Gilbert, E. C. Pinel, T. D. Wilson, S. J. Blumberg, and T. P. Wheatley, "Immune Neglect: A Source of Durability Bias in Affective Forecasting," *Journal of Personality and Social Psychology* 75 (1998): 617–638.
16. Y. Trope and N. Liberman, "Temporal Construal and Time-Dependent Changes in Preference," *Journal of Personality and Social Psychology* 79 (2000): 876–889. Y. Trope and N. Liberman, *Temporal Construal* (New York: New York University, Department of Psychology, 2001).
17. D. Dreman, S. Johnson, D. MacGregor, and P. Slovic, "A Report on the March 2001 Investor Sentiment Survey," *Journal of Psychology and Financial Markets* 2 (2001): 126–134.

18. Slovic et al., "The Affect Heuristic."

19. Sidney Cottle, Roger F. Murray, and Frank E. Block, *Graham and Dodd's Security Analysis,* 5th ed. (New York: McGraw-Hill, 1988).

CHAPTER 3: TREACHEROUS SHORTCUTS IN DECISION MAKING

1. Scott Plous, *Psychology of Judgment and Decision Making* (New York: McGraw-Hill, 1993).

2. "Death Odds," *Newsweek,* September 24, 1990, p. 10.

3. *Jaws.* Zanuck/Brown Productions Universal Pictures, 1975.

4. Amos Tversky and Daniel Kahneman, "Judgments Under Uncertainty: Heuristics and Biases," *Science* 185 (1974): 1124–1130.

5. Baruch Fischhoff, "Debiasing," in *Judgment Under Uncertainty: Heuristics and Biases,* ed. D. Kahneman, P. Slovic, and A. Tversky (New York: Cambridge University Press, 1982).

6. A. Tversky, P. Slovic, and D. Kahneman (eds.), *Judgment Under Uncertainty: Heuristics and Biases* (New York: Cambridge University Press, 1982).

7. Amos Tversky and Daniel Kahneman, "Availability: A Heuristic for Judging Frequency and Probability," *Cognitive Psychology* 5 (1973): 207–232.

8. Amos Tversky and Daniel Kahneman, "Intuitive Predictions: Biases and Corrective Procedures," *Management Science,* Spring 1981; Amos Tversky and Daniel Kahneman, "Causal Schemata in Judgments Under Uncertainty," in *Progress in Social Psychology,* ed. M. Fishbein (Hillsdale, N.J.: Lawrence Erlbaum Associates, 1973); Don Lyon and Paul Slovic, "Dominance of Accuracy Information and Neglect of Base Rates in Probability Estimation," *Acta Psychologica* 40, No. 4 (August 1976): 287–298.

9. Amos Tversky and Daniel Kahneman, "Belief in the Law of Small Numbers," *Psychological Bulletin* 76 (1971): 105–110.

10. Value Line New Issue Survey.

11. T. Loughran and J. Ritter, "The New Issues Puzzle," *Journal of Finance* 50, No. 1 (1995): 23–51.

12. J. R. Ritter, "The Long-Run Performance of Initial Public Offerings," *Journal of Finance* 46, No. 1 (1991): 3–27.

13. David Dreman and Vladimira Ilieva, "The Performance of IPO's during the Great Bubble 1996–2002," working paper, The Dreman Foundation, 2011.

14. H. Nejat Seyhun, "Information Asymmetry and Price Performance of IPOs," working paper, University of Michigan, 1992.

15. M. Levis, "The Long-Run Performance of Initial Public Offerings: The UK Experience 1980–88," *Financial Management* 22 (1993): 28–41.

16. Bharat Jain and Omesh Kini, "The Post-Issue Operating Performance of IPO Firms," *Journal of Finance* 49 (1994): 1699–1726.

17. Loughran and Ritter, "The New Issues Puzzle," 46.

18. Tversky, Slovic, and Kahneman, *Judgment Under Uncertainty.*

19. David Dreman, "Let's Hoard Crude Oil," *Forbes,* June 8, 2009, p. 104.

20. Tversky and Kahneman, "Belief in the Law of Small Numbers."

21. Tversky and Kahneman, "Judgment Under Uncertainty: Heuristics and Biases," pp. 1125–1126; Tversky and Kahneman, "Intuitive Predictions," pp. 313–327.

22. Looking back briefly to "Judgments of Risk and Benefit Are Negatively Correlated," on page 39, again we see this important psychological discovery played out clearly

in the market. Investors believed not only that the dazzling performance of stocks during the bubble would provide better returns but that these stocks would prove to be less risky than the far safer but less exciting stocks in the S&P 500. The psychologists' results in chapter 2 were thus dead-on. Neither investor assumption was correct: higher-performing stocks were not less but more risky than the far safer stocks in the S&P 500. Too, the S&P 500 didn't go down nearly as much as the "hot hand" stocks after the market's terrifying break. The S&P 500 also outperformed the "hot hand" stocks by a good margin over time.

23. Reed Abelson, "From Bulls to Bears and Back Again," *The New York Times,* July 28, 1996, p. D1.

24. Robert McGough and Patrick McGeehan, "Garzarelli Proves She Can Still Roil the Market," *The Wall Street Journal,* July 24, 1996, p. C1.

25. James Cramer, The Street, December 29, 1999.

26. Tversky and Kahneman, "Causal Schemata in Judgments Under Uncertainty"; Daniel Kahneman and Amos Tversky, "On the Psychology of Prediction," *Psychological Review* 80 (1973): 237–251.

27. Paul Slovic, Baruch Fischhoff, and Sarah Lichtenstein, "Behavioral Decision Theory," *Annual Review of Psychology* 28 (1977): 1–39.

28. Kahneman and Tversky, "On the Psychology of Prediction."

29. The reader may observe that this is the same course of action recommended in discussing the "inside view" versus the "outside view" in chapter 8.

30. Tversky and Kahneman, "Judgment Under Uncertainty"; Tversky and Kahneman, "Intuitive Predictions."

31. Kahneman and Tversky, "On the Psychology of Prediction."

32. Roger G. Ibbotson and Rex A. Sinquefield, *Market Results for Stocks, Bonds, Bills and Inflation for 1926–2010, 2011 Classic Yearbook* (Chicago: Morningstar, 2011); Roger G. Ibbotson and Rex A. Sinquefield, *Stocks, Bonds, Bills, and Inflation: The Past (1926–1976) and the Future (1977–2000)* (Charlottesville, Va.: Financial Analysts Research Foundation, 1977).

33. "The Death of Equities," *BusinessWeek,* August 13, 1979.

34. Tversky and Kahneman, "Intuitive Predictions."

35. Herbert Simon, "Theories of Decision Making in Economics and Behavioral Sciences," *American Economic Review* 49 (1959): 273.

36. Ibid., pp. 306–307.

37. B. Shiv and A. Fedorikhin, "Heart and Mind in Conflict: Interplay of Affect and Cognition in Consumer Decision Making," *Journal of Consumer Research* 26 (1999): 278–282.

38. Nelson Cowan, "The Magical Number 4 in Short-Term Memory: A Reconsideration of Mental Storage Capacity," *Behavioral and Brain Sciences* 24 (2000): 87–185.

39. Kahneman and Tversky, "On the Psychology of Prediction."

40. Tversky and Kahneman, "Judgment Under Uncertainty."

41. Benjamin Graham, David Dodd, Sidney Cottle, and Charles Tatham, *Security Analysis,* 4th ed. (New York: McGraw-Hill, 1962), p. 424.

42. See, e.g., George Katona, *Psychological Economics* (New York: American Elsevier, 1975).

43. S. C. Lichtenstein and Paul Slovic, "Reversals of Preference Between Bids and Choices in Gambling Decisions," *Journal of Experimental Psychology* 89 (1971): 46–55; S. C. Lichtenstein, B. Fischhoff, and L. Phillips, "Calibration of Probabilities: The State of

the Art," in *Decision Making and Change in Human Affairs,* ed. H. Jungermann and G. de Zeeuw (Amsterdam: D. Reidel, 1977).

44. Baruch Fischhoff, "Hindsight Does Not Equal Foresight: The Effect of Outcome Knowledge on Judgment Under Uncertainty," *Journal of Experimental Psychology: Human Perception and Performance* 1 (August 1975): 288–299; Baruch Fischhoff, "Hindsight: Thinking Backward?" *Psychology Today,* April 1975, p. 8; Baruch Fischhoff, "Perceived Informativeness of Facts," *Journal of Experimental Psychology: Human Perception and Performance* 3 (1977): 349–358; Baruch Fischhoff and Ruth Beyth, "I Knew It Would Happen: Remembered Probabilities of Once-Future Things," *Organizational Behavior and Human Performance* 13, No. 1 (1975): 1–16; Paul Slovic and Baruch Fischhoff, "On the Psychology of Experimental Surprises," *Journal of Experimental Psychology: Human Perception and Performance* 3 (1977): 511–551.

45. John F. Lyons, "Can the Bond Market Survive?" *Institutional Investor* 3 (May 1969): 34.

CHAPTER 4: CONQUISTADORS IN TWEED JACKETS

1. Winston Churchill, radio speech, 1939.

2. Edward Gibbon, *The History of the Decline and Fall of the Roman Empire,* Vol. 6, chap. 37, para. 619.

3. Louis Bachelier, "Théorie de la Speculation," trans. A. James Boness, in *The Random Character of Stock Market Prices,* ed. Paul H. Cootner (Cambridge, Mass.: MIT Press, 1964), pp. 17–78.

4. Harry V. Roberts, "Stock Market Patterns and Financial Analysis: Methodological Suggestions," *Journal of Finance* 14 (March 1959): 1–10.

5. M. F. M. Osborne, "Brownian Motion in the Stock Market," *Operations Research* 7, No. 2 (March–April 1959): 145–173.

6. Fischer Black, "Implications of the Random Walk Hypothesis for Portfolio Management," *Financial Analyst Journal* 27, No. 2 (March–April 1971): 16–22.

7. Arnold B. Moore, "Some Characteristics of Changes in Common Stock Prices," in *The Random Character of Stock Market Prices,* ed. Paul H. Cootner (Cambridge, Mass.: MIT Press, 1964), pp. 139–161.

8. Clive W. J. Granger and Oskar Morgenstern, "Spectral Analysis of New York Stock Market Prices," *Kyklos* 16 (1963): 1–27.

9. Eugene F. Fama, "The Behavior of Stock Market Prices," *Journal of Business* 38 (January 1965): 34–105.

10. Eugene F. Fama, "Efficient Capital Markets: A Review of Theory and Empirical Work," *Journal of Finance* 25 (May 1970): 383–417.

11. Fama, "The Behavior of Stock Market Prices."

12. Black, "Implications of the Random Walk Hypothesis."

13. Burton G. Malkiel, *A Random Walk Down Wall Street* (New York: Norton, 1973), p. 126.

14. Black, "Implications of the Random Walk Hypothesis."

15. Fama, "Efficient Capital Markets."

16. Benjamin Graham and David Le Fevre Dodd, *Security Analysis* (New York: McGraw-Hill, 1951).

17. Alfred Cowles III, "Can Stock Market Forecasters Forecast?" *Econometrica* 1, Issue B

(1933): 309–324; Alfred Cowles, "Stock Market Forecasting," *Econometrica* (1944): 206–214.

18. Irwin Friend, Marshall Blume, and Jean Crockett, *Mutual Funds and Other Institutional Investors: A New Perspective, Twentieth Century Fund Study* (New York: McGraw Hill, 1971).

19. Michael Jensen, for example, measured the record of 155 mutual funds between 1945 and 1964, adjusting for risk as the academics defined it, and found that only 43 of 115 funds outperformed the market after commissions. In 1970, Irwin Friend, Marshall Blume, and Jean Crockett of the Wharton School made the most comprehensive study of mutual funds to that time. They measured 136 funds between January 1, 1960, and June 30, 1968, and found that the funds returned an average of 10.7 percent annually. During the same time span, shares on the New York Stock Exchange averaged 12.4 percent annually. With value weighting for the number of outstanding shares of each company (which gave far more emphasis to the changes of the larger companies), the increase was 9.9 percent. See Michael C. Jensen, "The Performance of Mutual Funds in the Period 1945–1964," *Journal of Finance* 23 (May 1968): 389–416; and Friend, Blume, and Crockett, *Mutual Funds and Other Institutional Investors*.

20. No-load funds and funds with low sales charges perform marginally better.

21. Eugene F. Fama, Lawrence Fisher, Michael Jensen, and Richard Roll, "The Adjustment of Stock Prices to New Information," *International Economic Review* 10 (February 1969): 1–21; James H. Lorie and Mary T. Hamilton, *The Stock Market: Theories and Evidence* (Homewood, Ill.: Dow Jones-Irwin, 1973), pp. 171ff.

22. Ray Ball and Phillip Brown, "An Empirical Evaluation of Accounting Income Numbers," *Journal of Accounting Research* 6 (Fall 1968): 159–178.

23. Here the efficient-market theorists acknowledge a paradox. Since it is fundamental analysis that is largely responsible for keeping markets efficient, if enough practitioners believed the efficient-market hypothesis and stopped their analytic efforts, markets might well become inefficient.

24. Daniel Seligman, "Can You Beat the Stock Market?" *Fortune,* December 26, 1983, p. 84.

25. James H. Lorie and Victor Niederhoffer, "Predictive and Statistical Properties of Insider Trading," *Journal of Law and Economics* 11 (April 1968): 35–53.

26. Fama, "Efficient Capital Markets."

27. Eugene F. Fama, "Efficient Markets: II," *Journal of Finance* 46 (December 1991): 1575–1617.

28. Eugene F. Fama, "Market Efficiency, Long-Term Returns, and Behavioral Finance," *Journal of Financial Economics* 49 (1998): 283–306.

29. Fama, "Efficient Markets: II."

30. Ibid.

31. Seligman, "Can You Beat the Stock Market?"

32. Paul H. Cootner, "Stock Prices: Random Versus Systematic Changes," *Industrial Management Review* (Spring 1962): 25.

CHAPTER 5: IT'S ONLY A FLESH WOUND

1. Bob Tamarkin, *The New Gatsbys: Fortunes and Misfortunes of Commodities Traders* (New York: Morrow, 1985).
2. William Glaberson, "How Risk Rattled the Street," *The New York Times,* November 1, 1987.
3. Tamarkin, *The New Gatsbys.*
4. Ibid.
5. Hayne E. Leland, "Who Should Buy Portfolio Insurance?" *Journal of Finance* 35, No. 2 (May 1980): 581–594.
6. Barbara Donnelly, "Is Portfolio Insurance All It's Cracked Up to Be?" *Institutional Investor* II (November 1986): 124–139. Quote is on p. 126.
7. Roger Lowenstein, *When Genius Failed: The Rise and Fall of Long-Term Capital Management* (New York: Random House, 2000).
8. Ibid.
9. Ibid.
10. Ibid., p. 78.
11. Ibid., p. 159.
12. Paul Krugman, "How Did Economists Get It So Wrong?" *The New York Times,* September 6, 2009.
13. John Cassidy, "Rational Irrationality: Interview with Eugene Fama," *The New Yorker,* January 13, 2010. Online at www.newyorker.com.

CHAPTER 6: EFFICIENT MARKETS AND PTOLEMAIC EPICYCLES

1. Maurice A. Finocchiaro, *Retrying Galileo, 1633–1992* (London: University of California Press, 2007).
2. J. Michael Murphy, "Efficient Markets, Index Funds, Illusion, and Reality," *Journal of Portfolio Management* 4, No. 1 (1977): 5–20.
3. Ibid. See also Shannon Pratt, "Relationship Between Variability of Past Returns and Levels of Future Returns for Common Stocks, 1926–60," *Business Valuation Review* 27, No. 2 (Summer 2008); Fischer Black, Michael Jensen, and Myron Scholes, "The Capital Asset Pricing Model: Some Empirical Tests," in *Studies in the Theory of Capital Markets,* ed. M. Jensen (New York: Praeger, 1972); R. Richardson Pettit and Randolph Westerfield, "Using the Capital Asset Pricing Model and the Market Model to Predict Securities Returns," *Journal of Financial and Quantitative Analysis* 9, No. 4 (September 1974): 579–605 (published by the University of Washington School of Business Administration); Merton Miller and Myron Scholes, "Rates of Return in Relation to Risk: A Re-Examination of Some Recent Findings," in *Studies in the Theory of Capital Markets,* ed. M. Jensen (New York: Praeger, 1972); Nancy Jacob, "The Measurement of Systematic Risk for Securities and Portfolios: Some Empirical Results," *Journal of Financial and Quantititative Analysis* 6 (March 1971), pp. 815–833 (published by Cambridge University Press).
4. Dale F. Max, "An Empirical Examination of Risk-Premium Curves for Long-Term Securities, 1910–1969," unpublished Ph.D. thesis, University of Iowa, 1972, microfilm Order No. 73-13575.
5. Marshall Blume and Irwin Friend, "A New Look at the Capital Asset Pricing Model,"

in *Methodology in Finance-Investments,* ed. James L. Bicksler (Lexington, Mass.: Heath-Lexington, 1972), pp. 97–114.

6. Albert Russell and Basil Taylor, "Investment Uncertainty and British Equities," *Investment Analyst* (December 1968): 13–22.

7. Quoting J. Michael Murphy, "Efficient Markets" (the foregoing three citations are references made by Murphy within the quoted passage).

8. Robert A. Haugen and James A. Heins, "Risk and the Rate of Return on Financial Assets: Some Old Wine in New Bottles," *Journal of Financial and Quantitative Analysis* (December 1975): 775–784.

9. Paul Krugman, "How Did Economists Get It So Wrong?" *The New York Times,* September 6, 2009.

10. Eugene Fama and James MacBeth, "Risk, Return, and Equilibrium: Empirical Tests," *Journal of Political Economy* 81 (1973): 607–636; see also Eugene Fama, "Efficient Capital Markets: A Review of Theory and Empirical Works," *Journal of Finance* 25 (1970): 383–417.

11. See Eugene Fama and Kenneth French, "The Cross Section of Expected Stock Returns," *Journal of Finance* 67 (1992): 427–465.

12. See Eric N. Berg, "Market Place: A Study Shakes Confidence in the Volatile-Stock Theory," *The New York Times,* February 18, 1992, p. D1.

13. Bill Barnhart, "Professors Say Beta Too Iffy to Trust: A Substitute Stock Scorecard Is Proposed," *Chicago Tribune,* July 27, 1992, p. 3.

14. Terence P. Pare, "The Solomon of Stocks Finds a Better Way to Pick Them," *Fortune,* June 1, 1992, p. 23.

15. Bill Barnhart, "Professors Say Beta Too Iffy."

16. Mary Beth Grover, "Slow Growth," *Forbes,* October 12, 1992, p. 163.

17. David Dreman, "Bye-Bye to Beta," *Forbes,* March 30, 1992, p. 148.

18. Barnhart, "Professors Say Beta Too Iffy."

19. Eugene F. Fama and Kenneth R. French, "The CAPM Is Wanted Dead or Alive," *Journal of Finance* 5, Issue 5 (December 1996): 1947–1958.

20. Ibid.

21. Eugene F. Fama, "Market Efficiency, Long-Term Returns, and Behavioral Finance," *Journal of Financial Economics* 49 (1998): 208–306.

22. George M. Frankfurter, "The End of Modern Finance," *Journal of Investing* 3, No. 3 (Fall 1994).

23. The impact of beta went far beyond the market. The capital asset pricing model had long been used by corporate managers to determine the attractiveness of new ventures. Because the accepted wisdom holds that companies with higher betas must pay commensurately higher returns, chief financial officers of high-beta companies might be loath to invest in new plants unless they feel they can earn the extra dollop of return. As one business consultant said, "Dethroning the model may have been the best thing that has happened to American business" (Pare, "The Solomon of Stocks"). CAPM, it seems, resulted in bad business decisions in corporate America for a long time.

24. Jonathan Burton, "Revisiting the Capital Asset Pricing Model," interview with William Sharpe, *Dow Jones Asset Manager* (May–June 1998): 20–28. Cited with permission.

25. Milton Friedman, "The Methodology of Positive Economics," in *Essays on Positive Economics* (Chicago: University of Chicago Press, 1953), p. 15.

26. Fama, "Market Efficiency."

27. Fama, "Efficient Capital Markets."

28. EMH thus creates something of a paradox, for if professionals are important to the operation of the efficient market—if they do help to keep price synonymous with value—they must also, according to EMH, be dismal failures in the primary goal of their profession: helping their clients outperform the market.

29. J. Michael Murphy, "Efficient Markets, Index Funds, Illusion, and Reality."

30. Ibid., p. 10.

31. Michael C. Jensen, "The Performance of Mutual Funds in the Period 1945–1964," *Journal of Finance* 23 (May 1968): 389–416.

32. J. Michael Murphy, "Efficient Markets, Index Funds, Illusion, and Reality."

33. As indicated, this would exclude a minute number of extraordinarily skilled professionals using extensive resources for only their own benefit.

34. Tim Loughran and Jay Ritter, "The New Issues Puzzle," *Journal of Finance* 50, No. 1 (1995): 23–51.

35. Fama and French, "The Cross-Section of Expected Stock Returns."

36. Burton G. Malkiel, *A Random Walk Down Wall Street* (New York: Norton, 1973).

37. R. Ball and P. Brown, "An Empirical Evaluation of Accounting Income Numbers," *Journal of Accounting Research* 6 (1968): 159–178.

38. V. Bernard and J. Thomas, "Evidence That Stock Prices Do Not Fully Reflect the Implications of Current Earnings for Future Earnings," *Journal of Accounting and Economics* 13 (1990): 205.

39. Fama, "Market Efficiency."

40. Eugene Fama, Lawrence Fisher, Michael Jensen, and Richard Roll, "The Adjustment of Stock Prices to New Information," *International Economic Review* 10 (1969): 1–21.

41. See chap. 17 in *Contrarian Investment Strategies: The Next Generation* for more details and an examination of the chart.

42. David L. Ikenberry, Graeme Rankine, and Earl K. Stice, "What Do Stock Splits Signal?" *Journal of Financial and Quantitative Analysis* 31, No. 3 (September 1996): 357–375.

43. Hemang Desai and Prem C. Jain, "Long-Run Common Stock Returns Following Stock Splits and Reverse-Splits," *Journal of Business* 70 (1997): 409–433.

44. Ray Ball and Philip Brown, "An Empirical Evaluation of Accounting Income Numbers."

45. Myron S. Scholes, "The Market for Securities: Substitution Versus Price Pressure and the Effects of Information on Share Prices," *Journal of Business* 45 (1972): 179–211.

46. Eugene Fama, "Efficient Capital Markets: II," *Journal of Finance* 46 (1991): 1601.

47. Gregor Andrade, Mark Mitchell, and Erik Stafford, "New Evidence and Perspectives on Mergers," *Journal of Economic Perspectives* 15, No. 2 (2001): 103–120; Michael C. Jensen and Richard S. Ruback, "The Market for Corporate Control: The Scientific Evidence," *Journal of Financial Economics* 11 (1983): 5–50; Gregg A. Jarrell, James A. Brickley, and Jeffry M. Netter, "The Market for Corporate Control: The Empirical Evidence Since 1980," *Journal of Economic Perspectives* 2, No. 1 (1998): 49–68.

48. Roni Michaely, Richard H. Thaler, and Kent Womack, "Price Reactions to Dividend Initiations and Omissions: Overreaction or Drift?" NBER working paper series no. 4778 (Cambridge: National Bureau of Economic Research, 1994).

49. Victor Bernard and Jacob Thomas, "Evidence That Stock Prices Do Not Fully Reflect the Implications of Current Earnings for Future Earnings," *Journal of Accounting and*

Economics 13 (1990): 305–340; Victor Bernard and Jacob Thomas, "Post-Earnings-Announcement Drift: Delayed Price Response or Risk Premium?" *Journal of Accounting Research* 27(S) (1989): 1–36; George Foster, Chris Olsen, and Terry Shevlin, "Earnings Releases, Anomalies, and the Behavior of Security Returns," *Accounting Review* 59 (1984): 574–603; Ray Ball and Philip Brown, "An Empirical Evaluation of Accounting Income Numbers."

50. Jeffery Abarbanell and Victor Bernard, "Tests of Analysts' Overreaction/Underreaction to Earnings Information as an Explanation for Anomalous Stock Price Behavior," *Journal of Finance* 47 (1992): 1181–1206.

51. See, e.g., Tables 11-1 and 12-1.

52. Robert J. Shiller, "Do Stock Prices Move Too Much to Be Justified by Subsequent Changes in Dividends?" *American Economic Review* 71 (1981): 421–436.

53. Ibid., pp. 432–433.

54. Edward M. Saunders, Jr., "Testing the Efficient Market Hypothesis Without Assumptions," *Journal of Portfolio Management* (Summer 1994): 28.

55. Karl R. Popper, *The Logic of Scientific Discovery* (New York: Basic Books, 1959).

56. David N. Dreman, *Psychology and the Stock Market* (New York: AMACOM, 1977), p. 221.

57. Alfred W. Stonier and Douglas C. Hague, *A Textbook of Economic Theory* (London: Longmans, Green, 1953), p. 2.

58. Krugman, "How Did Economists Get It So Wrong?"

59. Joseph Stiglitz, "Information and the Change in the Paradigm in Economics," Nobel Prize lecture, December 8, 2001, pp. 519–520.

60. Tim Icano, "How Did Economists Fail Us So Badly?" *The Wall Street Journal,* November 30, 2010.

61. John Cassidy, "The Decline of Economics," *The New Yorker,* December 2, 1996, pp. 50–60.

62. Ibid.

63. Ibid.

64. Thomas S. Kuhn, *The Structure of Scientific Revolutions* (Chicago: University of Chicago Press, 1970).

65. Ibid., p. 23.

66. Ibid., p. 52.

CHAPTER 7: WALL STREET'S ADDICTION TO FORECASTING

1. Woody Guthrie, "Pretty Boy Floyd," *Dust Bowl Ballads,* 1939, RCA.

2. P. J. Hoffman, P. Slovic, and L. G. Rorer, "An Analysis of Variance Model for the Assessment of Configural Cue Utilization in Clinical Judgment," *Psychological Bulletin* 69 (1968): 338–349.

3. These can combine into fifteen possible two-way interactions, twenty possible three-way interactions, fifteen possible four-way interactions, six possible five-way interactions, and one six-way interaction.

4. L. G. Rorer, P. J. Hoffman, B. D. Dickman, and P. Slovic, "Configural Judgments Revealed," in *Proceedings of the 75th Annual Convention of the American Psychological Association* 2 (Washington, D.C.: American Psychological Association, 1967), pp. 195–196.

5. Lewis Goldberg, "Simple Models or Simple Processes? Some Research on Clinical Judgments," *American Psychologist* 23 (1968): 338–349.

6. Paul Slovic, "Analyzing the Expert Judge: A Descriptive Study of a Stockbroker's Decision Processes," *Journal of Applied Psychology* 53 (August 1969): 225–263; P. Slovic, D. Fleissner, and W. S. Bauman, "Analyzing the Use of Information in Investment Decision Making: A Methodological Proposal," *Journal of Business* 45, No. 2 (1972): 283–301.

7. Goldberg, "Simple Models or Simple Processes?"

8. Paul Slovic, "Behavioral Problems Adhering to a Decision Policy," IGRF Speech, May 1973.

9. Dale Griffin and Amos Tversky, "The Weighing of Evidence and the Determinants of Confidence," *Cognitive Psychology* 24 (1992): 411–435; S. Lichtenstein and B. Fischhoff, "Do Those Who Know More Also Know More About How Much They Know? The Calibration of Probability Judgments," *Organizational Behavior and Human Performance* 20 (1977): 159–183.

10. W. Wagenaar and G. Keren, "Does the Expert Know? The Reliability of Predictions and Confidence Ratings of Experts," in *Intelligent Decision Support in Process Environments,* ed. E. Hollnagel, G. Maneini, and D. Woods (Berlin: Springer, 1986), pp. 87–107.

11. Stewart Oskamp, "Overconfidence in Case Study Judgments," *Journal of Consulting Psychology* 29 (1965): 261, 265.

12. L. B. Lusted, *A Study of the Efficacy of Diagnostic Radiology Procedures: Final Report on Diagnostic Efficacy* (Chicago: Efficacy Study Committee of the American College of Radiology, 1977).

13. J. B. Kidd, "The Utilization of Subjective Probabilities in Production Planning," *Acta Psychologica* 34 (1970): 338–347.

14. M. Neal and M. Bazerman, *Cognition and Rationality in Negotiation* (New York: Free Press, 1990).

15. C. A. S. Stael von Holstein, "Probabilistic Forecasting: An Experiment Related to the Stock Market," *Organizational Behavior and Human Performance* 8 (1972): 139–158.

16. S. Lichtenstein, B. Fischhoff, and L. Phillips, "Calibration of Probabilities: The State of the Art to 1980," in *Judgment Under Uncertainty: Heuristics and Biases,* ed. D. Kahneman, P. Slovic, and A. Tversky (Cambridge, England: Cambridge University Press, 1982).

17. G. Keren, "Facing Uncertainty in the Game of Bridge: A Calibration Study," *Organizational Behavior and Human Decision Processes* 39 (1987): 98–114; D. Hausch, W. Ziemba, and M. Rubenstein, "Efficiency of the Market for Racetrack Betting," *Management Sciences* 27 (1981): 1435–1452.

18. J. Frank Yates, *Judgment and Decision Making* (Englewood Cliffs, N.J.: Prentice-Hall, 1990).

19. *Wall Street Transcript* 45, No. 13 (September 23, 1974).

20. Herbert Simon, *Models of Man: Social and Rational* (New York: Wiley, 1970).

21. The belief that all paranoid patients accentuate certain characteristics in their drawings belongs in the category of psychologists' old wives' tales.

22. L. Chapman and J. P. Chapman, "Genesis of Popular but Erroneous Psychodiagnostic Observations," *Journal of Abnormal Psychology* (1967): 193–204; L. Chapman and J. P. Chapman, "Illusory Correlations as an Obstacle to the Use of Valid Psychodiagnostic Signs," *Journal of Abnormal Psychology* (1974): 271–280.

23. Amos Tversky, "The Psychology of Decision Making," in *Behavioral Finance and Decision Theory in Investment Management,* ed. A. Wood, ICFA Continuing Education Series (Stanford, Calif.: Stanford University Press, 1995), pp. 2–6.
24. Ibid.
25. Ibid., p. 6.
26. Ibid.
27. Jennifer Francis and Donna Philbrick, "Analysts' Decisions as Products of a Multi-Task Environment," *Journal of Accounting Research* 31 (Autumn 1993): 216–230.
28. A Ph.D. in astrophysics who worked for the Dreman Foundation.
29. For details, please see David N. Dreman, *The New Contrarian Investment Strategy* (New York: Random House, 1982), app. I, pp. 303–307.
30. "Vanderheiden Choices Top Other Pickers," *The Wall Street Journal,* January 3, 1994, p. R34; John R. Dorfman, "'Value' Still Has Value, Says This Quartet of Stock Pickers," *The Wall Street Journal,* January 4, 1993, p. R8; John R. Dorfman, "Cyclicals Could Be the Right Way to Ride to New Highs in 1992," *The Wall Street Journal,* January 2, 1992, p. R24; John R. Dorfman, "New Year's Stock Advice in an Icy Economy: Insulate," *The Wall Street Journal,* January 2, 1991, p. R22; John R. Dorfman, "The Sweet Smell of Success Might Be One of Caution," *The Wall Street Journal,* January 2, 1990, p. R6; John R. Dorfman, "Champion Stock-Picker Is Facing 3 Challengers for Title," *The Wall Street Journal,* January 3, 1989, p. R6; John R. Dorfman, "Four Investment Advisors Share Their Favorite Stock Picks for 1988," *The Wall Street Journal,* January 4, 1988, p. 6B; John R. Dorfman, "Stock Pickers Nominate Big Gainers for 1987," *The Wall Street Journal,* January 2, 1987, p. 4B; Rhonda L. Rundle, "Stock Pickers Make Their Picks Public, Betting on Low Inflation, Falling Rates," *The Wall Street Journal,* January 2, 1986, p. R4.
31. Just as the theory holds that even professionals cannot outdo the market over time, it also holds that they cannot do substantially worse. After all, it is their very decision making that keeps prices at the proper level in the first place. The surveys, however, give us a different picture from the one assumed by the theorists. The massive underperformance in both up and down markets indicates that their most crucial assumption is inconsistent with a significant body of evidence. The hypothesis is made of straw.

CHAPTER 8: HOW BIG A LONG SHOT WILL YOU PLAY?

1. Ben White, "On Wall Street, Stock Doublespeak; Public, Private Talk at Odds, Papers Show," *The Washington Post,* April 30, 2003, p. E01.
2. Gretchen Morgenson, "Bullish Analyst of Tech Stocks Quits Salomon," *The New York Times,* August 16, 2002.
3. "The Superstar Analysts," *Financial World,* November 1980, p. 16.
4. Ibid.
5. Ibid.
6. David Dreman, "Cloudy Crystal Balls," *Forbes,* Vol. 154, Issue 8, October 10, 1994, p. 154; David Dreman, "Chronically Cloudy Crystal Balls," *Forbes,* Vol. 152, Issue 8, October 11, 1993, p. 178; David Dreman, "Flawed Forecasts," *Forbes,* Vol. 148, Issue 13, December 9, 1991, p. 342; David Dreman, "Hard to Forecast," *Barron's,* March 3, 1980, p. 9; David Dreman, "Tricky Forecasts," *Barron's,* July 24, 1978, pp. 4–5, 16,

18; David Dreman, "The Value of Financial Forecasting: A Contrarian's Approach," speech at Fortieth Annual Meeting of the American Financial Association, December 29, 1981. In June 1996, the study was updated again in collaboration with Eric Lufkin, formerly of the Dreman Foundation.

7. David Dreman and Michael Berry, "Analyst Forecasting Errors and Their Implications for Security Analysis," *Financial Analysts Journal* 51 (May–June 1995): 30–41.

8. The average of the forecasts of the analysts covering the company. Studies have shown that these estimates are reasonably closely bunched.

9. Before the early 1980s, the database used the forecasts of analysts in the Value Line Investment Survey, which normally were very close to consensus forecasts.

10. We used the database of Abel/Noser Corporation, which contains estimates from the leading forecast services: Value Line prior to 1981, Zacks Investment Research beginning in 1981, and I/B/E/S beginning in 1984. The utilized portion of the database includes 500,000 individual estimates. Eric Lufkin, formerly of the Dreman Foundation, updated the findings for the 1991–1996 period using Abel/Noser Corporation data through 1993Q3 and I/B/E/S estimates thereafter. Thomson First Call provided the data for 1997–2010.

11. The four separate error metrics:

> SURPE = (Actual earnings – Forecast) / |Actual earnings|
> SURPF = (Actual earnings – Forecast) / |Forecast|
> SURP8 = (Actual earnings – Forecast) / Standard deviation of actual earnings, eight quarters trailing
> SURPC7 = (Actual earnings – Forecast) / Standard deviation of change in actual earnings, seven quarters trailing.

All the results in the book are for SURPE: forecast error divided by actual earnings.

12. With signs removed. We recorded a total of 189,158 surprises in expansions (104,538 positive and 69,411 negative) and 36,901 surprises in recessions (19,477 positive and 14,941 negative). Note that positive surprises outnumbered negative surprises in both expansions and recessions. Surprises of zero, although not true surprises, have been retained in calculations of all surprises, because they count in assessing analysts' overall accuracy.

13. Dov Fried and Dan Givoly, "Financial Analysts' Forecasts of Earnings: A Better Surrogate for Market Expectations," *Journal of Accounting and Economics* 4 (1982): 85–107; Patricia C. O'Brien, "Analysts' Forecasts as Earnings Expectations," *Journal of Accounting and Economics* 10 (1988): 53–83; K. C. Butler and L. H. Lang, "The Forecast Accuracy of Individual Analysts: Evidence of Systematic Optimism and Pessimism," *Journal of Accounting Research* 29 (1991): 150–156; M. R. Clayman and R. A. Schwartz, "Falling in Love Again: Analysts' Estimates and Reality," *Financial Analysts Journal* (September–October 1994): 66–68; A. Ali, A. Klein, and J. Rosenfeld, "Analysts' Use of Information About Permanent and Transitory Earnings Components in Forecasting Annual EPS," *Accounting Review* 87 (1992): 183–198; L. Brown, "Analysts' Forecasting Errors and Their Implications for Security Analysis: An Alternative Perspective," *Financial Analysts Journal* (January–February 1996): 40–47.

14. J. G. Cragg and B. Malkiel, "The Consensus and Accuracy of Some Predictions of the Growth of Corporate Earnings," *Journal of Finance* 23 (March 1968): 67–84.

15. Ibid. You may recall the Meehl studies of clinical psychologists, where it was shown

that simple mechanical techniques performed as well as or better than the complex analytical diagnoses in twenty separate studies of trained psychologists. In fact, mechanical prediction formulas have been suggested in a number of fields, primarily psychology, as a direct result of these problems, and they will be a part of the strategies proposed in the following chapters.

16. I. M. D. Little, "Higgledy Piggledy Growth," *Bulletin of the Oxford University Institute of Economics and Statistics* (November 1962): 31.

17. I. M. D. Little and A. C. Rayner, *Higgledy Piggledy Growth Again* (Oxford: Basil Blackwell, 1966).

18. See, e.g., Joseph Murray, Jr., "Relative Growth in Earnings per Share—Past and Future," *Financial Analysts Journal* 22 (November–December 1966): 73–76.

19. Richard A. Brealey, *An Introduction to Risk and Return from Common Stocks* (Cambridge, Mass.: MIT Press, 1968).

20. François Degeorge, Jayendu Patel, and Richard Zeckhauser, "Earnings Management to Exceed Thresholds," *Journal of Business* 72, no. 1 (January 1999): 1–33.

21. John Dorfman, "Analysts Devote More Time to Selling as Firms Keep Scorecard on Performance," *The Wall Street Journal,* October 29, 1991, p. C1.

22. Ibid. See also Amitabh Dugar and Siva Nathan, "Analysts' Research Reports: Caveat Emptor," *Journal of Investing* 5 (Winter 1996): 13–22.

23. Michael Siconolfi, "Incredible Buys: Many Companies Press Analysts to Steer Clear of Negative Ratings," *The Wall Street Journal,* July 19, 1995, p. A1.

24. Ibid., p. 3; Debbie Gallant, "The Hazards of Negative Research Reports," *Institutional Investor* (July 1990): 73–80.

25. Siconolfi, "Incredible Buys."

26. E. S. Browning, "Please Don't Talk to the Bearish Analyst," *The Wall Street Journal,* May 2, 1995, p. C1.

27. Dugar and Nathan, "Analysts' Research Reports."

28. Siconolfi, "Incredible Buys."

29. Ibid.

30. D. Kahneman and A. Tversky, "On the Psychology of Prediction," *Psychological Review* 80 (1973): 237–251.

31. D. Kahneman and D. Lovallo, "Timid Choices and Bold Forecasts: A Cognitive Perspective on Risk Taking," *Management Science* 39 (January 1993): 1–16.

32. E. Merrow, K. Phillips, and C. Myers, *Understanding Cost Growth and Performance Shortfalls in Pioneer Process Plants* (Santa Barbara, Calif.: Rand Corporation, 1981).

33. J. Arnold, "Assessing Capital Risk: You Can't Be Too Conservative," *Harvard Business Review* 64 (1986): 113–121.

CHAPTER 9: NASTY SURPRISES AND NEUROECONOMICS

1. For greater detail, see David Dreman, "Don't Count on Those Earnings Forecasts," *Forbes,* Vol. 161, Issue 2, January 26, 1998, p. 110; David Dreman and Michael Berry, "Overreaction, Underreaction, and the Low-P/E Effect," *Financial Analysts Journal* 51 (July–August 1995): 21–30; David Dreman, "Nasty Surprises," *Forbes,* July 19, 1993, p. 246.

2. We formed the portfolios at the beginning of the first quarter and measured earnings surprises thereafter.

3. Compustat, provided by Standard & Poor's, is one of the largest stock databases available, giving price, earnings, and other information on more than 34,000 stocks. The studies reported here use the largest 1,500 companies in the Compustat database traded on the NYSE, AMEX, and NASDAQ exchanges, as measured by the total market value of all shares outstanding at the beginning of each calendar year. (This sample is referred to here as the Compustat 1500.) We use the Compustat database for all price and accounting information.

4. To control for negative earnings, we delete companies with no earnings or negative earnings. We also delete P/E multiples above 45 (over 75 from 1997 on), to control for stocks with nominal earnings as a result of poor quarters. In doing so, we also unfortunately lose some of the most highly favored issues.

5. Ibbotson® SBBI®, *2011 Classic Yearbook: Market Results for Stocks, Bonds, Bills and Inflation, 1926–2010.*

6. Jennifer Francis and Donna Philbrick, "Analysts' Decisions as Products of a Multi-Task Environment," *Journal of Accounting Research* 31 (Autumn 1993): 216–230.

7. The T-statistics show that the probability that these results are just chance is less than 1 in 1,000, often much less.

8. Jeffery Abarbanell and Victor Bernard, "Tests of Analysts' Overreaction/Underreaction to Earnings Information as an Explanation for Anomalous Stock Price Behavior," *Journal of Finance* 47 (July 1992): 1181–1208; V. Bernard and J. K. Thomas, "Evidence That Stock Prices Do Not Fully Reflect the Implications of Current Earnings for Future Earnings," *Journal of Accounting and Economics* 13 (1990): 305–340.

9. Eric Lufkin and I came up with findings similar to those of Abarbanell and Bernard. We also discovered that after the surprise quarter, stocks in the high-, low-, and middle-P/E groups (with positive surprises in that quarter) outperformed those stocks in the same groups without positive surprises for the next three quarters. (The same was true for price-to-book-value and price-to-cash-flow measures.) This seems to be caused by additional positive surprises, if the initial surprise was positive—or negative surprises, if the initial surprise was negative—in the three succeeding quarters, again indicating that analysts' forecasts do not adjust quickly to changing conditions.

10. Jason Zweig, *Your Money and Your Brain: How the New Science of Neuroeconomics Can Help Make You Rich* (New York: Simon and Schuster, 2007), p. 66.

11. Ibid., p. 64.

12. Ibid.

13. Pammi V. S. Chandrasekhar, C. Monica Capra, Sara Moore, Charles Noussair, and Gregory S. Berns, "Neurobiological Regret and Rejoice Functions for Aversive Outcomes," *NeuroImage* 39 (2008): 1472–1484.

14. Wolfram Schultz, Paul Apicella, Eugenio Scarnati, and Tomas Ljungberg, "Neuronal Activity in Monkey Ventral Striatum Related to the Expectation of Reward," *Journal of Neuroscience* 12 (1992): 4595–4610.

15. Jason Zweig, "Your Money and Your Brain."

16. W. Schultz and A. Dickinson, "Neuronal Coding of Prediction Errors," *Annual Review of Neuroscience* 23 (2000): 473–500.

17. Chandrasekhar et al., "Neurobiological Regret and Rejoice Functions," p. 1479.

18. Ibid. Though the fMRI has not yet been used on earnings surprise, dozens of similar tests have been done with parallel results in many areas, including finance, to investigate the neural correlates of regret and rejoice, disappointment and elation.

19. Zweig, "Your Money and Your Brain."

20. Schultz and Dickinson, "Neuronal Coding of Prediction Errors."
21. Chandrasekhar et al., "Neurobiological Regret and Rejoice Functions."

CHAPTER 10: A POWERFUL CONTRARIAN APPROACH TO PROFITS

1. Francis Nicholson, "Price-Earnings Ratios in Relation to Investment Results," *Financial Analysts Journal* 24, No. 1 (January–February 1968): 105–109.
2. Francis Nicholson, in an earlier test that eliminated companies with nominal earnings, measured the performance of high- and low-P/E stocks in the chemicals industry between 1937 and 1954. The results strongly favored the low-P/E stocks. James McWilliams used a sample of nine hundred stocks from the S&P Compustat tapes in the 1953–1964 period and found strong corroboration of the better performance of low-P/E stocks. McWilliams further discovered that although stocks having the highest individual appreciation in any given year appeared to be randomly distributed, those with the greatest declines were in the high-P/E group. William Breen used the 1,400 companies on the Compustat tapes for the 1953–1966 period. He eliminated all stocks with less than 10 percent earnings growth and then set up portfolios of ten stocks with the lowest P/Es relative to the market, comparing them with a series of randomly selected portfolios of ten stocks in each year. See Francis Nicholson, "Price/Earnings Ratios," *Financial Analysts Journal* 16 (July–August 1960): 43–45; James D. McWilliams, "Prices and Price-Earnings Ratios," *Financial Analysts Journal* 22 (May–June 1966): 137–142; William Breen, "Low Price/Earnings Ratios and Industry Relatives," *Financial Analysts Journal* 24 (July–August 1968): 125–127.
3. See Table 7-3, "A Workable Investment Strategy," in David Dreman, *Contrarian Investment Strategies: The Next Generation* (New York: Simon and Schuster, 1998), p. 147.
4. David Dreman, "A Strategy for All Seasons," *Forbes,* July 14, 1986, p. 118.
5. David Dreman, "Getting Ready for the Rebound," *Forbes,* July 23, 1990, p. 376.
6. We used the same methodology in all my studies, as is outlined in chapter 11.
7. David Dreman, "Cashing In," *Forbes,* June 16, 1986, p. 184.
8. Within the experimental design, we adjusted for methodological criticisms of previous studies, such as hindsight bias—selecting stocks, as Nicholson did, that had survived to 1962, something an investor of 1937 could not have known—and not using year-end earnings and prices, as previous studies did, when investors could not know earnings until several months later. I did not think those would markedly change the results, and our findings indicate that they didn't.
9. Sanjoy Basu, "Investment Performance of Common Stocks in Relation to Their Price-Earnings Ratios: A Test of the Efficient Markets Hypothesis," *Journal of Finance* 32 (June 1977): 663–682; Sanjoy Basu, "The Effect of Earnings Yield on Assessments of the Association Between Annual Accounting Income Numbers and Security Prices," *Accounting Review* 53 (July 1978): 599–625; Sanjoy Basu, "The Relationship Between Earnings' Yield, Market Value and Return for NYSE Common Stocks: Further Evidence," *Journal of Financial Economics* 12 (June 1983): 129–156.
10. Basu, "Investment Performance of Common Stocks."
11. B. Rosenberg, K. Reid, and R. Lanstein, "Persuasive Evidence of Market Inefficiency," *Journal of Portfolio Management* 13 (1985): 9–17; Dennis Stattman, "Book Values and Stock Returns," *Chicago MBA: A Journal of Selected Papers* 4 (1980): 25–45.

12. Eugene Fama and Kenneth French, "The Cross-Section of Expected Stock Returns," *Journal of Finance* 47 (June 1992): 427–465.
13. Ray Ball, "Anomalies in Relationships Between Securities' Yields and Yield-Surrogates," *Journal of Financial Economics* 6 (1978): 103–126.
14. Fama and French, "The Cross-Section of Expected Stock Returns."
15. Terence Pare, "The Solomon of Stocks Finds a Better Way to Pick Them," *Fortune*, June 1, 1992, p. 23.
16. J. Lakonishok, A. Shleifer, and R. Vishny, "Contrarian Investment, Extrapolation, and Risk," *Journal of Finance* 49 (December 1994): 1541–1578.
17. D. G. MacGregor, P. Slovic, D. Dreman, and M. Berry, "Imagery, Affect and Financial Judgment," Decision Research Report 97-11 (Eugene, Ore., 1997).

CHAPTER 11: PROFITING FROM INVESTORS' OVERREACTIONS

1. "Investors Lack Exposure to Contrarian Value Investing Strategies," presentation given to David Dreman of Dreman Value Management, LLC, by DWS Scudder Deutsche Bank Group. Sources: Deutsche Asset Management, Inc., and Morningstar, Inc., 2006.
2. Sanjoy Basu, "Investment Performance of Common Stocks in Relation to Their Price-Earnings Ratios," *Journal of Finance* 32, No. 3 (June 1977): 663–682.
3. Werner F. M. De Bondt and Richard Thaler, "Does the Stock Market Overreact?" *Journal of Finance* (July 1985): 793–805.
4. The original investor overreaction hypothesis was updated in David Dreman and Michael Berry, "Overreaction, Underreaction and the Low P/E Effect," *Financial Analysts Journal* (July–August 1995): 21–30.
5. David N. Dreman and Eric A. Lufkin. "Investor Overreaction: Evidence That Its Basis Is Psychological," *Journal of Psychology and Financial Markets* 1, No. 1 (2000): 61–75.
6. For an overview of standard risk-return models, see Zvi Bodie, Alex Kane, and Alan Marcus, *Investments,* 9th ed. (New York: McGraw-Hill/Irwin, 2010).
7. The Compustat database comprises most of the major companies traded in this country, as well as some hundreds of ADRs traded abroad.
8. The methodology is identical to that in our study described in chapter 9, page 219.
9. Back in Graham's time, investors used actual book value to price, whereas today most contemporary investors use relative book value, the book value of the company relative to its industry or the market. The reason is that with inflation increasing prices manyfold in the post–World War II period, the replacement costs of land, plant, and equipment are substantially higher than the values shown on most corporate balance sheets. The average company in the S&P 500 currently trades at 1.9 times its book value.
10. Although not shown in the chart, all three strategies continue to outperform for up to ten years. For those of a statistical bent, the t-tests are also high. For example, low P/E has only a 1 in 200 probability of being pure chance, low price to cash flow has 1 in 200, and price to book has 1 in 100. With the best stocks by each value measurement, the probability is 1 in 20. The t-tests are generally weaker on the high-P/E side, but 1 in 20 (the "95 percent confidence level") is generally considered the basic threshold for significance.

11. Financial studies have indicated that well-diversified portfolios of as few as sixteen stocks have an excellent chance of replicating approximately 85 percent to 90 percent of the return of the group from which they are selected, even if the group is the stock market as a whole.

12. The large-company rule is not etched in stone, however. As chap. 15 of *Contrarian Investment Strategies: The Next Generation* (1998) demonstrates, small contrarian companies provide somewhat higher returns over time than their larger siblings. But the small-cap strategy is entirely different and requires substantial resources to implement properly. It should normally be used for only a relatively small portion of your stock portfolio.

13. Andrew Ross Sorkin and Landon Thomas, Jr., "J.P. Morgan Acts to Buy Bear Stearns at Huge Discount," *The New York Times,* March 16, 2008.

14. Robin Sidel, David Enrich, and Dan Fitzpatrick, "WaMu Is Seized, Sold Off to J.P. Morgan, in Largest Failure in U.S. Banking History," *The Wall Street Journal,* September 26, 2008.

15. David Ellis and Jeanne Sahadi, "JPMorgan to Buy WaMu," CNN Money, September 26, 2008.

16. See the performance of contrarian strategies including bear markets in chapter 10. In *The New Contrarian Investment Strategy,* I gave a similar record of performance from the 1976–1982 period, one of moderate market decline. The approach significantly outperformed the S&P 500 during that earlier period, too.

17. The results are taken from the twenty-seven-year study from 1970 to 1996 that I did in collaboration with Eric Lufkin, which I have updated through 2010.

18. Other studies over sixty years come up with similar results.

19. This is for one quarter. For one year, there would be twenty-five draws with the card returned to the deck.

20. The numbers are startling but true. To follow up, we did a Monte Carlo simulation with 100,000 trials. Low P/E won 99,891 times.

CHAPTER 12: CONTRARIAN STRATEGIES WITHIN INDUSTRIES

1. This work is based in part on an exchange of ideas between Sanjoy Basu and myself. Basu produced preliminary results that, unfortunately, were lost after his untimely death in 1983.

2. The previous literature on whether contrarian strategies worked included William Breen, "Low Price-Earnings Ratios and Industry Relatives," *Financial Analysts Journal* (July–August, 1968): 125–127. Breen analyzed low-P/E stocks for one-year periods between 1953 and 1966. He found that stocks with low absolute P/E did only slightly better than stocks with the lowest P/E in an industry. However, the test used extremely small samples of ten stocks each. R. Fuller, L. Huberts, and M. Levinson, "Returns to E/P Strategies, Higgledy-Piggledy Growth, Analysts' Forecast Errors, and Omitted Risk Factors," *Journal of Portfolio Management* (Winter 1993): 13–24, found that low P/Es within industries outperform the market.

3. The original study by Eric Lufkin and me covered the period 1973–1996. We used a government industry classification system that was discontinued in the late 1990s. The industry taxonomy developed by Standard & Poor's and Morgan Stanley Capital International called Global Industry Classification Standard (GICS) classifies

industries more accurately for financial use. Reliable historical data for the newer classification start in 1995.

4. The industries that had the largest numbers of the absolutely cheapest stocks only marginally outperformed the averages, with returns well below those gained by the industry-relative strategy.

5. Benjamin Graham, David Dodd, Sidney Cottle, and Charles Tatham, *Security Analysis*, 4th ed. (New York: McGraw-Hill, 1962), p. 179.

6. Since I use large-cap companies in this strategy, the reader would be shielded from the frenetic small-cap concept stocks and IPOs, which were not a part of our study and which I doubt would come close to these results.

CHAPTER 13: INVESTING IN A NEW, ALIEN WORLD

1. Rob Iati, "The Real Story of Trading Software Espionage," *Advanced Trading*, July 10, 2009. Online at http://www.advancedtrading.com/algorithms/218401501.

2. Kambiz Foroohar, "Trading Pennies into $7 Billion Drives High-Frequency's Cowboys," *Bloomberg*, October 6, 2010.

3. Jim McTague, "The Real Flash-Crash Culprits," *Barron's*, October 9, 2010. Online at http://online.barrons.com/article/58500042405.html.

4. "Preliminary Findings Regarding the Market Events of May 6, 2010—Report of the Staffs of the CFTC and SEC to the Joint Advisory Committee on Emerging Regulatory Issues—May 18, 2010," p. 65.

5. Ibid.

6. Foroohar, "Trading Pennies into $7 Billion."

7. Whitney Kisling, "Fund Outflows Top Lehman at $75 Billion," *Bloomberg*, September 19, 2011.

8. Tom Lauricella, "Pivot Point: Investors Lose Faith in Stocks," *The Wall Street Journal*, September 26, 2011.

9. Jenny Strasburg, "A Wild Ride to Profits," *The Wall Street Journal*, August 16, 2011.

10. Nina Mehta, "High-Frequency Firms Tripled Trades Amid Rout, Wedbush Says," *Bloomberg*, August 12, 2011.

11. CNBC, *Fast Money*, August 8, 2011.

12. Kevin Drawbaugh, "SEC Head Eyes Fast Traders on Crash Anniversary," *Reuters*, May 6, 2011.

13. Jenny Strasburg and Jean Eaglesham, "Subpoenas Go Out to High-Speed Trade Firms," *The Wall Street Journal*, August 8, 2011.

14. Mehta, "High-Frequency Firms Tripled Trades Amid Rout, Wedbush Says."

15. Tim Cave, "European Regulator Moves to Limit High-Speed Trading," *Financial News*, July 21, 2011.

16. Jacob Bunge and Brendan Conway, "Regulators Hone Circuit-Breaker Proposals," *The Wall Street Journal*, September 28, 2011.

17. The record of these mutual funds can be found in the *Forbes 2010 Mutual Fund Guide*. Similar information on no-load funds can be found on Lipper, Morningstar, or Barron's.

CHAPTER 14: TOWARD A BETTER THEORY OF RISK

1. Frank H. Knight, *Risk, Uncertainty, and Profit,* Hart, Schaffner, and Marx Prize Essays, No. 31 (Boston and New York: Houghton Mifflin, 1921):

   > Uncertainty must be taken in a sense radically distinct from the familiar notion of Risk, from which it has never been properly separated. The term "risk," as loosely used in everyday speech and in economic discussion, really covers two things which, functionally at least, in their causal relations to the phenomena of economic organization, are categorically different. . . . The essential fact is that "risk" means in some cases a quantity susceptible of measurement, while at other times it is something distinctly not of this character; and there are far-reaching and crucial differences in the bearings of the phenomenon depending on which of the two is really present and operating. . . . It will appear that a measurable uncertainty, or "risk" proper, as we shall use the term, is so far different from an unmeasurable one that it is not in effect an uncertainty at all. We . . . accordingly restrict the term "uncertainty" to cases of the non-quantitative type.

2. Jeremy J. Siegel, *Stocks for the Long Term* (New York: Irwin), 1994.
3. FDIC, *Trust Examination Manual,* section 3, "Asset Management," Part 1, "Investment, Principles, Policies and Products."
4. Ibbotson® SBBT®, *2011 Classic Yearbook: Market Results for Stocks, Bonds, Bills and Inflation for 1926–2010.* Growth of $100,000 for long-term government bonds adjusted for inflation from 1946 to 2010.
5. Tax Foundation, "Federal Individual Income Tax Rates History," www.taxfoundation .org/files/fed_individual_rate_history-20110323.pdf.
6. An earlier version of this chart is found in David Dreman, *Contrarian Investment Strategies: The Next Generation* (New York: Simon and Schuster, 1998), p. 314.

CHAPTER 15: THEY'RE GAMBLING WITH YOUR MONEY

1. David Dreman, "Bailout Blues," *Forbes,* Vol. 182, Issue 10, November 17, 2008, p. 136.
2. Frank Partnoy, "The Case Against Alan Greenspan," *Euromoney Institutional Investor,* September 1, 2005, p. 2.
3. Lucette Lagnado, "After the Bubble, Beauty Is But Fleeting for Greenspan Portraits," *The Wall Street Journal,* February 19, 2010.
4. Alex MacCallum, "Want Alan Greenspan to Come to Dinner? That'll Be $250,000," Huffington Post, March 28, 2008.
5. Partnoy, "The Case Against Alan Greenspan."
6. "The Tragedy of Robert Rubin, the Fall of Citigroup, and the Financial Crisis—Continued," The Strange Death of Liberal America, November 30, 2008, http:// thestrangedeathofliberalamerica.com/the-tragedy-of-robert-rubin-the-fall-of-citi group-and-the-financial-crisis-continued.html.
7. Peter S. Goodman, "Taking a Hard Look at a Greenspan Legacy," *The New York Times,* October 9, 2008.
8. Marshall Auerback, "Robert Rubin Is Back: Noooooo!!!" Business Insider, January 5, 2010.
9. Robert Scheer, "The Rubin Con Goes On," *The Nation,* August 11, 2010.

10. Ibid.
11. Goodman, "Taking a Hard New Look at a Greenspan Legacy."
12. Ibid.
13. Ibid.
14. Ibid.
15. Souphala Chomsisengphet and Anthony Pennington-Cross, "The Evolution of the Subprime Mortgage Market," *Federal Reserve Bank of St. Louis Review* (January–February 2006): 38.
16. Board of Governors of the Federal Reserve System, "20-Year Treasury Constant Maturity Rate," May 31, 2011, www.federalreserve.gov/releases/h15/current/h15.pdf.
17. "Residential MBS Insurance," *Inside MBS and ABS, LoanPerformance, Amherst Securities,* 2010.
18. "Characteristics and Performance of Nonprime Mortgages" (Washington, D.C.: United States Government Accountability Office, July 28, 2009).
19. SEC Press Release, "Former Countrywide CEO Angelo Mozilo to Pay SEC's Largest-Ever Financial Penalty Against a Public Company's Senior Executive," October 15, 2010, www.sec.gov/news/press/2010/2010-197.htm.
20. Peter Ryan and Kym Landers, "I Didn't See the Subprime Crisis Coming: Greenspan," ABC News, September 17, 2007.
21. I. P. Greg, James R. Hagert, and Jonathan Karp, "Housing Bust Fuels Blame Game," *The Wall Street Journal,* February 27, 2008.
22. Jeremy W. Peters, "Fed Chief Addresses Foreclosures," *The New York Times,* May 18, 2007.
23. "The Economic Outlook," testimony by chairman Ben S. Bernanke before the Joint Economic Committee, U.S. Congress, March 28, 2009.
24. Ibid.
25. Guy Rolnik, interview with Nobel laureate Daniel Kahneman, "Irrational Everything," *Haaretz,* April 10, 2009.
26. Maurice Marwood, "That's Where the Money Is," Nassau Institute, January 18, 2004.
27. "Opening Remarks of Chairman Phil Angelides at the Financial Crisis Inquiry Commission Hearing on the Credibility of Credit Ratings," June 2, 2010.
28. Zeke Faux and Jody Shenn, "Subprime Mortgage Bonds Getting AAA Rating S&P Denies to U.S. Treasuries," *Bloomberg Businessweek,* August 31, 2011.
29. United States Senate Permanent Subcommittee on Investigations, Committee on Homeland Security and Government Affairs, "Exhibits: Hearing on Wall Street and the Financial Crisis—The Role of Investment Banks," Exhibit 105, e-mail from Tom Montag to Daniel L. Sparks, Washington, D.C., April 27, 2010.
30. Christine Harper and David Voreacos, "Goldman Sachs Chief Blankfein Hires Attorney Weingarten for Probe by U.S.," *Bloomberg Businessweek,* August 22, 2011.

CHAPTER 16: THE NOT-SO-INVISIBLE HAND

1. Adam Smith, *An Inquiry into the Nature and Causes of the Wealth of Nations* (London: W. Strahan and T. Cadell, 1776), Vol. 1, p. 349.
2. Ibid., p. 43.
3. T. G. Buchholz, *New Ideas from Dead Economists: An Introduction to Modern Economic Thought* (London: Penguin, 1999), p. 17.

4. David Ricardo, *On the Principles of Political Economy and Taxation* (London: John Murray, 1817).

5. Ibid.

6. John Harwood, "53% in US Say Free Trade Hurts Nation: NBC/WSJ Poll," CNBC, September 28, 2010.

7. Paul R. Krugman, "Is Free Trade Passé?" *Journal of Economic Perspectives* 1, No. 2 (1987): 131–144.

8. Ministry of Labour and State Statistical Bureau, "(DA) Labour-Related Establishment Survey." Survey. *Laborsta Internet.* ILO Department of Statistics. <http://laborsta.ilo.org> Midyear exchange rate was used to derive figures.

9. David Barboza, Christopher Drew, and Steve Lohr, "G.E. to Share Jet Technology with China in New Joint Venture," *The New York Times,* January 17, 2011.

10. Mark Lee and Bruce Einhorn, "Microsoft's Ballmer Says China Piracy Makes India a Better Bet," Bloomberg, May 25, 2010.

11. Ibid.

12. Shaun Rein, "Piracy from China: How Microsoft, Ralph Lauren, Nike and Others Can Cope," *Seeking Alpha,* April 9, 2007.

13. "Trade in Goods with China," U.S. Census Bureau: Foreign Trade, revised June 2009, 2011. Online at http://www.census.gov/foreign-trade/balance/c5700.html.

14. Senator Carl Levin at Congressional Executive China Commission Hearing, "Will China Protect Intellectual Property? New Developments in Counterfeiting, Piracy and Forced Technology Transfer," September 22, 2010.

15. Wayne M. Morrison, "China-U.S. Trade Issues," Congressional Research Service, CRS Report for Congress, January 7, 2011, p. 2.

16. Catherine Rampell, "Second Recession in U.S. Could be Worst Than First," *The New York Times,* August 7, 2011.

17. Grail Research, "Global Financial Crisis: Bailout/Stimulus Tracker," September 12, 2009. Stimulus announced by respective governments.

18. Jeannine Aversa, "Bernanke Hits Back at Critics of Bond-Buying Plan," Washington Associated Press, November 19, 2010.

19. Ibid.

20. Benjamin Graham and David L. Dodd, *Security Analysis: Principles and Technique* (New York: McGraw-Hill, 2005).

21. Richard J. Whalen, "Joseph P. Kennedy: A Portrait of the Founder," *Fortune,* April 10, 2011.

General References

CHAPTER 2: THE PERILS OF AFFECT

Aspara, Jaakko, and Henrikki Tikkanen. "The Role of Company Affect in Stock Investments: Towards Blind, Undemanding, Noncomparative and Committed Love." *Journal of Behavioral Finance* 11, No. 2 (2010): 103–113.

Bateman, I. J., S. Dent, E. Peters, P. Slovic, and C. Starmer. "The Affect Heuristic and the Attractiveness of Simple Gambles." *Journal of Behavioral Decision Making* 20, No. 4 (2007): 365–380.

Berns, Gregory S., C. Monica Capra, Jonathan Chappelow, Sara Moore, and Charles Noussair. "Nonlinear Neurobiological Probability Weighting Functions for Aversive Outcomes." *NeuroImage* 39 (2008): 2047–2057.

———, C. Monica Capra, Sara Moore, and Charles Noussair. "A Shocking Experiment: New Evidence on Probability Weighting and Common Ratio Violations." *Judgment and Decision Making* 2 (2007): 234–242.

Damasio, A. R. *Descartes' Error: Emotion, Reason, and the Human Brain*. New York: Penguin, 2005.

Davidson, Richard J., Klaus R. Scherer, and H. Hill Goldsmith, eds. *Handbook of Affective Sciences* (Series in Affective Science). New York: Oxford University Press, 2002.

Dreman, David N. "Analysts' Conflicts-of-Interest: Some Behavioral Aspects." *Journal of Behavioral Finance* 3, No. 3 (2002): 138–140.

———. "Bubbles and the Role of Analysts' Forecasts." *Journal of Behavioral Finance* 3, No. 1 (2002): 4–14.

———. "The Influence of Affect on Investor Decision-Making." *Journal of Behavioral Finance* 5, No. 2 (2004): 70–74.

———. "The Role of Psychology in Analysts' Estimates." *Journal of Behavioral Finance* 2, No. 2 (2001): 66–68.

———, and Michael A. Berry. "Analyst Forecasting Errors and Their Implications for Security Analysis." *Financial Analysts Journal* 51, No. 3 (1995): 30–41.

———, and Michael A. Berry. "Overreaction, Underreaction and the Low P/E Effect." *Financial Analysts Journal* 51, No. 4 (1995): 21–30.

———, and Eric A. Lufkin. "Do Contrarian Strategies Work Within Industries?" *Journal of Investing* 6, No. 3 (1997): 7–29.

———, and Eric A. Lufkin. "Investor Overreaction: Evidence That Its Basis Is Psychological." *Journal of Behavioral Finance* 1, No. 1 (2000): 61–75.

Engelmann, J. B., C. M. Capra, C. Noussair, and G. S. Berns. "Expert Financial Advice Neurobiologically "Offloads" Financial Decision-Making Under Risk." *PLoS One* 4, No. 3 (2009): e4957.

Fischhoff, B., S. Lichtenstein, P. Slovic, S. Derby, and R. Keeney. *Acceptable Risk.* New York: Cambridge University Press, 1981.

Hirshleifer, David, and Tyler Shumway. "Good Day Sunshine, Stock Returns and the Weather." *Journal of Finance* 58, No. 3 (2003): 1009–1032.

Hsee, C. K., and J. Zhang. "General Evaluability Theory: An Analysis of When What We Care About Matters." *Perspectives on Psychological Science* 5, No. 4 (2010): 343–355.

Johnson, E. J., and A. Tversky. "Affect, Generalization, and the Perception of Risk." *Journal of Personality and Social Psychology* 45 (1983): 20–31.

Kahneman, D., and A. Tversky. "Choices, Values, and Frames." *American Psychologist* 4 (1984): 341–350.

———. "Prospect Theory: An Analysis of Decision Under Risk." *Econometrica* 47 (1979): 263–291.

Knutson, B., A. Westdorp, E. Kaiser, and D. Hommer. "FMRI Visualization of Brain Activity During a Monetary Incentive Delay Task." *NeuroImage* 12, No. 1 (2000): 20–27.

Laibson, David, and Richard Zeckhauser. "Amos Tversky and the Ascent of Behavioral Economics." *Journal of Risk and Uncertainty* 16 (1998): 7–47.

Larsen, Jeff T., A. Peter McGraw, Barbara A. Mellers, and John T. Cacioppo. "The Agony of Victory and Thrill of Defeat: Mixed Emotional Reactions to Disappointing Wins and Relieving Losses." *Psychological Science* 15, No. 5 (2004): 325–330.

Levy, Adam. "Mapping the Trader's Brain." Bloomberg Markets, February 1, 2006, pp. 34–45.

Lowenstein, G., ed. *Exotic Preferences: Behavioral Economics and Human Motivation.* New York: Oxford University Press, 2007.

———. "Out of Control: Visceral Influences on Behavior." *Organizational Behavior and Human Decision Processes* 65, No. 3 (1996): 272–292.

———, Rick Scott, and Jonathan D. Cohen. "Neuroeconomics." *Annual Review of Psychology* 59 (2008): 647–672.

MacGregor, D. G. "Imagery and Financial Judgment." *Journal of Psychology and Financial Markets* 3 (2002): 15–22.

———, P. Slovic, D. Dreman, and M. Berry. "Imagery, Affect, and Financial Judgment." *Journal of Psychology and Financial Markets* 1, No. 2 (2000): 104–110.

Montague, P. Read. "Neuroeconomics: A View from Neuroscience." *Functional Neurology* 22, No. 4 (2007): 219–234.

———, and Gregory S. Berns. "Neural Economics and the Biological Substrates of Valuation." *Neuron* 36 (2002): 265–284.

Olsen, R. A. "Behavioral Finance as Science: Implications from the Research of Paul Slovic." *Journal of Psychology and Financial Markets* 2 (2001): 157–159.

Rangel, Antonio, Colin Camerer, and P. Read Montague. "A Framework for Studying the Neurobiology of Value-Based Decision Making." *Nature Reviews Neuroscience* 9 (2008): 545–556.

Shiv, B., and A. Fedorikhin. "Heart and Mind in Conflict: Interplay of Affect and Cognition in Consumer Decision Making." *Journal of Consumer Research* 26 (December 1999): 278–282.

Sloman, S. A. "The Empirical Case for Two Systems of Reasoning." *Psychological Bulletin* 119, No. 1 (1996): 3–22.

Slovic, Paul. "The Construction of Preference." *American Psychologist* 50 (1995): 364–371.

——. "Rational Actors and Rational Fools: The Influence of Affect on Judgment and Decision Making." *Roger Williams University Law Review* 6, No. 1 (2000): 163–212.

——. "What's Fear Got to Do with It? It's Affect We Need to Worry About." *Missouri Law Review* 69 (2004): 971–990.

——. "Risk as Analysis and Risk as Feelings: Some Thoughts About Affect, Reason, Risk, and Rationality." *Risk Analysis* 24, No. 2 (2004): 1–12.

——, and S. Lichtenstein. "Relative Importance of Probabilities and Payoffs in Risk Taking." *Journal of Experimental Psychology Monograph* 78, No. 3 (1968): 1–18.

——, and E. Peters. "Risk Perception and Affect." *Current Directions in Psychological Science* 15, No. 6 (2006): 322–325.

Starr, Chauncey. "Social Benefit Versus Technological Risk." *Science* 165, No. 3899 (1969): 1232–1238.

Statman, Meir. "Characteristics, Affect, and Stock Returns." Santa Clara University Leavey School of Business Research Paper No. 10-06.

CHAPTER 3: TREACHEROUS SHORTCUTS IN DECISION MAKING

Fischhoff, Baruch, Paul Slovic, and Sarah Lichtenstein. "Knowing with Certainty: The Appropriateness of Extreme Confidence." *Journal of Experimental Psychology: Human Perception and Performance* 3 (1977): 552–564.

Kahneman, Daniel, and Amos Tversky. "Subjective Probability: A Judgment of Representativeness." *Cognitive Psychology* 3, No. 3 (July 1972): 430–454.

Lichtenstein, S., Paul Slovic, B. Fischhoff, M. Layman, and B. Combs. "Judged Frequency of Lethal Events," *Journal of Experimental Psychology: Human Learning and Memory* 4 (1978): 551–578.

Nisbett, Richard E., and Timothy DeCamp Wilson. "Telling More Than We Can Know: Verbal Reports on Mental Processes." *Psychological Review* 84, No. 3 (1977): 231–259.

CHAPTER 4: CONQUISTADORS IN TWEED JACKETS

Dieckmann, N. F. "Numeracy: A Review of the Literature." Report No. 08-2. Eugene, Ore.: Decision Research, 2008.

Faro, David, and Yuval Rottenstreich. "Affect, Empathy, and Regressive Mispredictions of Others' Preferences Under Risk." *Management Science* 52, No. 4 (2006): 529–541.

Gilovich, Thomas, Dale Griffin, and Daniel Kahneman, eds. *Heuristics and Biases: The Psychology of Intuitive Judgment.* New York: Cambridge University Press, 2002.

Kahneman, Daniel, and Jonathan Renshon. "Why Hawks Win." *Foreign Policy* (January–February 2007): 34–38.

Kahneman, D., and A. Tversky. "Subjective Probability: A Judgment of Representativeness." *Cognitive Psychology* 3 (July 1972): 430–454.

Peters, E., and P. Slovic. "The Springs of Action: Affective and Analytical Information Processing in Choice." *Personality and Social Psychology Bulletin* 26 (2000): 1465–1475.

——, Daniel Västfjäll, Paul Slovic, C. K. Mertz, Ketti Mazzocco, and Stephan Dickert. "Numeracy and Decision Making," *Psychological Science* 17, No. 5 (2006): 407–413.

Slovic, Paul. "Psychological Study of Human Judgment: Implications for Investment Decision Making." *Journal of Psychology and Financial Markets* 2 (2001): 160–172.

CHAPTER 5: IT'S ONLY A FLESH WOUND

Denes-Raj, V., and S. Epstein. "Conflict Between Intuitive and Rational Processing: When People Behave Against Their Better Judgment." *Journal of Personality and Social Psychology* 66 (1994): 819–829.

CHAPTER 6: EFFICIENT MARKETS AND PTOLEMAIC EPICYCLES

Cassidy, John. "After the Blowup." *The New Yorker,* January 11, 2010.

Dunbar, Nicholas. *Inventing Money: The Story of Long-Term Capital Management and the Legends Behind It* (New York: Wiley, 2001).

Nocera, Joe. "Poking Holes in a Theory on Markets." *The New York Times,* June 5, 2009.

CHAPTER 7: WALL STREET'S ADDICTION TO FORECASTING

Dreman, David N. "Bubble Jr." *Journal of Behavioral Finance* 4, No. 4 (2003): 188–190.

Fox, Justin. *The Myth of the Rational Market: A History of Risk, Reward, and Delusion on Wall Street.* New York: Harper Paperbacks, 2011.

Michel-Kerjan, Erwann, and Paul Slovic, eds. *The Irrational Economist: Decision Making in a Dangerous World.* New York: Public Affairs Press, 2010.

Simon, H. A. "Rational Choice and the Structure of the Environment." *Psychological Review* 63 (1956): 129–138.

CHAPTER 8: HOW BIG A LONG SHOT WILL YOU PLAY?

Cummins, L. F., M. R. Nadorff, and A. E. Kelly. "Winning and Positive Affect Can Lead to Reckless Gambling." *Psychology of Addictive Behavior* 23, No. 2 (2009): 287–294.

Kuo, W. J., T. Sjöström, Y. P. Chen, Y. H. Wang, and C. Y. Huang. "Intuition and Deliberation: Two Systems for Strategizing in the Brain." *Science* 324, No. 5926 (2009): 519–522.

Van Dillen, L. F., D. J. Heslenfeld, and S. L. Koole, "Tuning Down the Emotional Brain: An fMRI Study of the Effects of Cognitive Load on the Processing of Affective Images." *NeuroImage* 45, No. 4 (2009): 1212–1219.

CHAPTER 9: NASTY SURPRISES AND NEUROECONOMICS

Bayer, H. M., and P. W. Glimcher. "Midbrain Dopamine Neurons Encode a Quantitative Reward Prediction Error Signal." *Neuron* 47 (2005): 129–141.

Berns, Gregory S., Samuel M. McClure, Giuseppe Pagnoni, and P. Read Montague. "Predictability Modulates Human Brain Response to Reward." *Journal of Neuroscience* 21, No. 8 (2001): 2793–2798.

Chua, H. F., R. Gonzalez, S. F. Taylor, R. C. Welsh, and I. Liberzon. "Decision-Related Loss: Regret and Disappointment," *NeuroImage* 47, No. 4 (2009): 2031–2040.

Cowen, T. "Enter the Neuro-Economists: Why Do Investors Do What They Do?" *The New York Times,* April 20, 2006, p. C3.

Cromwell, H. C., and W. Schultz. "Effects of Expectations for Different Reward Magnitudes on Neuronal Activity in Primate Striatum." *Journal of Neurophysiology* 89 (2003): 2823–2838.

Daw, N. D., and K. Doya. "The Computational Neurobiology of Learning and Reward." *Current Opinion in Neurobiology* 16 (2006): 199–204.

Doya, K. "Modulators of Decision Making." *Nature Neuroscience* 11, No. 4 (2008): 410–416.

Dunn, B. D., T. Dalgleish, and A. D. Lawrence. "The Somatic Marker Hypothesis: A Critical Evaluation." *Neuroscience and Biobehavioral Reviews* 30, No. 2 (2006): 239–271.

Elliott, R., K. J. Friston, and R. J. Dolan. "Dissociable Neural Responses in Human Reward Systems." *Journal of Neuroscience* 20, No. 16 (2000): 6159–6165.

Fiorillo, C. D., P. N. Tobler, and W. Schultz. "Discrete Coding of Reward Probability and Uncertainty by Dopamine Neurons." *Science* 299 (2003): 1898–1902.

Hollerman, J. R., and W. Schultz. "Dopamine Neurons Report an Error in the Temporal Prediction of Reward During Learning." *Nature Neuroscience* 1 (1998): 304–309.

Kobayashi, S., and W. Schultz. "Influence of Reward Delays on Responses of Dopamine Neurons." *Journal of Neuroscience* 28 (2008): 7837–7846.

Lee, D. "Neural Basis of Quasi-Rational Decision Making." *Current Opinion in Neurobiology* 16, No. 2 (2006): 191–198.

Liu, X., D. K. Powell, H. Wang, B. T. Gold, C. R. Corbly, and J. E. Joseph. "Functional Dissociation in Frontal and Striatal Areas for Processing of Positive and Negative Reward Information." *Journal of Neuroscience* 27, No. 17 (2007): 4587–4597.

Livet, P. "Rational Choice, Neuroeconomy and Mixed Emotions." *Philosophical Transactions of the Royal Society, London (B: Biological Sciences)* 365, No. 1538 (2010): 259–269.

Loewenstein, George, Scott Rick, and Jonathan D. Cohen, "Neuroeconomics." *Annual Review of Psychology* 59 (2008): 647–672.

Martin, L. E., G. F. Potts, P. C. Burton, and P. R. Montague. "Electrophysiological and Hemodynamic Responses to Reward Prediction Violation." *Neuroreport* 20, No. 13 (2009): 1140–1143.

Mirenowicz, J., and W. Schultz. "Importance of Unpredictability for Reward Responses in Primate Dopamine Neurons." *Journal of Neurophysiology* 72 (1994): 1024–1027.

——. "Preferential Activation of Midbrain Dopamine Neurons by Appetitive Rather Than Aversive Stimuli." *Nature* 379 (1996): 449–451.

Montague, P. R. "Neuroeconomics: A View from Neuroscience." *Functional Neurology* 22, No. 4 (2007): 219–234.

——, P. Dayan, and T. Sejnowski. "A Framework for Mesencephalic Dopamine Systems Based on Predictive Hebbian Learning." *Journal of Neuroscience* 16, No. 5 (1996): 1936–1947.

Sanfey, A. G., G. Loewenstein, S. M. McClure, and J. D. Cohen. "Neuroeconomics: Cross-Currents in Research on Decision-Making." *Trends in Cognitive Sciences* 10, No. 3 (2006): 108–116.

Schultz, W. "Behavioral Theories and the Neurophysiology of Reward." *Annual Review of Psychology* 57 (2006): 87–115.

——. "Introduction. Neuroeconomics: The Promise and the Profit." *Philosophical Transactions of the Royal Society, London (B: Biological Sciences)* 363, No. 1511 (2008): 3767–3769.

——. "Predictive Reward Signal of Dopamine Neurons." *Journal of Neurophysiology* 80 (1998): 1–27.

——, P. Dayan, and P. R. Montague. "A Neural Substrate of Prediction and Reward." *Science* 275 (1997): 1593–1599.

Shiv, B., G. Loewenstein, and A. Bechara. "The Dark Side of Emotion in Decision-Making: When Individuals with Decreased Emotional Reactions Make More Advantageous Decisions." *Brain Research. Cognitive Brain Research* 23, No. 1 (2005): 85–92.

Tobler, P. N., C. D. Fiorillo, and W. Schultz. "Adaptive Coding of Reward Value by Dopamine Neurons." *Science* 307 (2005): 1642–1645.

Werner, N. S., S. Duschek, and R. Schandry. "Relationships Between Affective States and Decision-Making." *International Journal of Psychophysiology* 74, No. 3 (2009): 259–265.

Wu, C. C., P. Bossaerts, and B. Knutson. "The Affective Impact of Financial Skewness on Neural Activity and Choice." *PLoS One* 6, No. 2 (2011): e16838.

CHAPTER 10: A POWERFUL CONTRARIAN APPROACH TO PROFITS

Basu, Sanjoy. "The Effect of Earnings Yield on Assessments of the Association Between Annual Accounting Income Numbers and Security Prices." *Accounting Review* 53 (1978): 599–625.

——. "Investment Performance of Common Stocks in Relation to Their Price-Earnings Ratios: A Test of the Efficient Markets Hypothesis." *Journal of Finance* 32 (1977): 663–682.

——. "The Relationship Between Earnings' Yield, Market Value and Return for NYSE Common Stocks: Further Evidence." *Journal of Financial Economics* 12 (1983): 129–156.

Dreman, David. *Contrarian Investment Strategies: The Next Generation.* New York: Simon and Schuster, 1998.

——. *Contrarian Investment Strategy.* New York: Random House, 1979.

——. *The New Contrarian Investment Strategy.* New York: Random House, 1982.

——, and Michael Berry. "Overreaction, Underreaction and the Low P/E Effect." *Financial Analysts Journal* (1995): 21–30.

————, and Eric Lufkin. "Investor Overreaction: Evidence That Its Basis Is Psychological." *Journal of Psychology and Financial Markets* 1, No. 1 (2000): 61–75.

CHAPTER 11: PROFITING FROM INVESTORS' OVERREACTIONS

Abarbanell, J. S., and V. L. Bernard. "Tests of Analysts' Overreaction/Underreaction to Earnings Information as an Explanation for Anomalous Stock Price Behavior." *Journal of Finance* 47 (1992): 1181–1207.

Amir, Eli, and Yoav Ganzach. "Overreaction and Underreaction in Analysts' Forecasts." *Journal of Economic Behavior and Organization* 37 (1998): 333–347.

Daniel, K. D., D. Hirshleifer, and A. Subrahmanyam. "Investor Psychology and Security Market Under- and Overreactions." *Journal of Finance* 53, No. 6 (1998): 1839–1886.

De Bondt, Werner F. M., and Richard Thaler. "Does the Stock Market Overreact?" *Journal of Finance* 40, No. 3 (1985): 793–805.

————. "Do Security Analysts Overreact?" *American Economic Review* 80, No. 2 (1990): 52–57.

————. "Further Evidence on Investor Overreaction and Stock Market Seasonality." *Journal of Finance* 42, No. 3 (1987): 557–581.

Drehmann, Mathias, Jörg Oechssler, and Andreas Roider. "Herding and Contrarian Behavior in Financial Markets: An Internet Experiment." *American Economic Review* 95, No. 5 (2005): 1403–1426.

Dreman, David N., and Michael A. Berry. "Overreaction, Underreaction, and the Low-P/E Effect." *Financial Analysts Journal* 51, No. 4 (1995): 21–30.

————, and Eric A. Lufkin. "Do Contrarian Strategies Work Within Industries?" *Journal of Investing* 6, No. 3 (1997): 7–29.

Jegadeesh, N., and S. Titman. "Overreaction, Delayed Reaction, and Contrarian Profits." *Review of Financial Studies* 8 (1995): 973–993.

Lakonishok, J., A. Shleifer, and R. Vishny. "Contrarian Investment, Extrapolation, and Risk." *Journal of Finance* 49, No. 5 (1994): 1541–1578.

CHAPTER 12: CONTRARIAN STRATEGIES WITHIN INDUSTRIES

Bali, Turan G., K. Ozgur Demirtas, Armen Hovakimian, and John J. Merrick, Jr. "Peer Pressure: Industry Group Impacts on Stock Valuation Precision and Contrarian Strategy Performance." *Journal of Portfolio Management* 32, No. 3 (2006): 80–92.

Dreman, David N., and Eric A. Lufkin. "Do Contrarian Strategies Work Within Industries?" *Journal of Investing* 6, No. 3 (1997): 7–29.

CHAPTER 14: TOWARD A BETTER THEORY OF RISK

Coleman, William Oliver. *The Causes, Costs, and Compensations of Inflation: An Investigation of Three Problems in Monetary Theory.* Northampton, Mass.: Edward Elgar Publishing, 2007.

CHAPTER 15: THEY'RE GAMBLING WITH YOUR MONEY

Acharya, Viral V., Thomas F. Cooley, Matthew P. Richardson, Richard Sylla, and Ingo Walter. *Regulating Wall Street: The Dodd-Frank Act and the New Architecture of Global Finance.* New York: Wiley Finance, 2010.

Tatom, John A. *Financial Market Regulation: Legislation and Implications.* New York, Dordrecht, Heidelberg, London: Springer, 2011.

CHAPTER 16: THE NOT-SO-INVISIBLE HAND

Fletcher, Ian. *Free Trade Doesn't Work: What Should Replace It and Why,* 2011 Edition. Washington, D.C.: U.S. Business and Industry Council.

Index

About the Author

DAVID DREMAN is regarded as the "dean" of contrarians by many on Wall Street and in the national media. Dreman is the chairman and managing director of Dreman Value Management, LLC, of Jersey City, New Jersey, a firm that pioneered contrarian strategies on the Street and manages over $5 billion of individual and institutional funds. The author of the critically acclaimed *Psychology and the Stock Market* and *Contrarian Investment Strategy,* Dreman is also a senior investment columnist at *Forbes* magazine. Articles dealing with the success of his methods have appeared in *The New York Times, The Wall Street Journal, Fortune, Barron's, Bloomberg Businessweek, Newsweek,* and numerous other national publications. Dreman is also on the editorial committee of the *Journal of Behavioral Finance.* He resides with his wife and daughter in Aspen, Colorado, and on the family yacht, *The Contrarian.*